From Reaction to
Conflict Prevention

A project of the International Peace Academy

From Reaction to Conflict Prevention

OPPORTUNITIES FOR THE UN SYSTEM

EDITED BY
Fen Osler Hampson
David M. Malone

LYNNE
RIENNER
PUBLISHERS

BOULDER
LONDON

Published in the United States of America in 2002 by
Lynne Rienner Publishers, Inc.
1800 30th Street, Boulder, Colorado 80301
www.rienner.com

and in the United Kingdom by
Lynne Rienner Publishers, Inc.
3 Henrietta Street, Covent Garden, London WC2E 8LU

Library of Congress Cataloging-in-Publication Data
From reaction to conflict prevention : opportunities for the UN system / edited by Fen
Osler Hampson and David M. Malone.
    p. cm.
    A project of the International Peace Academy.
    Includes bibliographical references and index.
    ISBN 1-58826-043-7—ISBN 1-58826-019-4 (pbk.)
    1. Pacific settlement of international disputes.   2. Conflict management.   3. United
Nations.   I. Hampson, Fen Osler.   II. Malone, David, 1954–
JZ6010.F76   2001
341.5'23—dc21

                                   2001041774

British Cataloguing in Publication Data
A Cataloguing in Publication record for this book
is available from the British Library.

Printed and bound in the United States of America

    The paper used in this publication meets the requirements
    of the American National Standard for Permanence of
    Paper for Printed Library Materials Z39.48-1984.

    5 4 3 2 1

Contents

Preface

David M. Malone

Conflict prevention is much discussed at the United Nations and elsewhere but, sadly, little practiced. Nevertheless, it is widely accepted that more of it would be a very good thing, particularly for a world organization sagging under the strain of multiple complex peace operations supported restlessly by sometimes unreliable funders.

Sweden has long been preoccupied with the peaceful settlement of disputes and with techniques for conflict management. In recent years, its government's attention has turned to conflict prevention, with a particular focus on preventive diplomacy and related approaches to short-term crisis management that attempt to forestall full-blown conflict. Jan Eliasson, recently state secretary at the Ministry of Foreign Affairs in Sweden and previously under-secretary-general of the United Nations Department of Humanitarian Affairs, having observed the United Nations from the inside, knew of the UN's potential in this area as well as its constraints on effective action. He knew that the challenge of moving from reaction to prevention would not be easy to overcome on the East River. With admirable confederates Anders Bjürner and Ragnar Ängeby, Jan urged the International Peace Academy (IPA) to tackle the barriers to effective conflict prevention. This Swedish initiative aiming to achieve traction during Sweden's presidency of the European Union in the first six months of 2001 was principally brought to fruition by Elizabeth Cousens, IPA's director of research currently on leave with the Office of the United Nations Special Coordinator in the Occupied Territories in Gaza, with significant contributions by Andrew Mack, then head of the UN Secretary-General's Strategic Planning Unit and now at Harvard University. Their combined effort, which culminated in an international policy conference in April 2000, is the genesis of this volume.

IPA's follow-on work regarding conflict prevention, which is being carried forward under the direction of Chandra Lekha Sriram, seeks further to strengthen efforts by the United Nations and its member states to act preventively. At its outset, it received tremendous encouragement from Mukesh Kapila, director of the Conflict and Humanitarian Affairs Division of the Department for International Development in London. Beyond generous support from the UK government, it has been supported by the governments of Germany, the Netherlands, Denmark, Sweden, Portugal, and Italy. These governments, and many allies within the UN system, believe that the United Nations can do more and better on conflict prevention in the years ahead, overcoming occasionally daunting obstacles to effective and speedy UN action in virtually any field, not least decisionmaking processes and management structures aimed not so much at efficiency as at initiative and response politically acceptable to the majority of member states. Kofi Annan's first term as UN Secretary-General, crowned by the Nobel Peace Prize in October 2001, has been most impressive at redefining the international terms of debate on the primacy of fundamental human rights and the imperative of humanitarian action. It remains to be seen whether member states are capable of drawing conclusions from the undoubted desire of peoples everywhere to live free from the scourge of war.

The editors would like to thank Karin Wermester for her splendid editorial assistance. They are also very grateful to Lynne Rienner and her helpful, highly professional, and friendly team for their commitment to this project.

1

Introduction: Making Conflict Prevention a Priority

Fen Osler Hampson,
Karin Wermester, and David M. Malone

Prevention of conflict is the first promise in the Charter of the United Nations. Yet it is a promise that is constantly betrayed by local parties, governments, international organizations, and to some extent the scholarly community, which until quite recently had been unable to generate policy-relevant analysis of the circumstances in which this goal might be achieved.[1] This edited volume brings together scholarly perspectives and findings that shed practical light on the challenge of moving from reaction to conflict prevention within the UN system.

The United Nations, specifically the UN Security Council, lies at the heart of the post–World War II collective security system that, despite functioning imperfectly, no doubt prevented more cataclysmic conflict among states. Although the Security Council has become much active, passing resolutions and improvising new techniques to address the spate of intrastate conflicts that it was not created to resolve, its effectiveness has nonetheless been limited.[2] Such limitations and shortcomings—which exist despite the dramatic increase in the number of resolutions passed—have highlighted, sometimes in dramatic fashion, the need for a *comprehensive* approach to conflict prevention.

Geostrategic balancing exercises were the hallmark of the Cold War era. Crises arose primarily between the great powers or their surrogates and were usually the culmination of strategic ventures prepared in secret and executed with stealth. Multifaceted preventive measures and action of the kind considered today, therefore, were rarely an option. The United Nations itself possessed neither the resources sufficient to intervene effectively in conflicts between these great powers or their clients, nor the mandate with which to do so.[3] Even so, the United Nations was able to improvise some instruments for preventive action through the constant hybridization of peacekeeping missions.[4]

With the collapse of the Soviet Union, the risk of disputes escalating to the global level has greatly diminished. Furthermore, interstate conflicts are today fewer in number. Occasionally a new interstate conflict will surprise the international community, for example, the senseless and murderous border war between Ethiopia and Eritrea that erupted at the end of the 1990s. But these are relatively rare. A single superpower, or "supreme power," dominates the global scene.[5] The remaining significant powers have largely refrained from jousting with each other, although certain familiar international hotspots (the India-Pakistan dispute over Kashmir, the Israeli-Arab conflict) continue to defy peaceful resolution.

Much contemporary conflict stems from *within* states, even though it may spill across borders, and typically occurs in desperately impoverished regions. Today's wars are driven by local elites—often those in government—maneuvering to corner as large a share of the inadequate national complement of power and wealth as possible, further impoverishing the poor and marginalized sectors of society and destroying avenues for nonviolent change. They also tend to unfold in slow motion over a period of several months, if not years, following familiar patterns that, given any genuine interest on the part of the outside world and a concomitant willingness to expend resources, might be arrested. As a result, some of the most violent conflicts of the late twentieth century continue to fester, absorbing economic potential, social progress, and many lives while mortgaging the futures of nations.

In the early 1990s, the international community, and the United Nations in particular, was deeply engaged in many of these conflicts. But enthusiasm for intervention waned in the aftermath of perceived peacekeeping failures in Somalia, Bosnia, and elsewhere. At the same time, however, there was growing interest in designing strategies aimed at prevention rather than management, even though skeptics asserted the futility and even impossibility of effective preventive action to forestall conflict. Given the scope and depth of the challenge, governments, international institutions, and academics rose to the challenge. The *study* of conflict prevention flourished and was complemented by some notable successes in the *practice* of conflict prevention. Many findings most pertinent to the UN role in conflict prevention related to how and why these conflicts start, what sustains them, and what kinds of intervention measures might be adopted to prevent them from occurring, escalating, and recurring are presented in this volume.

Although every conflict is complex and unique, there are general characteristics of contemporary violent conflict that emerge from the chapters and that are of relevance to policy development and implementation within the UN system. The first is the importance of economic factors in both contributing to and prolonging war.[6] Resource scarcity relating to high population growth, the legacies of land distribution, uneven food distribution, and a lack of access to freshwater are all potential sources of conflict. Conversely, a plethora of natural resources can also increase the probability and duration of violent conflict as actors seek to enrich themselves through illicit means (e.g., those engaged in massive looting of treasuries, embezzlement of state revenues from oil and mineral exploration or production, small-arms trafficking, and the mining of so-called conflict-supporting minerals such as diamonds). The second significant characteristic is the role of belligerent groups—some of which exist at the substate level but many of which are in fact elites acting concertedly with government forces or on behalf of the state itself—and the manner in which they are able to foment and perpetuate violence. Their ability to manipulate populations through the instrumental use of ethnicity, religion, history, and myths in support of the goals they seek is one of the key factors that determines how a conflict will unfold, and hence what can be done to arrest it. The third characteristic is the fungible nature of contemporary conflict. Whereas during the Cold War conflict was *either* interstate *or* intrastate, today it has a tendency to shift along a sliding scale between interstate and intrastate. So-called civil wars permeate easily across existing territorial borders to form *regional conflict complexes*; conversely, regional conflict dynamics can impact rapidly on the internal processes of neighboring states.[7] Conflicts in the 1990s and early 2000s have a nasty habit of spilling over (as in the Great Lakes region since 1997, and Liberia/Sierra Leone/Guinea in 1999–2001) and spilling in, as demonstrated by extensive external involvement in the Democratic Republic of the Congo's civil war in the early 2000s. The role of neighbors is thus extremely important, as they can act as mitigators of violence just as easily as they can fuel and prolong it.

The UN system, including its large family of agencies, has sought to address these challenges, with varying degrees of success. Through its case-by-case decisions and statements, the Security Council has chipped away at arguments in favor of absolute sovereignty and has thus managed to expand the perception of what is legitimate relating to preventive action undertaken by the United Nations.[8] As early as 1991, actions mandated by the Security Council in Resolution 687 imposed a highly intrusive and complex regime of monitoring on Iraq in an effort to prevent it from seeking again to produce weapons of mass destruction.[9] Thereafter, Security Council members tended to use the threat to international peace and security that flows of refugees could pose to neighboring countries to authorize preventive action. Such arguments were advanced, notably, in the early stages of the disintegration of the former Yugoslavia, Somalia, Haiti, and in the Council's deliberations in early 2001 regarding the overflow of refugees in Guinea from neighboring Liberia and Sierra Leone. Where action was taken (in the former three cases at the time of writing), Council decisions aimed at preventing even worse outcomes. Earlier and more explicitly preventive action includes the Council's decision in 1995 to authorize a solely preventive deployment of UN peacekeepers to the Former Yugoslav Republic of Macedonia and the deployment of a peace-keeping force to the Central African Republic in 1998.[10]

Yet in general at the UN, prevention is preached (by the UN Secretary-General) more often than it is practiced (certainly by the member states). Preventive measures tend to be intrusive, and governments object to the examination of their internal affairs even as national intelligence services and globalized media do so constantly and with considerable success. Enthusiasm for early warning may have peaked at the Security Council summit of January 1992, when its members urged the UN Secretariat to "collect and analyze pertinent information in order to alert relevant inter-governmental organs about impending crises."[11] This invitation led to the creation of the UN Department of Political Affairs (DPA), which was charged with early warning as well as the support of the Secretary-General's good offices. However, in spite of strong leadership by Marrack Goulding until 1997 and Kieran Prendergast since then, and an increasingly professional and capable staff, the preventive drive of the UN has been held in check, largely by its members. This was readily apparent in the UN General Assembly debate on the "Report of the Panel on UN Peace Operations" (the Brahimi Report) that was released in August 2000.[12] The debate—often quite heated—revealed many concerns and fears harbored by developing countries. These concerns included the selectivity of peace-keeping deployments, their increasing intrusiveness, and the likelihood that they would divert resources from the more urgent developmental needs of the so-called global south. The report called for a radical overhaul of the UN Department of Peacekeeping Operations (DPKO) and the creation of an information and strategic analysis unit to complement and assist the Secretary-General, DPA, and DPKO in, inter alia, preventive action. Although the General Assembly was able to agree on additional resources for DPKO, it punted into the (possibly distant) future the recommendations aimed at enhancing the analytical capacity of the Secretariat, inter alia, for preventive purposes.[13]

This book represents the culmination of the International Peace Academy's research project entitled "From Reaction to Prevention: Opportunities for the UN System in the New Millennium." The purpose of the project was to identify opportunities for making existing and nascent capacity for conflict prevention more effective operationally within the UN system at large. In this light, Part 1 begins with an examination of recent quantitative and qualitative findings regarding conflict trends and their causes with a view toward better informing conflict prevention initiatives and implementation. Part 2 looks at conflict prevention instruments and capacities as they have developed since the end of the Cold War, then offers practical suggestions for future such initiatives with a view to informing the UN system's role. In Part 3, the focus of conflict prevention is broadened to examine the work of practitioners beyond the UN system in the world of donors and nongovernmental organizations (NGOs).

The Dynamics of War

The chapters in Part 1 present recent research findings on the dynamics of war in the post–Cold War era in order to better understand how they might be prevented. Chapter 2 by Anne-Marie Gardner begins with a survey of the recent literature on conflict's causes and trends, pointing out where there is convergence and divergence among researchers. Gardner identifies four interrelated and prominent causes of conflict that appear throughout the literature: insecurity, inequality, private incentives, and perceptions, where variance among cases is explained by the historical legacies of conflict, the pace and depth of political and economic change, and external, often regional dynamics. In addition, she reveals that many of the findings from current research on conflict trends run contrary to conventional wisdom. Although experience would suggest that intrastate armed conflicts have increased in number and intensity in the post–Cold War era, almost all quantitative studies demonstrate that there has been a rather dramatic decrease in the number of armed conflicts since the end of the Cold War, with a slight rise recorded by some since 1998.

Gardner's chapter lays the foundation for the themes that are developed in the following three chapters. Conflict trends and the causes and implications of them are presented in detail by Ted Robert Gurr in Chapter 3 and Monty Marshall in Chapter 4. A negative reading would suggest that declining intrastate conflict trends could be due to diminishing external support for factors that facilitate violent conflict. In this case, the reduction in conflict probably more closely correlates to reduced support and funding for unwholesome allies and superpower proxy wars, as well as the increase (albeit nominal perhaps) in democratic regimes across the world. However, Gurr argues instead that the overall declining trend reflects improved efforts by the international community to actively promote mediation of disputes, deploy force in the face of gross human rights violations, and develop postconflict peacebuilding initiatives. Marshall, in a related study of the societal and systemic impact of war, looks at the conventional measures of the scale and impact of war. He finds that there has also been a reduction in the impact and/or intensity of war within the same time frame. Furthermore, he discounts claims of increased conflict in the late 1990s, pointing out that generally they were escalations of existing conflicts rather than eruptions of new ones. The findings of both Gurr and Marshall suggest that preventive action by the international community may have been much more widespread and successful than previously thought, but they point to the urgent need, in order to better inform future such efforts, to develop more rigorous assessment of measures that were in fact taken.

In Chapter 5, Frances Stewart demonstrates the importance of understanding the interconnectedness of social, economic, and political factors and how they can coalesce to cause violence. Her research focuses on the structural causes of conflict with a view toward better informing development policy. She challenges the conventional wisdom that emerged among development actors at the end of the 1990s—poverty causes conflict because violence erupts predominantly in poor pockets of the world—finding it simplistic and indeed dangerous. Instead, she argues that the multifaceted measure of horizontal inequality (i.e., the political, social, and economic disempowerment of certain groups in a society relative to others) is a significant cause of violent conflict. Her chapter concludes with a series of proposals for policymakers.

Conflict Prevention: The State of the Art

As the causes of conflict are interrelated and interact over what can be a prolonged time frame, it follows that effective prevention requires integrated strategy across different sectors (diplomatic, military, political, economic, social) and periods of engagement. However, most current prevention efforts are isolated within a particular international organization or sector of international actors. Several new tools are starting to bridge traditional sectoral and bureaucratic divisions with an explicit view toward conflict prevention: complex peacekeeping operations, coercive diplomacy, targeted sanctions, aid conditionality, civil society peacebuilding, and socioeconomic approaches to development. However, in order to be effective, intervention strategies must be targeted at specific conflict variables, or causes, recognizing that the salience of any given set of factors is likely to vary from one setting to another. Coherent strategies also require ably planned, implemented, and coordinated strategies in order to anticipate and avoid, to the extent possible, unintended consequences that exacerbate rather than alleviate the causes of violent conflict.[14] The chapters in Part 2 examine recent practice and emerging trends in conflict prevention with a view toward strengthening the capacity for action in the future.

Chapter 6 by Fen Osler Hampson begins with a review of the growing body of scholarly and policy literature on preventive diplomacy. There are essentially two views about the United Nations' own role and potential to

engage in preventive diplomacy. Some studies argue that several UN entities, the Security Council and the Executive Office of the Secretary-
General in particular, have a vital role to play that is currently underuti-
lized. Others believe that these bodies carry with them significant
institutional liabilities that outweigh their assets, especially in the case of
the Security Council. Hampson argues that although there is an increasingly sophisticated understanding of the potential strengths and limitations of
preventive diplomacy, including the challenges of operationalizing the concept within the United Nations, there is increasing skepticism about its utility and narrow scope.

Chapters 7 and 8 provide useful guidelines for policymakers attempting to develop and implement preventive strategy. In Chapter 7, Michael
Lund examines the evolution of prevention action in the 1990s and argues
that the most problematic obstacles to conflict prevention relate more to
effectiveness and the institutionalization of regular mechanisms for prevention than to understanding causation or mobilizing political support for
action—both of which are eminently resolvable. He disaggregates the different levels of preventive action and, on the basis of lessons learned from
recent practice, offers priorities for the future. He then suggests some key
ingredients for preventive engagements as a complement to his toolkit of
preventive instruments. John Cockell (Chapter 8) concurs, highlighting the
need to develop multifaceted preventive operations that address the specific
causes of conflict in a given situation. However, rather than focusing on
what instruments and tools might be most useful, Cockell instead looks at
the elements of good preventive strategy. In particular, he examines the
issues of causal complexity and cross-sectoral implementation of operational action, as well as the planning connection between these two points:
preventive action strategy.

In Chapter 9, Peter Wallensteen introduces the distinction that is the
focus of Chapters 10 and 11: direct conflict prevention, which is taken to
reduce or eliminate the immediate manifestations of violence; and structural prevention, which seeks to address the underlying causes.[15] Wallensteen
goes on to identify a set of candidates for conflict prevention analysis in the
1990s, an attempt to disaggregate what kinds of policies might be most
effective, at what time, and in what sequence given the different types of
conflict prevalent in the post–Cold War era: interstate disputes, intrastate
disputes over government, and state formation conflicts. He argues that
whereas direct preventive action tends to be the norm, when there is action
at all, international actors might well focus their efforts on structural prevention as a complement to, and sometimes instead of, direct measures.

The question of scope—and whether the United Nations ought to focus
more on direct or structural prevention—is the subject of Chapters 10 and
11. In Chapter 10, Tobi Dress and Gay Rosenblum-Kumar offer a maximal-

ist strategy and propose a systemwide approach to structural prevention for the UN system. They begin with an examination of the institutional requirements of the UN system for conflict prevention based on the economic, social, and political-developmental needs of partners from the community level upward, then go on to argue for a focus on global, regional, and national capacity-building and dialogue aiming to render more systematic, long-term peace planning.

A major caveat to such a broad view of conflict prevention is whether the UN system, including its development and donor agencies, can realistically adopt it. Moreover, the goal of conflict prevention risks being subsumed among myriad others—such that the United Nations mainstreams an ideal it is unable to live up to. Edward Luck, in Chapter 11, raises serious concerns regarding whether those UN bodies best placed to address the root causes of conflict are even up to the challenge of structural prevention. Rather than abandoning prevention outright, he argues for a minimalist approach that would focus UN efforts on direct prevention—that is, pressing challenges relating to the imminent collapse of governments or territorial disputes.

Comparative Advantages: Practitioner Perspectives Beyond the United Nations

Actors beyond the UN system and its family of agencies have an important role to play as a complement to—and sometimes instead of—the preventive efforts of the United Nations. The research and policy development community, which includes scholars, NGOs, and think tanks from around the world, has developed a wealth of knowledge on a range of cross-cutting topics that can usefully inform the practice of preventive action. This work by non-UN actors on conflict theory has begun to see practical application by nontraditional preventive actors such as lenders and donors, as well as actors charged with humanitarian, development, human rights, and refugee tasks. By dint of their weight in resources and/or expertise and experience that can be brought to bear, such actors' comparative advantage tends to lie in early and long-term preventive action relating to the management of resource scarcity and abundance, processes of political transition and democratization, and socioeconomic issues such as horizontal inequality.

The research community has been instrumental in widening the focus of peace and security to include developmental, socioeconomic, and health issues. Nonetheless, although there is an increasing range of policy-oriented research that seeks to bridge the gap between theory and practice—that is, identifying best practices and lessons learned and applying them to a range of policy issues—more work and new initiatives are required to build bridges between the research and policy communities. This is the subject of Chapter 12 by Maureen O'Neil and Necla Tschirgi. They set the stage for the practical demonstration of how research and practice are being mutually informed and operationalized by practitioners in the remaining chapters in Part 3.

For instance, major donors have begun to apply some of the quantitative and qualitative insights relating to the causes of conflict and how to prevent them. Mukesh Kapila and Karin Wermester in Chapter 13 describe recent initiatives that are being adopted to this end by the Department for International Development of the government of the United Kingdom, spearheaded by the newly created Conflict and Humanitarian Affairs Department. In particular, the United Kingdom has placed security sector reform at the top of its sustainable development agenda in an effort to stem potential sources of violent conflict following research indicating that insecurity is a strong concern for the poor. In addition, the World Bank began at the end of the 1990s to undertake a major research project on conflict indicators that seeks to establish, among other things, a categorization of at-risk countries that can be used to inform the Bank's lending practices in those countries. The structure of this project, and some initial findings, are presented by Patricia Cleves, Nat Colletta, and Nicholas Sambanis in Chapter 14.

In Chapter 15, Bengt Säve-Söderbergh and Izumi Nakamitsu Lennartsson emphasize the importance of efforts to support good governance and democratization, informed by the experiences of an NGO that engages in just such work, the International Institute for Democracy and Electoral Assistance. They argue that traditional preventive action—short-term preventive diplomacy in particular—has become increasingly ineffective in the face of complex crises and conflicts. What is needed, then, is a more comprehensive democratization assistance strategy for prevention, as well as a longer-term one that addresses root causes.

Conclusion

The devastating terrorist attacks on the World Trade Center and the Pentagon of September 11, 2001, and their aftermath have brought to prominence a further challenge for the UN system in the field of prevention. There may be little the UN can do to affect the nihilist strategies of some terrorist groups (although these groups need to be combated energetically). However, international actors need to understand, reflect on, and counter-act wherever possible the support some of the most virulent terrorist groups enjoy among disaffected populations. Many of the issues discussed in this volume are relevant to longer-term strategies of conflict prevention and management, including measures that will alleviate the societal tensions that transnational terrorist networks can exploit for their own narrow ends. Improved strategies of conflict prevention are essential in the UN's toolkit to combat global terrorism, which threatens the safety of peoples everywhere. This volume seeks to strengthen the *potential* of the UN and member states to effect preventive action. What is required is a concomitant shift moving the system from promise to practice; a topic discussed further in Chapter 16.

Notes

The authors are especially grateful to Chandra Lekha Sriram for her substantive insights and editorial comments.

1. Chapter 1, Article 1 of the Charter of the United Nations states that the purposes of the United Nations are: "To maintain international peace and security, and to that end: to take effective collective measures for the prevention and removal of threats to the peace, and for the suppression of acts of aggression or other breaches of the peace, and to bring about by peaceful means, and in conformity with the principles of justice and international law, adjustment or settlement of international disputes or situations which might lead to a breach of the peace."

2. For a more in depth discussion of the role of the Security Council in the post–Cold War era, see David M. Malone, "The Security Council in the Post–Cold War Era," in *International Security Management and the United Nations,* eds. Muthiah Alagappa and Takashi Inoguchi (Tokyo: United Nations University Press, 1999): 394–408.

3. See Lilly R. Sucharipa-Berhman and Thomas M. Franck, "Preventive Measures," *New York University Journal of International Law and Politics* 30, 3–4 (spring-summer 1998): 485.

4. For instance, the deployment of UN peacekeeping forces in the 1956–1957 Suez crisis was a form of conflict prevention designed, in part, to prevent conflicts from intensifying and drawing in the superpowers. The First United Nations Emergency Force was authorized by the General Assembly—as the Security Council was paralyzed on the issue—and was deployed in November 1956 "to secure and supervise the cessation of hostilities, including the withdrawal of the armed forces of France, Israel and the United Kingdom from Egyptian territory and, after the withdrawal, to serve as a buffer between the Egyptian and Israeli forces." See http://www.un.org/Depts/dpko/dpko/co_mission/unefi.htm, accessed on February 26, 2001, and Brian Urquhart, *Ralph Bunche: An American Life* (New York: W. W. Norton, 1993).

5. Nabil Elaraby, interview with David M. Malone, New York, January 1996.

6. A recent International Peace Academy (IPA) volume examines some of the economic factors at play in contemporary wars. See Mats Berdal and David M. Malone, eds., *Greed and Grievance: Economic Agendas in Civil Wars,* a project of the International Peace Academy (Boulder: Lynne Rienner Publishers, 2000). Debate in this area has been heavily influenced by the work of Paul Collier, (now at the World Bank), who offered a chapter to the cited volume, and also by Frances Stewart (published in this volume; see Chapter 5), the World Institute of Development Economics Research in Helsinki, and a number of other research

institutions. IPA has now launched a major policy development project of its own on economic factors in civil wars, focusing on the economic activities of belligerents, on corporate motivations in theaters of conflict, and on what an effective international regulatory and legal framework would need to encompass in order to address meaningfully white-collar crime under the cover of civil wars.

7. See Chapter 9 by Peter Wallensteen in this volume and Barnett R. Rubin, *Blood on the Doorstep: The Politics of Preventive Action* (New York: Century Foundation and the Council on Foreign Relations, 2001).

8. See David M. Malone, *Decision-Making in the UN Security Council: The Case of Haiti, 1990–1997* (Oxford: Clarendon Press, 1998).

9. See UN Security Council Resolution 687, April 3, 1991.

10. The United Nations Preventive Deployment Force, the first of its kind, was authorized by UN Security Council Resolution 983, March 31, 1995, superseding earlier deployment of UN peacekeepers there. In the Central African Republic (CAR), the initial request for international preventive action came from President Ange-Félix Patassé himself as early as December 1996 and was based on the potential for escalation of the internal situation, as well as the possibility that instability emanating from within the CAR would spread to an already troubled region. The United Nations Mission in the Central African Republic was subsequently established by Security Council Resolution 1159, March 27, 1998.

11. See the Statements by the President of the Security Council on behalf of the Council, and especially the Statement by the President of the Security Council, S/23500, January 31, 1992.

12. See United Nations, "Report of the Panel on United Nations Peace Operations," UN Doc. A/55/305-S/2000/809, August 21, 2000.

13. For a cogent articulation of the view, strongly held by some developing countries, that the United Nations' capacity in this area is in no need of strengthening, see Statement by H.E. Mr. Kamalesh Sharma, Permanent Representative of India to the United Nations on the Comprehensive Review of the Whole Question of Peacekeeping Operations in All Their Aspects (Agenda Item 86), in the Special Political and Decolonization Committee (Fourth Committee) of the UN General Assembly, New York, November 9, 2000.

14. For instance, several experts have argued that the programs of some international institutions (and in particular the international financial institutions) may have indirectly contributed to the exacerbation of horizontal inequality and, hence, to the probability of violence. In particular, see Susan L. Woodward, *Balkan Tragedy: Chaos and Dissolution After the Cold War* (Washington, D.C.: Brookings Institution Press, 1995).

15. The distinction is articulated as between structural and *operational* prevention in the Carnegie Commission on Preventing Deadly Conflict, *Preventing Deadly Conflict: Final Report* (New York: Carnegie Corporation of New York, December 1997), xvii-xlvi, but structural and *direct* prevention by Wallensteen and others.

PART I

The Dynamics of War

2

Diagnosing Conflict: What Do We Know?

Anne-Marie Gardner

Since 1990, interest in intrastate conflict has surged as an intriguing academic puzzle as well as a persistent practical problem. Though it is difficult to draw a definitive line between intrastate and interstate conflict, as most internal wars contain regional or international dimensions, the focus here will be on the internal dynamics at the heart of intrastate conflict. Many of the most perplexing conflicts in the 1990s—Bosnia, Somalia, Rwanda—have centered on ethnic violence within state borders, new roles for United Nations (UN) peacekeeping in the aftermath of civil wars, and other aspects of internal conflict. A proliferation of recent studies has analyzed the issue from theoretical and policy perspectives, attempting to understand the root causes of such conflicts as well as the underlying trends in the incidence and magnitude of intrastate wars. The goal of this chapter is not a comprehensive review of the literature on the causes of conflict and conflict trends—either of which could fill entire volumes—but rather a focused review of several studies conducted in the 1990s in order to highlight emerging areas of convergence and divergence in the literature.[1] The underlying mission is to map out where the efforts of scholars converge, with special emphasis on findings that challenge conventional wisdom and/or traditional policy approaches. This analysis might then serve as a first step—outlining key potential topics for discussion—as we attempt to offer policy prescriptions for effective prevention efforts by the UN system.

The first section in this chapter will concentrate on causes of conflict, assessing the level of agreement among several theories. Despite wide variation in approaches and focal points, there appears to be convergence in two fundamental areas. First, four factors appear repeatedly as especially prominent causes of conflict: insecurity, inequality, private incentives, and perceptions. These factors often work in tandem: economic inequalities may exacerbate security concerns, and perceptions fuel incentives to initiate or support conflict. Increasingly emphasized in the literature is the role played by economic factors, such as economic inequalities or the economic incentives of subnational actors. Prevention efforts must therefore utilize a multipronged approach, addressing multiple factors in a coordinated fashion, and emphasize previously neglected economic factors. Second, these causes interact with each other across time. Scholars designate some factors as structural causes and some as mobilizing factors that more directly precipitate the outbreak of war. *Structural factors* are the deeply rooted, underlying causes of conflict that may not always develop into violence. *Mobilizing factors* are more immediate to the conflict and often involve the actions of elites and/or masses. Thus, prevention should target underlying causes with long-term approaches and mobilizing factors with short-term prevention efforts—the latter focused on the role played by local actors.

The second section briefly presents key insights from a divergent approach to studying conflict: the literature on causes of peace. Though much of this literature has developed from theories of interstate conflict, the interest here will be on the implications for intrastate conflict. Some scholars have suggested how the democratic peace thesis as well as hypotheses on interdependence or deterrence might be applied to intrastate conflict. Others are investigating recent efforts at postconflict peacebuilding in order to understand conditions conducive to long-term peace and prevention of conflict recurrence.

The third section reviews theories on conflict trends, focusing on analyses of the post–Cold War period. Conventional wisdom—that the Cold War produced stability and the succeeding era has witnessed an unchecked conflagration of civil violence—will be compared to two types of measures of intrastate conflict in the 1990s. One tracks the incidence of war over time (the number of interstate and intrastate wars occurring each year); the other traces trends in the magnitude of war (the number of wars combined with a measure of each war's impact on society). Both undermine the conventional wisdom and in fact highlight the decreasing frequency and intensity of conflict in the 1990s. Understanding these trends and what is driving them may offer clues as to what types of prevention measures might be successful in the future.

In the fourth section, potential topics for discussion are offered in order to set the stage for formulating actionable recommendations for the United Nations. What are the implications for prevention efforts of recent findings on causes of conflict and causes of peace? What is the relation between conflict trends and the potential for international action? How can these learnings be operationalized into policy? Even if one were to embrace the points of convergence and trends identified in this literature review as the basis for action, there remains much work to be done and many tough questions to answer in order to improve conflict prevention in the UN system.

Causes of Conflict: Emerging Consensus

If scholars who study intrastate conflict agree on nothing else, they have reached consensus on the complexity of their subject and the fact that it is exceedingly difficult to generalize about causes when myriad, interrelated factors are involved and each conflict is to some extent context-specific.[2] Perhaps even the word "causes" is somewhat of a misnomer; some experts such as Ted Robert Gurr describe conflict as akin to disease—we should look for symptoms instead of causes.[3] At first glance, there is wide divergence in the literature on what precisely those symptoms are (collapsed states, economic change, human rights abuses), how they interact (with each other and across time), how to undertake diagnosis (methodology for analysis), and even the name of the disease (ethnic conflict, civil war, etc.). (See Appendix 2.1.) Commenting on the state of ethnic conflict research, David Carment and Patrick James note the following: "Agreement exists that some combination of economic, political and psychological factors can explain ethnic conflict. Consensus, however, ends at that point."[4]

Even though exact causal mechanisms are in dispute, there seem to be two main points of convergence in the literature reviewed:

1. *Key variables:* despite wide variation across specific arguments appearing in the literature, four factors appear repeatedly in causal explanations: insecurity, inequality, private incentives, and perceptions. Many studies emphasize the influence of economic factors that have been underemphasized by past academic and policy efforts. Prevention should be multidimensional—combining security, economic, and other concerns into a coordinated approach—with special emphasis on previously underemphasized economic factors.

2. *Structural and mobilizing causes:* myriad and interrelated factors combine to cause conflict, but one can break down factors by type to understand the difference between underlying, or structural, causes of conflict and more proximate, or mobilizing, causes. Prevention should address underlying factors with long-run prevention strategies and proximate causes with short-run prevention strategies, the latter targeted at substate actors whose actions often directly precipitate violent conflict.

Key Variables

From the lengthy list of potential causes, four factors stand out in many studies: insecurity, inequality, private incentives, and perceptions.[5] Although each will be discussed individually in the following pages, most scholars agree that these factors operate together in various combinations to cause or exacerbate conflict. For example, insecurity may be a result of conscious elite policies to solidify their own power at the expense of other societal groups (inequality and private incentives leading to insecurity) and perceptions may exacerbate or fuel inequalities. These links, as well as the individual causes, need to be addressed in order for prevention to be effective.

Insecurity

Insecurity is mentioned as a key variable by several analysts in the form of the security dilemma.[6] One academic school of thought argues that intrastate conflict can be conceived of as interstate conflict writ small, borrowing learnings from analyses of the international system on the effects of anarchy. Under this view, government collapse, or the inability of the state to protect all groups within its borders, spurs various groups to elevate the provision of security to a primary concern. As in the international system, attempts to increase security by one group may decrease the perceived security of another group, and these actors find themselves locked into a security dilemma under which their actions could spiral unintentionally into war. Barbara Walter highlights situations in which such security fears alone may be sufficient to cause conflict without aggressive aims from elite leadership: government collapse, geographic isolation of a minority group, and shifts in the political or economic balance of power.[7] In the extreme, government collapse produces a situation of anarchy that increases insecurity for all and triggers conflicts.[8] For this and other similar theories, the necessary condition underlying intrastate war is anarchy; the path to violent conflict is a result of security-seeking behavior under this condition.

In other cases, the security dilemma may be a prelude to state collapse instead of resulting from it. Actors seek to maximize security when other conditions besides anarchy obtain weak state institutions,[9] lack of institutional capacity,[10] breakdown of conflict management mechanisms,[11] and crises of state legitimacy[12]—all point to the inability of the state to provide security for diverse groups within its borders. A posited connection also appears in the literature between overtly strong states and the same underlying weaknesses if one measures institutional strength as legitimacy. David A. Lake and Donald Rothchild argue that repressive tactics are used by inherently weak states: "States that use force to repress groups, for instance, may appear strong, but their reliance on manifest coercion rather than legitimate authority more accurately implies weakness."[13] Monty Marshall draws on Hannah Arendt's distinction between power (which she defines as the human ability to act in concert) and violence: the concepts are often incorrectly linked but in reality are opposites—violence appears when power so understood is in jeopardy (i.e., when insecurity increases).[14] The problem for prevention—traditionally the international community dealing with existing state institutions—is how to address the security concerns of all groups when those institutions are too weak to act effectively or are themselves the crux of the problem.

Inequality

Another ubiquitous concept in the literature is inequality. The absolute amount of deprivation (such as overall poverty or education levels) is not as salient as what E. W. Nafziger, Frances Stewart, and Raimo Väyrynen, in a study of complex humanitarian emergencies, define as horizontal inequality—differentials or deprivation across recognizable groups in society. This inequality can be measured across multiple dimensions: political participation, economic assets, income or education, and social situation (see Chapter 5 by Frances Stewart in this volume). Gurr defines the similar notion of collective disadvantage as socially derived inequalities in material well-being or political access.[15] Elsewhere, he and Barbara Harff describe inequality as relative deprivation—highlighting political and economic discrimination as examples—and argue that unequal access to political power often lies at the heart of other types of discrimination or disadvantage.[16] Such inequality works in conjunction with deteriorating economic conditions and problems of state legitimacy (which fuel insecurity or private incentives) as the roots of conflict.

Although usually not a sufficient cause of conflict in isolation, group inequalities underpin grievances that are key to mobilization for conflict. Several authors focus on relative deprivation or inequality across economic as well as political dimensions as the primary condition upon which elite action builds. A study by the Clingendael Institute (known in English as the Netherlands Institute for International Relations) suggests that inequalities in both areas—exclusionary political and economic policies—can form the basis of grievances utilized by leaders to mobilize support. Leaders incite followers by using inequalities to construct or enhance group identity.[17]

The focus on inequalities, especially economic deprivation, challenges a common tendency for policymakers to distill the role of economics into a simplistic maxim: poverty leads to conflict and war. According to some, this formula is deeply entrenched in UN thinking. The ideas of, first, integrating development with security and other factors and, second, targeting group-specific deprivation instead of general poverty constitute new approaches to prevention. These ideas need to be articulated and implemented as different from current practice, as many of the chapters in this volume suggest. As one example, prior to 1994 Rwanda was by many accounts responding well to overall development programs despite the fact that insecurity and inequality continued to fester. The traditional development approach neither emphasized integration nor addressed inequalities, suggesting how prevention might be improved in the future.

Private Incentives

The political and economic incentives of potential leaders as well as potential followers are crucial to understanding conflict. Some local actors may react to legitimate security concerns, whereas other leaders have more predatory designs. Carment and James stress the importance of understanding both the structural underpinnings of conflict (e.g., uneven economic development, which creates or enhances inequalities) as well as the motivations of leaders who may see conflict as the most preferable option available.[18] Leaders can be motivated by political goals (most often to attain or retain power) or economic gain. Gurr suggests that discriminatory policies are used instrumentally by elites to protect power, whereas Michael Brown as well as Rui de Figuieredo and Barry Weingast posit that vulnerable leaders seek to secure power through conflict.[19] Similarly, Harvey Waterman argues that those in power are likely to initiate conflict when they feel threatened and those not in power use violence when presented with opportunities to gain power.[20]

Often elites are motivated by opportunities for private accumulation and use shared ethnic ties and discrimination primarily for their own achievement of power. Stewart describes how ethnicity and ideology are used as instruments by leaders pursuing political goals. Paul Collier models the greed factor of both leaders and followers, showing that when the incentives for group leaders to fight over control of the state are high (large proportion of gross domestic product in commodities—that is, "lootable" resources) and the costs of recruiting followers are low (many young men in the population with few other opportunities for income), then the seeds of conflict are sown.[21] Those who choose to follow leaders may have direct incentives for economic or other benefits if they are widely distributed. Leaders become less important in the path to conflict when the potential advantages will be conferred directly on group members; conversely, followers are most likely to support elites when they lack alternative sources of income.[22] Additionally, others who profit from conflict (e.g., business opportunists or criminals) may prefer continued conflict to resolution, thus erecting obstacles to or spoiling settlement.

Prevention or resolution of conflict must address private incentives of leaders *and* followers in order to be effective, as well as remove potential spoilers from the equation. The final report of the Carnegie Commission on Preventing Deadly Conflict emphasizes that conflict arises from deliberate political decisions; leaders can be persuaded or coerced to use peaceful means of conflict resolution and followers' incentives to fall prey to violent arguments can be averted by alleviating the basis for grievances.[23] Prevention efforts can succeed only when the nature and incentives of local actors are considered, especially actions that incite groups to violence.

Perceptions

Finally, perceptions are a key contributing factor in many studies—especially for ethnic conflict. The salience of group identity and the degree of group cohesion are factors that facilitate mobilization.[24] Taisier M. Ali and Robert O. Matthews list ethnic cleavages as a predisposing structural condition and note how inequalities can create or aggravate perceived differences.[25] Harff and Gurr point to differential success among ethnic groups as a factor that increases perceptions of discrimination and heightens the risk of conflict.[26] Antagonistic group histories or recent prior conflict increase the likelihood of conflict under Brown's and Stewart's models and are implicit in the security fears that underpin the security dilemma.[27] Such histories also color how development efforts are interpreted; investments by Indonesia into East Timor were greeted with suspicion because of the bitter history between them. Carment and James, Brown, Walter and Snyder, and Lake and Rothchild all describe the functional use of fear or myths (derived from insecurity or grievances) that are intensified to political advantage by opportunistic leaders.[28] These histories or fears are often institutionalized in schools and textbooks—especially if group discrimination exists in the education system. Intrastate conflict is caused in part by "fear of the future, lived through the past."[29] Thus, one must not only take security, economic inequality, and incentives into account but also understand how perceptions magnify these factors or are used instrumentally to create or exacerbate other causes.

Structural and Mobilizing Causes

Despite wide surface variation across studies, most authors agree that the interaction of multiple factors across time—some structural, or underlying, conditions and some mobilizing, or more immediate, causes—is important to understand the outbreak of violent conflict. Brown charts two types of causal factors: permissive (underlying conditions that alone are not sufficient to cause conflict) and proximate (the factors of immediate or direct causal importance), arguing that prevention must address both by combining long-run and short-run approaches. He also notes how change—especially rapid change—can turn permissive forces into proximate causes, often by making elites vulnerable and prone to power struggles.[30] Likewise, the Clingendael study lists four roles that factors can play: trigger, pivotal, mobilizing, or aggravating. The structural roots of conflict are embodied in pivotal factors (which must be addressed to ultimately resolve the conflict), and mobilizing factors capture the role of leaders. The study also states that power transitions, as one example of a trigger factor, can intensify the effects of the pivotal and mobilizing factors. Clingendael's pivotal and mobilizing roles are roughly equivalent to Brown's permissive and proximate causes.[31] Other authors, without laying out a full theoretical framework for types of causes, stress that certain factors are important underlying conditions—sometimes necessary but not sufficient causes— that are acted upon by elites or masses when political opportunities arise. In a comprehensive articulation of this interplay—centering on the key factors mentioned in the previous section—Gurr and Harff have argued that conflict results from relative deprivation (in their study, ethnicity-based) and group mobilization (on the basis of political or material interests).[32] Ethnopolitical conflict arises from "peoples' deep-seated grievances about their collective status in combination with the situationally determined pursuit of political interests, as articulated by group leaders and political entrepreneurs."[33] In other words, conflict emerges from a combination of underlying insecurity and inequality, colored by perceptions and acted upon by individuals with private incentives. Thus, neither underlying conditions nor human mobilizing actions alone are sufficient explanations, but rather both are necessary to describe the incidence of intrastate conflict.

Breaking conflicts into this type of life cycle—from preconflict to outbreak to postconflict—provides clues for how to increase the effectiveness of prevention. The Carnegie Commission's report offers two types of prevention to match different types of causes: operational (which addresses immediate crises) and structural (which aims to prevent the occurrence or recurrence of crises). The Carnegie report also advocates a complete prevention package that includes early reaction to signs of trouble (necessitating a robust early warning system), as well as an effort to address root causes (long-term planning and solutions).[34] Other studies also advocate long-run prevention aimed at permissive or underlying conditions, short-run prevention targeting mobilizing or proximate factors, and better early warning systems. Challenges to implementing these prescriptions include institutionally uniting long- and short-term strategies; defining and articulating the mandate for prevention, especially long-term; dealing with recalcitrant states, often both the crux of structural problems as well as the conduit for international prevention efforts; and understanding the incentives driving local leaders and followers to mobilize.

Structural Causes

Within the causal milieu, some analyses emphasize structural or systemic factors in order to show that aggressive and/or charismatic leaders are not necessary for conflict to occur—while certain structural factors are—or to highlight the role of macro-level phenomena (e.g., poverty) on conflict. Though the object of study is intrastate conflict, some underlying conditions are found at the regional or international level (such as weak international institutions), and other systemic factors outside the state may influence internal conditions (for instance, a state's performance in the world economy affects poverty levels and distribution of benefits domestically). Brown stresses that ethnic conflict arises from a combination of systemic, domestic, and perceptual factors, but he identifies two structural conditions that are necessary—though not sufficient—for conflict to occur: two or more groups existing in close proximity and national, regional, and international institutions too weak to provide security for those groups.[35] Likewise, Lake and Rothchild identify state weakness as the necessary precondition for conflict before arguing that political entrepreneurs magnify the intergroup strategic dilemmas born under the lack of legitimate state authority.[36] The Clingendael study offers two political-military factors (lack of institutional capacity—i.e., weak or illegitimate state institutions—and unequal access to decisionmaking) and two socioeconomic factors (poverty or economic decline and relative economic deprivation) as contributors to conflict.[37]

Other studies acknowledge the important influence of leaders or political entrepreneurs on the factors they describe—or even the culpability of government elites in creating or exacerbating these conditions—but emphasize salient underlying conditions. Joan Nelson assesses the relation of poverty and inequality on civil conflict while noting the necessity of intervening variables (e.g., legitimacy of elite and political institutions) to transform poverty into conflict. After reviewing several theories that seek to link economic conditions to conflict, she argues that economic factors—especially relative deprivation across groups—can contribute to or exacerbate conflict.[38] Waterman, writing in a collection of essays devoted to the settlement of civil wars, argues that civil wars by definition begin with the failure of state institutions: a breakdown of conflict management mechanisms. Mobilization to violent conflict—a matter of "idiosyncratic choice" by leaders—could be averted if the type of effective conflict management mechanisms found in a stable polity were operating. Thus, war occurs as a result of weakness in underlying structures that sets the stage for incentive-based choices of political leaders and masses.[39]

Existing prevention efforts rarely consider structural causes directly; they tend to be addressed in contexts other than prevention or not at all. One goal of the Early Warning and Preventive Measures Project at the UN Staff College in 1999 was to highlight the prevention measures the United Nations might already be undertaking at the working level and to identify them as such. For example, the United Nations engages in establishing facilitation workshops (Moldova), monitoring transitional elections (South Africa), providing assistance to nongovernmental organizations (NGOs) for monitoring human rights (Cambodia), and other activities that address structural factors but may not have been identified as prevention in the past. Not only does the United Nations need the capacity to identify categories of conflict-prone states—targets of prevention—but it also needs an awareness of its own capabilities to effect change in structural conditions. And even with improvements in these areas, one remaining obstacle to enhancing structural prevention is securing the cooperation of the affected state, the elites of which may draw power from weak structures or institutions.

Mobilizing Causes

Some scholars may include structural factors in their overall explanations but focus on elite action or the process of mobilization either because this part of the equation has been neglected or because leaders' and followers' private incentives are deemed necessary to turn static structural problems into active conflict. The emphasis in parts of the literature has been on elites' attempts to mobilize support for conflict and, to a lesser degree, masses' decisions to mobilize with and without leaders. Within the scope of this review, the strongest articulation of this type of explanation—or, in his words, the prominence of "greed" over "grievance"—is Paul Collier.[40] Based on his quantitative model, individual incentives (greed) motivate conflict more than underlying conditions that disadvantage or divide society (grievance).[41] The roots of intrastate war lie in the private incentives of group leaders and their potential followers: those who benefit from conflict initiate and sustain it.

Brown as well as Ali and Matthews emphasize the aspect of elite choice and action because, in their views, previous literature had been focused almost exclusively on structural factors.[42] Though societal cleavages may exist, according to Ali and Matthews, it is the actions and policies of political elites that can either exacerbate or mitigate potential conflicts. Ethnic divisions, economic disparities, and weak state institutions are often underlying causes of conflict, but alone they are not sufficient explanations—one must examine how political leadership manages such structural problems. Mismanagement may result from an effort by elites to retain power by trampling on the economic, cultural, or political rights of the marginalized. Similarly, Brown argues that many studies have mistakenly highlighted domestic economic or other problems as the root of conflict without considering the important role of "bad leaders." Vulnerable elites engaged in power struggles, he argues, are at the heart of many internal conflicts. Likewise, the Carnegie Commission's report attributes conflict to long-standing grievances exploited by political demagogues. Worsening political or economic conditions and antagonistic histories may set the stage for conflict, but the actions of elites attempting to retain or attain power is a key—and often overlooked—catalyst.

Walter and Snyder see security fears underpinning most intrastate conflict but note that few conflicts occur in the presence of such fears alone; in most cases they are combined with elites' predatory goals (leaders set expansionary goals to increase their group's security or prey upon existing fears to mobilize followers).[43] In the same volume, de Figueiredo and Weingast demonstrate how, given an underlying insecurity and conditions of uncertainty, vulnerable leaders can utilize the fear and incomplete information of their constituents in order to garner support. For example, if negotiations between two conflicting sides fail and the majority of people don't know why, leaders' claims of the other side's aggressive intentions become more plausible. Mobilizing behind these leaders may be a rational response to uncertainty as well as to the high costs of supporting conflict resolution should the other side turn out to be the aggressor.[44] The actions of leaders and of the masses are thus key to causing and sustaining conflict and must be addressed by prevention strategies. Current practice targeting primarily state actors must be infused with knowledge of local actors and their incentives as well as with strategies for engaging them in prevention.

Causes of Peace

Although much recent literature has focused on trying to identify causes of conflict, a separate but related literature has tackled the question of what causes lasting and stable peace. This section will briefly review four strands of this latter literature: three theories that developed mostly in reference to interstate relations (democratic peace, interdependence, and deterrence), and learnings from a new generation of UN peacekeeping operations that engage in peacebuilding activities to prevent the recurrence of conflict. The interest will be to understand the implications of these theories for preventing intrastate conflict.

The democratic peace literature seeks to explain the empirical finding that democracies tend not to go to war with other democracies but do engage in conflict with nondemocracies. Scholars have advanced three hypotheses that operate alone or in combination to explain this phenomenon: norms, institutions, and trade. In the first argument, the domestic norm of peaceful conflict resolution (which obtains in democratic regimes) is externalized to a state's international relations. Democratic states will use peaceful means of resolving conflict with other democracies because they expect reciprocal behavior; a shared normative basis for relations prevails and averts conflict.

Another piece of the puzzle is the function of democratic institutions, which are based on representation as well as checks and balances. Leaders who might otherwise carry the state into war are constrained by the need to garner approval from a legislative body (for a declaration of war or appropriation of funds to conduct the war) and to win public support for the action (affecting mobilization or influencing government decisions through the shadow of reelection). When dealing with other democratic states, a democracy can expect similar constraints that not only decrease the likelihood that a war will be declared but also produce a time delay that allows peaceful avenues of resolution to be explored. These expectations are absent in dealings with nondemocracies because those states lack such internal conflict management mechanisms.[45]

The third part of the democratic peace is related to a more general argument about interdependence. This argument holds that democracies tend to trade more with each other than with nondemocracies and, hence, will avoid conflict because it would be extremely costly. Others outside the democratic peace literature have made similar arguments, asserting that a higher degree of interdependence—which implies mutual vulnerability, not simply interconnectedness—leads to peaceful relations because the cost to one's own economy of using military force is prohibitively high. A state would not want to risk the adverse consequences of severing relations upon which it is dependent for its own growth. The more symmetric the relationship, the greater its stabilizing influence.

Drawing from interdependence literature, regime theorists argue that international regimes increase transparency and information in interstate relations, thus removing some perceived conflicts of interest and—in the case of security regimes—replacing security dilemmas with cooperative relations. Other potential solutions to security dilemmas that are based on forging interdependent security links include alliances and collective security. The spread of democratization and globalization—domestic liberalization and forging more interdependent links, primarily economic—may be driven in part by the underlying notion that democracy and interdependence bring peace to war-prone areas. However, except for studies that cite the instability of democratizing regimes, scholars have not directed their efforts into translating these learnings from interstate relations to the resolution of internal conflict.[46]

Yet another theory that seeks to explain interstate peace is deterrence. Proponents of nuclear deterrence argue that the Cold War did not erupt into World War III due to the second-strike capability of the two sides—the assurance of mutual destruction kept either side from initiating violent conflict, according to this view. Alliances can extend deterrence if the threat to retaliate as if it were one's own territory being attacked is credible; this would arguably enlarge the zone of peace. A functioning collective security arrangement is also based upon deterrence—threatening a preponderance of power ("all against one") brought to bear against any aggressor. Stabilization through deterrence has recently been attempted in resolving intrastate conflict as well. One aspect of the Dayton Accords for Bosnia was to create a military equilibrium by equipping and arming the Bosniac army and instituting an enclave system to prevent secession—striving for parity in capabilities and vulnerability as a way to establish peace through deterrence. Others have argued that if the insecurity cannot be alleviated (e.g., when antagonistic identities are too ingrained) the only route to peace may be to separate groups into defensible enclaves.[47] Power-sharing arrangements in Bosnia and elsewhere can also be considered a form of institutional deterrence.[48]

Finally, the articulation by UN Secretary-General Boutros Boutros-Ghali in his 1992 *Agenda for Peace* of a new type of peacekeeping activity—namely, peacebuilding—reflects a UN effort to prevent recurrence of conflicts.[49] Long-term postconflict engagements focus on rebuilding society (instilling human rights into peace agreements and constitutions, establishing and training judiciary and police, restructuring the armed forces, holding elections) and reconciling the past (establishing truth commissions, reintegrating insurgents into government and the military). The goal of these comprehensive missions is to address the root causes of the original conflict and to set the context for a lasting, stable peace. One issue that requires specific attention is mitigating the insecurity that underpins many conflicts. Disarmament of insurgents, integration of rebels into army and society, third-party guarantees of the peace agreement, and peacekeeping forces to monitor the cease-fire are all techniques to overcome security dilemmas that could potentially trigger a recurrence of violence. Other aspects of peacebuilding tackle inequality, private incentives, and perceptions as well: attention to minority rights and representation in government, integration of insurgents into the regular army, and establishment of inclusive educational and judicial systems. In this respect, the integrated approach of peacebuilding missions serves as a model for the type of multidimensional strategy necessary for successful prevention.[50]

Conflict Trends

Conventional wisdom—especially as informed by the dominant school of thought in the academic literature—holds that the end of the Cold War ushered in a new world disorder. According to this view, the international system had been divided neatly into two spheres of influence and the conflict fault line was known. Internal conflict was contained or limited for fear that escalation and international involvement could eventually spiral into a superpower conflict. Lacking the stabilizing influence of bipolarity, the post–Cold War era is marked by multiple fronts of potential conflicts— adding complexity to international relations and increasing the number of disputes that erupt into violent conflict. Superficial musing on the events of the last ten years seems to uphold this thesis. The wars and associated atrocities, devastation, and humanitarian crises in Bosnia, Kosovo, Chechnya, Somalia, Rwanda, and elsewhere all seem to attest to the proliferation of conflict as well as to an increase in the overall level of violence and destruction. Policymakers' perceptions also support the conventional wisdom: as conflicts move closer to home or the international community becomes more involved in conflicts, it may seem as if the overall number of conflicts is increasing.

But some analysts disagree with the assessment that the international system has become a hotbed of conflict since the end of the Cold War. (See Appendix 2.1 for an overview of the studies in this section.) Citing numerous data sets in a review essay, Stephen R. David notes that the number and intensity of intrastate conflicts did not increase dramatically in the 1990s; rather, the increase in academic interest in this topic stems from the relative decline in importance of interstate conflict with the collapse of the Soviet Union and with the proximity of recent wars to Western states.[51] Other quantitative studies tracking the number of ongoing ethnopolitical wars (see Chapters 3 and 4 in this volume)[52] or armed conflicts (see also Peter Wallensteen and Margareta Sollenberg)[53] show a trend line that underscores David's assessment: rising steadily throughout the Cold War but falling after 1992. Gurr's "ethnopolitical" wars are internal ethnic conflicts in which one party is the government, and Wallensteen and Sollenberg's data include both interstate conflict and internal conflict when one party is the state. Gurr also notes decline in the number of new wars as well as in the number of groups engaged in serious conflict. According to the Wallensteen and Sollenberg data, intrastate conflict has consistently comprised the vast majority of armed conflicts over the past ten years; using 1998 as a representative year, only two out of thirty-six ongoing conflicts were fought between states.[54] These data imply that David's assessment is correct: the reason intrastate conflict is at the forefront of academic and policy agendas is not due to a surge in the number of such wars—quite the contrary—but derives from the relative prevalence of intrastate conflicts over interstate conflicts in the international system today.

Other studies take issue with the conventional belief that the Cold War kept intrastate conflicts contained and that we are witnessing an upswing in the overall level of violence and destructiveness of intrastate war. Wallensteen and Sollenberg's data distinguishes three levels of armed conflict: minor armed conflict (<1,000 total battle deaths); intermediate armed conflict (>1,000 total battle deaths, but <1,000 in any given year); and war (>1,000 battle deaths in any year). They note that the gradual decline in overall armed conflict is driven by a marked decrease in war.[55] This is especially notable for intrastate conflict, as their data also show the vast majority of conflicts over the past decade were intrastate.

The Center for International Development and Conflict Management at the University of Maryland has undertaken an extensive effort to track and code the relative destructive power of ongoing conflicts since 1946 (see Chapter 4 in this volume by Monty Marshall).[56] Marshall includes interstate and intrastate conflicts (state versus ethnic group or between rival political groups); the main criterion for inclusion is organized political violence (not incidental or accidental clashes between armed forces or nonsystematic campaigns). Factors such as fatalities and casualties, resource depletion, infrastructure destruction, and population dislocations (refugees) are combined with subjective elements (psychological trauma or adverse changes to political culture) to assign an ordinal measure on a scale of 1-7 that reflects the impact of the violence on the society experiencing the conflict. These scores can be used to gauge the intensity of an individual conflict (a score of 2, for example, can be very roughly considered as up to 20 percent of a society's annual potential invested in or consumed by the conflict) or to compare the intensity of several conflicts. For each year during 1946–1998, Marshall has also aggregated the ordinal scores of ongoing conflicts to construct a trend line for overall destructive impact that parallels the pattern in the number of wars for the same period: rising steadily until 1992 and falling dramatically thereafter. This overall trend holds for both civil and interstate war, demonstrating that not only the number of internal conflicts but also their aggregate intensity is falling over time.

What might be driving these trends? Gurr as well as Wallensteen and Sollenberg have suggested that an increasing number of peace agreements and better conflict management techniques may be contributing to the decline of conflicts by preventing renewal of old conflicts or arresting conflict before it escalates to the most violent levels (see Chapters 3 and 9).[57] If these scholars are correct, the downward trend in incidence and intensity of conflict reflects the success of conflict prevention and conflict management in the 1990s and similar prevention efforts should be wholeheartedly embraced to maximize these benefits in the future.

Policy Relevance

What impact can these recent findings on causes of conflict and trends in conflict patterns have on the potential for prevention? The review above identified several areas of emerging consensus as to causes of conflict and highlighted studies that challenge conventional wisdom regarding conflict trends. How might these findings impact the formation of prevention policies? This section raises several potential topics for discussion:

1. *Key variables:* the influences of insecurity, inequality, private incentives, and perceptions as causes of conflict point to two policy prescriptions: an integrated approach to prevention addressing all four areas, and an emphasis on economic factors. Peacebuilding missions offer an example of an integrated approach. How can such a multidimensional strategy be applied to prevention efforts? The UN system is already engaging in activities across these four areas—military and defense responses, development and economic incentives, diplomatic coercion, and supporting local efforts by NGOs. But it lacks coordination and, in many cases, a focus on these activities as prevention. How might these efforts be better coordinated? Who ought to be involved—the United Nations, individual states, international financial institutions, NGOs? How especially can economic factors be identified and addressed?

2. *Structural and mobilizing causes:* scholars can agree on a list of structural factors that predispose societies to conflict (weak governance, inequalities across groups), but many societies that exhibit these conditions do not succumb to violence because mobilizing causes are weak or absent. How can the UN system identify where to target prevention—and should we focus on the areas most prone to conflict, or the states that pose the greatest danger of large-scale conflict if it erupts into violence? Moreover, variables do not neatly divide into structural and mobilizing causes; weak or collapsed states—treated as a structural factor—may result from corruption or other elite policies. How can the international community treat structural problems in the face of state—or elite—resistance? Can attempts to address structural problems create fertile ground for mobilizing factors? For example, an established democracy offers stable government and political participation, which decrease the risk associated with weak institutions and political discrimination and are associated with causes of peace; but the process of democratization is identified as destabilizing because it creates opportunities for elite manipulation of new institutions, parties, and the media.

3. *Causes of peace:* which of these causes of peace can be applied to intrastate conflict before it occurs? Although some learnings from this literature have been studied in the context of internal conflict, offering solu-

tions such as power-sharing (deterrence) or integrated missions (peace-building), more research is needed in this area. What other lessons from the causes of peace are transferable to intrastate conditions as preventive measures? Do these prescriptions imply radically divergent—or merely different but complementary—approaches?

4. *Conflict trends:* the disagreement between conventional wisdom and the data suggests two broad areas for discussion. First, how disputable and how significant is the downward trend? Other studies use slightly different measures or methods and may not arrive at the same conclusion; the Arbeitsgemeinschaft Kriegsursachenforschung at the University of Hamburg, for example, uses a different definition of conflict—with no minimum level of battle deaths—and shows an increasing number of conflicts in recent years. Another data set (from the PIOOM Foundation) also includes lower-level conflicts—or microconflicts—and shows a similar upswing in recent years. These data may reflect an increase in the amount of data available, including data on conflicts that previously had not been counted; the increase may be an increase in types of conflicts being counted rather than an increase in the number of actual ongoing conflicts. Even if we agree that we are witnessing a decline in the incidence of armed conflict, how significant is the decline? Has there been a permanent change in the patterns of global warfare, or does 1998 indeed represent a trend break, as the increase in Wallensteen and Sollenberg's measure of wars may indicate? Assuming we accept the trend and deem it worthy of further study, the second issue for discussion is to ask what it suggests for policy. Can the trend data help identify where conflicts are likely to occur and where the United Nations should focus its activities? Marshall and Gurr juxtapose charts of declining conflict with charts of increasing democratization, but is the latter a cause of the former, or are both merely an artifact of the end of the Cold War? If Gurr as well as Wallensteen and Sollenberg are correct that an increasing number of peace agreements and better conflict management techniques may be contributing to the decline of conflicts, how can the UN system maximize these benefits?

The academic literature thus offers several prescriptions for improving future prevention efforts: an integrated approach with an emphasis on economic factors; a phased approach that addresses both structural and mobilizing causes, focusing on the role of local actors; and using trend data to identify targets for prevention and strategies for resolving ongoing conflicts. The trick is to combine these multiple policies into an approach to prevention that is adaptable as well as coherent, timely as well as strategic, and above all effective.

*   *   *

Appendix 2.1 Literature on Causes of Intrastate Conflict

Author, Title	Permissive Causes	Possible Triggers	Proximate Causes/Process	Methodology	Dependent Variable
Taisier M. Ali and Robert O. Matthews, *Civil Wars in Africa*	Ethnic cleavages, economic disparities, weak state institutions (these conditions not sufficient)		Elite action that exacerbates or mismanages underlying cleavages; elites motivated by need to stay in power	Edited volume of case studies	Civil war
Michael E. Brown, *Ethnic Conflict and International Security*	Two necessary systemic conditions: 2+ groups in close proximity and weak national, regional, and international institutions	Democratization	Domestic and perceptual factors layered onto systemic conditions; opportunistic leaders can use myths to mobilize followers	Edited volume of case studies; levels of analysis approach in introduction	Ethnic conflict
Michael E. Brown, *International Dimensions of Internal Conflict*	Structural (weak states), political/military (political discrimination), economic/social (economic stagnation), cultural/perceptual (group histories)	Rapid change to permissive factors—focus on internal elite-triggered conflict (bad leaders)	Power struggle led by vulnerable elites underscored by antagonistic group histories and growing economic problems	Edited theoretical/case study volume; editor's framework divides causes into permissive and proximate	Ethnic conflict
David Carment and Patrick James, *Peace in the Midst of Wars*	Uneven development, self-determination versus multiculturalism issues	International spillover (contagion and diffusion)	Interdependence of variables (not structure alone)—leaders may see conflict as preferable to loss of power; use of fear as instrument of elites	Edited theoretical volume	Ethnic conflict

Author, Title	Permissive Causes	Possible Triggers	Proximate Causes/Process	Methodology	Dependent Variable
Carnegie Commission on Preventing Deadly Conflict, *Preventing Deadly Conflict: Final Report*	Weak states, repression, discrimination, colonial legacies, resource scarcity, regional threats	Indicators of imminent violence: human rights abuses, oppression, propaganda in media, arms buildup	Grievances plus deliberate political action	Culmination of three-year project examining causes of conflict and prevention	Deadly conflict
Paul Collier, "Doing Well Out of War"	Factors that provide economic incentives to leaders and followers (proxies: share of commodity exports in GDP, proportion of population male 15–24, average years education)		Group that sees opportunity to benefit from conflict initiates and sustains it	Statistical analysis (probit model)	Intrastate conflict
Stephen R. David, "Internal War: Causes and Cures"	Neorealism: anarchy and security fears produce security dilemma	Government collapse	Security dilemma (sometimes unintentional spiral to conflict)	Review of Licklider and Brown (highlights limits of neorealism and difficulties of acting based on either set of findings)	Internal war
Douma, Frerks, and van de Goor, "Causes of Conflict in the Third World"	Political/military: lack of institutional capacity and exclusionary politics Socioeconomic: inequality, poverty, slow or unequal economic growth	Power transitions	Relative deprivation: political exclusion and socioeconomic inequality plus group losing power; interdependence of multiple levels and actors	Analysis of causes of conflict and policy recommendations	Intrastate conflict

(continues)

Appendix 2.1 continued

Author, Title	Permissive Causes	Possible Triggers	Proximate Causes/Process	Methodology	Dependent Variable
Ted Robert Gurr, *Minorities at Risk*	Disadvantage across groups (material well-being or political access), repressive government control, group identity and cohesion	Global political change (e.g., statebuilding leads to assimilation policies), democratization, international spread (diffusion and contagion)	Grievances (relative deprivation) combined with pursuit of political interests (group mobilization)—but contextually dependent	Theoretical study based on data analysis of ethnopolitical groups worldwide	Ethnopolitical protest and rebellion
Ted Robert Gurr and Barbara Harff, *Ethnic Conflict in World Politics*	Competition for resources, discrimination (in social well-being or political access), identity, group cohesion, external support	Differential success that increases discrimination	Ethnic identity along with material or political interests (primordialism plus instrumentalism)	Theoretical study based on data analysis of ethnopolitical groups worldwide	Ethnic conflict
Jeni Klugman, "Social and Economic Policies to Prevent Complex Humanitarian Emergencies"	Horizontal inequality, crisis of state legitimacy, worsening economic conditions; also: resource wealth, external shocks	Inequitably distributed growth, political transition, economic failure	Interaction of political and economic factors; keys are group mobilization (based on horizontal inequality) and individual incentives (private accumulation); elites use ethnicity or ideology as instrument	Part of UNU/WIDER study of complex humanitarian emergencies	Complex humanitarian emergency
David A. Lake and Donald Rothchild, *The International Spread of Ethnic Conflict*	Necessary: weak state Other: ethnic groups in competition for resources, economic slowdown	Combination of ethnicity, social uncertainty and fear (security or assimilation) through three strategic dilemmas (e.g., information failure) magnified by political leaders (myths)		Edited volume; editors describe linkage across levels of analysis (intergroup and intragroup dynamics)	Ethnic conflict

Author, Title	Permissive Causes	Possible Triggers	Proximate Causes/Process	Methodology	Dependent Variable
Joan M. Nelson, "Poverty, Inequality, and Conflict in Developing Countries"	Economic factors: relative deprivation (not absolute deprivation)		Poverty or worsening economic trends need intervening variables (e.g., perceptions of unfairness)	Review of theories relating economic factors to the outbreak of civil conflict (as well as trends in global poverty and inequality)	Civil conflict
Frances Stewart, Chapter 5 in this volume	Past conflict, horizontal inequality, low income, economic stagnation	Change in one or more of the following: access to political participation, economic assets, employment and income, or social situation	Elites mobilize groups based on differences (e.g., horizontal inequality) in order to secure or sustain power	Overview of findings from UNU/WIDER study of complex humanitarian emergencies	Complex humanitarian emergency
Barbara F. Walter and Jack Snyder, Civil Wars, Insecurity, and Intervention	Security dilemma	Government collapse, change in economic resources distribution or change in balance of power	Security fears combine with predatory goals of leaders; in some cases security dilemma alone sufficient (government collapse, geographic isolation, shift in economic or political power)	Edited volume of case studies; De Figueiredo and Weingast use game theory to model effect of uncertainty on security dilemma	Civil war
Harvey Waterman, "Political Order and the 'Settlement' of Civil Wars"	Weak polity (lacks effective conflict management mechanisms)	Those in power threatened or those not in power see new opportunity (change in incentives)	Combination of structure and idiosyncratic choice; group mobilization tied to breakdown of conflict management mechanisms	Part of edited volume on resolution or settlement of civil wars	Civil war

Appendix 2.2 Conflict Trends: An Overview

Study	Dependent Variable	Definition/Criteria for Inclusion of Data	Measure of Intensity
Stephen R. David	Internal war	Qualitative assessment of trend using datasets from Gurr, Wallensteen and Sollenberg, Brown, and Licklider	Qualitative assessment of trend referencing Gurr
Ted Robert Gurr	Ethnopolitical conflict (other work also includes ethnopolitical protest and intercommunal conflict)	Ethnopolitical conflict involving government	Rebellion measured by ordinal scale (0-7) that takes into account the number of people involved and intensity of their actions—from banditry to guerrilla activity to protracted civil warfare (similar scales used for levels of protest and for intercommunal conflict)
Peter Wallensteen and Margareta Sollenberg	Armed conflict	Interstate conflict, Intrastate conflict when one party is in government, Minimum twenty-five battle deaths per year	Three levels of armed conflict: Minor (<1,000 total battle deaths), Intermediate (>1,000 total battle deaths but <1,000 in any given year), and War (>1,000 battle deaths in any year)
Monty G. Marshall	Interstate and civil warfare (recent work adds colonial or extrasystemic wars)	Interstate war, Intrastate conflict (state versus ethnic group or between rival political groups), Main criterion is organized political violence (incidental clashes or non-systematic campaigns not included)	The following are considered in assigning an ordinal measure (1-7): fatalities and casualties, resource depletion, infrastructure destruction, population dislocations (refugees), psychological trauma, adverse change to political culture
Arbeitsgemeinschaft Kriegsursachenforschung (AKUF)	War	Two or more armed forces, one of which is government, Organized violence (no minimum number of battle deaths)	

Notes

This chapter was initially commissioned by the International Peace Academy (IPA) to serve as a background paper for the Expert Workshop and International Policy Conference under the rubric of IPA's prevention project "From Reaction to Prevention: Opportunities for the UN System in the New Millennium," June 1999–April 2000. The findings of the project and related research are presented in this edited volume.

1. See Appendixes 2.1 and 2.2 for a list of the main pieces reviewed for the purposes of this chapter. Others are also cited below.

2. The studies reviewed here differ in the definition of their subject matter. Those that seek to explain intrastate conflict, civil war, ethnic conflict, or ethnopolitical conflict will be treated as discussing the same phenomenon, noting that ethnicity is one of several fault lines along which societies divide into conflictual groups (others being clans, religion, tribes). From the studies that center on complex humanitarian emergencies (CHEs), the causes of intrastate war—a precursor to or cause of CHEs—are extracted. From other studies (on prevention or the effects of international involvement), those causal arguments that bear upon explaining intrastate conflict are distilled.

3. See Ted Robert Gurr, *Peoples Versus States: Minorities at Risk in the New Century* (Washington, D.C.: United States Institute of Peace Press, 2000).

4. See David Carment and Patrick James, "Ethnic Conflict at the International Level: Theory and Evidence," in *Wars in the Midst of Peace: The International Politics of Ethnic Conflict*, eds. David Carment and Patrick James (Pittsburgh: University of Pittsburgh Press, 1997), 2.

5. See Appendix 2.1.

6. See Stephen R. David, "Internal War: Causes and Cures," *World Politics* 49, 4 (1997): 552–576; Michael E. Brown, "Causes and Implications of Ethnic Conflict," in *Ethnic Conflict and International Security,* ed. Michael Brown (Princeton: Princeton University Press, 1993); Barbara F. Walter, "Introduction," in *Civil Wars, Insecurity, and Intervention,* eds. Barbara F. Walter and Jack Snyder (New York: Columbia University Press, 1999).

7. See Walter, "Introduction."

8. Jack Snyder and Robert Jervis, "Civil War and the Security Dilemma," in *Civil Wars, Insecurity, and Intervention,* eds. Walter and Snyder; David, "Internal War."

9. Michael E. Brown, "The Causes and Regional Dimensions of Internal Conflict," in *The International Dimensions of Internal Conflict*, ed. Michael E. Brown (Cambridge: MIT Press, 1997).

10. P. Douma, G. Frerks, and L. van de Goor, "Major Findings of the Research Project 'Causes of Conflict in the Third World,'" (The Hague: Clingendael Institute [Netherlands Institute for International Relations], 1999).

11. Harvey Waterman, "Political Order and the 'Settlement' of Civil Wars," in *Stopping the Killing: How Civil Wars End,* ed. Roy Licklider (New York: New York University Press, 1993).

12. E. W. Nafziger, F. Stewart, and R. Väyrynen, eds., *The Origin of Humanitarian Emergencies in the Third World* (Oxford: Oxford University Press, 2000).

13. See David A. Lake and Donald Rothchild, "Spreading Fear: The Genesis of Transnational Ethnic Conflict," in *The International Spread of Ethnic Conflict: Fear, Diffusion, and Escalation,* eds. David A. Lake and Donald Rothchild (Princeton: Princeton University Press, 1998): 8.

14. Monty G. Marshall, "Systems at Risk: Violence, Diffusion, and Disintegration in the Middle East," in *Wars in the Midst of Peace,* eds. Carment and James.

15. See Ted Robert Gurr, *Minorities at Risk: A Global View of Ethnopolitical Conflicts* (Washington, D.C.: United States Institute of Peace Press, 1993).

16. Ted Robert Gurr and Barbara Harff, *Ethnic Conflict in World Politics* (Boulder: Westview Press, 1994).

17. Douma, Frerks, and Goor, "Major Findings."

18. See David Carment and Patrick James, "Ethnic Conflict at the International Level: An Appraisal of Conflict Prevention and Peacekeeping," in *Peace in the Midst of Wars,* eds. Carment and James.

19. Rui de Figueiredo and Barry Weingast, "The Rationality of Fear: Political Opportunism and Ethnic Conflict," in *Civil Wars, Insecurity, and Intervention,* eds. Walter and Snyder; also see Gurr, *Minorities at Risk,* chapter 2.

20. Waterman, "Political Order."

21. Paul Collier, "Doing Well Out of War," in *Greed and Grievance: Economic Agendas in Civil Wars,* eds. Mats Berdal and David M. Malone, a project of the International Peace Academy (Boulder: Lynne Rienner Publishers, 2000).

22. See Collier, "Doing Well Out of War," and Chapter 5 by Frances Stewart in this volume.

23. Carnegie Commission on Preventing Deadly Conflict, *Preventing Deadly Conflict: Final Report* (Washington, D.C.: Carnegie Commission on Preventing Deadly Conflict, 1997).

24. Gurr and Harff, *Ethnic Conflict in World Politics.*

25. See Taisier M. Ali and Robert O. Matthews, "Conclusion: Conflict, Resolution, and Building Peace," in *Civil Wars in Africa: Roots and Resolution,* eds. Taisier Ali and Robert O. Matthews (Montreal: McGill-Queen's University Press, 1999).

26. Barbara Harff and Ted Robert Gurr, "Systematic Early Warning of Humanitarian Emergencies," revised version of a paper presented at the Conference on the Political Economy of Humanitarian Emergencies, convened by the World Institute for Development Economics Research, Helsinki, Finland, October 6–8, 1996.

27. Brown, "The Causes and Regional Dimensions of Internal Conflict," in *The International Dimensions of Internal Conflict,* ed. Brown; Chapter 5 by Frances Stewart in this volume.

28. Carment and James, "Ethnic Conflict at the International Level: Causation, Prevention, and Peacekeeping," in *Peace in the Midst of Wars,* eds. Carment and James; Brown, "Causes and Implications of Ethnic Conflict," in *Ethnic Conflict and International Security,* ed. Brown; Lake and Rothchild, "Spreading Fear: The Genesis of Transnational Ethnic Conflict," in *The International Spread of Ethnic Conflict,* eds. Lake and Rothchild; Snyder and Jervis, "Civil War and the Security Dilemma" in *Civil Wars, Insecurity, and Intervention,* eds. Walter and Snyder.

29. Vesna Pesic, quoted by Lake and Rothchild, "Spreading Fear: The Genesis of Transnational Ethnic Conflict," in *The International Spread of Ethnic Conflict,* eds. Lake and Rothchild, 7.

30. Brown, "The Causes and Regional Dimensions of Internal Conflict" and "Internal Conflict and International Action," in *The International Dimensions of Internal Conflict,* ed. Brown.

31. Clingendael defines "trigger factors" as events that trigger conflict but are

neither necessary nor sufficient to sustain it; "aggravating factors" are those that add weight to other factors but do not cause conflict on their own. See Douma, Frerks, and Goor, "Major Findings."

32. Gurr and Harff, *Ethnic Conflict in World Politics*.

33. In a 1997 study, these authors outline factors that, when present, increase the likelihood that a politically active ethnic group will initiate a rebellion against the state: group incentives (perceived disadvantages, e.g., arising from economic or political discrimination), group capacity (factors that aid mobilization), and opportunities for initiation (regime transition and/or external support). Gurr and Harff, "Systematic Early Warning of Humanitarian Emergencies," variables summarized in Appendixes 38–40.

34. Carnegie Commission on Preventing Deadly Conflict, *Preventing Deadly Conflict: Final Report*.

35. Brown, "Causes and Implications of Ethnic Conflict," in *Ethnic Conflict and International Security*, ed. Brown.

36. Lake and Rothchild, "Spreading Fear: The Genesis of Transnational Ethnic Conflict," in *The International Spread of Ethnic Conflict*, eds. Lake and Rothchild, 19–20.

37. Douma, Frerks, and Goor, "Major Findings."

38. Joan M. Nelson, "Poverty, Inequality, and Conflict in Developing Countries," Project on World Security (New York: Rockefeller Brothers Fund, 1998).

39. Waterman, "Political Order and the 'Settlement' of Civil Wars."

40. Collier, "Doing Well Out of War."

41. What is unclear, however, is the exact relationship between his proxy variables for grievance—which seem to measure overall deprivation in society—and horizontal inequality or group discrimination—where grievance derives specifically from deprivation or differentiation linked to ethnic or other identifiable groups.

42. Brown, "The Causes and Regional Dimensions of Internal Conflict," in *The International Dimensions of Internal Conflict*, ed. Brown; and Ali and Matthews, "Conclusion: Conflict, Resolution and Building Peace," in *Civil Wars in Africa: Roots and Resolution*, eds. Ali and Matthews.

43. Walter, "Introduction," in *Civil Wars, Insecurity, and Intervention*, eds. Walter and Snyder.

44. Ibid.

45. For an introduction to the democratic peace debate, see, e.g., Michael W. Doyle, "Liberalism and World Politics," *American Political Science Review* 80, 4 (December 1986): 1151–1169; and Michael E. Brown, Sean M. Lynn-Jones, and Steven E. Miller, eds., *Debating the Democratic Peace: An International Security Reader* (Cambridge: MIT Press, 1996).

46. On regime theory and interdependence, see, e.g., Robert O. Keohane, *After Hegemony: Cooperation and Discord in the World Political Economy* (Princeton: Princeton University Press, 1984); Stephen D. Krasner, ed., *International Regimes* (Ithaca: Cornell University Press, 1983); and Robert Keohane and Joseph S. Nye, *Power and Interdependence*, 2nd ed. (Glenview, Ill.: Scott Foresman, 1989).

47. See Chaim Kaufman, "Possible and Impossible Solutions to Civil Wars," *International Security* 20 (spring 1996): 265–304.

48. For an introduction to deterrence theory, see, e.g., Thomas Schelling, *Arms and Influence* (New Haven: Yale University Press, 1966), and Alexander L. George and Richard Smoke, *Deterrence in American Foreign Policy: Theory and Practice* (New York: Columbia University Press, 1974). On the Dayton Accords, see Susan

Woodward, *Implementing Peace in Bosnia and Herzegovina: A Post Dayton Primer and Memorandum of Warning* (Washington, D.C.: Brookings Discussion Paper, May 1996).

49. Boutros Boutros-Ghali, *An Agenda for Peace* (UN document A/47/277-S/2411, June 17, 1992).

50. There is a host of literature on this subject; for an overview, see Elizabeth M. Cousens and Chetan Kumar with Karin Wermester, eds., *Peacebuilding as Politics: Cultivating Peace in Fragile Societies,* a project of the International Peace Academy (Boulder: Lynne Rienner Publishers, 2000).

51. Drawing on data through 1995, David describes the post–Cold War era as merely a continuation of a trend toward more intrastate conflict that began in the 1960s. He cites, among others, earlier works by the authors reviewed here: Wallensteen, Sollenberg, and Gurr. See David, "Internal War: Causes and Cures."

52. Gurr, *Peoples Versus States.*

53. Peter Wallensteen and Margareta Sollenberg, "Armed Conflict, 1989–1998," *Journal of Peace Research* 36 (1999): 593–606, and the website: http://www.pcr.uu.se/.

54. See Wallensteen and Sollenberg, "Armed Conflict, 1989–1998," table 2. The total number of wars fell from forty-seven in 1989 to thirty-six in 1998; the number of interstate wars ranged from one to three before 1992 and zero to two after that year.

55. The number of wars fell from twenty to seven from 1993–1997 but rose to thirteen in 1998.

56. See also Monty G. Marshall, *Third World War: System, Process, and Conflict Dynamics* (Boulder: Rowman and Littlefield, 1999).

57. See also Gurr, *People Versus States;* Wallensteen and Sollenberg, "Armed Conflict, 1989–1998."

3

Containing Internal War in the Twenty-First Century

Ted Robert Gurr

The conventional view is that armed conflicts within states and their attendant humanitarian emergencies surged upward at the end of the Cold War
and continued to increase during the 1990s. That view is not supported by
the evidence. On the contrary, quantitative and qualitative changes have
occurred in the severity and settlement of deadly societal conflicts during
the last decade, including a decline in new wars beginning in the mid-1990s
and continuing through the end of that decade into the next. This chapter
briefly reviews those changes and assesses their implications for international responses to future threats to regional and global security.

Global Evidence:
The Declining Trend in Armed Conflicts

Trends in wars and lesser conflicts within and among states from 1945 to
1999 are tracked by Monty G. Marshall (see Chapter 4 in this volume).[1]
His analysis uses a ten-category indicator of the severity of violent conflict—a Richter scale of conflict—that takes into account the scope,
destructiveness, and human costs of each episode. A graph of trends in
these data shows a long-term increase in the magnitude of violent internal
conflicts that accelerated from the 1950s to a maximum in the early 1990s,
followed by a decline.

In a more detailed analysis, Marshall breaks out the annual magnitudes
of three different kinds of violent conflict: interstate war and, within states,
political and ethnic warfare. The distinction between political and ethnic
conflict is to some degree arbitrary. Some are revolutionary struggles for

41

state power, with or without an ethnic or communal base; others are eth-nonationalist campaigns for independence or regional autonomy. For purposes of this analysis, internal wars aimed at seizing state power are categorized as revolutionary, even if ethnic groups provide the basis for group action.[2] The results are shown in Figure 3.1.

The dotted line at the bottom of Figure 3.1 tracks the trend in magnitude of international warfare, which was low during most of the Cold War era. The late Cold War surge is mainly due to the Iran-Iraq War (1980–1988) and Israel's intervention in Lebanon (1982–1990). The upward bump after 1997 is principally due to the 1998–2000 war between Ethiopia and Eritrea.

The dashed line shows the changing magnitude of political warfare, that is, violent struggles for state power. The magnitude of political warfare increased steadily during the Cold War but declined in the 1990s, mainly because of the settlement of intense and protracted wars like those in El Salvador (1979–1992), Mozambique (1981–1992), and Tajikistan (1992–1998). Significant new episodes of political war began and ended in two states during the late 1990s, in Congo-Brazzaville (1997–1999) and Guinea-Bissau (coup and civil war in 1998–1999). At the beginning of

Figure 3.1 Trends in Violent Political and Ethnic Conflict and Interstate Warfare, 1946–1999 (summed magnitude scores)

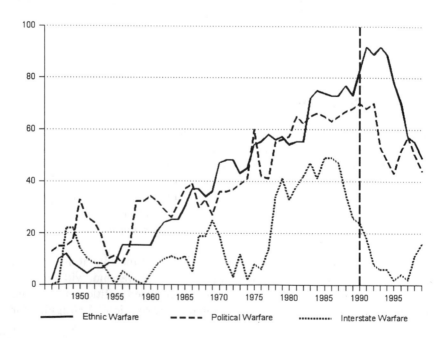

2001 seven medium- to high-magnitude political wars were being fought (i.e., conflicts registering 03 or higher on Marshall's ten-point scale). Five were protracted conflicts that have persisted despite many efforts at settlement: Angola (the quarter-century-long war against the government waged by the National Union for the Total Independence of Angola [UNITA]), Afghanistan (the latest phase of a conflict that began with the Marxist seizure of power in 1977), Colombia (where the current phase in insurgency began in 1984), Sierra Leone (a multisided insurgency begun by the Revolutionary United Front [RUF] in 1991), and Algeria (an Islamist insurgency since 1991). Two other high-magnitude political wars began during the late 1990s: the political (and ethnic) warfare that has wracked Congo-Kinshasa since 1996, and rebellions against President Charles Taylor's regime in Liberia since 1998.

Finally, the solid line tracks the magnitude of ethnic wars. The trends and magnitude of political and ethnic war parallel one another until the early 1980s, after which armed ethnic conflict surged sharply upward to a peak in 1991–1993, followed by an equally sharp decline. Further evidence on the decline is offered in the next section. At the beginning of 2001 eight medium- to high-magnitude ethnic wars were being fought (conflicts of magnitude 03 or higher). Six were secessionist wars that have been highly resistant to both counterinsurgency campaigns and efforts at negotiated settlement. The protagonists are: Moros in the southern Philippines (since 1972); Tamils in Sri Lanka and southerners in Sudan, both beginning in 1983; the Kurdish-based Kurdistan Workers' Party in Turkey (since 1984); Kashmiris in India (since 1990); and Chechens in Russia (since 1994). The other two serious ethnic wars were being fought by clan rivals in Somalia (since 1991) and in Burundi by Hutus who oppose the Tutsi-dominated regime (since 1993). Regional ethnic conflicts in Indonesia escalated during winter of 2000–2001, but at the time of writing none had yet reached magnitude 03.

In summary, fifteen serious wars were under way late in 2000, with an average duration of fifteen years. About half seemed to be winding down, especially in Angola, Turkey, and Afghanistan, and perhaps also in Sierra Leone, Somalia, and Chechnya. The containment or settlement of many other wars during the 1990s is no basis for complacency, though. Some internal wars disconcertingly morph from one form to another: the actors and issues shift but warfare continues, as happened in Afghanistan after the Soviet withdrawal in 1989 and in Congo-Kinshasa after President Mobutu Sese Seko was overthrown in 1997. "Settled" wars also have the potential to resume, depending on domestic and international political developments. Contenders may resume fighting when one or both parties defect from a negotiated agreement, as in Sudan in 1983 and the Israeli-Palestinian conflict in 2000. Rebels may continue fighting despite a cease-fire (e.g., in

Kashmir in summer 2000), or take up arms after the failure of long-term negotiations (e.g., some Moros in the Philippines in mid-2000). Other internal wars resume when spoilers challenge a negotiated settlement or election that had brought fighting to a stop (as in Angola in 1993 and 1998, or Liberia in 1998). Withdrawal of international forces may also trigger renewed fighting, as in Somalia in 1993.

The consequences are paradoxical: as settlements and containment reduce the magnitude of societal warfare, the number of potential hotspots of future conflict may in fact increase.

Global Evidence: Wars of Self-Determination

We can sharpen our understanding of the global decline in ethnic wars during the 1990s by examining one particular type of conflict: armed separatist conflicts. These ethnonational wars, as they are also known, are exemplified by conflicts in Kosovo (Serbia), Aceh (Indonesia), Tamil Nadu (India), and southern Sudan.[3] Their protagonists claim the right to their own national state or autonomous region. Whereas some such claims are settled with little or no violent conflict, like the breakup of the Soviet Union and the devolution of power to Scotland in the United Kingdom, Wallonia in Belgium, and Catalonia in Spain, many others have led to warfare. Separatist wars have been among the most deadly and protracted of all violent conflicts within states during the last half-century, and spillovers from them—the movement of fighters, arms, refugees, and doctrines of armed struggle across porous boundaries—have posed the greatest regional security threats of the post–Cold War era.

These conflicts have been analyzed by the Minorities at Risk project from the 1950s onward.[4] Figure 3.2 summarizes the findings about trends in the initiation and settlement of armed separatist conflicts from 1956 through 2000.

The upper line tracks the number of ethnonational wars ongoing at the end of each period from 1956–1960 through 1996–2000. The general pattern is a steady increase during and immediately after the Cold War that peaked in the early 1990s. The bars along the baseline indicate, from left to right, the number of new ethnonational wars in each period; the wars contained in each period; and the wars settled. "Containment" signifies that fighting was largely ended by some combination of government military victory (Serbs in Croatia), the introduction of peacemaking forces (Kosovo), and cease-fires and ongoing negotiations (Nagorno-Karabakh, Azerbaijan). "Settlements" include only negotiated agreements that largely or entirely ended fighting (Afars in Djibouti, Chakmas in Bangladesh) or that ended in sovereign independence for the separatist region (Slovenia,

Figure 3.2   Trends in Armed Conflicts for Self-Determination, 1956–2000

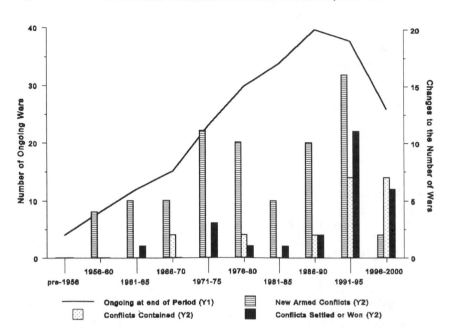

Croatia, Eritrea). In a case where agreement has diminished but not ended fighting, the cases are "contained." If major fighting continues, for example, by Moro factions in the Philippines and Palestinians in Gaza and the West Bank, the war is ongoing.

The results provide striking confirmation of the trends in the Marshall scale. During the 1990s, seventeen armed separatist conflicts were settled by negotiated peace agreements, and fourteen others were checked by cease-fires and ongoing negotiations. Fewer armed separatist conflicts were being fought at the end of 2000—twenty-five by our count—than at any time since the early 1970s.[5] This steep decline helps put the rebellion of Kosovar Albanians in perspective. The armed conflict that began with a few bombings and ambushes by the Kosovo Liberation Army in late 1997 was the only new ethnic war in Europe after 1994, one of only four new separatist wars anywhere in the world between 1995 and 2000. The others were a brief episode of renewed fighting among separatist Muslims in southern Thailand (1995–1998), a new separatist phase in the Afghan Uzbeks' conflict with the Taliban (1996 to the present), and a shift in strategy among militant Ijaws in the Nigerian Delta, from demands for reform to regional autonomy (1995 to the present).[6] The armed uprising of Albanians in Macedonia began—and was contained—after this comparative analysis was completed.

The validity of the evidence about trends in armed conflicts within states can be questioned on several grounds. One possibility is that the long-term rise in numbers of societal wars is a function of the changing number of states in the international system. On the contrary, the percentage of independent states with armed conflicts, graphed over time, shows the same general trend as Figures 3.1 and 3.2. A tenth of states had armed conflicts in the mid-1950s, 20 percent in the early 1970s, 33 percent in 1991, but only 18 percent in 1999.[7] Another consideration is that the long-term upward trend may be inflated by the proliferation of internal wars in a few large and heterogeneous states like Burma, India, and Indonesia. But the governments of India and Burma also contained or negotiated settlements that ended a half-dozen separatist wars during the 1990s, so they contributed as much to the global trend of declining conflict as to its long-term increase.

A further argument is that ethnic and other internal conflicts since the end of the Cold War have been more intense and deadly than those of earlier decades. Marshall's magnitude data suggest otherwise, as does William Ayers's recent analysis of seventy-seven ethnonational wars fought between 1945 and the late 1990s. When Ayres compares wars that began before 1989 and those beginning in 1989 or after, he finds that "neither fighting intensity, total deaths, deaths per month, nor deaths per 1,000 population showed any significant differences between Cold War and post–Cold War conflicts."[8]

A third possibility is that new forms of violent internal conflict have emerged in the 1990s that are not reflected in the trends analyses. In particular, deadly intercommunal rivalries may be on the increase, especially in the global south, due to such factors as ecological pressures and competition for power among communal rivals in weak, multiethnic states. Conflicts like those between Muslims and Christians in Indonesia's Ambon, indigenous Dayaks and Madurese settlers in Kalimantan (Borneo), and between tribal rivals in East Central Africa may be on an upward trajectory that is masked by the downward trend in separatist wars. An initial answer to this possibility is summarized in Figure 3.3.

From 1990 to 1998 the Minorities at Risk project collected annual information on open hostilities between each of 275 groups in the survey and other communal groups (including majority groups, but not the state itself). The number of conflict dyads (pairs of antagonistic groups) increased from about 90 in 1990 to 140 in 1995, then leveling off at about 100 later in the decade. The figure traces the most serious of these, *mass conflict dyads*, defined to include demonstrations against rival groups; rioting and armed attacks; and communal warfare.[9] The same rise-and-decline pattern is evident, steadying at about thirty mass conflicts per annum among the 275 groups. This evidence is not decisive because we examined

Figure 3.3   Trends in Mass Conflict Between Pairs of Communal Contenders, 1990–1998 (number of dyads)

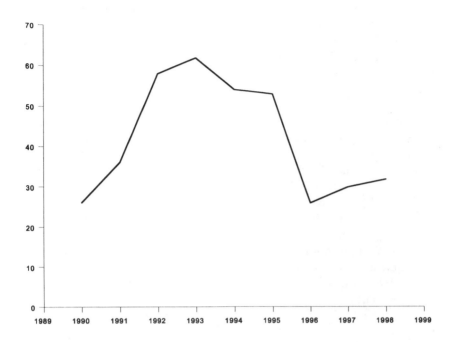

only intercommunal conflicts of the 275 groups already engaged in conflict with governments. The warring Christians and Muslims in Ambon, for example, would not be counted because neither one is on the project's roster of 275 at-risk groups. The evidence is suggestive, nevertheless. It shows that serious intercommunal conflict in the 1990s followed the same rise-and-fall path of violent ethnic challenges to states.

Interpreting the Trends

In the face of this evidence, why are so many observers convinced that the world is threatened by a tidal wave of internal warfare? Part of the answer is selective attention; because they are preoccupied with immediate crises, most policymakers and journalists—as well as most scholars—find it difficult to see the larger trends.[10]

   Another part of the explanation is that observers tend to fixate on the most persistent conflicts that have lasted for decades, like those between Palestinians and Israelis, and between the north and south in Sudan. In fact, as Ayers points out, the median length of all ethnonational conflicts that ended during the last half-century is less than five years. By contrast, the average length of the fifteen medium- to high-magnitude internal wars being fought in 2000 is fifteen years, as noted above. It is unsurprising that the latter attract greater international concern, more intense efforts at containment, and greater frustration about their persistence.

A third factor is that settlements of ethnic conflicts are not as newsworthy as warfare itself. The war in Chechnya is an example. Both phases of the war have attracted intense media attention and international criticism. There is scant recognition that beginning in 1994 the Russian Federation peacefully negotiated power-sharing agreements with Tatarstan, Bashkiria, and some forty other regions in the federation.[11] It is true enough that some agreements attract intense international attention, especially when the United States plays a prominent role. Examples are the 1998 Good Friday agreement in Northern Ireland and the Oslo and Wye Plantation agreements (1994, 1999) between Israel and the Palestinians. By contrast, very little attention has been paid to recent accords that ended open conflicts between the Tuaregs and the Niger government (1995), the Trans-Dniester Slavs and the Moldovan government (1997), the Chakma people and the Bangladesh government (1997), Bougainvillians and the Papua New Guinea government (1998), and Naga separatists and the Indian government (2000). Most of these conflicts had lasted a decade or more and inflicted more casualties—sometimes many more—than the turf war between Catholics and Protestants in Northern Ireland.

A fourth factor is the novelty of new forms and dynamics of internal war and especially the "criminalization" of war—the shift from conflict motivated by ideology and ethnic claims to predatory warfare and armed banditry. The best-known contemporary examples are predatory wars in Colombia, Sierra Leone, and Angola. Insurgency in Colombia began in the 1970s with revolutionary objectives that still motivate some participants, but both social revolutionaries and right-wing militias have been drawn into cooperation with drug producers and traffickers. Foday Sankoh's RUF in Sierra Leone in the early 1990s capitalized on rural resentment against Mende dominance of the government but soon became more interested in diamonds than revolution. Control of diamond mines in northeast Angola became the main source of revenue sustaining UNITA's war with the Luanda government after South African and U.S. assistance was cut off in 1988.

There is, however, nothing new about predatory warfare. The Katanga secession from newly independent Congo in 1961 aimed to protect local and Belgian access to copper wealth. The Wa and other ethnic rebels in northern Burma have benefited from drug trafficking for decades. The political and strategic challenge posed by predatory warfare is that it is more resistant to containment and settlement as compared to other internal wars. The rebels use their resources to buy arms and advisers that make them much more resilient fighters. Their predatory motives make it more difficult to negotiate settlements. Why settle for power-sharing at the center, or for regional autonomy in a federal state, when the rebel army already controls significant sources of wealth?

How commonly are internal wars motivated by predation? Paul Collier and Anke Hoeffler have reported statistical evidence that countries whose economies are dominated by primary product exports have been four times more likely, since 1965, to have internal wars. This is widely cited as evidence that greed motivates most societal wars.[12] But the indicator used is little more than a proxy for underdevelopment, and the results appear merely to confirm the widely observed regularity that armed societal conflict is most common and severe in poor countries. Of the fifteen serious internal wars being fought at the end of 2000, only the four cited above—Colombia, Sierra Leone, Angola, and Burma—are wars of predation, in the sense that they are sustained mainly by the rebels' trade in scarce resources, and all began as political or ethnic wars. Predation occurs during almost all political and ethnic wars: Crops and stores are confiscated; banks and armories are looted; foreigners are held for ransom. These are the "normal" means by which rebel fighters sustain themselves while they, or at least their leaders, pursue larger objectives. I suggest that generalizations about greed or predation as motives for internal war be restricted to conflicts in which rebel control and exploitation of scarce resources have, on the evidence, become a primary objective.

A fifth factor seems to be equally or more important than any of the above in explaining the perception that civil and ethnic wars are a growing threat to international security. It is not the objective number or magnitude of warfare that sustains this view; it is rather the increased awareness of foreign policy makers and observers that local wars threaten regional and international security. This awareness is in turn a reflection of new international realities. The ripple effects of internal wars are substantially greater now than they were twenty years ago, for a number of mostly familiar reasons. Russia cannot contain armed conflict in the Caucasus and Central Asia as effectively as could the Soviet Union. Rump Yugoslavia has fomented rather than restrained ethnic conflict in the Balkans. The mobility of arms and fighters in East and Central Africa means that ethnic rivalries once confined within a single state have spread outward to create a conflict-ridden "bad neighborhood" encompassing ten states or more. These security threats emerged during the same decade that saw an explosion of international news coverage, a rapid expansion of international trade and investment, and a proliferation of nongovernmental organizations (NGOs) and politically active publics demanding that the United Nations (UN) and the major powers take proactive responsibility for local and regional security. NGOs concerned with humanitarian crises and underdevelopment have made frequent and successful use of their close links with the media to publicize the plight of conflict victims.[13] Hence, the paradox. Internal wars are less numerous but objectively more threatening to regional and international security, and responsibility for containing them has moved up on the policy agenda of the United Nations, regional organizations, and the major powers.

The Evolution of New International Policies to Contain Internal Warfare

Both the norms and practices of international response to internal war changed during the 1990s. Norms that prescribed international responsibility for managing internal wars were asserted more forcefully, reinforcing the perception—noted immediately above—that internal wars posed a greater security threat than heretofore. And international actors did in fact engage more frequently and directly in preventive diplomacy, negotiated settlements of internal wars, and collective peacekeeping, peace enforcement, and humanitarian intervention. The net effect of international engagement is evident in the trends depicted at the outset of this chapter. Numerous internal wars have been contained or settled, and a less obvious, unknowably large number of other conflict situations has been defused short of open warfare.[14]

My view is that these norms and practices constitute the elements of a new international doctrine. It incorporates the following principles of good practice about how to manage violent conflict in divided societies, principles that can be expected to drive international policy during the early years of the twenty-first century.[15]

Implementing International Norms About Individual and Group Rights

Standard-setting texts specify individual political rights and minorities' cultural, economic, and political rights that the international community is obliged, in principle, to implement. Among them are the International Bill of Human Rights as well as agreements signed by member states of the Organization for Security and Cooperation in Europe (OSCE) in the early 1990s. These texts are not binding, but they provide the legal basis for a political program that includes proactive advocacy of individual and group rights by individual states, regional organizations, NGOs, and minority groups themselves. The texts are worded so as to endorse the rights of individual members of ethnic and religious minority groups and do not specify that groups as such have rights. Nonetheless, it is a widely accepted corollary of this package of rights that the right to organize and act politically implies the right of regionally concentrated minorities to seek self-governance within existing states.

Promoting Institutions for Democratic Power-Sharing

Democratic institutions are the preferred domestic means for protecting group rights in heterogeneous societies and for pursuing political programs to redress inequalities. Within the context of democratic institutions, mutual accommodation is the optimal strategy for managing conflicts between challenging groups and states, rather than suppression or forced assimilation of groups that claim separate identities and interests. These preferences are both normative and practical. Normatively, the leading states in the international community operate on democratic principles and strongly support the establishment and continuation of democratic institutions elsewhere.[16]

In practice, democracy and power-sharing are not a one-size-fits-all solution to the political tensions of heterogeneous states. In poor states with a history of protracted interethnic conflict, externally induced power-sharing may contribute to political disasters, as they did in Burundi and Rwanda in the early to mid-1990s.[17] But the weight of evidence favors democratic approaches to ethnic conflicts rather than authoritarian rule or, as Chaim Kaufman has argued, partition.[18] I have shown elsewhere that democracies have less ethnic rebellion (but more ethnic protest) than other kinds of regimes. Moreover, in third world countries that underwent democratic transitions between 1980 and 1995, ethnic rebellion was more likely to decrease than increase. In addition, the new democratic states established during this period have a strong record of acknowledging and promoting minority rights. Finally, democracies did substantially better than authoritarian regimes in reaching negotiated settlements of internal wars. Out of twenty-five settled armed conflicts for self-determination between 1956 and 2000, nineteen were settled by democratic governments—often after new leaders came to power during transitions from autocracy to democracy.[19]

International Engagement in Containing Internal Wars

The emergent norm is that international and regional organizations, and individual states, have responsibilities to mediate internal wars and to engage, using force if necessary, to check gross violations of human rights. As a practical consequence, the protagonists in internal war are very likely to face multilateral and bilateral pressures to reach negotiated settlements.

Some such efforts are highly publicized, not necessarily to good effect, whereas others take less visible diplomatic forms.

The UN Security Council has authorized fifty-two peacekeeping operations during the past half-century, fifteen of them current, and most of these aimed at containing armed conflicts within states.[20] Current debates within and about the United Nations' responsibility to address internal conflicts focus on two issues: first, improving the capacity of the United Nations to anticipate and respond proactively to emerging crises (the focus of several chapters in this volume; see Part 2); and second, improving the effectiveness of UN peace operations. Improving peace operations is the objective of the "Report of the Panel on UN Peace Operations" (the Brahimi Report, named for the chair of the panel that prepared it).[21] This report to the UN Secretary-General recommends comprehensive reforms, including long-term strategies for conflict prevention; better Secretariat capacity for strategic analysis, planning, and support of peace operations; the need for bigger, better-equipped peacekeeping forces with robust rules of engagement; and means to support more rapid and effective deployment, preferably within thirty days, of a Security Council resolution authorizing a peace operation. This ambitious set of proposals illustrates the current evolution of the doctrine of international engagement. Its acceptability was signaled when the Security Council adopted a resolution that endorsed the report's key recommendations on November 13, 2000.[22]

The United Nations has often suggested that regional organizations take more responsibility for conflict management. Some have done so with Security Council authorization and some have not—most recently and notably the 1999 intervention in Kosovo by the North Atlantic Treaty Organization (NATO). In general there is great variability in the willingness and ability of regional organizations to engage in societal conflicts. European organizations—the European Union and the OSCE—have been proactive in identifying and reacting to potential as well as current conflicts. The Organization of American States and, in the last decade, the Organization of African Unity (OAU) have also sought to prevent and mitigate armed conflicts. No such regional efforts are evident in Asia. Also at issue is the role of individual states in peacekeeping operations. The United States and Russia have engaged in unilateral peacekeeping operations, and Nigeria and South Africa have done so through the guise of subregional organizations. The criticism inevitably leveled at such operations, whatever their rationale, is that they aim at advancing the initiating countries' national interests. Nonetheless, they can be expected to recur whenever the United Nations and regional organizations fail to act.

Another issue is the fact that some regional powers, like India and China, cannot initiate preventive or peacekeeping measures without raising profound suspicions among neighbors about their motives. Russia, China, and India are also examples of regional powers whose policies toward domestic challengers are all but impervious to international engagement. There is little chance that an international cavalry will ride to the rescue of rebellious Chechens, Uighers, or Kashmiris. The examples in this and the previous paragraph suggest that application of the principle of international engagement is and will continue to be constrained by realist considerations.

Threats of international use of force and military presence have a critical and expanding role in the process of engagement. Bruce Jentleson argues vigorously for what he calls "coercive prevention," saying that "while coercion rarely is sufficient for prevention, it often is necessary," and without it "we will continue to do too little too late to prevent ethnic wars and other deadly conflicts."[23] The doctrine of coercive prevention means the use of credible threats of military action to deter fighting and gross human rights violations, as well as to compel an end to them once under way. Coercive prevention may include preventive deployment of military forces, as was done in Macedonia in 1993; as Jentleson points out, this should have been done in East Timor before or immediately after the August 30, 1999, independence referendum there.

When preventive means fail to deter conflicts that pose serious threats to regional security or cause gross violations of human rights, the United Nations and some regional organizations have come to accept the obligation to respond with military sanctions and peace enforcement operations. Historically, most UN-authorized peacekeeping forces were used to ensure implementation of agreements that had largely ended hostilities, whereas *peace enforcement* refers to the evolving doctrine and strategies by which force is used proactively to contain ongoing conflict even in the absence of agreement by the contenders. A recurring criticism of the UN Security Council during the 1990s has been its authorization of peacekeeping missions in situations where missions should have been authorized, manned, and equipped for robust peace enforcement operations, for example in Bosnia (UNPRFOR, 1992–1995), Rwanda (UNAMIR, 1993–1996), Sierra Leone (UNOMSIL, 1998–1999), and in eastern Congo (2000–2001).[24]

One further step in the evolution of international doctrine of engagement is acceptance of the principle that when authority and security have collapsed, multilateral force can be used to maintain international protectorates while civil governance is reestablished. In effect, this has happened in Kosovo and East Timor, but it is too soon to suggest that the precedents establish a general principle.

Proactive international engagement in societal conflicts implies long-term responsibilities. Once settlements have been brokered and civil order reestablished, outside actors have an obligation to provide the material assistance and political guarantees needed to ensure that peace is sustained. A case can be made that if international actors use political and military means to contain internal conflict, they have a normative obligation to help pick up the pieces afterward. As a practical matter, early withdrawal risks losing all the gains achieved by intervention. In fact, political and military engagement has been sustained, more often than not, in most international-ized civil conflicts of the 1990s. The sustained engagement of the United States in the respective peace processes in Northern Ireland and the Middle East is one example. The continued presence of peacekeepers and civilian advisers in Bosnia, Kosovo, and East Timor is another. But there also are counterexamples. One was the 1994 withdrawal of UN forces from Somalia, after the deaths of 100 peacekeepers (including eighteen U.S. Rangers). Outside parties also gave up on implementation of peace accords in Angola in late 1998; peacekeepers were pulled out and diplomatic efforts suspended in view of overwhelming evidence that both UNITA and the Luanda government wanted to fight on.

There is considerable ambiguity about how best to implement the prin-ciples of this emerging doctrine for managing internal wars. For example, not enough is known about the relative effectiveness of different strategies of engagement. Who should engage? Regional powers may be more accept-able to the parties to conflict but have less leverage than major powers. When should engagement begin? Early engagement is better in principle, but it may provoke counterproductive resistance. Should coercion be part of the strategy of early engagement? Should engagement be multilateral or bilateral? Multilateral engagement is preferred in principle but may take too long to organize. What is the optimum mix of inducements, sanctions, and threats? What strategies of prevention and accommodation are most likely to forestall impending internal wars? They probably are different from the strategies that help end ongoing wars.

If any general principal applies, it is that there is no one package of strategies and tactics that is appropriate in all circumstances. It is essential to devise solutions tailored to the specific identity and security needs of each particular set of contenders.

Some Implications for Peacekeeping and Peace Enforcement Doctrine and Planning

I have suggested how international responsibilities for managing internal conflict expanded during the 1990s. The question addressed in this section is whether and how military establishments, especially the European and North American forces that usually are called upon to take the lead in peacekeeping and peace making operations, are equipped to deal with a complex set of changes in security strategies and objectives. It is said that military strategists make plans to fight the last war. For NATO forces, the last war was either the Cold War or the Gulf War, depending on who was involved, and those wars provide no lessons relevant to dealing with internal wars. The Indian army probably has had more experience fighting internal wars compared to all of NATO's armies together.

Below I outline some of the implications that changes in security strategies and objectives carry for military strategists and planners:

• Western military units are far more likely to be committed to peace-keeping and peace enforcement operations than any other kind of combat or near-combat situation. Therefore, these operations should have high priority in national decisions about allocation of defense resources and contingency planning. A corollary is that military promotion and retention policies should favor personnel with training and experience in these operations.

• There is a compelling need for standing multinational forces that can be deployed quickly in crisis situations. The European members of NATO are developing a joint force for these kinds of deployments, and a similar force has been proposed for Africa. Prominent international diplomats like Brian Urquhart and Jonathan Dean have urged the United Nations to establish a standing peacekeeping force, despite resistance from permanent members of the Security Council. Some such multilateral forces will be in place within the next few years under the auspices of regional organizations.[25]

• Internal wars are political wars. This means that military strategy and tactics are almost invariably subordinate to political objectives. Most peacekeeping and peace enforcement operations are multilateral, which further complicates the political constraints on military operations. The political constraints operate in the war zone itself, as well as in the civilian political arenas of the states providing forces. Clear strategic priorities and vigorous international leadership are needed to keep multilateral operations on track.

• The paramount goal of avoiding military casualties, which constrained NATO strategy in Kosovo, was a reflection of civilian leaders' concerns more than those of military strategists. Military planners need to convince their civilian leaders of the importance of taking calculated risks when seeking to contain internal wars, just as risks are taken on the battlefield in interstate wars.[26] Barbara Harff, who has written widely on humanitarian intervention, points out that it is often necessary to risk lives to save lives—and the lives at risk should include military personnel, not just civilians who suffer from collateral damage.[27]

• The UN Security Council and the major powers have in the past been reluctant to authorize vigorous military action in internal wars where the antagonists are intransigent. The recent shift in Security Council views is reflected in the adoption of Resolution 1327 in response to the recommendations of the Brahimi Report.[28] It is increasingly likely that more peace-keeping operations will be recognized at the outset as peace enforcement operations and given the appropriate resources and rules of engagement. Parallel efforts are needed in the countries most likely to provide units for such operations. In addition, military leaders experienced in peacekeeping and peace enforcement need to better educate civilian decisionmakers on the contingencies.

• Internal wars sustained by predation are probably not susceptible to the kinds of settlements that have ended revolutionary and separatist wars, as suggested above. It may not be possible to contain them other than by military means. But Western publics and policymakers are likely to be reluctant to commit troops to ensure that Angola's diamonds and Congo's mineral and agricultural wealth are exploited to the benefit of those countries' corrupt and ineffective governments. Executive Outcomes (EO), a private security organization led and staffed mainly by South African mercenaries, was quite effective in wresting control of the diamond mines from rebels in both Sierra Leone and Angola. It operated in Sierra Leone from spring 1995 until January 1997 with a high level of military success, suffered minimum casualties (reportedly, four casualties out of 350 personnel), and gained much political and public support—until, under international pressure, the Sierra Leone government terminated its agreement with EO.[29] Unless and until the United Nations and OAU establish their own rapid reaction forces, the international community may want to reconsider its condemnation of member states' reliance on mercenaries to contain predatory wars.

• Politically, many in the international community recognize that temporary protectorates may be needed in places like Bosnia and Kosovo in order to reconstruct the conditions of self-government. This means a vigorous military presence to check potentially warring factions. It also requires a more active police presence. Security threats in postconflict situations typically include riots, isolated attacks, and killings by vengeful antagonists who have no controlling political authority. Lightly armed, mobile, and proactive police are better suited to providing security in such situations than heavily armed peacekeepers. Observers in the United States have proposed that the United Nations establish a standing police force of 5,000 or so volunteers, suggesting that it would be politically less controversial than a UN rapid reaction force, and have introduced a resolution in the U.S. Congress endorsing such a force. A non-UN multinational police force is an alternative.[30]

• Finally, military personnel should be better trained for the special political requirements of peacekeeping and peace enforcement operations. The special requirements include working effectively with multilateral forces; close cooperation with international civilian officials and NGO representatives; and proactive engagement with local civilian populations. And in the absence of a multinational police force or constabulary, there is a clear need for peace enforcement units with training and functions like the French *Gendarmerie*, whose primary task is to provide security for civilian populations.

Lessons Learned:
International Containment of Internal Wars

If my interpretation is correct, the criss-crossing trends of declining internal warfare and increasing numbers of settlements during the 1990s are the result of concerted efforts at conflict management by the United Nations, by major powers, by regional organizations, by NGOs, and by members of civil society in countries divided by political and ethnic cleavages. The international doctrine and practice of engagement remains a work in progress. It has evolved through a trial-and-error process that will continue for the foreseeable future. Each new diplomatic offensive, each new peace enforcement operation aimed at internal conflict situations, is in part a political experiment whose success or failure shapes and constrains future engagement. Some of the major lessons learned thus far:

- The most effective strategies of engagement are usually those that are applied early, *before* the onset of armed conflict or gross violations of human rights. Prevention by political and diplomatic means is less costly than coercive intervention and reconstruction. The point is widely recognized by policymakers, observers, and scholars but not yet consistently acted upon. The problem is twofold. One issue is the lack of reliable and convincing risk assessments about crises that lie more than a year or two away. The second is that UN and major power policymakers focus most of their limited political and material resources on responding to immediate crises.[31]
- The most effective kinds of engagement are both multilateral and multidimensional. The multilateral principle is well established with regard to peacekeeping and peace enforcement operations. Less widely recognized is the principle that effective engagement requires collaborative planning among interested states to design strategies that integrate diplomatic, political, economic, and military moves.
- Strategies should be designed with fall-back objectives. The first objective is to forestall violent conflict in high-risk situations. When prevention fails (or is not attempted), the second-best objective is to induce the warring parties to negotiate an end to conflict. If efforts to induce settlement fail, plan three should be to contain spillovers from armed conflict

into neighboring states. Plan four is a peace enforcement mission, worth consideration where humanitarian costs and security threats are high. Successful peace enforcement missions, as suggested at several points above, presuppose a high degree of resolve (or political will) on the part of states that lead such missions and a long-term commitment of resources.

• Military options should always be on the table, not as separate strategies but as part of the metastrategy of engagement. The options range from coercive deterrence, to rescue and training missions, to peacekeeping and peace enforcement, to air and ground warfare. Any threat or use of these actions in specific conflict situations should be integrated vertically with the larger political strategy designed to deal with the conflict, as well as horizontally across all participating states and international organizations.

• There are no fixed scenarios of political and military engagement. Sierra Leone requires different strategies than Kosovo, eastern Congo, or northern Iraq. It is possible to profile high-risk situations, identifying countries and regions at high risk of humanitarian crises and ethnic wars with reasonable accuracy.[32] It is much more difficult to design optimum responses except in the context of a given region, country, and conflict situation. There is always the risk that policymakers will learn the wrong lessons from a particular success or failure, using it as a simple guide about what (not) to do next time. "Next time" in fact is likely to differ significantly from "last time."

Limits to the Doctrine and Practice of Engagement

It is important to recognize that current doctrine and practice of engagement cannot be expected to contain all internal wars. Intense and protracted conflicts like those in Sudan, Afghanistan, and Chechnya have a momentum that is very difficult to check. Antagonists may not want their conflicts settled; quite the opposite, they may be determined to win at any cost. Others do not accept the basic principles of power-sharing and democratic governance that are essential to most negotiated settlements.

Despite the best efforts of international actors to shore up weak states, failed states will continue to provide both incentives and opportunities for future wars. The Democratic Republic of Congo (DRC) is an example. Like Somalia and Sierra Leone, the DRC is not even a "state"—rather, it has become a political arena in which a multiplicity of local and foreign contenders are fighting for control of resources and local power.

It also is the case that some parts of the world are off-limits to the more assertive forms of engagement because regional hegemons like India, Russia, and China reject intervention in their spheres of influence. This does not mean that engagement is irrelevant in these regions. On the contrary, quiet but persistent diplomatic and political initiatives should be pursued, not because they are likely to succeed in the short run but because they increase the long-term prospects for proactive peacemaking in places like Kashmir and Tibet, if and when a regime change or regional crisis provides a political opening.

Toward an Uncertain Future

The evolution of an international doctrine and practice of engagement in internal wars and humanitarian crises is one of the signal accomplishments of the international community during the post–Cold War era. It has inspired many sustained and creative efforts to contain and settle serious internal conflicts that once were thought to be intractable. And it has many successes to its credit: internal wars ended in southern Africa and Central America; humanitarian crises checked in Timor and Kosovo; serious ethnic conflicts deflected in the Baltic states. These successes should be enough to offset skepticism induced by the failure to end warlord rule in Somalia, or halt genocide in Rwanda, or dissuade Pakistan and India from fighting a proxy war in Kashmir. There is, however, a long-term threat to continued engagement by the world community in efforts to contain internal wars and humanitarian disasters. It is not the occurrence of failures per se. Rather, it is that selective attention to failures may be used in domestic politics, especially in the United States, to justify disengagement.

Notes

1. See also Ted Robert Gurr, Monty G. Marshall, and Deepa Khosla, *Peace and Conflict 2001: A Global Survey of Armed Conflicts, Self-Determination Movements, and Democracy* (College Park: Center for International Development and Conflict Management, University of Maryland, 2001).

2. Internal wars in Afghanistan, Guatemala, and Uganda have all drawn support from specific ethnic groups—the Pashtuns, Tajiks, and Uzbeks in Afghanistan, Mayans in Guatemala, the Acholi in Uganda—but because their leaders have fought mainly for control of the state, we categorize them as political rather than ethnic wars. The leaders of Mexico's Chiapas uprising talked revolution but were mainly concerned about empowering indigenous communities; therefore that conflict is categorized as an ethnic war. For a list and categorization of all recent armed conflicts, and their magnitude scores, see the appendix in Gurr, Marshall, and Khosla, *Peace and Conflict 2001*.

3. Marshall's analysis of trends in ethnic wars includes separatist wars but also instances of ethnopolitical violence that have different objectives such as rivalry, revenge, or power-sharing.

4. The Minorities at Risk (MAR) project, based at the University of Maryland's Center for International Development and Conflict Management, tracks the status and conflicts of some 300 politically active minority and national peoples. This analysis of trends in separatist movements is drawn from Ted Robert Gurr, *Peoples Versus States: Minorities at Risk in the New Century* (Washington, D.C.: United States Institute of Peace Press, 2000): chap. 6, updated in Gurr, Marshall, and Khosla, *Peace and Conflict 2001*, 14–18.

5. The count of twenty-five includes the eight intense separatist wars listed above plus seventeen other low-magnitude separatist conflicts, for example by the Basque ETA organization in Spain, some Oromos and Somalis in Ethiopia, Ijaw in Nigeria, and Uighers in China. A roster of all current and recent separatist conflicts, categorized according to their current status, is provided in Gurr, Marshall, and Khosla, *Peace and Conflict 2001*, note 1, 29–32.

6. In addition, some separatist conflicts that appeared to have been contained in the mid-1990s resumed late in the decade, notably in Chechnya and the West Bank and Gaza, and also among the Papuans of Irian Jaya and the Karenni in Burma.

7. See Chapter 4 by Monty G. Marshall in this volume and Gurr, Marshall, and Khosla, *Peace and Conflict 2001*, 9.

8. R. William Ayers, "A World Flying Apart? Violent Nationalist Conflict and the End of the Cold War," *Journal of Peace Research* 37 (January 2000): 105–117, quotation: 112.

9. Each of the 275 groups in the MAR survey was coded each year for open conflict with up to three antagonist groups on a seven-point scale ranging from individual acts of harassment to communal warfare. Because Figure 3.3 shows the total number of conflict dyads, ethnic groups with more than one antagonist are counted two or three times. Analysis of the average magnitude (or intensity) of conflict among all dyads, not shown here, shows a gradual decline from 1992 onward. For details on the coded data used, see the MAR data set and codebook at www.bsos.umd.edu/cidcm/mar.

10. Other studies that show declining global trends in armed conflict from a peak in the early 1990s are Klaus Jürgen Gantzel, "War in the Post–World War II World: Some Empirical Trends and a Theoretical Approach," in *War and Ethnicity: Global Connections and Local Violence*, ed. David Turton (Rochester, NY: University of Rochester Press, 1997), and annual surveys from 1989 to 2000 by Peter Wallensteen and Margareta Sollenberg, the most recent of which is "Armed Conflict, 1989–2000," *Journal of Peace Research* 38 (September 2001): 629–644. The Wallensteen and Sollenberg study shows an increase in Africa in 1996–1999 but a sustained decline in other world regions. A more substantial late 1990s increase is claimed by A. J. Jongman, "Downward Trend in Armed Conflicts Reversed," *PIOOM Newsletter* 9, 1: 28–34, but the PIOOM procedures for categorizing and counting internal conflicts have changed over time in ways that preclude reliable cross-time comparisons.

11. The estimate that agreements have been negotiated with more than forty of Russia's eighty-nine regions appears in the *Washington Post*, February 26, 1999. A detailed analysis is Daniel S. Treisman, *After the Deluge: Regional Crises and Political Consolidation in Russia* (Ann Arbor: University of Michigan Press, 1999).

12. Paul Collier and Anke Hoeffler, "On the Economic Causes of Civil War," *Oxford Economic Papers* 50 (1998): 563–573; also Paul Collier, "Doing Well Out of War: An Economic Perspective," in *Greed and Grievance: Economic Agendas in Civil Wars*, eds. Mats Berdal and David M. Malone (Boulder: Lynne Rienner Publishers, 2000): 91–112.

13. See Warren P. Strobel, *Late Breaking Foreign Policy: The News Media's Influence on Peace Operations* (Washington, D.C.: United States Institute of Peace Press, 1997).

14. The most successful instances of international engagement in internal conflict situations are usually the least known. It is much easier to document wars settled than wars prevented. Recent case studies and commentaries include Chester Crocker, Fen Osler Hampson, and Pamela Aall, eds., *Herding Cats: Multiparty Mediation in a Complex World* (Washington, D.C.: United States Institute of Peace Press, 1999); P. Terrence Hoppman, *Building Security in Post–Cold War Eurasia: The OSCE and U.S. Foreign Policy* (Washington, D.C.: United States Institute of Peace Press, 1999); and Bruce W. Jentleson, ed., *Opportunities Missed, Opportunities Seized* (Lanham, MD: Rowman and Littlefield, 2000).

15. Elsewhere I propose that these principles are the heart of an emergent international regime for the management of conflict in heterogeneous societies; see Ted Robert Gurr, "Ethnic Warfare on the Wane," *Foreign Affairs* 79:3 (May–June 2000): 52–64; and Gurr, *Peoples Versus States,* chap. 8.

16. Leading NGOs in North America and Europe, notably the National Endowment for Democracy in the United States and the International Institute for Democracy and Electoral Assistance in Sweden, promote these principles. A good statement of the norms and practices alluded to in the text is Peter Harris and Ben Reilly, eds., *Democracy and Deep-Rooted Conflict: Options for Negotiators* (Stockholm: International IDEA, 1998).

17. On Burundi, see Michael S. Lund, Barnett R. Rubin, and Fabienne Hara, "Learning from Burundi's Failed Democratic Transition, 1993–1996: Did International Initiatives Match the Problem?" *Cases and Strategies for Preventive Action,* ed. Barnett R. Rubin (New York: Century Press for the Center for Preventive Action, 1998), 47–92.

18. Chaim Kaufman, "Possible and Impossible Solutions to Civil Wars," *International Security* 20 (spring 1996): 265–304.

19. Based on global comparisons using the MAR data set, summarized in Gurr, *Peoples Versus States,* 163–174 and 204–206, and in Gurr, Marshall, and Khosla, *Peace and Conflict 2001,* note 1, 20–21.

20. A recent analysis of the legal basis for forceful intervention in societal conflicts is Edward B. Davis, Sheila M. Davis, and Terry Mays, "International Law and the Legitimate Use of Force," paper presented to the International Studies Association Annual Meeting, Chicago, February 2001. The paper includes a roster and analysis of UN-authorized and other peacekeeping operations. Another such study is Steven Haines, "Genocide, Humanitarian Intervention, and International Law," in *The Ottawa Papers,* ed. Stan Windass, prepared by the Foundation for International Security for the Ottawa Forum (Canada: Canadian Center for Foreign Policy Development, 2001). *The Ottawa Papers* will be republished as *Just War and Genocide* (London: Palgrave Press, 2002).

21. See United Nations, "Report of the Panel on United Nations Peace Operations," UN Doc. A/55/305-S/2000/809, August 21, 2000.

22. UN Security Council Resolution 1327, November 13, 2000.

23. Bruce W. Jentleson, "Coercive Prevention: Normative, Political, and Policy Dilemma," *Peaceworks* 35 (Washington, D.C.: United States Institute of Peace, October 2000): 5.

24. Many factors, political as well as military, internal as well as international, contribute to the failures of UN-authorized peacekeeping missions. See, for example, Dennis C. Jett, *Why Peacekeeping Fails* (New York: St. Martin's, 1999).

25. See Michael Hirsch, "Calling All Regio-Cops: Peacekeeping's Hybrid Future," *Foreign Affairs* 79, 6 (November-December 2000).

26. During NATO's war in Kosovo, half or more of Americans questioned in various polls thought it was worth risking U.S. soldiers' lives to bring peace to the region; see Jentleson, *Coercive Prevention,* note 20, 26.

27. See Barbara Harff, "Rescuing Endangered Peoples: Missed Opportunities," *Social Research* 62 (spring 1995): 23–40.

28. See United Nations, "Report of the Panel on United Nations Peace Operations," UN Doc. A/55/305-S/2000/809, August 21, 2000.

29. A thoroughly documented account is Jonah Schulhofer-Wohl, "The Use of a Private Military Company: A Case Study from Sierra Leone," appendix 2 in *The Ottawa Papers*.

30. For example, see Jonathan Dean, "A Strategy for Ending War," in *The Ottawa Papers*, note 20, and Saul Mendlovitz and John Fousek, "A UN Constabulary to Enforce the Law on Genocide and Crimes Against Humanity," also in *The Ottawa Papers*. Mendlovitz and Fousek's concept calls for a robust force that might be deployed early in a conflict instead of military peacekeepers. A detailed discussion is William H. Lewis and Edward Marks, "Strengthening International Civilian Police Operations," (Washington, D.C.: Center for Strategic and International Studies, Preventive Diplomacy Program Report, December 2000).

31. European institutions are something of an exception to this generalization. They have been relatively effective in anticipating and heading off potentially serious ethnic conflicts in the postcommunist states of Eastern and Central Europe; see the references in endnote 14.

32. Social scientists have a growing capacity to provide empirically based risk assessments of internal wars that complement the more conventional expert-based assessments used by foreign policy makers. For a review of approaches see John L. Davies and Ted Robert Gurr, eds., *Preventive Measures: Building Risk Assessment and Crisis Early Warning Systems* (Lanham, MD: Rowman and Littlefield, 1998). Two recent studies that use structural models to provide global risk assessments are Ted Robert Gurr and Monty G. Marshall, "Assessing Risks of Future Ethnic Wars," chap. 7 in Gurr, *Peoples Versus States*, note 4; and reports of the U.S. government-sponsored State Failure Task Force, some of them available online at www.bsos.umd.edu/eidcm/statefail.

4

Measuring the
Societal Impact of War

Monty G. Marshall

War is perhaps the most distinctive, dramatic, documented, and studied phenomenon in the social sciences, yet it remains one of the most problematic concepts to quantify and compare, rivaling the concept of the "state" in its capacity to confound analysis. In order to better understand the problem of warfare from a systemic perspective, so that systemic conflict management and prevention strategies may be better designed, implemented, and evaluated, it is necessary to develop measures of the societal and systemic impact of warfare that can better inform analyses of social conflict and political violence at the global level. The conventional analysis of warfare that evolved during the era of state-centric internationalism unduly prioritizes state sovereignty, military strategy, and international anarchy in its preoccupation with issues of national security. These priorities are clearly inadequate for defining security analysis in the emerging era of globalization.

The contemporary period has been characterized mainly by protracted civil warfare, intense humanitarian crises, and regional disorder; outbreaks of classic interstate warfare have largely been avoided. Strategies for increasing global security in this century must take into account the full range of effects of episodes of warfare on individuals, local societies, regional communities, and the world system. The success of global security policies will be evaluated not by measuring individual successes and failures but by a systematic assessment of net systemic gains and losses in terms of human security concerns and global resources expended. Global conflict management demands answers to the questions: Is there more or less warfare in the world today than yesterday? Is global human security improving or deteriorating? Who and where are the winners and the losers under the current policies?

Under the tenets of conventional security analysis, few attempts were made to measure the general societal and systemic impact of warfare (Lewis Richardson made a notable, early attempt).[1] Tabulations of military victories, threats, and defeats were compiled individually by states under the conditions of global anarchy, but the world system is much more than simply a sum of its parts and cannot be adequately assessed from a particularistic perspective. A global organization that could apply a broader perspective to common concerns was envisioned. Although charged at its inception with "maintaining international peace and security," the United Nations (UN) was largely precluded from developing a proactive global conflict management system by the predominance of the state-centric Cold War between rival superpowers. The fortuitous end of the Cold War has reinvigorated the impetus to globalization and reinfused the need for a global perspective on human security.

This chapter proposes and applies a measurement scheme to major episodes of political violence in the contemporary era, 1946–1999, to facilitate assessment of progress toward greater global security. The study presents an elaboration and update of ideas and research originally published by the author in the book *Third World War*.[2] The first section explains the impact of warfare (or warfare magnitude) measurement scheme for individual episodes of warfare, that is, the societal impact of warfare. The second section uses the warfare measures to compile and examine global warfare trends; special attention is given to the controversies surrounding perceptions of Cold War and post–Cold War trends in warfare. The global aggregation of the number and magnitude of societal warfare effects gives us a sense of the more general, systemic impact of warfare and how the problem of warfare affects the further development of an effective, global conflict management and prevention regime. The third section focuses on an assessment of the current trend in global warfare and examines the claims by some researchers that the observed, substantial decrease in global warfare levels and events since the end of the Cold War has been reversed in the late 1990s and that warfare is increasing once again. The final section provides concluding remarks.

Measuring the Societal Effects of Warfare

The conventional measures used to capture the magnitude of warfare for application in quantitative analysis typically include an event count (identifying individual actors), a duration count (a time span usually measured in months or years), and some form of casualty count directly associated with fighting among organized combatant groups (battle deaths, battle-related deaths, or total deaths). The resulting figures appear to be comparable across cases (as actors, time, and violent death comprise the most distinguishing, common, and fundamental traits of warfare), but their implied precision is in most cases little more than an illusion, especially when used in combination. Although the identification of an event, the relevant actors, and its duration are by far the least controversial measures applied to the study of warfare phenomena, even these attributes are not immune to measurement errors. These types of measurement errors and an alternative measurement scheme will be discussed below.

A related issue concerns the categorization of warfare events according to actors, actor types, and relational status (e.g., distinguishing interstate events from intrastate or systemic events, ethnic wars from revolutionary wars, terrorism from genocide, etc.). These distinctions inject nuanced meanings to the analysis of warfare that shift the focus away from generalizations concerning warfare's effects on societies toward more particular, specialized foci on means, methods, and the changing nature of relationships (i.e., applied technologies of warfare). These issues have been the subject of an earlier study and will not be repeated here.[3] The measurement of a warfare event's time span is, perhaps, the least problematic of the conventional measures of a warfare episode, yet the identification of an event's beginning and ending point is not without controversy. Episodes often escalate and deescalate incrementally over time, and the intensity of the interaction fluctuates substantially over its course. Analysts very often disagree over the date, even the year, that pinpoints the outbreak and termination of war. Disagreement also surrounds the significance and method of accounting for variations in intensity over time: how does it matter that there are lulls and flurries, escalations and shifting locations, sustained and erratic conduct by the opposing forces? What is of particular concern in this regard is the measurement of the magnitude of a warfare event: the death count. Estimates of warfare death counts vary wildly, as such counts are often purely speculative and always political.

Death counts are the least accurate and least reliable measure of the impact of warfare. The intensive analysis of warfare based, in whole or in part, on this measure is fundamentally flawed on this account. Few cases provide accurate, reliable, and comprehensive body counts of combatants, and in most cases the incentives to distort such reports are enormous. The deaths measurement is most often little more than a rough estimate of the intensity, duration, and course of warfare based on observations and evaluations of the event with only the most rudimentary, comparative perspective. And the death of combatants, although important to military-strategic analysis, is arguably the least problematic and least enduring effect of warfare for the larger societies consumed by these events. By far, the overwhelming majority of the victims of warfare are those directly and indirectly affected by the far-reaching ravages of warfare, short of outrageous death. War ends abruptly for the dead but gains immortality in the disturbed minds of the survivors. A simple accounting of the dead trivializes and distorts war's impact on societal systems, violates statistical assumptions, and does a grave injustice to the full, humanistic analysis of war.

There have been few attempts to quantify the full range of event-related casualties among combatants and noncombatants, even though that measure can be argued to contain a quality of the broadest and most enduring effect of warfare, that is, its meta-effect on normal social dynamics and societal systems. Our greatest insight into the full spectrum of warfare's ravages comes from accounts of World War II, but few events since that catastrophe have been recorded in such open, broad, and vivid detail. Casualties among noncombatants have not been systematically counted and so are rarely included in quantitative analyses. War has both direct and indirect effects on the living as well as the dead; injuries to human agents and damage to social structures may not be remedied for many years after the actual battles have ceased; some effects are even considered generational, as they cannot be fully remedied for the individuals so afflicted.

Some recent studies have examined and attempted to quantify a much wider range of the effects of warfare on societies and systems. Researchers at Saferworld have attempted to calculate the true cost of conflict by examining a broader range of war externalities and applying cost-benefit analysis to several contemporary warfare events.[4] In that groundbreaking treatment, researchers examined the negative impact of war on various aspects of societal development, civil and political rights, and the economy of affected states and involved third parties. Michael Brown and Richard Rosecrance applied similar analysis and accounting techniques to examine systemic responses to warfare events.[5] They focused their analyses of the costs of conflict on the costs to outside powers in order to press their concern for prioritizing conflict prevention strategy alternatives over conflict reaction alternatives to systemic (or third-party) conflict management techniques. Brown and Rosecrance examined five general, categorical effects on outside parties: refugee costs; direct economic costs and economic opportunity costs; military costs; instability costs; and the costs of international peacekeeping operations.

Both studies provide thought-provoking rather than systematic analysis; both studies make strong contributions by revealing the importance of expanding the scope of inquiry and revealing the enormity and complexity of comprehensive cost accounting in assessing the rationality of societal warfare and systemic conflict management. However, systematic compilation and measurement of these broad societal and systemic effects remains an abstract and challenging goal. And even if such a precise and comprehensive measure could be developed, it could not be readily applied to historical cases. Yet the importance of this information is crucial to a full comprehension and accounting of war and the establishment of appropriate systemic priorities and policies.

In order to overcome the problems associated with quantitative analysis of poorly measured social phenomena, such as warfare events, this study has undertaken an extensive analysis, comprising both theoretical and empirical components, that establishes patterns of corroborating evidence for effects and trends. Applying this methodology to the study and measurement of warfare requires the consideration of the full range of known conditions and effects in the assessment of the magnitude of warfare events. Among the societal effects that must be considered in such an assessment are the following:

• *Human resources:* direct deaths (combatant and noncombatant); indirect deaths (e.g., from collateral fire, induced famines and droughts, epidemics, medical shortages); direct injuries (both physical and psychological, permanent and temporary); indirect injuries (e.g., crime and victimization, experiential trauma, grief, diminished health and capabilities, increased insecurity); sexual crimes and intimidation (e.g., rape, prostitution, child molestation, gender domination).

• *Population dislocations:* costs, traumas, inefficiencies, and indirect effects associated with the displacement, whether for personal safety, logistic, predatory, retaliatory, or strategic policy considerations, of large numbers of domiciled people, either within the parameters of the affected society (e.g., internally displaced, forcibly relocated, or sequestered persons) or across societal borders (e.g., refugees, asylum-seekers, emigrants). The practice commonly known as "ethnic cleansing" contains elements of both as group boundaries are redrawn by conflict.

• *Societal networks:* damage and distortions to the fragile fabric of interpersonal associations and the disintegration of relationships and identities based on amity, trust, exchange, mutual benefit, comity, reciprocity, and deferred gratification; relations necessary for the proper and effective functioning of normative systems (social cooperation, cohesion, coherence, and coordination in politico-legal, economic, professional, and sociocultural subsystems).

• *Environmental quality:* direct and indirect damage and destruction to general ecosystem; use or release of explosive, corrosive, and devegetative chemical compounds and mechanical devices that limit utilization of agricultural resources, foul surface and subterranean water resources, pollute atmosphere, disseminate toxic substances and hidden explosive devices, and destroy wildlife and habitats.

• *Infrastructure damage and resource diversions:* direct damage, destruction, and overconsumption of material and mechanical infrastructure, resources, and surpluses such as production facilities, storage, transport networks, vehicles, water supplies, croplands, food, medical supplies, and the like; indirect damage to the society's resource and infrastructure bases (opportunity costs) through the official diversion of resources and funding to the war effort and away from infrastructure construction and maintenance and the provision of social services and unofficial diversions to illicit trade in tangible, transportable commodities such as drugs, gold and diamonds, labor and sex, weapons, art and treasures, and the like.

• *Diminished quality of life and nonreciprocal resource transfers:* tangible and intangible losses (both short- and long-term) associated with general deterioration in the immediate, aesthetic quality of life, access to basic needs, and future prospects in affected societies; humanitarian crises; capital outflows (e.g., "brain drain," "capital flight"); devaluation and unequal terms of exchange; lack of investment and exchange; losses in human potential due to lowered self-esteem and lowered expectations, self-destructive behaviors, alienation and introversion, and within-group factionalization and victimization.

Unfortunately, few of the effects listed above are systematically measured or consistently recorded outside the contemporary *zone of peace*—that is, the thirty advanced industrial economy states in which, during the period 1946 to present, almost *no* major armed conflict has been located and so contribute few, if any, data points to the analysis of warfare. The measurement principle thus has to be consistent with the known level of imprecision inherent in the factors included in the measurement. Benchmarks can be located in estimates of forces available or committed (e.g., national material capabilities, military personnel and expenditures, troop strength), territorial size of the area of operations, casualties, refugees, and internally displaced or relocated persons. Figures for these items are commonly generated for strategic policy, academic, and journalistic purposes. Equally important in the full assessment of war magnitudes are the more numerous narrative accounts and case studies (academic, journalistic, and literary), as the communication and information media are more amenable to reporting complex and case-specific effects, although those sources lack the comparable systematic treatment of the more general quantitative studies.

A ten-point categorical measurement scale of war magnitude and its impact on societal systems was developed and applied to major episodes of political violence for the period 1946–1999.[6] Assessments have been made and scale values have been assigned for all states directly affected by major episodes of violence and destruction (the indirect, mediated effects on societal systems resulting from their leaders' decision to intervene in warfare events taking place in remote societies are not included). The coded values have been compiled and recorded in a data set for comparative analysis across time, place, and typologies of warfare (e.g., interstate warfare, wars of independence, civil warfare, ethnic warfare, genocide). The data can be aggregated annually for presentation in a series of global and regional warfare trend graphs and used for assessing global, regional, and local contexts and their effects in quantitative conflict research (i.e., event interdependence and the quality of "neighborhoods"). The data also can be used in assessing systemic trends in conflict management.

The scale is roughly logarithmic, and the orders of magnitude can be considered a ratio scale for analytic purposes. Warfare, like most human collective endeavors, exhibits economies of scale at the greater magnitudes; whereas long-term social costs of providing security and attendant damage to societal networks and human capabilities are strongly affected at the lower magnitudes, immediate effects such as deaths, dislocations, and physical damage increase dramatically at higher magnitudes. In holistic terms, warfare's effects on societal systems are additive: two category 03 events are roughly equivalent to one category 06 event, and thus the values can be aggregated and compared in meaningful ways. In order to establish and maintain confidence and consistency in the assignment of comparative measures for complex social phenomena, both general and specific qualities and combinations must be taken into account, including an event's duration, or time span, (some events are very short, others protracted), as well as an event's conflict potential. *Conflict potential* is best expressed as the combination of goals and relative means of the conflicting parties, which determines the realized effects of a warfare event over the course of the event.[7] It is assumed to remain generally constant despite periodic fluctuations among actualized activities and realized effects.

In order to aid comprehension of the ten-point categorical warfare scale, descriptive, representative scenarios of the several categorical values are included below. Referent figures for population displacements and direct deaths are listed for each category, but it must be emphasized that these figures are approximate for conventional scenarios under standard conditions. The total effects of warfare result from intensity over time and vary accordingly. For example, direct deaths may be inflated under conditions where combatants' lives are undervalued, and refugee flows and humanitarian crises will be much higher under conditions of general poverty, the brutal victimization of civilians, and/or more transient or subsistence livelihoods. What is more important in determining the magnitude of the impact of warfare on a society are the relational goals, available technologies, and relative means of the combatant groups. Of course, the combination and levels of effects vary from case to case, but levels across effects will usually coincide.

Warfare is an inherently self-limiting event. Population and technical capabilities determine the potential for warfare intensity, whereas actual warfare's consumption and destruction of material infrastructure and human resources make its continuation dependent on the continued production, procurement, and capture of sufficient quantities of essential war materials. As such, both the conduct and resolution of warfare are especially dependent on external sources of support and recovery, both strategic and humanitarian. Unfortunately, there has been little systematic study of the external "sustenance" of protracted warfare, and so both the capacities of war actors as well as external linkage dynamics remain implicit in the categories below. The range of contemporary events (1946–1999), fortunately, does not provide any examples of categorical values greater than seven (07), as the necessary military technologies are not present in most contemporary warfare locations; some historical events are used for illustration of these more extreme values. (The complete list of Major Episodes of Political Violence, 1946–1999, is provided in Appendix 4.1.)

• *Category 10: extermination and annihilation.* Extensive, systematic, and indiscriminate destruction of human resources and/or physical infrastructure with persistent, adverse effects. The social identity itself is the target of destruction. Greatly disparate power and weapons technologies and singularity of intent between adversarial groups make this category possible. Historical events that illustrate this category include Japan for a period when it became the location of nuclear warfare in 1945 and German territories during the Holocaust.

• *Category 09: total warfare.* Massive, mechanized destruction of human resources and physical infrastructure in a war of attrition, with intentional targeting of both combatant and noncombatant societal factors resulting in widespread destruction and long-term effects. Whole societies are the target for destruction, that is, their capacity for both action and reaction; adversaries are of comparable strength and compromise is unacceptable. Population dislocations often exceed 20 million; deaths exceed 5 million. Perhaps 90 to 100 percent of societal production is consumed in the war effort. Military victory (unconditional surrender) is prioritized over all other societal and humanitarian values. Historical examples include Germany (1941–1945) and the Soviet Union (1940–1944).

• *Category 08: modern warfare.* Massive, mechanized destruction of human resources and physical infrastructure in a war of attrition with medium-term effects; noncombatants are not systematically targeted, although great numbers are directly affected by violence. The adversary's military capabilities are the target for destruction; adversaries are of comparable strength. Population dislocations often exceed 10 million; deaths often exceed two million. About 60 to 90 percent of societal production is consumed by the war effort. Society and human capital are prioritized over military victory (capitulation or stalemate are possible). Historical examples are France (1914–1918), Germany (1914–1918), and Russia (1914–1917).

• *Category 07: pervasive warfare.* Technology of destruction is extensive but resources and productive capacity are limited, with continued war effort frequently dependent on supplemental resources from external suppliers. Effects are persistent, and development is arrested over the medium to long term. Social roles and mobilization are almost entirely determined by the culture of warfare. No location within the society is secure from attack, including the largest cities. Population dislocations often exceed 5 million; deaths exceed 1 million. More than 50 percent of societal production is consumed by the war effort. Core issues are considered nonnegotiable. Contemporary examples include Vietnam (1958–1975), Cambodia (1975–1979), Afghanistan (1978 to the present), and Rwanda (1994).[8]

• *Category 06: extensive warfare.* Technology of destruction is extensive but limited; supplemental resources from external supporters are limited. Effects are persistent, and development is arrested over the medium term. Social mobilization is largely determined by warfare, but crucial areas are fairly secure from attack. Population dislocations often exceed 2 million; deaths often range from 500,000 to 1 million. More than 40 percent of societal production is consumed by the war effort. Issues of contention are perceived as vital, but terms are somewhat negotiable, as neither war party has the capacity to unilaterally impose and enforce a lasting settlement. Ethnic cleansing is often viewed as a strategic imperative in the struggle to control a territorial and resource base. Contemporary examples include Ethiopia (1974–1991), Iran-Iraq (1980–1988), Sudan (1983 to the present), and Bosnia (1992–1995).

• *Category 05: substantial and prolonged warfare.* Technology of destruction is at a high level, but goals are limited and often ill-defined. Impetus to warfare is often sustained by issue complexities that make negotiation and compromise difficult. Warfare is intense but mostly confined to particular regions. Population dislocations may exceed 1 million; deaths range from 100,000 to 500,000. More than 25 percent of societal production is consumed by the war effort. For challengers, local autonomy may be preferred over complete separation or predominance, allowing negotiated outcomes. Contemporary examples include Guatemala (1966–1996), Lebanon (1975–1991), Sri Lanka (1983 to the present), and Somalia (1988 to the present).

• *Category 04: serious warfare.* Available technologies of destruction are at a lower level and/or applications remain limited; challenger groups' authority, discipline, and objectives are often diffuse and/or indistinct. Areas affected by warfare may be extensive, but the intensity and the effects are limited; otherwise, warfare is confined to distinct areas and/or periods of time. If armed conflict is protracted, long periods of dormancy will be punctuated by sporadic operations (re)establishing opposing group boundaries. Population dislocations may exceed 100,000 in affected regions; deaths range from 50,000 to 100,000. Contemporary examples include Angola (1961–1975), the Israeli-Arab theater (1967–1970), and Liberia (1990–1997).

• *Category 03: serious political violence.* Technologies of destruction are limited; objectives are usually focused on strategic authority, including control of human and/or material resources. Long periods of relative quiescence may be punctuated by focused operations targeting armed factions, group leaders, and/or symbols of defiance. Population dislocations respond to specific, localized operations and may be counted in the tens of thousands; deaths range from 10,000 to 50,000. Effects of political violence are unevenly distributed, mainly targeting militias, leaders, and symbolic targets. Contemporary examples include Chile (1974–1976), Turkey (1984 to the present), and Sierra Leone (1991–1998).

• *Category 02: limited political violence.* Applied technologies are limited. Objectives may be limited and clearly defined, allowing warfare to remain confined; general support for warfare and/or the nature of the opposition may be weak or resistant to provocation. Events are confined to short periods or specific areas of operation or may involve sporadic acts of terrorism over longer periods. Population dislocations of short duration may occur; attributable deaths range from 3,000 to 10,000. Contemporary examples include Cuba (1957–1959), Northern Ireland (1969–1994), Cyprus (1974), and Georgia (1991–1993).

• *Category 01: sporadic or expressive political violence.* Applied technologies are relatively low-level; objectives are often diffuse and ill-defined, and violent actions occur mainly as an expression of general dissatisfaction and/or social control. Oppositional violence is achieved mostly by small militant groups or confined to a very specific time, target, or location. Small population dislocations of short duration may occur from areas directly affected by violence; deaths usually are less than 2,000. Contemporary examples include the United States (urban ghetto riots, 1965–1968), Argentina–United Kingdom (Falkland Islands, 1982), and Moldova (1991–1997).

Contemporary Trends in Global Warfare

The illusion of stability lent by the Cold War superrivalry distorted perceptions of the real dynamics and actual trends in armed conflict during the period. In fact, nothing could be farther from the truth or more dangerous to the prospects for world peace than the unfounded romanticization of the

Cold War period as a mythical era of global stability and a long peace. Rather, the ideology of the Cold War lent a veil of civility and stasis that served as a cover for increasing incidence and magnitudes of political violence, mostly civil wars, that gradually decimated large areas of the world, led many states to the brink of structural failure (and even beyond), and imprisoned vast numbers of peoples in humanitarian crises.

The end of the Cold War, circa 1990, led to an important shift in world attention away from ideological/apocalyptic images of conflict to focus on an alternative reality plagued by sectarian conflict and warfare, the flames of which were often fanned and fueled by political support and armaments by the rival superpowers and their cohorts. Many people, including important media commentators and world policymakers, were induced by the dramatic shift in viewpoints from singular cold war to myriad hot wars into believing that the end of the Cold War had ushered in a period of global instability and increasing levels of warfare, largely characterized as ethnic or "civilization" warfare.[9] During the 1990s, conflicts in these areas shifted from wars for separation or supremacy to wars for elimination or survival, that is, wars of desperation—an ironic complement to the concentration of wealth and prosperity in the West.

Of great and immediate importance to the formulation of an appropriate global policy for conflict prevention is the aggregate effect that decentralized (local) warfare has had on the global system. In a systems analysis of warfare, the focus moves from particular events and societal effects to cumulative effects and general trends. To this end, multiple sources of compiled information regarding various forms of armed conflict in the contemporary period have been consulted, cross-referenced, and reconciled to produce a comprehensive list of the period's major episodes of political violence. Using the ten-point measurement scheme described above, each warfare episode was assigned a single (net) magnitude score (see Appendix 4.1), which was then summed for each year to produce the annual trend lines shown in Figure 4.1.

Whereas the Cold War shadowed an enormous increase in the number and intensity of localized wars, the trend lines illustrate, significantly, that the overall magnitude and incidence of warfare episodes have decreased sharply and steadily since the Cold War ended.[10] This observation of a recent, sharp downward trend in global warfare is supported by downward trends in ethnic rebellion,[11] in forcibly dislocated populations,[12] and in autocratic authority[13] since the end of the Cold War. The general downward trend noted for major episodes of political violence is further complemented by upward trends in the spread of democracy and increases in conflict settlements.[14]

There is, nonetheless, a great deal of resistance to the notion that global armed conflict is decreasing.[15] It is common for well-informed policy-

Figure 4.1   Armed Conflict and Intervention (ACI) Global Warfare Trends, 1946–1999 (summed conflict magnitude scores)

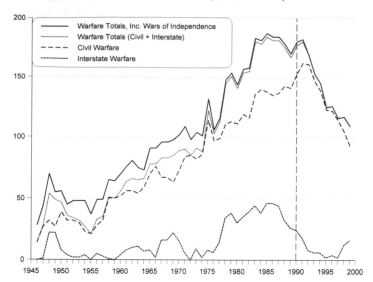

makers and commentators to assume and even insist that armed conflict and related humanitarian crises are becoming more of a problem in world politics, rather than less. This reverse viewpoint highlights perceptual distortions on the salience of global conflict due to greater flow of information and communication; greater attention to previously ignored conflicts in more marginal areas; an increase in appreciation of the relative importance of "minor" conflicts because of their potential spillover effects; greater sensitivity to transnational issues; greater expectations of "civility" in the postindustrial world; and increasing impatience with persisting conflicts in areas considered to be of no strategic importance. Do the apparently counterintuitive empirical trends described above provide any evidence to explain, if not support, the intuitive assessment?

The recognition of a decreasing trend in global warfare does not necessarily negate a concurrent realization that the problem of warfare is of increasing importance in world politics. Declining breadth and/or intensity of a phenomenon and its increasing importance are not contradictory, especially as the sense of conflict's potential and the possibility of renewed hostility linger in the aftermath of war's abatement. Fewer hot wars present the possibility of more lingering hotspots and, with this, a greater sense of urgency, challenge, and vulnerability for an emerging, global conflict management and prevention system. Direct external involvement is in greater demand in hotspots than in hot wars, as are public expectations of meaningful results from that involvement.[16] This is particularly true in the aftermath of civil wars, as the state is usually one of the victims of warfare and so cannot provide the necessary security and framework for economic activity without external assistance.

The prominence of civil warfare is the first element supporting the perception of increasing global violence. Civil wars are the most common form of contemporary warfare, and such situations necessarily involve complex societal and systemic development issues. Interstate wars are often thought to strengthen the capacity of warring states, as states must either affirm their viability and marshal their capabilities to act in pursuit of national interests, including response to external threats, or succumb to their inherent weaknesses and disappear. Civil wars, by contrast, more often undermine the capacity of the state by diminishing its resources, dividing its population, and limiting the scope and nature of its (legitimate) authority, often making it more vulnerable to both external and internal challenges and more dependent on external support. Civil warfare creates tensions for the international norm of noninterference in the internal affairs of states and thus presents additional challenges for the state system and additional complexities in conflict management.

The increasing challenge to the international system of effectively responding to and managing conflict is a second reason for perceptions of increasing armed conflict. The Cold War period experienced a long-term linear increase in the number of conflicts and general magnitude of warfare. During the course of warfare, substantial social resources are diverted to the war effort, even to the complete exclusion of (lower-order) social development priorities. Large areas of the world system have thus experienced an extended drain on available resources, seriously eroding the international capacity to recover from conflict experiences.

The effects of warfare do not disappear with the last shot fired in anger; many societal effects persist over time. The detrimental effects of warfare's harm and destruction must be undone, redone, and overcome. In the aftermath of warfare, political healing is often prioritized over social development programs. Wealth and assets, which flee troubled areas to perceived safe havens, must be enticed to return—a monumental, if not insurmountable, task. Prewar levels of production may not be regained for years or even decades. War-torn societies therefore often experience arrested development. Under such circumstances, greater demands may be placed on diminished capacity, mobilizing competing interest groups and fueling potential conflict. Thus, warfare over a long period of time may challenge a country's capacity to recover and transform its pathologies.

Casual observers are intuitively aware that episodes of violence, although perhaps not immediately observable in global warfare trends, cluster spatially in bad neighborhoods; the unresolved problems of conflict generate spillover effects beyond a state's borders. Over time, the extent of warfare's effects increase and widen, drawing neighboring countries in, triggering past grievances or generating new tensions within and between states. War- and insecurity-affected regions thus become self-reinforcing conflict systems prone to repeated and prolonged episodes of violence.[17]

The emergence of these bad neighborhoods may be a disincentive to external peacebuilding initiatives. External support for postconflict peacebuilding suffers from logistical challenges as resources are far removed from their place of application. This problem is compounded by the frequent unwillingness of external actors to be involved in complex problems seemingly confined to distant locations and remote cultures. Systematic assaults within societies with low productive capacities will quickly result in humanitarian crises and other disasters because people are already living on the edge. In these situations, limited local resources are quickly depleted, and there are serious constraints on the interest and willingness of outside parties to lend assistance, whether in prevention, reaction, or recovery. Thus, the alternatives to warfare in affected regions are few and fragile.

If global warfare is becoming more concentrated in poorer societies, the perception that warfare is a growing problem, and one more resistant to resolution, may be strengthened. Extensive global analysis of civil warfare events by the State Failure project has highlighted a very strong and robust correlation between low state capacity and low quality-of-life measures with armed conflict and governance failure.[18] The question of whether diminished state capacity is causal or consequential in the statistical relationship is peripheral to the present discussion; it is quite likely both cause and effect, making it even more difficult for societies to move away from warfare.

Figures 4.2 and 4.3 recast the global warfare trend data to highlight evidence that state capacity is associated with the occurrence of armed conflict. They present separate global warfare trends (using magnitude scores) for the five quintiles of states based upon an arbitrary but compelling measure of societal capacity: energy consumption per capita.[19] Figure 4.2 displays the warfare trends of the lowest three quintiles of states/societies, and Figure 4.3 displays the trends for the upper three quintiles (the middle quintile is reproduced in both graphs to provide a common point of reference). A comparison of the two graphs reveals the importance of societal capacity in the distribution of warfare: the lowest two quintiles (40 percent) of states account for the majority (65 percent) of the world's armed conflict, whereas the lowest three quintiles account for more than 88 percent of total global warfare. The upper two quintiles together provide location for about 12 percent of the warfare in the contemporary period. The largest share accrues to societies composing the second quintile of states, that is, those states possessing some capacity to wage war but limited capacity for managing conflicts. These second-tier states experienced nearly 40 percent

Figure 4.2   ACI Global Warfare Magnitude Totals by Societal Capacity: Lowest Quintiles

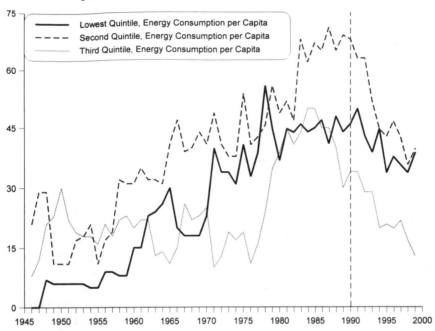

Figure 4.3   ACI Global Warfare Magnitude Totals by Societal Capacity: Highest Quintiles

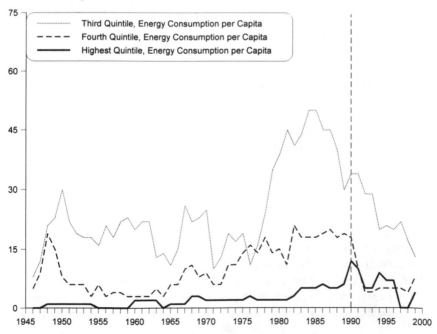

of post–World War II warfare. The highest-capacity states, in contrast, have experienced very few and very limited outbreaks of major armed conflict within their respective jurisdictions.

This study has argued that a substantial portion of the perceptual distortion that warfare is increasing rather than decreasing in the post–Cold War period may arise from the increasing concentration of conflict in the world's poorest countries. It has also argued that when wars occur there under generally dire circumstances, then perceptions of underdevelopment, insecurity, and violence are likely to be conflated and confused, stark images of the brutality of warfare exaggerated, and cultural differences pronounced in the minds of the increasingly removed and distanced witnesses to warfare. But what is the nature of post–Cold War changes in the annual magnitudes of warfare?

Two trends help to condition our perceptions of the problem of warfare and our expectations of its future course: changes in the relevant magnitudes of warfare; and changes in the relative warfare shares across the societal capacity quintiles. As noted in Figure 4.1, the general global trend in warfare since the end of the Cold War has been sharply downward. However, this general decline is not distributed equally across the five quintiles. Comparing the peak period of global warfare (1984–1988) with the more recent period (1994–1998), one finds quite different changes: warfare in the lowest quintile declined the least, about 17 percent; warfare in the second quintile decreased 35 percent; there is a 57 percent decrease in third quintile warfare; and an incredible 74 percent drop in the fourth quintile (the highest quintile decreased the least, 12 percent, but generally had little or no warfare during the entire period). As such, the relative market share for the lowest-capacity societies increased from 61 percent in the peak period to more than 73 percent in the most recent period (climbing to 77 percent in 1998), just in time to become a focal point for the information and communication revolution—and thus a real coffee-table tragedy.

Comparison of Data on Current Trends in Global Warfare in the 1990s

The discussion of global warfare trends has concentrated, so far, on examining the contrast between current *perceptions* of increasing global instability, warfare, and humanitarian crisis and *measures* of the societal and systemic impact of warfare that present a global warfare trend that, although steadily increasing throughout the Cold War period, has been diminishing substantially in both the incidence and magnitude since the end of the Cold War. However, in the late 1990s, some researchers such as Peter Wallensteen and Margareta Sollenberg, and A. Jongman, have presented evidence that the observed downward trend in serious armed conflicts may have been short-lived and is now reversed and appears to be increasing once again as we begin this century.[20] Such claims appear to contradict the continuing downward trend presented by the Armed Conflict and Intervention data (ACI data) above.[21]

Much of the disagreement regarding current warfare trends centers on the method of identifying individual, distinct armed conflict events and the comparability of measures used in the articulation of general trends. Those studies indicating a reversal in the trend (i.e., Wallensteen and Sollenberg; Jongman) use categorical action-event counts (i.e., all events that meet the minimum definitional threshold count as equivalent units). This study used episode counts combined with magnitude scores to suggest that the total impact of warfare continues to decline and, using only the numbers of states experiencing armed conflicts (without magnitude scores), to suggest in addition that the global incidence of armed conflict continued to diminish through the 1990s.[22] However, as any reversal in the downward trend would be cause for alarm in the global community, updated current trends in global warfare should be continually examined.

All that being said, one should expect to find a fair amount of disagreement among the research reports on conflict trends but also to identify a substantial fundamental agreement across analyses. Despite methodological differences and procedural difficulties, there are points of comparability in the armed conflict data sources by which to make some important assessments of the current global warfare trends. Event counts can be compared across data sources by shifting the analytic focus from events to states and assessing the number of states affected by serious armed conflicts in a given year. Of course, interest in the fact of armed conflict is qualified by the seriousness or intensity of conflict events, changes in event intensity over time, and how events affect a state's ability to maintain political performance.

An annual tally of the number of states affected by major armed conflicts is provided for comparison in Table 4.1. The ACI data, which compile and assign societal impact (magnitude) scores by the state in which the conflict event actually occurs, provide a single societal impact score for each state for each year covered (scores for multiple events in a given state are summed for the year). Both the SIPRI/PRIO (a joint project between the Stockholm International Peace Research Institute and the International Peace Research Institute in Oslo) and State Failure data were reworked from their original event count to an affected state format to make them comparable with the ACI data.

The ACI, State Failure,[23] and SIPRI/PRIO[24] data cover the entire 1990s and are generally comparable on raw annual events counts; in addition, the State Failure and SIPRI/PRIO data are roughly comparable on the subset of annual events that exceed a 1,000 battle-related death threshold.[25] The PIOOM Foundation's *high-intensity conflict* (HIC, the flipside of low-

Table 4.1 Number of States Experiencing Armed Conflict, 1989–1999

	1989	1990	1991	1992	1993	1994	1995	1996	1997	1998	1999
Wallensteen and Sollenberg (SIPRI/PRIO): > 1,000 deaths	16	17	16	19	13	7	6	6	7	14	15
State Failure problem set: > 1,000 deaths (rev.)	24	23	27	27	23	20	18	12	13	19	20
Jongman (PIOOM): > 1000 deaths							22	20	20	16	22
Wallensteen and Sollenberg (SIPRI/PRIO): all armed conflicts	37	40	40	42	33	34	31	29	27	32	28
State Failure problem set: all armed conflicts (rev.)	41	38	45	44	39	36	34	34	31	33	26
Marshall (ACI): major political violence episodes	43	44	50	47	46	43	38	38	36	33	29
Jongman (PIOOM): combined events (high-intensity conflict [HIC] and low-intensity conflict [LIC])							61	51	79	86	99
Jongman (PIOOM): violent political conflict (VPC)							40	44	45	114	151

intensity conflict, or LIC) events should compare with SIPRI/PRIO *war events* and State Failure *high-intensity events*. The combined number of PIOOM HIC and LIC events should compare with the *major armed conflict* annual events counts for the years 1995–1999. There is no comparable data for the PIOOM category of violent political conflict (VPC).[26]

Several comments are suggested by the data comparisons presented in Figure 4.4. First, for the subset of events that cross the 1,000 battle-related deaths threshold in a given year, there are substantial differences across the three data sources listed. However, all three sources note an increase in the incidence of high-intensity warfare in the latter 1990s. State Failure and SIPRI/PRIO plot similar trend lines, with a substantial dip in the number of cases of the most intense warfare in the mid-1990s and an upswing beginning in 1997.[27] The PIOOM figures indicate a slightly later dip and an upswing in 1999. In sum, there appears to be consistent evidence that there are increasing numbers of states experiencing intense warfare in the late

Figure 4.4 Comparison of Data on Current Trends in Global Warfare

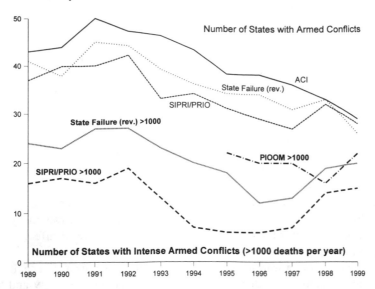

1990s, following a peculiar lull in the mid-1990s. More research is necessary before this particular dynamic can be explained fully.

The complex patterns that emerged in the 1990s could certainly contribute to the general *perception* of increasing warfare in the world. Moreover, the annual numbers of states affected by "all armed conflicts" are similar across three of the four data sources listed: SIPRI/PRIO, State Failure, and ACI. Although the SIPRI/PRIO and State Failure data both denote a slight increase in the number of affected states in 1998, there is not enough evidence to support a claim that the general downward trend in global warfare has been reversed. On the contrary, the substantial decrease in the State Failure data for 1999 appears to support the continuing downward trend noted in the ACI data (and also noted in the Arbeitsgemeinschaft Kriegsursachenforschung data).[28] The PIOOM data appears to support a claim that a downward trend in armed conflicts has been reversed, although little evidence of this is recorded in its brief coverage.[29] In sum, there is substantial evidence that the general downward trend in the number of armed conflicts, and the number of states experiencing armed conflicts, in the 1990s is continuing into the twenty-first century.[30]

Conclusion: Future Trends

The preceding discussion has charted the rise and fall of global warfare in the last half of the twentieth century. The warfare trend thus charted, in many ways, runs contrary to intuitive perspectives of a long peace during the Cold War and greater global instability with its passing. Although it is beyond the scope of this study to speculate on the reasons why the incidence and magnitude of global warfare has diminished so dramatically since the end of the Cold War or to prognosticate future trends, some general observations can be made on the strength of the evidence collected here. The general global trend argues for both optimism and caution; the circumstances present both an opportunity and a dilemma.

• Although the number of hot wars has decreased, the number of hotspots has increased. The probability of renewed fighting following the breakdown of peace settlements is great and diminishes only after long periods of proactive conflict management. In conflict management terms, then, the decrease in open warfare creates pressures for increased involvement by the global community in reversing the ravages wrought by warfare, reconstruction of social relations and infrastructure in affected societies, and the prevention of a relapse to armed conflict.

• Years of open warfare have exhausted the resources and capacities of states and societies and disrupted the complex network of amity and trust upon which societies might be rebuilt. In many locations, development processes have been arrested and even reversed. Entire regions have been devastated by warfare, and some remain immersed in a culture of violence that will be difficult to transform. Many of the most seriously affected societies have either lost, or never gained, viability and vitality. The prospects for many of these weaker societies remain dim without substantial assistance from the stronger societies and the larger community.

• The role of ideas and ideology should not be overlooked or underestimated in our understanding of the dynamics of social conflict and the resort to violence. The ideology of struggle and the acceptance of inhumanity coincide with the rationalization of injustice.

• Future trends in global warfare will reflect not only the quality of the human mind and spirit but also the nature of external influence and involvement in local conditions and conflicts. Wars do not occur in a vacuum; they must consume ever greater numbers of human lives and livelihoods to continue their existence. Misguided or misdirected external support can help to ignite passions, fuel armed conflict, and prolong the disaster. Errors of omission or commission by the global community are crucial in determining the fate of societies in crisis.

A cursory examination of the countertrend of increasing incidents of serious warfare within the general global context of decreasing warfare reveals some additional clues for the future of global (systemic) conflict management and the emerging culture of prevention. The increase in serious warfare in the late 1990s is characterized by four sets of circumstances:

1. *Escalation of long-standing disputes or rivalries:* nearly all of the armed conflicts that crossed the threshold to serious warfare in the late 1990s involved an escalation in a long-standing dispute rather than an outbreak of a new conflict.

2. *Separatism:* many of the most serious incidents of warfare in the late 1990s involved escalations in attempts by distinct ethnic groups to gain (or maintain) separation from a central authority unwilling to accept it.

3. *Black market control:* most serious wars of the late 1990s involved conflicts over the control of black-market commodities and assets that could be easily liquidated through illicit trade, such as drugs and diamonds. Wars have become a pay-as-you-go proposition as the global arms trade becomes increasingly privatized.

4. *Bad neighborhood effects:* only five new armed conflicts broke out in the late 1990s, and each occurred in regions already beset by warfare: armed conflicts in Albania and Kosovo in the Balkans and Congo (Brazzaville), Ethiopia/Eritrea, and Guinea-Bissau in Africa. In general, new outbreaks and escalations of serious warfare in the late 1990s tended to occur in particular regions, or bad neighborhoods, where ongoing, serious armed conflicts were already taking place just as they have throughout the contemporary period.

With the passing of the Cold War, many of the world's warriors have lost their sources of external support and supply and exhausted their own resources and resolve. Consequently, a real opportunity exists to discourage and contain the resort to warfare in human social relations. Providing immediate relief for the victims of warfare is not enough. One of the most effective methods for transforming violent conflict events to negotiated conflict processes involves proactive global scrutiny of and involvement in local conflict dynamics, with observers and caretakers on the ground in and near these trouble spots. Brutality thrives in anonymity and finds its natural corollary in the brutality of daily life in severely underdeveloped societies. A strong global presence seriously dampens the local incentives to accept and escalate brutality and provides viable alternatives to armed conflict.[31] The first step in establishing a preventive conflict management regime for the future of the global community is to draw a clear and accurate picture of the present danger so that the opportunities associated with it can be identified and understood. The challenge remains to comprehend the dynamics underlying the contemporary trends in warfare and to capitalize on the unique opportunity thus presented.

Appendix 4.1:
Major Episodes of Political Violence, 1946–1999

The following table lists 291 episodes of armed conflict that constitute the global, major armed conflict and inform the study. The variables listed are as follows:

Inclusive years (begin and end): the beginnings and endings of most political violence episodes are difficult to determine exactly; various researchers "pinpoint" and denote various dates. The "begin" and "end" years listed for each episode (below) are those considered by the author to be those most likely to capture the transformative "moments" (beginning and ending) of the episodes, according to a comparison of the varying claims of the sources noted. No end year is listed for episodes that began and ended in the same year.

Episode type (type): episode type is listed according to two character codes. The first character denotes either a (C)ivil-intrastate involving rival political groups; (E)thnic-intrastate involving the state agent and a distinct ethnic group; or (I)nternational event–interstate, usually two or more states, but may denote a distinct polity resisting foreign domination (colonialism). The second character connotes either an episode of (V)iolence—the use of instrumental violence without necessarily exclusive goals; (W)ar—violence between distinct, exclusive groups with the intent to impose a unilateral result to the contention; or i(N)dependence—an attempt to forcibly remove an existing foreign domination.

Magnitude of societal-systemic impact (magnitude): the rationale and methodology for assessing the societal and systemic impact of warfare episodes is discussed and described in detail in the accompanying text. The number listed represents a scaled indicator of the destructive impact, or magnitude, of the violent episode on the directly affected society or societies on a scale of 1 (smallest) to 10 (greatest). Magnitude scores reflect multiple factors including state capabilities, interactive intensity (means and goals), area and scope of death and destruction, population displacement, and episode duration. Scores are considered to be consistently assigned (i.e., comparable) across episode types and for all states directly involved.

Episode location (states directly involved): countries listed are only those upon whose territory the political violence episode actually takes place, that is, those state-societies directly affected by the warfare. Countries intervening in the episodes are not listed as the violence does not take place on their territory and, so, these intervening actors are considered to be indirectly, or remotely, affected by the violence.

Estimates of "directly related" deaths (deaths): accountings of the number of deaths resulting directly from an episode of political violence are difficult to determine, and estimates often vary widely. This difficulty is especially problematic as the distinction between combatants and noncombatants has grown increasingly obscure as "less formal" civil conflict interactions in less institutionalized societal systems predominate in the contemporary era. As argued in the text, such estimates of "battle-related deaths" should be regarded simply as estimates of the general magnitude of the violence. The numbers listed here reflect the median or mean of often widely disparate estimates listed in the various sources and are provided solely as a reference point. Casualties among noncombatants directly related to the violent conflict are inconsistently estimated (if at all) in the various source estimates. Far more problematic than "battle-related deaths" for societal systems are the much larger numbers of persons directly and indirectly, physically and psychologically, distorted and disturbed by violence during episodes of armed conflict (for this we have no estimation procedure).

Information sources (references): there is no general agreement among scholars as to what constitutes a major episode of armed conflict. The most common divisions in the relevant research center on episode type or interstate-intrastate conflict distinctions, further complicating the comprehensive compilation of episodes of all types. The reference letters list those from the following sixteen sources that include the episode with the purview of their particular classification scheme.

a. Sivard, Ruth Leger. 1991. *World Military and Social Expenditures 1991*. 14th ed. Washington, DC: World Priorities. (Also consulted 16th ed., 1996; see letter m below.) Criteria: "Armed conflict involving one or more governments and causing the death of 1,000 or more people per year" (Sivard 1991, 25).

b. Brogan, Patrick. 1989. *World Conflicts: Why and Where They Are Happening*. London: Bloomsbury. Criteria: "Includes all the major wars and insurrections since 1945, but leaves out many lesser insurrections and riots, many of which resulted in the deaths of thousands of people."

c. Small, Melvin, and J. David Singer. 1982. *Resort to Arms: International and Civil Wars, 1816–1980*. Beverly Hills, CA: Sage. Criteria: *Interstate wars* during which the total "battle-connected fatalities among military personnel" for all participants was at least 1,000 per year; *extrasystemic wars* during which battle deaths exceeded the 1,000 per year threshold for the system-member; *civil wars* that resulted in at least 1,000 deaths per year including both civilian and military personnel (Small and Singer 1982, 71).

d. Stockholm International Peace Research Institute (SIPRI). 1968–1993. *World Armaments and Disarmament: SIPRI Yearbook*. Annual series. Stockholm: SIPRI. Criteria: Major armed conflicts, defined as "prolonged combat between the military forces of two or more governments or of one government and at least one organized armed group, involving the use of weapons and incurring battle-related deaths of at least 1,000 persons" (SIPRI 1992, 417).

e. Harff, Barbara, and Ted Robert Gurr. 1988. "Toward Empirical Theory of Genocides and Politicides: Identification and Measurement of Cases Since 1945." *International Studies Quarterly* 32: 359–371. Criteria: Cases of "massive state repression" that are "sustained episodes in which the state or its agents impose on a communal or political group 'conditions of life calculated to bring about its physical destruction in whole or in part.'"

f. Kaye, G. D., D. A. Grant, and E. J. Emond. 1985. *Major Armed Conflict: A Compendium of Interstate and Intrastate Conflict, 1720 to 1985.* Ottawa, Canada: Department of National Defense. Criteria: "In a general sense, the conflict modes involve two or more groups (nations and/or actors) in which the use of force was a significant factor in the event. This includes both internal and international events. At least one nation is involved in every conflict listed."

g. Tillema, Herbert K. 1991. *International Armed Conflict Since 1945: A Bibliographic Handbook of Wars and Military Interventions.* Boulder: Westview. Criteria: "An international armed conflict is operationally defined to include all directly related foreign overt military interventions undertaken by one or more states within one or more foreign political territories. . . . Onset of the first directly related foreign overt military intervention and cessation of the last intervention are taken as the beginning and the end of an international armed conflict" (Tillema 1991, 12, n. 8).

h. Singer, J. David, and Melvin Small. 1993. *The Correlates of War Project: International and Civil War Data, 1816–1992.* Computer file. Ann Arbor: University of Michigan. Criteria: See source reference letter c above, except that the criteria for "extrasystemic" wars has been changed from "1,000 annual average battle deaths per year" to "1,000 battle deaths total for all participating interstate system members and the troop commitment criterion."

i. List of International and Civil Wars Excluded (1980–1988). Personal correspondence with Ricardo R. Rodriguiz, Data Management Assistant, Correlates of War Project (COW), dated May 25, 1993. Criteria: Recognized in the literature as an episode of "armed conflict" but fail to meet minimum criteria for definition as one of the three COW categories; see source reference letter c above.

j. Gurr, Ted Robert. 1994. "Peoples Against States: Ethnopolitical Conflict and the Changing World System." *International Studies Quarterly* 38: 347–377. Criteria: Serious ethnopolitical conflicts involving armed violence and resulting in large numbers of casualties and dislocated populations.

k. State Failure Task Force. 1998. "State Failure Problem Set." Ted

Robert Gurr, principal investigator. Available from the State Failure project's website: http://www.bsos.umd.edu/cidcm/stfail. Criteria: The State Failure Problem Set includes four types of events: ethnic wars, revolutionary wars, geno/politicides, and abrupt or disruptive regime transitions. Only the first three types of events meet the general criteria to be considered a major armed conflict for cross-referencing here. Ethnic wars are "episodes of violent conflict between governments and national, ethnic, religious, or other communal minorities (ethnic challengers) in which the challengers seek major changes in their status." Revolutionary wars are "episodes of violent conflict between governments and politically organized groups (political challengers) that seek to overthrow the central government, to replace its leaders, or to seize power in one region." Geno/politicide is "the promotion, execution, and/or implied consent of sustained policies by governing elites or their agents–or, in the case of civil war, either of the contending authorities–that result in the deaths of a substantial portion of a communal and/or politicized communal group." Episodes of geno/politicide must have lasted six months or more to be included. Revolutionary and ethnic wars are included if they pass a minimum threshold wherein each party must mobilize 1000 or more people (armed agents, demonstrators, troops) and average 100 or more fatalities per year during the episode.

l. Wallensteen, Peter, and Margareta Sollenberg. 1998. "Armed Conflict and Regional Conflict Complexes, 1989–1997." *Journal of Peace Research* 35: 621–634. Criteria: Wallensteen and Sollenberg include three types of events in their study: minor armed conflict, intermediate armed conflict, and war. Only the latter two types meet the general criteria for inclusion here. Intermediate armed conflicts have "more than 1,000 battle-related deaths recorded during the course of the conflict, but fewer than 1,000 in any given year." Wars have "more than 1,000 battle-related deaths during any given year" (Wallensteen and Sollenberg 1998, 621).

m. Sivard, Ruth Leger. 1996. *World Military and Social Expenditures 1996*. 16th ed. Washington, DC: World Priorities. Criteria: "Armed conflict involving one or more governments and causing the death of 1,000 or more people per year." (Updates letter a source above.)

n. Correlates of War. 1994. *Militarized Interstate Disputes*. Computer file. ICPSR version. Ann Arbor: University of Michigan. Criteria: Fatality category 5 and 6 cases were chosen for cross-referencing; category 5 includes disputes where fatalities range from 501 to 999 (1 case) and category 6 includes disputes with more than 999 fatalities (24 cases).

o. Regan, Patrick M. 1996. "Conditions of Successful Third-Party Intervention in Intrastate Conflicts." *Journal of Conflict Resolution* 40: 336–359. Criteria: Regan defines episodes of intrastate conflict as "armed, sustained combat between groups within state boundaries in which there are at least 200 fatalities" (Regan 1996, 338). Appendix lists only the eighty-five conflicts that had at least one intervention (of 138 total); only three of the conflicts listed fall below the standard 1,000 fatalities threshold.

p. Marshall, Monty G. 2000. "Updated State Failure Problem Set." Report to State Failure Task Force.

*   *   *

Appendix 4.1 continued

Begin	End	Type	Magnitude	States Directly Involved	Brief Description	Deaths	References
1945	1946	IN	2	Indonesia	Independence	10,000	a b c f g h
1945	1947	EV	2	Iran	Azerbaijani and Kurd rebellions	2,000	c f g
1945	1949	CW	5	Greece	Greek civil war	150,000	a b c f g h o
1945	1954	IN	6	Vietnam	Indochina independence	500,000	a b c f g h
1946		CV	1	Bolivia	Civil violence	1,000	c f o
1946	1948	EW	6	India / Pakistan	"Partition"—Muslims vs. Hindus/Sikhs	1,000,000	a b c d f g
1946	1950	CW	6	China	Chinese civil war	1,000,000	a b c f h o
1947		IV	1	China	Taiwan invasion	1,000	a c h o
1947		CW	3	China	Repression of Taiwan dissidents	20,000	a c e f
1947		CV	1	Paraguay	Civil violence (Liberals)	1,000	a c f h o
1947	1948	IN	4	Yemen AR	Civil violence (Yahya clan coup attempt)	5,000	a c h o
1947	1948	CW	4	Madagascar	Colonial repression	40,000	a b c e f g h
1947	1949	EV	2	India	Kashmir rebellion	4,000	a c f g h n
1948		CV	1	Israel	Independence	4,000	b
1948		CV	1	Colombia	Civil violence (Conservatives)	1,000	a b c f h o
1948		CV	1	Costa Rica	Civil violence (National Union)	2,000	a c f g h o
1948		CV	1	South Korea	Civil violence (Army)	1,000	a c f
1948		CV	1	India	Civil violence (Hyderabad)	200	a c f g h
1948	1949	IW	5	Egypt / Israel / Jordan / Lebanon / Syria	Palestine-Israel war	10,000	a b c d f g h
1948	1954	IV	1	Myanmar	International violence	na[a]	c
1948	1956	EW	2	Malaysia	Repression of Chinese by Malay militia	12,500	e
1948	1999+	EW	4	Myanmar	Ethnic war (Karen, Shan, and others)	100,000	a b c d e f h j k l o p
1949	1962	CV	1	Indonesia	Colonial violence (West Irian)	1,000	c f g
1949	1962	CW	5	Colombia	"La Violencia" civil war (Liberals)	250,000	a b c f h
1950		IV	2	China / Taiwan	International violence (Formosa Straits)	5,000	f g

(continues)

Appendix 4.1 continued

Begin	End	Type	Magnitude	States Directly Involved	Brief Description	Deaths	References
1950		EV	2	Indonesia	Ethnic violence (Moluccans)	5,000	a b c f h o
1950	1951	IW	2	China	Tibet invasion[b]	2,000	a c f g h k
1950	1952	CV	3	Philippines	Civil violence (Huks)	10,000	a b c f h o
1950	1953	CW	6	North Korea South Korea	Korean War (civil war)	2,000,000	a b c f g h n
1950	1960	CV	3	Malaysia	Independence and civil violence[c]	15,000	a b f g h o
1951		CV	1	Thailand	Civil violence	na	c
1952		CV	1	Egypt	Civil violence (Nasser coup)	1,000	f
1952		CV	2	Bolivia	Civil violence	2,000	a c f h
1952	1954	IN	2	Tunisia	Independence	3,000	a c f g h
1952	1963	IN	3	Kenya	Independence (Mau Mau rebellion)	20,000	a b c f g h
1952	1999+	EW	2	India	Ethnic war (northeast tribals)	25,000	c k o
1953		CV	1	Indonesia	Civil violence (Darul Islam)	1,000	a b c h o
1953	1954	CV	3	Vietnam	Repression of landlords	15,000	e
1953	1956	IN	2	Morocco	Independence	3,000	a c f g h
1954		IV	1	China Taiwan	International violence	na	c
1954		CV	1	Guatemala	Civil violence (coup against Arbenz)	1,000	a c h o
1954	1955	EV	2	Taiwan	Ethnic violence (Native Taiwanese vs. KMT)	5,000	a c
1954	1962	IN	5	Algeria	Independence	100,000	a b c f g h k
1955		CV	1	Costa Rica	Civil violence	1,000	c f
1955		CV	2	Taiwan	Civil violence (Taiwanese vs. KMT)	5,000	a
1955		CV	2	Argentina	Civil violence (army rebellion)	3,000	a c h k
1955	1960	IN	3	Cameroon	Independence	30,000	a b c f h
1956		IW	2	Egypt	Suez War	3,000	a c d f g h n
1956		IW	3	Hungary USSR	International war	20,000	a b c f g h o
1956	1957	CV	1	North Vietnam	Civil violence	na	c
1956	1960	CV	1	Haiti	Civil violence	na	c
1956	1960	EV	1	Yemen AR	Ethnic violence (Yemeni-Adenese clans)	1,000	c f
1956	1965	EW	3	Rwanda	Repression of Tutsis	75,000	a b c e f g h k o

Begin	End	Type	Magnitude	States Directly Involved	Brief Description	Deaths	References
1956	1967	EW	4	China	Ethnic war (Tibetans)	100,000	a b c e f g h j o
1956	1972	EW	5	Sudan	Ethnic warfare (Islamic vs. African)	500,000	a b c e f g h k o
1957		CV	1	Oman	Civil violence	na	c
1957		IV	1	Honduras Nicaragua	International violence (border dispute)	1,000	c f
1957	1958	IV	1	Mauritania Morocco	International violence (border dispute)	1,000	f g
1957	1959	CW	2	Cuba	Civil war (Castro ousts Batista)	5,000	a b c f h k o
1957	1961	CV	3	Indonesia	Civil violence (dissident military)	30,000	a b c f h k o
1957	1968	CV	1	Venezuela	Civil violence	na	c
1958		CV	1	Lebanon	Civil violence	2,000	a c f g h k o
1958		CV	1	Iraq	Civil violence (coup ousts monarchy)	2,000	a c g o
1958		CV	1	Jordan	Civil violence	na	c
1958	1975	CW	7	North Vietnam South Vietnam	"Vietnam War" (civil war)	2,000,000	a b c e g h k n o
1959		CV	1	Iraq	Civil violence (Shammar tribe)	2,000	a c h
1959	1961	CW	2	China	Repression of counter-revolutionaries	50,000	k
1960	1961	EV	1	Pakistan	Ethnic violence (Pushtun)	1,000	k
1960	1963	IV	2	Cuba United States	International violence	na	c
1960	1965	CW	4	Zaire	Katanga civil war	100,000	a b c e g h k o
1960	1973	CW	3	Laos	Civil war	25,000	a b c e f h k o
1961		CV	1	Tunisia	Colonial violence	1,000	c f
1961		IV	2	India Portugal	International violence	na	c
1961	1975	IN	4	Angola	Independence	50,000	a b c e f g h
1961	1993	EW	5	Iraq	Ethnic warfare (Kurds)	150,000	a b c d e f h j k l o
1962		IV	1	China India	International violence (border dispute)	2,000	a b c f g h n
1962	1963	CV	1	Algeria	Civil violence (rebel factions)	2,000	a c e h o
1962	1964	IV	1	Burundi Rwanda	International violence	na	c
1962	1966	IV	1	Indonesia Malaysia	International violence (north Borneo)	1,500	c g

(continues)

Appendix 4.1 continued

Begin	End	Type	Magnitude	States Directly Involved	Brief Description	Deaths	References
1962	1970	CW	3	Yemen AR	Civil war (following coup)	40,000	a b c f h k o
1962	1974	IN	3	Guinea-Bissau	Independence	15,000	h m
1963		CV	1	Iraq	Civil violence	na	c
1963		CV	1	Iran	Civil violence (land reform)	1,000	k
1963	1964	IV	1	Somalia Egypt	International violence	1,000	c f
1963	1964	IV	1	Algeria Morocco	International violence (border dispute)	1,000	c f g
1963	1968	CV	2	Cyprus	Civil violence (Makarios crisis)	2,000	k o
1963	1993	EW	2	Indonesia	Ethnic warfare (Papuan–West Irian)	15,000	j o
1964		CV	1	Guatemala	Civil violence	na	c
1964		CV	1	Zambia	Civil violence	1,000	a c
1964		CV	1	Gabon	Civil violence	na	c
1964		CV	1	Uganda	Civil violence	na	c
1964		CV	1	Tanzania	Civil violence	na	c
1964		CV	1	Kenya	Civil violence	na	c
1964		CV	1	Brazil	Civil violence	na	c
1965		EV	2	Burundi	Ethnic violence (failed coup; Hutu/Tutsi)	5,000	k
1965		CV	2	Dominican Republic	Civil violence	3,000	a b c h k o
1965		IW	3	India Pakistan	2nd Kashmir War	20,000	a b c d f g h n
1965		CV	1	Peru	Civil violence	na	c
1965	1966	CW	5	Indonesia	Repression of Chinese/Communists	500,000	a b c e f k o
1965	1968	CV	1	United States	Civil violence (urban Afro-American unrest)	1,000	k
1965	1975	IN	3	Mozambique	Independence (FRELIMO)	30,000	a b f g h
1965	1990	IN	3	Namibia	Independence	25,000	b c f g
1965	1994	CW	4	Chad	Civil war	75,000	a b c f g h j k l o
1965	1998	EW	2	Israel	Ethnic war (Arab Palestinians/PLO)	15,000	d f g j k l o p
1966		CW	3	Nigeria	Repression of Ibo	20,000	c e
1966		EV	1	Uganda	Ethnic violence (Buganda)	2,000	a b c h o

Begin	End	Type	Magnitude	States Directly Involved	Brief Description	Deaths	References
1966		CV	1	Zaire	Civil violence	na	c
1966	1970	EW	6	Nigeria	Ethnic warfare (Biafra separatism)	200,000	a b c f h k o
1966	1975	CW	5	China	"Cultural Revolution"	500,000	a c e f h k
1966	1996	EW	5	Guatemala	Repression of indigenous peoples	150,000	a b c d e f h j k l o
1967	1970	IV	4	Egypt Israel Jordan Syria	"Six-Day War" and war of attrition	75,000	a b c d f g h n
1967	1983	EV	1	Thailand	Ethnic violence and repression (Malay)	na	k
1968		CV	1	France	Civil violence (student and labor unrest)	3,000	f
1968		CV	1	Czechoslovakia	"Prague Spring" civil violence	1,000	c f g
1968		CV	1	India	Repression of Naxalites	2,000	e
1968	1982	EV	1	Spain	Ethnic violence (Basque separatism)	1,000	f j l o
1969	1999+	IV	1	USSR China	Ussuri River border dispute	1,000	a c f g
1969		IW	2	El Salvador Honduras	"Soccer War"	5,000	a b c f g h n
1969	1994	EV	2	United Kingdom	Ethnic violence (Northern Ireland/IRA)	3,000	b c d f j k l o
1970		CV	3	Jordan	Civil violence (Palestinians)	10,000	a b c f g h k o
1970	1975	CV	1	Oman	Civil violence (Dhofar rebellion)	3,000	g k o
1970	1975	CW	5	Cambodia	Civil war	150,000	a b c f h k o
1970	1982	EV	1	Italy	Ethnic violence (Sardinians)	2,000	f
1970		CV	1	Honduras	Civil violence (peasant insurgency)	1,000	f
1970	1990	CV	2	Sri Lanka	Civil violence (attempted coup)	10,000	a b c f h k o
1971		EW	6	Bangladesh Pakistan	Ethnic war (Bengali independence)	1,000,000	a b c e f g h k o
1971		IW	3	India Pakistan	International war	11,000	a b c d g h n
1971	1978	EW	5	Uganda	Ethnic warfare (Idi Amin regime)	250,000	a b e k o
1972		EV	2	Burundi	Ethnic violence (Hutus target Tutsis)	2,000	b f g o
1972	1973	EW	4	Burundi	Repression of Hutus	100,000	a b c e f g h k o
1972	1979	EV	3	Zimbabwe	Ethnic violence (ZANU/ZAPU vs. whites)	20,000	a b f g h k o
1972	1999+	CW	3	Philippines	Civil warfare (New Peoples Army)	40,000	a b c d h l o p
1972	1999+	EW	3	Philippines	Ethnic warfare (Moros)	50,000	a b c d e f h j k l o p

(continues)

Appendix 4.1 continued

Begin	End	Type	Magnitude	States Directly Involved	Brief Description	Deaths	References
1973		IW	3	Egypt Israel Syria	"Yom Kippur War"	16,000	a b c d f g h n
1973		CV	2	Chile	Civil violence (army ouster of Allende)	5,000	a b c f
1973	1977	EW	2	Pakistan	Ethnic warfare (Baluch separatism)	12,000	a b e f h k o
1974		CV	2	Cyprus	Civil violence	5,000	a b c f g h k n o
1974	1975	IV	1	Iran Iraq	International violence (Shatt el Arab)	1,000	f g
1974	1976	CW	3	Chile	Repression of dissidents ("disappeared")	20,000	a b e k
1974	1985	CV	2	Turkey	Civil violence	8,000	f
1974	1991	EW	6	Ethiopia	Ethnic warfare (Eritreans and others)	750,000	a b c d e f h j k l o
1975		CV	1	Portugal	Civil violence	na	c
1975	1978	CW	6	Cambodia	Khmer Rouge repression of dissidents	1,500,000	a b e g k
1975	1979	IV	1	Mozambique Zimbabwe	International violence	na	i
1975	1979	IW	2	Cambodia Vietnam	International war	10,000	h n
1975	1989	CW	3	Mauritania (1979) Morocco	Colonial war (Western Sahara)	15,000	a b c d f g h j k l o
1975	1990	CV	2	Laos	Civil violence (rebel Lao and Hmong)	10,000	d f g k l
1975	1991	EV	2	Indonesia	Ethnic violence (Aceh)	15,000	j l o
1975	1991	EW	5	Lebanon	Ethnic war (Various sects)	100,000	a b c d g h k l o
1975	1992	EW	2	Bangladesh	Ethnic war (Chittagong Hills)	25,000	d j l o
1975	1999+	CW	6	Angola	Civil war (UNITA)	1,000,000	a b c d f g h j k l o p
1976		EV	1	South Africa	Ethnic violence	1,000	a d k o
1976	1980	CW	3	Argentina	"The Dirty War" repression of dissidents	20,000	a b e f k
1976	1992	CW	5	Indonesia	Colonial war (East Timor)	200,000	a b c d e f g h j k l o
1977		IV	1	Angola Zaire	International violence (dispute over Shaba)	1,000	f g
1977	1979	IV	1	Zambia	International violence	na	i

Begin	End	Type	Magnitude	States Directly Involved	Brief Description	Deaths	References
1977	1979	EW	2	Zimbabwe, Ethiopia	"Ogaden War" ethnic violence (Somalis)	10,000	b c f g h n o
1977	1980	EV	2	Turkey	Ethnic violence (Armenians)	5,000	a b
1977	1983	CW	2	Zaire	Repression of dissidents	10,000	e k
1977	1987	IV	1	Cambodia, Thailand	International violence	1,000	i n
1977	1991	IV	1	Egypt, Libya	International violence	na	i
1978		IV	2	Israel, Lebanon	International violence (PLO factions)	5,000	d
1978		IV	1	Angola, Zaire	International violence (dispute over Shaba)	1,000	f g
1978	1979	IV	1	Yemen AR, Yemen PDR	International violence	na	i
1978	1979	CW	3	Nicaragua	Civil war (Sandinistas)	40,000	a b c f g h k o
1978	1979	IW	2	Tanzania, Uganda	International war (ouster of Idi Amin)	3,000	a b c g h n
1978	1989	IW	5	Cambodia, Vietnam	International war (ouster of Khmer Rouge)	65,000	a b c d f g h o
1978	1993	CW	4	Iran	Civil war (Islamic state)	50,000	a b c d e f h k l o
1978	1999+	CW	7	Afghanistan	Civil war	1,000,000	a b c d e f g h j k l o p
1979		IW	4	China, Vietnam	International war	30,000	a b c f g h n
1979	1980	CV	1	South Korea	Unrest, riots, and government repression	1,000	a k
1979	1981	IV	1	Afghanistan, Pakistan	International violence	na	i
1979	1985	EW	3	Iran	Ethnic war (Kurds)	40,000	j k o
1979	1992	CW	6	El Salvador	Civil war (FMLN)	75,000	a b c d e f g h k l o
1979	1998	EV	3	Iraq	Ethnic violence (Shias)	25,000	f h j o p
1980		IV	1	Ethiopia, Somalia	International violence	na	i
1980		CV	1	Brazil	Repression of dissidents (death squads)	1,000	a
1980		CV	1	Jamaica	Civil violence (elections)	1,000	a f

(continues)

Appendix 4.1 continued

Begin	End	Type	Magnitude	States Directly Involved	Brief Description	Deaths	References
1980	1981	CV	2	Nigeria	Civil violence (Islamic groups)	8,000	a f h k o
1980	1988	IW	6	Iran Iraq	International war	500,000	a b c f g h n
1980	1998	EV	2	China	Ethnic violence (Uighurs, Kazakhs)	10,000	j k o p
1981		CV	1	Ghana	Civil violence (Konkomba vs. Nanumba)	1,000	a f
1981		IV	1	Ecuador Peru	International violence	na	i
1981		IV	1	China Vietnam	International violence	na	i
1981	1982	CW	3	Syria	Repression of dissidents (Muslim)	25,000	a b e f k
1981	1985	EV	2	Zimbabwe	Ethnic violence (Ndebele)	3,000	a f k o
1981	1986	CW	4	Uganda	Repression of dissidents	100,000	a e f h k o
1981	1986	IV	1	Honduras Nicaragua	International violence	na	i
1981	1990	CW	3	Nicaragua	Civil war (Contras)	30,000	a b d f g h k l o
1981	1992	CW	6	Mozambique	Civil war (RENAMO)	500,000	a b d f g h k l o
1982		IV	1	Israel Syria	International violence	1,000	h n
1982		IW	1	Argentina United Kingdom	Falklands-Malvinas War	1,000	a b f g h n
1982	1990	IW	4	Israel Lebanon	International war	50,000	a b
1982	1997	CV	3	Peru	Civil violence (Sendero Luminoso)	30,000	a b d f h j k l o p
1983		CV	2	India	Civil violence (elections in Assam)	3,000	a
1983		IV	1	India Pakistan	International violence	na	i
1983		IV	1	Chad Nigeria	International violence	na	i
1983		IV	1	China Vietnam	International violence	na	i
1983	1984	CV	2	China	Repression of dissidents	5,000	a

Begin	End	Type	Magnitude	States Directly Involved	Brief Description	Deaths	References
1983	1987	IV	1	Afghanistan / Pakistan	International violence	na	i
1983	1993	EW	3	India	Ethnic warfare (Sikhs)	25,000	a b d f h j k l
1983	1996	EW	3	South Africa	Ethnic/civil warfare	20,000	a d j k l o
1983	1998	EV	1	Pakistan	Ethnic violence (Sindhis; Muhajirs)	5,000	k
1983	1999+	EW	5	Sri Lanka	Ethnic war (Tamils)	70,000	a b d e f g h j k l o p
1983	1999+	EW	6	Sudan	Ethnic war (Islamic vs. African)	1,000,000	a b d f h j k l o p
1984		EV	1	Zaire	Ethnic/civil warfare	1,000	k
1984		CV	1	Nigeria	Civil violence (Islamic groups)	1,000	a h o
1984	1999+	EW	3	Turkey	Ethnic warfare (Kurds)	40,000	d g h j k l p
1984	1999+	CV	4	Colombia	Civil violence (insurgency and drug lords)	50,000	a d f h k l o p
1985		IV	1	India / Pakistan	International violence	na	i
1985		CW	2	Liberia	Repression of dissidents (failed coup)	5,000	a
1985	1986	IV	1	Burkina Faso / Mali	International violence	na	i
1985	1987	IW	2	China / Vietnam	International war	4,000	h n
1986		IV	1	Libya / United States	International violence	na	i
1986	1987	CW	2	Yemen PDR	Civil war	10,000	a b h k o
1986	1993	EV	2	Nigeria	Ethnic violence (Muslim-Christian)	10,000	j o
1986	1999+	EV	2	Uganda	Ethnic violence (Langi and Acholi)	10,000	d j k l o p
1987		IV	1	China / Vietnam	International violence	1,000	a i
1987		IV	1	India / Pakistan	International violence	na	i
1987		CV	2	Chile	Civil violence	3,000	a b
1987	1990	CW	4	Sri Lanka	Civil war (JVP–Sinhalese extremists)	25,000	h k l o
1988		CV	1	Myanmar	Civil violence (student protests)	2,000	k
1988		EV	3	Burundi	Ethnic violence (Tutsis against Hutus)	10,000	a b h k o
1988	1997	EW	1	Papua New Guinea	Ethnic warfare (Bougainville)	1,000	k l o p
1988	1999+	CW	5	Somalia	Civil war	100,000	a b d h j k l o p

(continues)

Appendix 4.1   continued

Begin	End	Type	Magnitude	States Directly Involved	Brief Description	Deaths	References
1989		CV	1	China	Civil violence (Tiananmen protests)	2,000	a k
1989		IV	1	Panama United States	International violence	1,000	a l
1989		CV	1	Romania	Civil violence	1,000	a h k l o
1989	1990	IV	1	India Pakistan	International violence	na	l
1989	1990	IV	1	Mauritania Senegal	International violence	na	l
1990		CW	1	China	Repression of dissidents	2,000	a
1990	1991	EV	1	Mali	Ethnic violence (Tuareg)	1,000	k o
1990	1991	EV	2	USSR	Sporadic ethnic/communal violence	5,000	k l
1990	1991	IW	5	Iraq Kuwait	Gulf War	100,000	h l n
1990	1994	EW	3	Rwanda	Ethnic warfare (Tutsis vs. Hutu regime)[d]	15,000	h j k l o
1990	1994	IW	3	Armenia Azerbaijan	International war (Nagorno-Karabakh)	10,000	h j k l n o
1990	1997	CW	4	Liberia	Civil war	40,000	a d h j k l o p
1990	1997	EW	3	Azerbaijan	Ethnic war (Nagorno-Karabakh)	15,000	h j k l n o p
1990	1997	EV	1	Niger	Ethnic violence (Azawad and Toubou)	1,000	l o
1990	1997	CW	2	Cambodia	Civil warfare (Khmer Rouge)	5,000	l
1990	1999+	EW	3	India	Ethnic war (Kashmiris)	30,000	j k l o p
1991		CW	2	Croatia	Civil war (Croatian independence)	10,000	h k l
1991		CV	1	Burundi	Civil violence	1,000	h l
1991		CV	1	Haiti	Civil violence (Aristide presidency)	na	k l
1991	1993	CW	1	Georgia	Civil war	1,000	h k l
1991	1993	EV	1	Kenya	Ethnic violence (Kalenjin, Masai, Kikuyu, Luo)	2,000	j k o
1991	1993	EW	2	Georgia	Ethnic war (Abkhazians-Ossetians)	3,000	h j k l o
1991	1993	EV	1	Bhutan	Ethnic violence (Drukpas vs. Nepalese)	na	j
1991	1994	CV	1	Djibouti	Civil violence	1,000	l o
1991	1995	EW	3	Croatia	Ethnic war (Serbs)	40,000	j k l o
1991	1997	EV	1	Moldova	Ethnic violence (Trans-Dniester Russians)	2,000	j k l o p
1991	1999	EV	1	Senegal	Ethnic violence (Casamance)	3,000	l p

Begin	End	Type	Magnitude	States Directly Involved	Brief Description	Deaths	References
1991	1999+	CW	3	Sierra Leone	Civil/ethnic warfare (Mende)	25,000	k l m p
1991	1999+	CW	4	Algeria	Civil warfare (Islamic militants)	60,000	k l o p
1991	1999+	EV	2	India	Ethnic violence (Hindu vs. Muslim)	2,500	j
1992		IV	1	India Pakistan	International violence	na	l
1992	1995	EW	6	Bosnia	Ethnic war (Serbs, Croats, Muslims)	200,000	h j k l o
1992	1996	EV	2	Zaire	Ethnic violence	10,000	j k o
1992	1998	CW	3	Tajikistan	Civil warfare	25,000	h k l o p
1992	1999	CV	1	Egypt	Civil violence (Islamic militants)	2,000	k o p
1993		EV	1	Congo-Brazzaville	Ethnic violence	2,000	m
1993	1999+	EW	4	Burundi	Ethnic warfare (Tutsis against Hutus)	100,000	j k l p
1994		EW	7	Rwanda	Ethnic violence (Hutus target Tutsis)	500,000	k l o
1994		EV	1	Ghana	Ethnic violence	1,000	m
1994		EW	1	Yemen	Ethnic warfare (south Yemenis)	3,000	l o
1994	1996	EW	4	Russia	Civil war (Chechnya secession)	40,000	k l o
1994	1997	EV	1	Mexico	Ethnic violence (Chiapas)	1,000	l o p
1994	1998	EW	3	Rwanda	Ethnic warfare (ousted Hutu vs. Tutsi regime)	15,000	p
1995		IV	1	Ecuador Peru	International violence (border dispute)	1,000	l
1996		IV	1	Cameroon Nigeria	International violence (Bakassi)	na	l
1996	1997	IV	1	India Pakistan	International violence	na	l
1996	1997	CV	1	Uganda	Civil violence	na	l
1996	1998	EW	1	Iraq	Ethnic warfare (Kurds)	2,000	k l p
1996	1999+	CV	1	Nepal	Civil violence (UPF "People's War")	2,000	p
1996	1999+	CW	5	Zaire	Civil war (ouster of Mobutu and aftermath)	100,000	k l p
1997	1999	CW	3	Congo-Brazzaville	Civil warfare	10,000	l p
1997		CV	2	Albania	Civil violence (Pyramid schemes)	2,000	p
1997	1999+	EV	1	Indonesia	Ethnic violence (Aceh, Moluccas, W. Papua)	2,000	l p
1998		CV	1	Lesotho	Civil violence (May elections)	1,000	p
1998	1999	EW	4	Yugoslavia	Ethnic war (Kosovar Albanians)	15,000	p
1998		CV	2	Indonesia	Civil violence (ouster of Suharto)	2,000	p
1998		EW	1	Georgia	Ethnic warfare (Abkhazia)	1,000	p

(continues)

Appendix 4.1 continued

Begin	End	Type	Magnitude	States Directly Involved	Brief Description	Deaths	References
1998	1999	CW	2	Guinea-Bissau	Civil war (coup attempt)	6,000	p
1998	1999+	IW	5	Eritrea Ethiopia	Interstate war	100,000	p
1998	1999+	IV	1	Iraq	International violence (US/UK airstrikes)	1,000	p
1999		IV	1	India Pakistan	International violence (Kargil clashes)	1,500	p
1999		CV	2	Indonesia	Ethnic violence (East Timor independence)	3,000	p
1999		IV	3	Yugoslavia	International violence (NATO airstrikes)	1,000	p
1999	1999+	EW	1	Ethiopia	Ethnic war (Oromo separatists)	2,000	p
1999	1999+	EV	1	Nigeria	Ethnic violence (Delta and northern regions)	1,500	p
1999	1999+	EW	4	Russia	Ethnic war (Chechen separatists)	15,000	p

Source: This comprehensive compilation is a substantial revision and update of earlier work published in the following source: Monty G. Marshall. 1999. *Third World War: System, Process, and Conflict Dynamics.* Boulder: Rowman and Littlefield.

Notes: a. The code "na" means that no estimate of "directly related deaths" is available in the above named sources. The Correlates of War Project (COW) holds to a very stringent definition of war (see source references c and h above). Particularly problematic are the focus on "fatalities among military personnel" and the limitation for inclusion to "system-members." Political violence in the post-1945 era is characterized by increasing confusion about what constitutes military personnel, combatants in general, and noncombatants, especially in regard to civil violence and warfare and interstate acts of terrorism. This confusion makes it increasingly difficult to make intellectual distinctions, or limitations, concerning human casualties, especially as the destructiveness of advanced technological weaponry includes ever greater collateral damage. The second limitation, to "system-members," unnecessarily discounts the lives of people fighting colonial domination in wars of independence and self-determination: those deaths are not tabulated in the category of "extra-systemic war." The COW studies also list "wars" that don't meet their criteria for various reasons. It is assumed that the mere fact that a "war" is acknowledged by the COW project points to that episode's significance in the societal relations of participants. These "wars that do not meet COW standards" are included in the above list even though there is no estimated indicator of deaths. For the purposes of this study, all such episodes are coded "1" in intensity unless further information is presented by alternate sources.

b. In cases where the sovereignty of a distinct territory is ambiguous and contested by the parties in conflict, the episode is coded as an international conflict until authority has either been successfully imposed or resisted, after which subsequent episodes are coded according to the sovereignty thus established.

c. The case of Malaysian independence and civil violence is continuous and coded IN3 for the period prior to official independence in 1957 and CV3 afterward (i.e., 1958–1960).

d. The Rwanda case is unique in that it involves a sudden and complete transference of political power as the Tutsi insurgency mounts an offensive and seizes power following the Hutu regime-instigated genocide. Former members of the Hutu regime and, especially, those responsible for the genocide then take up arms against the new Tutsi-dominated regime. This situation is listed as two separate episodes but is coded as though it were a continual episode (i.e., with no overlap of the two episodes).

Appendix 4.2 Countries Composing the Societal Capacity Quintiles (based on energy consumption per capita)

Lowest Quintile	Second Quintile	Third Quintile	Fourth Quintile	Highest Quintile
Afghanistan	Angola	Albania	Argentina	Australia
Bangladesh	Bolivia	Algeria	Bulgaria	Austria
Benin	Cameroon	Brazil	Chile	Bahrain
Bhutan	Congo (Brazzaville)	China	Cuba	Belgium
Burkina Faso	Dominican Republic	Colombia	Cyprus	Canada
Burma/Myanmar	El Salvador	Costa Rica	Greece	Czechoslovakia
Burundi	Ghana	Djibouti	Hungary	Denmark
Cambodia	Guatemala	Ecuador	Ireland	Finland
Central Africa Republic	Guinea	Egypt	Israel	France
Chad	Honduras	Fiji	Italy	Germany
Comoros	India	Gabon	Jamaica	Kuwait
Congo (Kinshasa)/Zaire	Indonesia	Guyana	Japan	Luxembourg
Equatorial Guinea	Ivory Coast	Iran	Korea, North	Netherlands
Ethiopia	Kenya	Iraq	Lebanon	New Zealand
Gambia	Liberia	Jordan	Libya	Norway
Guinea-Bissau	Mauritania	Korea, South	Mexico	Poland
Haiti	Morocco	Malaysia	Mongolia	Qatar
Laos	Nigeria	Mauritius	Oman	Russia
Madagascar	Pakistan	Nicaragua	Romania	Singapore
Malawi	Papua New Guinea	Panama	Saudi Arabia	South Africa
Mali	Paraguay	Peru	Spain	Sweden
Mozambique	Philippines	Portugal	Taiwan	Switzerland
Nepal	Senegal	Syria	Uruguay	Trinidad and Tobago
Niger	Sri Lanka	Tunisia	Venezuela	United Arab Emirates
Rwanda	Sudan	Turkey	Yugoslavia	United Kingdom
Sierra Leone	Thailand	Yemen, South		United States
Somalia	Vietnam (North and South)	Zambia		USSR
Tanzania	Yemen	Zimbabwe		
Togo				
Uganda				
Yemen, North				

Notes

1. The Correlates of War Project, under the direction of J. David Singer and Melvin Small, conducted the first systematic study identifying and compiling information on the world's major warfare events. This seminal project was designed with a strongly statist orientation that limits its applicability to systems analysis.

2. Monty G. Marshall, *Third World War: System, Process, and Conflict Dynamics* (Boulder: Rowman and Littlefield, 1999).

3. See ibid., chap. 2.

4. See Michael Cranna, ed., *The True Cost of Conflict* (New York: New Press, 1994).

5. See Michael E. Brown and Richard N. Rosecrance for the Carnegie Commission on Preventing Deadly Conflict, *The Costs of Conflict: Prevention and Cure in the Global Arena* (Lanham, MD: Rowman and Littlefield Publishers, 1999).

6. This measurement technique follows from earlier applications developed, with Ted Gurr, for assessing nonviolent protest, violent protest, and rebellion by minority groups for the Minorities at Risk project. See Ted Robert Gurr, *Minorities at Risk: A Global View of Ethnopolitical Conflicts* (Washington, D.C.: United States Institute of Peace Press, 1993), 93–98. This scaling technique has become fairly common in the assessment of conflict magnitudes in comparative analysis and is similar to the technique used in meteorology to assess the magnitudes of atmospheric macrophenomena such as hurricanes and tornadoes.

7. See Marshall, *Third World War*, 38–54.

8. The instigators and perpetrators of the 1994 genocide in Rwanda lacked both the technological and organizational means for systematic extermination of the target populations.

9. See, for instance, Charles William Maynes, "Containing Ethnic Conflict," *Foreign Policy* 90, 2 (spring 1993): 3–21; Samuel P. Huntington, "The Clash of Civilizations?" *Foreign Affairs* 72, 3 (summer 1993): 22–49.

10. The decrease in warfare episodes has also been noted by research at AKUF (Arbeitsgemeinschaft Kriegsursachenforschung); see Klaus Jürgen Gantzel, "War in the Post–World War II World: Some Empirical Trends and a Theoretical Approach," in *War and Ethnicity: Global Connections and Local Violence*, ed. David Turton (Rochester, NY: University of Rochester Press; San Marino, CA: Center for Interdisciplinary Research on Social Stress, 1997). The AKUF global warfare trend graph can be viewed on the AKUF website, available at http://www.sozialwiss.uni-hamburg.de/Ipw/Akuf/home.html.

11. Noted by the Minorities at Risk Project; see Ted Robert Gurr, Monty G. Marshall, and Deepa Khosla, *Peace and Conflict 2001: A Global Survey of Armed Conflicts, Self-Determination Movements, and Democracy* (College Park, MD: Center for International Development and Conflict Management, 2000).

12. United States Committee for Refugees, *World Refugee Survey 1999* (Washington, D.C.: United States Committee for Refugees, 1999), table 3.

13. See Kofi Annan, *We the Peoples: The Role of the United Nations in the 21st Century*, Millennium Report of the United Nations Secretary-General (New York: United Nations, Department of Public Information, 2000).

14. Graphs of contemporary global trends in civil and interstate warfare, ethnic rebellion, forcibly dislocated populations, regime authority characteristics, and conflict settlements, as well as regional trends in warfare and rebellion, can be viewed on the Center for Systemic Peace website at http://members.aol.com/csp-mgm.

15. The depiction of global warfare presented in Figure 4.1 offers only one perspective on the global trend in warfare. This view has been criticized as reflecting simply a statistical artifact of changes in the organization of the world's state system and, especially, of decolonization. Over the same period of time, the number of state units composing the global system increased dramatically—the United Nations today has 189 members. Some argue that the growth in the number of state units may account for the plotted increase in the global warfare trend until the Cold War's end. However, when the number of states experiencing war events is plotted as a percentage of the total number of states, the steady increase in warfare during the Cold War and decrease since the early 1990s denoted in Figure 4.1 is corroborated (see Gurr, Marshall, and Khosla, *Peace and Conflict 2001*). Other critics question the methodology for compiling warfare magnitude scores. This is discussed in greater detail below in the third section.

16. Although external attention is drawn to crisis situations and external support is an important factor in the outcomes of crisis events, the actual conduct of a hot war is most often left to the indigenous actors. External interventions into hot wars, such as the U.S. intervention in Vietnam and Soviet intervention in Afghanistan, have proven very costly for the intervening powers. Once the fighting has stopped, hot wars become hotspots as the potential for new outbreaks of fighting between antagonists remains high for several years following cessation of open warfare. These hotspots present a ripe moment for less-risky external involvement in ameliorating conditions and forestalling future outbreaks of violence.

17. Marshall, *Third World War*.

18. See Daniel C. Esty, Jack A. Goldstone, Ted Robert Gurr, Pamela T. Surko, and Alan N. Unger, "Working Papers: State Failure Task Force Report" (McLean, VA: Science Applications International Corporation, 1995); and Daniel C. Esty, Jack A. Goldstone, Ted Robert Gurr, Barbara Harff, Marc Levy, Geoffrey D. Dabelko, Pamela T. Surko, and Alan N. Unger, "State Failure Task Force Report: Phase II Findings," (McLean, VA: Science Applications International Corporation, 1998).

19. Figures for energy consumption and population are from the Correlates of War "National Material Capabilities" data set; the data set covers nearly all independent states for all years over the relevant period, 1946–1991. Missing values were imputed whenever possible by averaging preceding and succeeding values. Notable in this regard is the fact that there are no figures available for the successor states to the Soviet Union and Yugoslavia and, so, these new states were removed from the analysis. States were scored annually over the coverage period, and then the annual scores were converted to a percent of a standard progressive score, based on the energy consumption of the leading Western European industrial states. The annual percentage scores were averaged over the full time period to derive the general percentage scores that were then separated into quintiles; see Appendix 4.2 for a list of countries in each quintile.

20. See Peter Wallensteen and Margareta Sollenberg, "Armed Conflict, 1989–1998" *Journal of Peace Research* 36 (1999): 593–606; and A. J. Jongman, "Downward Trend in Armed Conflicts Reversed," *PIOOM Newsletter* 9, 1 (2000): 28–34.

21. Although the ACI data reference the SIPRI/PRIO historical data on major political violence episodes (and thereby subsume their event data points), the ACI data do not reveal this same reversal of fortune. Differences in accounting procedures must account for the discrepancy.

22. The AKUF study (see above), which concurs with the ACI trend, used a

mobilization criterion, rather than a battle-death criterion, for identifying an armed conflict episode. Group mobilization for armed conflict captures the group's political potential rather than its actions. This conception comes closer to the broader conceptualization used in the ACI study than the others examined here.

23. The vast majority of armed conflict events during the contemporary period have been domestic, or civil, conflict events, thus the fact that the State Failure project covers only domestic events does not jeopardize its suitability as an independent data resource. The State Failure data were revised to include information on interstate warfare events.

24. Peter Wallensteen and Margareta Sollenberg (SIPRI/PRIO) include three categories of armed conflict events identified according to threshold numbers of battle-related deaths; they are minor armed conflict, intermediate armed conflict, and war. Major armed conflicts involve "more than 1,000 battle-related deaths recorded during the course of the conflict," and minor armed conflicts have less than 1,000 during their course.

25. SIPRI/PRIO war events and State Failure events with annual fatality scores (MAGFATAL) greater than 1.

26. PIOOM records midyear event counts, whereas the other sources record year-end event counts.

27. In general, it appears that the SIPRI/PRIO death estimates are more conservative than those of either State Failure or PIOOM.

28. An early assessment of armed conflict in the year 2000 (through June 1) indicates that, if current situational trends continue, the number of armed conflicts in 2000 reported by State Failure may drop to as low as twenty-one. See Monty G. Marshall, "Current Status of the World's Major Episodes of Political Violence: Hot Wars and Hot Spots," Report to the State Failure Task Force (College Park, MD: Center for Systemic Peace, 2001).

29. The huge increases in LIC and VPC events noted by PIOOM researchers are contrary to the expectations generated by any of the other studies. However, as Jongman provides no information on the cases included in the PIOOM study except the high-intensity conflicts, no independent assessment or verification of numbers or procedures concerning PIOOM's low-intensity conflict and violent political conflict categories could be conducted.

30. A detailed analysis of discrepancies across the several studies was conducted to increase the author's understanding of the differences and confidence in his assessments. The results of that analysis are not reported here.

31. Establishing and maintaining such a presence is not without risks. Having a global presence on the ground carries with it the implication of a global police presence that can and will provide security, protection, and prosecution for violations of that presence. Local warriors often view a global presence as a constraint on military tactics and an obstacle to military victory.

5

Horizontal Inequalities as a Source of Conflict

Frances Stewart

Civil wars are a major source of poverty. Eight of the ten countries with the worst Human Development Index (HDI), and similarly eight out of ten countries with the lowest gross national product (GNP) per capita, have had major civil wars in the recent past.[1] About half of low-income countries have been subject to major political violence. Causality works both ways, as low incomes lead to conditions that are conducive to violence.[2] But the evidence suggests that major civil wars are associated with markedly worse performance in economic growth, food production per capita, and human indicators such as infant mortality rates, school enrollment, and so on.[3] Hence, any comprehensive strategy to tackle poverty must give central focus to the prevention of conflict. In the past, this has not been the case.

Conflict prevention has been regarded as desirable as a political objective, but it has not been part of the poverty reduction or human development agendas. For example, the World Bank's Poverty Reduction Strategy documents do not deal centrally (and often not at all) with this issue; neither has the United Nations Development Programme (UNDP)'s Human Development Report treated it as a focal point.[4] Yet recognizing prevention as central for poor societies may alter the design of policies substantially.

This chapter explores how economic and social policymaking would be affected by focusing on conflict prevention in low-income countries, in addition to related development issues. I start from the premise that crisis prevention is essential for poverty reduction as well as to alleviate immediate human suffering; policies aimed at reducing political violence are needed for *all* low-income countries given their high propensity for strife. Of the forty-eight countries classified as least-developed by the United Nations, twenty-four experienced serious conflict during the period between 1970 and 1996.⁵ Similar policies are also needed for some middle-income countries, but the incidence of civil war is substantially lower among them. This partly reflects the fact that they have succeeded in graduating to the middle-income level as a result of having avoided conflict. Hence, for middle-income countries, special crisis prevention policies may be needed only in especially vulnerable cases. Such vulnerability arises where there are severe horizontal inequalities, that is, inequality in political, economic, and/or social conditions among culturally and/or geographically distinct groups.

My main argument is that horizontal inequalities are one of the major causes of conflict and vulnerability to conflict. The aim is to suggest how introducing crisis prevention into policymaking would alter the normal design of policy for low-income countries. The first section is a general analysis of conflicts, partly drawn from the findings of a recent research program into the economic and social causes of conflict.⁶ Next I elucidate the concept of *horizontal inequalities*, a key element in understanding and preventing conflict. Third, I illustrate the applicability and relevance of the concept of horizontal inequalities with three cases: Uganda, Northern Ireland, and Sri Lanka. Finally, I provide an overview of the policy recommendations that emerge from the analysis.

Motivation, Mobilization, and Conflict

The human motivation of the participants is at the heart of any violent situation. If a conflict is to be avoided or stopped, this motivation must be understood and the conditions leading to a predisposition to conflict reduced or eliminated. This section aims to sketch elements that determine such motivation. Although the focus is on economic motivation, other factors (i.e., political, cultural) are also of obvious importance. In fact, it is rarely possible to disentangle political, cultural, and economic elements, as each is embedded in the other.

The type of conflicts with which we are concerned are *organized group* conflicts, those conflicts that are not exclusively a matter of individuals randomly committing violence against others. What is involved is *group mobilization,* and we need to understand its underlying motivation. "Groups" here are defined as collections of people who, for certain purposes, identify with each other as against those outside the group, which often involves identifying the characteristics and membership of some other group with whom they are in conflict. Group organization may be quite informal, but it implies a degree of agreement (often implicit) on purposes and activities within the group. Normally there are those within any group instigating conflict who lead or orchestrate the conflict through the use of perceptions of group identity to achieve mobilization, as well as those who actively carry out the fighting or give it some support. We shall call these two categories "leaders" and "followers," although there can be considerable overlap between the two. The violence is generally instrumental, used in order to achieve other ends. Usually, the declared objective is political—to secure or sustain power—while power is desired for the advantages it offers, especially the possibilities of economic gain. However, especially as wars persist, political motivation may disappear or become less important. The continuation of war, then, results from the economic advantages conferred directly on those involved, the gain from looting being one among several sought-after prizes.[7] But even so, conflicts remain predominantly group activities. The group element, and the fact that the conflicts are instrumental, usually with political objectives, is what differentiates violent conflict from crime, although in the extreme case, where fighting parties disintegrate into gangs whose efforts are devoted to maximizing their short run economic gains, the distinction between the two becomes blurred.[8]

Accepting that groups are central to violent conflict, the questions become why and how they are mobilized. In order to mobilize groups, there must be some way in which groups are differentiated from one another. Studies show a number of contemporary examples. In central Africa, ethnic identity has been the major source of group definition and mobilization; in Central America, group identification and organization occurred along class lines, but with some overlapping ethnic dimensions; in Somalia, the cultural source of group differentiation and mobilization was the clan (different lineages within broadly the same ethnic group); in Northern Ireland and the Balkans, religion is the major categorizing feature. Another source of differentiation often arises from regional location, which can, but does not always, coincide with ethnic or language divisions—for example, in Biafra, Eritrea, and eastern Pakistan (Bangladesh).

The question of how groups are formed and when they become salient is complex and contested, and it cannot be treated adequately here.[9] The view adopted here is that group identity is "constructed" by political leaders via a strategy of "reworking historical memories" and acts as a powerful mechanism in the competition for power and resources. Numerous examples have shown how "ethnicity was used by political and intellectual elites prior to, or in the course of, wars."[10] Yet as D. Turton points out, "neither the constructedness nor the instrumentality of ethnicity [or other similar sources of identity which are used to make groups cohere such as religion or class] can be explained unless we are prepared to see it as an independent as well as a dependent variable in human affairs."[11] Some shared circumstances are needed for group construction—for example, speaking the same language, sharing cultural traditions, living in the same place, and facing similar sources of hardship or exploitation. Past group formation, although possibly constructed for political purposes at the time, also contributes to present differences. Hence, what was a dependent variable at one point in history can act as an independent variable in contributing to current perceptions.[12]

For the emergence of group conflict, a degree of similarity of circumstance among potential members is not by itself enough to bring about group mobilization. Several other conditions must be present. Leaders must see the creation or enhancement of group identity as helpful to the realization of their political ambitions and work actively to achieve this, using a variety of strategies, including education or propaganda. In many cases, it has been shown that political leaders set out to create group consciousness in order to achieve a basis for power. J. Lonsdale points out that in Kenya "conflict between political elites for state (and hence economic) power led to the emergence of 'political tribalism.'"[13] Government policies, particularly toward education, frequently play a role by discriminating in favor of some category and against others.

The story of how differences between the Hutu and Tutsi were possibly created and certainly strongly enhanced by colonial and postcolonial governments is powerfully illustrated in studies of Burundi and Rwanda.[14] In the case of Rwanda, the *interhamwe*—the extremist leaders of the Hutu massacre of the Tutsi population—deliberately and efficiently cultivated Hutu consciousness and fear of Tutsis for several years before the disaster. Yet some group mobilization is a defensive reaction, in response to discrimination and attacks by others. Often people do not recognize themselves as members of a group until this is pointed out by outsiders. However, differences in actual underlying conditions with respect to political and economic control are important for the development of group identity and mobilization. Without such inequalities, group identification is likely to be weak and remain a cultural rather than political or conflict-creating phenomenon. For example, ethnic or religious differences in Tanzania, Uruguay, and Costa Rica have not become a source of violent conflict, as economic differences between major ethnic groups are not substantial.

The hypothesis is that in any society there are some differences in individuals' circumstances—including cultural, geographic, economic—that provide the potential for the construction of group identity as a source of political mobilization. Political leaders, within government or outside it, may use this potential in their competition for power and resources, in the course of which they enhance group identification by reworking history and introducing new cultural symbols. However, cultural differences alone are not sufficient to bring about violent group mobilization. As A. Cohen points out, "Men may and do certainly joke about or ridicule the strange and bizarre customs of men from other ethnic groups, because these customs are different from their own. But they do not fight over such differences alone." Cohen continues: "When men *do,* on the other hand, fight across ethnic lines it is nearly always the case that they fight over some fundamental issues concerning the distribution and exercise of power, whether economic, political, or both."[15]

Economic and political differentiation among groups is thus of fundamental importance to group mobilization. This is the reason that the *relative,* rather than *absolute,* position is more often observed to be the underlying determinant of conflict.[16] If a whole society is uniformly impoverished, there may be despair, but there is no motivation for group organization. Even if political leaders hoped to use group mobilization as a source of power, they would find it difficult to secure sufficient adherence among followers without some underlying economic differences among the people they hoped to mobilize. Hence, in general, if there is group conflict, we should expect sharp economic differences between conflicting groups associated (or believed to be associated) with differences in political control.

Relevant economic differences vary according to the nature of the economy (e.g., land may be irrelevant in modern urban societies and employment relevant, but the converse could be true in rural-based economies). Although the prime cause of group conflict arises from inequalities among groups—that is, their *relative* position—the *absolute* situation may also be relevant, since an absolute deterioration in conditions may force attention onto the relative situation (e.g., when water becomes a scarce resource people may fight over it, but not when it is plentiful). Conversely, when incomes/resources are increasing, the relative position may matter less. The latter situation obtained in Kenya in the 1960s and 1970s and has been argued to be one reason why persistent relative inequality among tribal groups did not result in large-scale conflict.[17] But in some contexts, improving conditions, if the improvements are regarded as being unfairly shared, can give rise to conflict, as in Nigeria in the late 1960s.

Political power is an important instrument of economic power, setting the rules and determining allocation of employment, of government economic and social investments, and of incentives for private investment. In general, one would expect that political power would be a compelling means of securing (or, conversely, being deprived of) economic resources. It is plausible to argue that the role of the state relative to the market, as well as the discretionary decisions of government, may initially increase and is then likely to fall as development proceeds. In very underdeveloped societies, government expenditures and employment are low, but these increase alongside government's discretionary economic power as countries industrialize. During later stages of industrialization, the market tends to take a larger role, and government decisions are less discretionary and more rule-based. This would suggest that struggles to control state power might be greatest in the middle stages of development. Another relevant dimension is the nature of state resources: in rentier economies, where the bulk of state resources comes from levies on mineral production or from aid resources, the potential for personal economic enrichment arising from public office is much higher than where resources come from taxation.[18]

It should be noted that it is not necessarily the relatively deprived who instigate violence. The privileged may do so, fearing loss of position. For example, the prospect of possible loss of political power can act as a powerful motive for state-sponsored violence with the aim of suppressing opposition and maintaining power. Since the government has access to an organized force (police/army) and to finance, state terrorism is sometimes an important source of humanitarian emergencies. This was the case, for example, in most of the major episodes of violence in Uganda, in Haiti, and in Iraq's suppression of the Kurds. K. Holsti points out that state violence is more often than not the initiating cause of recent conflicts.[19]

In many societies, some level of organized violence persists over very long periods. Given conducive underlying conditions, there may be low-level struggle for certain periods, and then periods of fighting on a greater scale (civil war), sometimes culminating in major catastrophes. The memory of violence thereby contributes to group identification, animosities, and mobilization, increasing the likelihood of future conflict. This has been shown statistically by J. Auvinen and E. W. Nafziger.[20] Such a long history of violence of fluctuating strength appears to have occurred in many recent cases—Somalia, Rwanda, and Burundi among them. Hence a full understanding of causes must include an explanation both of the underlying vulnerability to conflict as well as the particular triggers that lead to sharp escalation. The trigger involves some change—possibly in relative deprivation or, frequently, in the activities of a particular political leader. However, a trigger event is likely to lead to a large scale conflict only in the presence of powerful underlying causes. Preventive policies should first and foremost address these underlying causes while being alert to the potential for, and trying to avoid, trigger events.

Dimensions of Differentiation in the Political, Economic, and Social Positions of Groups

Leaders often seize upon, change, and exaggerate cultural or religious differences—or symbolic systems—as a mechanism of group mobilization.[21] But it is suggested here that to make these symbolic systems work effectively in the mobilization of violence, parallel differences in political and/or economic dimensions are also necessary. For simplification, we can categorize the latter into four areas: political participation; economic assets; incomes and employment; and social aspects. Each contains other elements. For example, political participation can occur at the level of the cabinet, the bureaucracy, the army, and so on; economic assets comprise land, livestock, human capital, and the like.

The four categories and the main elements are presented in Table 5.1, with a column for each category. Each of the categories is important in itself, but most are also instrumental for achieving others. For example, political power is both an end and a means; control over economic assets is primarily a means to secure income, but it is also an end. As noted earlier, the relevance of an element varies according to whether it forms an important source of incomes or well-being in a particular society. The allocation of housing, for example, is generally more relevant in industrialized countries, where high-quality accommodation is expected and the government plays a role in its provision, in contrast to societies where most people construct their own basic accommodation; land is of huge importance where agriculture accounts for most output and employment. Water, as a productive resource, can be very important in parts of the world where rainwater is inadequate. Access to minerals can be a source of great wealth, and gaining such access may be an important source of conflict in countries with mineral resources.[22] Inequality between groups in any element is defined as constituting *horizontal inequality*.

Table 5.1   Sources of Differentiation Among Groups

Categories of Differentiation			
Political Participation	Economic Assets	Employment and Incomes	Social Access and Situation
Political parties	Land	Government	Education
	Livestock		
Government ministers, senior	Human capital	Private	Health services
Government ministers, junior	Communal resources, including water	Elite employment	Safe water
Army	Minerals	Rents	Housing
Parliament	Privately owned capital/credit	Skilled	Unemployment
Local government	Government infrastructure	Unskilled	Poverty
Respect for human rights	Security against theft	Informal-sector opportunities	Personal and household security

Table 5.2 summarizes the major horizontal inequalities identified in thirteen case studies of serious conflict carried out in the research program conducted by the United Nations University/World Institute for Development Economics Research on humanitarian emergencies. Evidence from these and other conflicts shows that group inequalities on the political dimension are virtually universal in countries where there has been serious conflict and that they tend to arise on each of the elements of political participation identified in the matrix, so as to permeate political power.

It must be noted that democratic institutions are not sufficient to prevent horizontal inequalities arising on the political dimension, partly because majorities can discriminate against minorities, and partly because even with power being shared at the top, inequalities may persist at lower levels. Inequalities in political power often lead to (but also stem from) similar inequalities in economic dimensions. Biased distribution of government jobs, infrastructure, and so on is common, with the group in power discriminating in its favor. For example, in Burundi in the 1990s, half of government investment went to Bujumbura and its vicinity, home of the elite Tutsi. In some countries, the president and his coterie take a massive share of state resources for their private use—as, for example, the Duvaliers in Haiti and the Somoza family in Nicaragua. Education has been shown to be a very common source of inequality, one that of course strengthens other economic inequalities. Unequal access to education was

Table 5.2   Some Examples of Horizontal Inequalities in Conflict-Prone Countries

Case	Relevant Groups	Source of Horizontal Inequality
Afghanistan	Ideological (Communism vs. Islam); ethnic (Pashtun vs. non-Pashtun); factional	Control over external resources
Bosnia and Herzegovina	Ethnic differences: Serbian, Croatian, and Muslims	Political power and jobs
Burundi	Hutu; Tutsi (and Twa—small and irrelevant) (Tutsi minority)	Political; distinction between farming (Hutu) and cattle rearing (Tutsi); severe imbalances favoring Tutsi in land; education; government jobs; army; government investment; privatization
Cambodia	Peasants; elite (some overlapping ethnic dimension—peasants Khmer and some newly educated; elite Sino-Khmer and Vietnamese; also Muslim Cham targeted by Khmer Rouge)	Location—urban/rural; Occupation—elite and salaried versus peasants; education; All associated with large differences in incomes

Case	Relevant Groups	Source of Horizontal Inequality
Congo	Power-holder versus others in Mobutu era; also some ethnic divisions; post-Mobutu more distinctions and conflicts according to ethnicity	Ethnic divisions created by colonial state, but became less important in early postcolonial era. Ethnic conflict and regional polarization did not emerge in the 1970s and 1980s on a major scale because of the patronage system Mobutu institutionalized; ethnicity more salient post-Mobutu.
El Salvador	Landlords, peasants (landlord minority)	Political; land distribution highly unequal between classes; communal property abolished 1882
Haiti	Elite surrounding president versus others (mainly peasants; also black middle class)	Control over state resources among nineteenth-century cliques, favored in education; language; land; economic opportunities
Liberia	Strongmen and factions; Americo-Liberians; locals	Political; control over state resources; natural resources
Rwanda	Hutu; Tutsi; Twa—very small group (Tutsi minority)	Political; colonial era, sharp inequalities favoring Tutsi—in education, employment, political participation. Postcolonial Hutus gained political power. Economically privileged class of Tutsi remained. All policies—employment, aid projects, army, diplomatic service, parliament—gave priority to Hutus. Access of Tutsi to higher education and state jobs limited by quota.
Sierra Leone	Strongmen; factions	Political; control over state resources; natural resources
Somalia	Clans (key); Classes (state dependent modern petite bourgeoisie/bureaucrats and ordinary Somali); Agriculturalists/pastoralists	Control over state resources; agriculturalists favored relative to pastoralists; land reform favored modern elites against traditional agriculturalists
Transcaucasia	Religious, ethnic, and among clans	Soviet supported "nominated" nationalist elite, and discriminated against minorities, politically, and economically
Zimbabwe (Matabeleland)	Political, geographic, and ethnic	Political power

Source: Country studies in Wayne E. Nafziger, Frances Stewart, and Raimo Väyrynen (eds.). *War, Hunger, and Displacement: The Origins of Humanitarian Emergencies (Wider Studies in Development Economics),* vol. 2 (Oxford: Oxford University Press, 2000).

prevalent from colonial times onward in Rwanda, Burundi, and until the Khmer revolution in Cambodia. In postcolonial Burundi there were deliberate attempts to limit educational access to the Hutu, and educated Hutu were targeted for killing in the 1970s.

Unequal access to state resources is often paralleled by inequalities in access to private assets, employment, and income, partly because the state resources (including education as well as rents) are a major source of private accumulation. But in some societies, private accumulation may benefit groups that are relatively deprived of state power and benefits (like the Kikuyu in Kenya, or minority religions or ethnicities, such as the Chinese in many Asian countries, or the Huguenots or Jews in Europe). This divergence may reduce tensions as far as the groups excluded from the state are concerned, but it can also enhance the likelihood of state terrorism against the economically privileged minority.

Other Elements to Be Considered
in an Analysis of the Causes of Conflict

In addition to these factors—that is, the existence of horizontal inequalities—four other elements also contribute to the causes of conflict: perceptions; private costs and benefits; constraints; and finance and opportunities.

First, we have already noted the important role of perceptions. People are not born with a sense of which group they belong to, who are friends and who enemies—this is socially constructed by family, community, and state. As noted above, each category may accentuate differences or reject them, changing perceptions and hence group mobilization.

Second, although social influences are especially important in conflict, there are also "rational" choice–type private benefits and costs of conflict to group members. Individual action is taken partly (the extreme neoclassical position would argue entirely) as a result of a calculus of individual or private costs and benefits of action. Of course, especially at times of high tension, group gains or losses also enter individual welfare functions. In some situations, people take action that is completely counter to their private interests—for example, rioters burn down factories in Sri Lanka where they themselves work, thereby destroying their own employment.[23] The role of leaders is to see that group considerations coincide with or override private ones, either by changing private incentives or through the use of propaganda and force.

Individuals and groups may also *gain* from conflict, for example, by looting, the use of forced labor, changes in the terms of trade in their favor, the creation of new economic opportunities, and controlling emergency aid. David Keen has analyzed such gains in the Sudan and elsewhere.[24] However, many people lose from the physical violence, disrupted markets, reduced state benefits, theft, and looting. The private calculus of costs and benefits also depends on the gains from avoiding conflict in terms of potential economic rewards and state-provided services from development in a peaceful environment. Hence, the general prospects for economic development, and the extent to which the individual and the group to which that individual belongs are likely to share in development gains, are important considerations; these may also be differentiated by gender. If the gains are low, the calculation is more likely to come out in favor of conflict.

The cost-benefit calculation often differs for leaders and followers as well as between those actively involved and the rest of the population. Leaders are generally seeking to form a government, control resources, secure high office, and so on. But they can do little without followers. However, if the followers—those providing the manpower and other resources—are strongly supportive of conflict, against the views of their existing leaders, new leaders may emerge.

Third, conflicts can result from a breakdown in state constraints. Even with strong motives for conflict on the basis of individual and group calculations, an effective repressive state (or other authority) can prevent, eliminate, or reduce conflict, whereas a weak authority may not be able to constrain violence. Some of the conflicts in the former Soviet Union can be seen as primarily due to the weakening of state authority and its ability to suppress conflicts so that underlying conflicts may again be openly expressed. In some of the African conflicts, too, the weakening of the state—for example, in Somalia and Sierra Leone—has permitted conflicts to erupt and enlarge, which might have been suppressed with a stronger state. In Kenya, in contrast, a relatively strong state has kept violent conflict to a fairly low level.[25] But as noted earlier, the state can also deliberately foster violence to undermine opposition groups, often provoking violent reactions to its actions. The state quite often has instigated violence by attacking opposition groups (again, in Haiti, Rwanda, Burundi, and Uganda in the 1970s and 1980s).

And finally, conflicts need resources, including arms, soldiers, and food. Some can be seized from the local territory—more readily if the conflict is popular locally, which again depends on whether the group involved regards itself as being seriously disadvantaged. Fighting groups can survive without foreign resources, but the availability of support from outside—credit, food, technical advice, and arms—helps the resource situation and thus feeds the conflict. The Cold War conflicts were largely financed from outside: since the end of the Cold War, external support has continued to be important—from governments (outside and within the region), from nongovernmental organizations (NGOs), and from the private sector. External resources supplied by governments played a considerable financing role in the wars in Central America, Afghanistan (from the United States, Pakistan, and Russia during the Cold War era, and subsequently from Pakistan and NGOs), Sudan, and Cambodia, for example. Private finance—from companies seeking mineral resources, from the sale of drugs, and from international crime—have been important in Afghanistan, Guatemala, the Congo, Angola, and the Balkans.[26] Finance is rarely an effective constraint, partly because wars do not always cost much (a low-level conflict, like that in Somalia, does not use expensive weapons), partly because they create opportunities for money-making (via theft and looting, black markets, and other crimes), and partly because there seem to be generous sources of credit for those at war.[27]

The same *reality* in terms of the relative and absolute position of groups in political and economic terms may have different effects in terms of conflict occurrence according to the four other elements just discussed. For example, a poor objective situation in terms of group inequality may not translate into conflict if there is a strong state that suppresses it, or if ideological elements are such that the inequalities are not widely perceived. A new conflict may emerge if either objective conditions change or if some of the other elements change—for example, the state weakens, new sources of external support for conflict develop, or leaders emerge who powerfully and effectively communicate the actual inequalities to the members of the group.

Trigger Events

Where there is high potential for conflict because of group inequalities and animosities, a trigger event may lead to eruption or escalation of conflict. A trigger may arise from a change in relative access to any important resource in the table, or because of endogenous or policy changes. Most commonly, however, it seems that a political event (as in Afghanistan with the Russian invasion) occurs in an environment in which there is a high potential for conflict because of perceived underlying inequalities.

The underlying reality about the absolute and, especially, the relative position of the group is of paramount importance. This is because the other factors just considered are all *permissive* and would not bring about a conflict in the *absence* of these inequalities. The next section will elaborate on the concept of horizontal inequality, which is critical to the analysis presented in this chapter.

Horizontal Versus Vertical Inequality

This analysis of the causes of conflict places overriding emphasis on inequality among groups along several dimensions. Yet societies we consider to be highly unequal are not invariably ridden by major conflict, as can be seen in Kenya, Thailand, Pakistan, and Brazil. This is partly because other potential causes of conflict may actually counter the high inequality and lead to an improvement in absolute conditions, or a repressive authoritarian state is able to suppress potential violent struggle. But it is also because the measurement of inequality does not correspond to the type relevant to conflict—inequality is normally assessed in relation to the distribution of private *income* only, and measured as *vertical* rather than *horizontal* inequality.

However, private income forms just one aspect of the numerous types of assets and resources potentially relevant as sources of conflict. Table 5.1 depicts a matrix of twenty-eight potentially relevant dimensions of inequalities, made up of four broad categories: political access; economic assets; incomes and employment; and social dimensions. Each of these categories included a vector of seven different elements. The selection was illustrative. It would have been possible to select more. As noted, the relevant elements are likely to vary across societies. Measures of inequality relevant for understanding the causes of conflict should include measures of horizontal inequality of each of the elements relevant in that society, in all four categories.

In contrast, inequality in income distribution—economists' normal basis for measuring inequality—is a summary measure of the incomes/ employment dimension but fails to capture, or gives only a partial indicator of, other relevant factors. Moreover, of greater significance, income distribution is a vertical measure, which takes everyone in society from top to bottom, recording incomes and the consequent inequality. What is needed for an analysis of conflict is a horizontal measurement of inequality between groups, defined by region/ethnicity/class/religion, according to the most appropriate type of group identification in the particular society.

There is, nonetheless, necessarily some connection between vertical and horizontal inequality, for any overall measure of societal inequality of income distribution (like the Gini or the Theil coefficients as vertical measures) can be divided into the weighted sum of two elements: intergroup inequality and intragroup inequality.[28] However, it is possible to have sharp vertical inequality in any dimension without any horizontal inequality—for example, if the average income of all groups was the same and distribution within each group was highly unequal. Conversely, it is possible to have considerable intergroup inequality while overall societal vertical inequality is moderate because intragroup inequality is small.

In fact, strong intragroup vertical inequality may actually *reduce* the potential for intergroup conflict for any given degree of horizontal inequality, because it may be more difficult to get group cohesion where there is high intragroup inequality, and because elite members may identify more with members of the elite from other groups than with lower-income members of their own group. This may help to explain the situation in Kenya. However, this is not always the case; strong vertical inequality within groups can lead to intragroup resentments that group leaders buy off by directing animosity against other groups. This crudely summarizes the case in Rwanda.

There are a number of ways of measuring horizontal inequality. Given availability of average data across groups, these may be summarized using such measures as the Gini coefficient, the Theil index, or the coefficient of variation—applied to groups rather than individuals, as is normal in measuring vertical inequality—to indicate the dispersion of achievements among groups. Where there are rather few relevant groups (sometimes, for example, just two or three), these are excessively complex measures. In that case, what is needed is to measure horizontal inequality by comparing the performance of one group with the average for the whole society or that of the other major group(s).

The consistency of deprivation over a number of dimensions is relevant in determining whether horizontal inequalities are likely to lead to conflict. This may be measured by looking at rankings in performance over different dimensions. Persistence in inequalities over time, and the trend in the differential (i.e., whether this is widening or narrowing), is also relevant. Major horizontal inequalities may give rise to conflict from different sources. The most obvious case is where those consistently on the losing side take up arms to correct the inequalities. However, if policies are adopted that lead the gaps between groups to narrow or reverse, even though this clearly reduces their potential to cause conflict from the perspective of the relatively deprived, it may lead to resentment among the losing group, something that can itself become a source of conflict. This was the case among the Tamils in Sri Lanka (discussed below). Moreover, the groups that gain can take preemptive action to protect their privileges—the white minority government in apartheid South Africa was an example of this kind of countermove.

Whether high levels of horizontal inequality are likely to cause serious conflict also depends on the size and political salience of the various groups. Where groups are small numerically, their potential to cause conflict on a substantial scale is generally limited, even when they suffer persistent discrimination.

Identifying the appropriate groups for measuring horizontal inequality can present some rather fundamental difficulties. In most conflicts, group differentiation is not based on some obvious objective differences between people (e.g., all people taller than six feet versus all those shorter than six feet) but is constructed or created in order to mobilize people for political purposes. Group construction is dynamic and fluid, changing with circumstances. In some situations, group identification may nonetheless be obvious (e.g., where a conflict has been ongoing for many years and the lines of differentiation are clearly drawn), but in others groups may split or new ones emerge in response to the developing situation. Then identification of groups for the purpose of measuring horizontal inequality may be not only difficult but also actually change the on-the-ground situation, either by reinforcing distinctions, or by creating some perceived political advantages in new alliances and groupings. Moreover, the announcement of the existence of a large degree of horizontal inequality may itself be conflict-provoking. It is extremely important that the act of measurement, and the subsequent policies, avoid worsening a conflict situation. But to avoid any assessment of horizontal inequality altogether for these reasons would be to lose a fundamental tool for analysis of the causes and prevention of conflict. My conclusion is that measurement of horizontal inequality and the uses to which it is put should be conducted with sensitivity to the considerations just discussed.

Three Examples of Horizontal Inequalities

Examination of horizontal inequalities in three cases of conflict—Uganda, Northern Ireland, and Sri Lanka—illustrates the usefulness of such an approach; but it also highlights some problems, especially with respect to policy.

Uganda

Uganda has suffered violent conflict on a major scale over the last forty years. Greatly oversimplifying the situation, one can say that divisions between the center and south and the more peripheral areas, especially the north, have been at the heart of most conflicts, although, of course, specific events and personalities have been responsible for particular developments. Table 5.3 presents some measures of horizontal inequality over time for Uganda.

It is apparent that there are significant, consistent, and persistent horizontal inequalities in Uganda over economic and social dimensions. Yet for much of the period these run counter to the political dimensions. This may explain why most of the violence over the first twenty-five years was state-instigated, by the northerners who controlled the political system against the economically privileged southerners. The narrowing of some differentials between 1969 and 1991 is the consequence of this—to some extent due to differential investment, but more to the destruction of central facilities during the political instability and fighting.[29] Since 1986, the govern-

Table 5.3   Horizontal Inequalities in Uganda (ratio of south and central Uganda to northern Uganda)

Indicator	Around 1959	Around 1969	Around 1991
Economic			
Cash crops, % of agricultural income	—	—	2.1
% taxpayers > 2,500 sh. income	—	2.9	—
Average household expenditure	—	—	1.7
Real GDP per capita	—	—	2.1
Increase in employment	—	1.3 (1962–1970)	5.6 (1970–1991)
Social			
Nurses per person	—	—	2.5
Distance to rural clinic	—	—	1.2
Primary enrollment	—	1.03	0.85
Secondary enrollment	—	1.4[a]	1.5
Infant mortality[b]	1.3	1.5	1.3
Human development index	—	—	1.5
Political			
General	Northerners	Northerners	Integrated
Military	Northerners	Northerners	Integrated

Source: J.-M. Matovu and F. Stewart, "The Social and Economic Consequences of Conflict: A Case Study of Uganda," in *War and Underdevelopment,* eds. F. Stewart and E. K. V. FitzGerald (Oxford: Oxford University Press, 2001).
   Notes: a. Population having completed secondary education.
   b. This is the ratio of the inverse of the infant mortality rate.

ment has been much more inclusive; for this period, violence has come mostly from the underprivileged in the north, stimulated and supported by various outside forces.

Northern Ireland

In Northern Ireland horizontal inequalities were large, persistent, and consistent over all dimensions over a long time period, providing an example of how such horizontal inequalities can lead to violence.[30] The case, however, also indicates how policies to correct such inequalities can provide conditions conducive to peacemaking.

   Horizontal inequalities in Ireland date back to the sixteenth and seventeenth centuries, when Protestants took the best land for themselves and introduced a variety of sources of legal discrimination, preventing Catholics from owning land or acquiring wealth, for example, and forcibly displacing Gaelic with English. "By the end of the nineteenth century Protestants controlled the vast bulk of the economic resources of east Ulster—the best of its land, its industrial and financial capital, commercial and business networks, industrial skill."[31] After the division of the island, when the Republic of Ireland was created in 1922, political control by the Protestants in the province of Northern Ireland—where they formed the majority—ensured the continuation of economic dominance. Assessments suggest that there was no narrowing of the gap between the communities from 1901 to 1951, with Catholics disadvantaged at every level.[32] Indeed, along certain dimensions there appears to have been a worsening between 1911 and 1971, with a rising proportion of unskilled workers in the Catholic community and a falling proportion among Protestants; the relative unemployment ratios also appear to have worsened over this period.

Considerable and consistent horizontal inequalities were present throughout the twentieth century with respect to economic, social, and political life. Unemployment rates, for example, were consistently more than twice the rate among Catholics than Protestants; educational qualifications were worse; the employment profile strongly favored Protestants; incomes were lower and housing access worse. Some aspects of horizontal inequalities in Northern Ireland are summarized in Table 5.4.

In addition to the systematic economic and social disadvantages, the Catholic community was politically disadvantaged at times when responsibility for government was devolved to the province, since majoritarian democracy meant that as a minority Catholics had no right to participate in government. There was also acute disadvantage with respect to participation in the security forces and the police, as illustrated in Table 5.4. For example, the Catholics, with roughly 40 percent of the population, accounted for only 8 percent of the membership of the Royal Ulster Constabulary (RUC). The consistency of the inequalities across political, economic, and social dimensions—with most evidence suggesting little change in the first three-quarters of the twentieth century—provided fertile ground for the outbreak of the troubles in the late 1960s. The relative disadvantage of the Catholic community was particularly prone to generate violence in the context of the high rates of impoverishment that prevailed: almost 60 percent of Catholic households had incomes below £6,000 per annum; 37 percent were dependent on income support; and in the early 1980s 30 percent of males were unemployed.

Yet the evidence recorded in Table 5.4 as well as the comments of many observers point to a reduction in horizontal inequalities over time, especially from the mid-1980s.[33] This is true on every dimension—for example, inequality in access to higher education was eliminated by the 1990s; inequality in incomes was reduced; the housing inequality was significantly reduced; the employment profile became more equal; even the imbalance in recruitment to the RUC was slowly being reversed. According to Joseph Ruane and Jennifer Todd, "The Catholic position is one of relative disadvantage; Protestants are stronger at all levels. But Protestant eco-

Table 5.4   Horizontal Inequalities in Northern Ireland

	Catholics	Protestants	Ratio of P benefits to C benefits[a]
Education			
% population leaving school without any qualifications			
1980s	20	16	1.25
% of population leaving school with two or more A-levels			
1980s	25.7	30.9	1.20
Numbers entering higher education			
1973	25,000	65,000	2.6
1985	155,000	205,000	1.3
1991	255,000	260,000	1.01
Employment and unemployment			
% unemployed (males)			
1917	17.3	6.6	2.6
1981	30.2	12.4	2.4
1991	28.4	12.7	2.2
% professional or managerial positions			
1971	21	33	1.6
1991	30	40	1.3
% of the police force (regular members of RUC)			
1995	8.2	91.8	11.2
% of new appointments to the police force			
1990	11.4	88.6	7.8
1995	14.4	85.6	5.9
Incomes			
Gross household incomes < £6,000, % of households in each community			
1986–1987	59	47	1.25
1988–1991	49	42	1.17
Gross household incomes >£10,000, % of households in each community			
1986–1987	19	34	1.8
1988–1991	31	39	1.3
Dependence on income support from state, % of households in each community			
1985–1987	37	20	1.85
1988–1991	30	16	1.88
Housing			
% of houses without inside toilet			
1971	33	26	1.3
1991	2	2	1.0
% of houses with less than three rooms			
1971	20.5	10.3	2.0
1991	7.5	6.8	1.1
% of houses with six or more rooms			
1971	25.3	36.4	1.4
1991	43.0	46.1	1.1

Source: A variety of investigations brought together on the Cain web service.

Note: a. The ratios have been calculated so as to show the ratio of benefits, rather than the ratio of the actual achievements; where the achievement is a negative one (e.g., housing without inside toilet) the ratio has been inverted.

nomic power has declined significantly over the past twenty-five years."[34] This narrowing of horizontal inequality is in part at least the outcome of British government policy, exemplified by a strengthened Fair Employment Act (1989),[35] a relatively generous housing policy, and efforts to ensure equality of education among the communities.[36] Systematic efforts to correct horizontal inequalities are one element explaining the readiness of the Catholic community to bring the conflict to an end. They also help explain the resistance of some Protestant groups to the more inclusive government which is being introduced.

Sri Lanka

Sri Lanka has suffered major civil war since the early 1980s, as Sri Lankan Tamils have sought political independence for the northeastern region of the country.[37] The situation with respect to horizontal inequalities within the island is a complex one. The Sri Lankan Tamil minority (accounting for 12.6 percent of the population in 1981) had been favored by the British colonial administration and had enjoyed relatively privileged access to education and to government employment in the first half of the twentieth century.[38] For example, although their overall university admissions were roughly in line with their share of population in 1964, Sri Lankan Tamils held around 40 percent of the university places in science, engineering, medicine, agriculture, and veterinary science (see Table 5.5). Tamils also gained from the use of English as the official language where they outperformed the Sinhalese majority (74 percent of the population in 1981). Yet there was much differentiation within both communities, with intragroup differentials greatly exceeding intergroup, and the relatively privileged Tamils being greatly outnumbered by impoverished members of the community.[39]

When the Sinhalese gained power, they sought to correct the perceived horizontal inequalities disadvantageous to them—through educational quotas, the use of Sinhalese as the official national language, and regional investment policy. The consequence was a major change in the extent and even direction of horizontal inequalities.[40] From 1963 to 1973, the incomes of the Sinhalese rose while those of the Tamils fell quite sharply, eliminating the previous differential between the two groups. By the end of the 1970s, differentials in access to education had been eliminated, with Sinhalese gaining more than proportionate places at university, although Tamils continued to be favored in science up to 1977. Civil service recruitment policies, particularly the use of the Sinhalese language in examinations, also favored the Sinhalese; by the end of the 1970s, Sinhalese recruitment in relation to population was four times more favorable than that of Tamils.

Sinhalese policies were undoubtedly effective in correcting prior hori-

Table 5.5 Horizontal Inequalities in Sri Lanka

	Sinhalese	Sri Lankan Tamils	Ratio of Sinhalese to Sri Lankan Tamils
Per capita income, two monthly, 1963 rupees			
1963	62.2[a]	105.9	0.59
1973	75[a]	75.8	0.99
Mean per capita income, rupees	all island	NEP[b]	
1963	134	157	0.85
1973	228	273	0.84
1981/82	1,111	1,113	0.99
Share of university admissions in relation to 1981 share of population: Science			
1969–1970	0.78	2.20[c]	0.35
1977	0.99	1.30[c]	0.76
Share of university admissions in relation to 1981 share of population: Total			
1969–1970	1.09	0.86[c]	1.26
1977	1.10	0.81[c]	1.36
Educational attainment: no schooling			
1978/79	21.9	23.5	1.07
Educational attainment: A levels			
1978/79	1.6	1.6	1.00
Civil service employment: % in relation to 1981 share of population			
1955	0.77	1.44[c]	0.53
1963	0.96	1.29[c]	0.74
1979	1.15	0.72[c]	1.60
Share of top grades state employment in relation to 1972 share of population			
1972	0.94	1.39[c]	0.68
Recruitment to civil service in relation to 1981 population share			
1970–1977	1.18	0.61[c]	1.93
1978–1981	1.26	0.31[c]	4.01

Source: Data quoted in D. Sriskandarajah, "The End of Serendipity: Politico-economic Explanations of Ethnic Conflict in Sri Lanka." M. Phil. thesis. Oxford, Queen Elizabeth House, 2000.
Notes: a. This represents the average of Kandyan Sinhalese and low-country Sinhalese.
b. The NEP (Northeast Province) is where Sri Lankan Tamils are concentrated, accounting for 72 percent of the population.
c. Includes Indian Tamils.

zontal inequalities, but they went overboard and instead introduced new horizontal inequalities in their favor. The result was to provoke the Sri Lankan Tamils, who felt politically excluded and economically threatened. "The political impact of the district quota system [introducing quotas on university access] has been little short of disastrous. It has convinced many

Tamils that it was futile to expect equality of treatment with the Sinhalese majority. . . . It has contributed to the acceptance of a policy campaigning for a separate state."[41] Similarly, the recruitment policies to the civil service in the 1970s, previously an important source of employment for Tamils, were strongly biased against the Tamils. Only 8 percent of the 23,000 new teachers recruited from 1971 to 1974 were Tamils.[42] In 1977–1978, *no* Tamils succeeded in the Ceylon administrative service examinations.[43] Moreover, political and cultural exclusion coincided with these adverse changes, making it easy for extremist leaders to use the growing resentment to gain support.

The Sri Lankan case indicates the care that is needed in pursuing policies to correct horizontal inequalities: sharp changes can create new sources of conflict, especially where they go beyond correcting prior inequalities and create new ones.

Policy Implications

This analysis of the sources of conflict contains some strong implications for policy formulation aimed at preventing or ending conflict. Policy needs to address the underlying causes of conflict systematically. Policies aimed at various permissive elements (resources that can fuel conflict, for example) are also relevant but cannot have lasting effects unless the root causes are tackled. As a first priority, policy formulation needs to consider both the issues of horizontal inequality among groups and that of the private incentives of leaders and followers. These two sets of issues—the conditions of groups and private incentives—overlap but are not the same.

Policy change is particularly difficult to achieve in the context of a country prone to violence, currently experiencing it, and/or having a history of conflict. In this context there are inherited memories and grievances, as well as entrenched group identity and intergroup animosities. The government is rarely broad-based and normally represents only a subset of the groups potentially involved in conflict. It would often be naive to think that the government even wants to promote peace, given the prevalence of state-instigated violence. This was illustrated by the three cases explored above. In the case of Uganda, the governments of Idi Amin and Milton Obote were actually responsible for much of the violence. In contrast, Yoweri Museveni has been much more peace-oriented. In Northern Ireland, an outside agent (the British government) was responsible for correcting the entrenched inequalities. In Sri Lanka, the majoritarian Sinhalese governments have systematically corrected the disadvantages faced by their own community, but in so doing they have provoked violent rebellion among the Tamils. In other cases, proposals have been put forward by external agents to correct horizontal inequalities, but they were unsuccessful, partly because they were not negotiated and accepted by the parties themselves. This was the case with the 1960 constitution for Cyprus and the Arusha Accords for Rwanda. Yet in all of these cases the solutions were mainly addressed at political dimensions; the underlying social and economic inequalities need to be tackled over a longer period with palpable results (as in Northern Ireland) before parties may be ready to accept a political settlement. Hence, the policies suggested below are most appropriate for long-term prevention rather than short-term solutions to ongoing conflicts.

These policies may fall on hostile ears as far as governments are concerned. The same may be true of the international community, which has its own reasons for pursuing the actions it has taken, many of which have been conflict-provoking themselves. Hence, it must be recognized that the context for introducing policy change is structurally unfavorable. Nonetheless, it is worth elucidating policies liable to reduce vulnerability to conflict, for some governments may wish to pursue them, as would some international donors, at least judged by their rhetoric; and for others, these policies can act as a standard against which actual policies may be judged.

Group (or Horizontal) Inequalities

The general direction of policy change to avoid violence must be to reduce group inequalities. To achieve this it is essential to have inclusive government—politically, economically, and socially. Politically this means that all major groups in a society participate in political power, the administration, the army, and the police. Inclusive government economically implies that horizontal inequality in economic aspects (assets, employment, and incomes) is moderate. And inclusive government socially means that horizontal inequality in social participation and achieved well-being is also moderate. "Moderate" is a loose term. Group equality would be the ideal. In contrast, a ratio of more than two in average achievements between groups would constitute severe inequality. The importance of any measure of inequality is increased if it occurs systematically over a number of dimensions and grows over time. Hence, such consistency (or otherwise) and developments over time should enter into considerations when determining what is an acceptable degree of horizontal inequality. "Horizontal equity" describes an acceptable degree of horizontal inequality.[44]

The general objective of inclusivity and moderate horizontal inequality will translate differently into specific policy recommendations, in particular cases depending on the relevant groups in the society, the dimensions of importance in the particular society, and those in which there is substantial horizontal inequality.

Political Inclusivity

The most universal requirement is for political inclusivity because it is monopolization of political power by one group or another that is normally responsible for many other inequalities. Yet achieving political inclusivity is among the most difficult changes to bring about. It is not just a matter of democracy, defined as rule with the support of the majority, as majority rule can be consistent with abuse of minorities, as, for example, in the recent history of Rwanda, Cambodia, and Zimbabwe. In a politically inclusive democratic system, particular types of proportional representation are needed to ensure participation by all major groups in the elected bodies. For inclusive government, representation of all such groups is essential not only at the level of the cabinet but also other organs of government. For political inclusivity to be achieved, members of major groups also need to be included at all levels of the civil service, the army, and the police.

Every case of conflict we have observed lacks such political inclusivity. Moreover, politically inclusive policies have been adopted by well-known peacemaking regimes (e.g., the Chilean government that followed Augusto Pinochet, Museveni in Uganda, and South Africa under Nelson Mandela).

These political requirements for conflict-prone countries do not currently form part of the dialogue of political conditionality adopted by many bilateral donors. The usual political conditionality includes rule with the consent of the majority, multiparty democracy, and respect for human rights. At times, the requirement of political inclusivity may even be inconsistent with proposed political conditionalities. Political conditions for avoiding conflict certainly include the requirement of respect for human rights. But the requirement for majority rule is not a sufficient condition for conflict-avoidance, as noted above, and multiparty democracy may not be consistent with conflict prevention, for political parties are often formed along ethnic (or other group) lines and can encourage group animosity.[45]

Economic and Social Inclusivity

Some of the appropriate economic and social recommendations may differ among countries. Those concerning government expenditure and jobs, however, are universal:

1. To ensure balance in group benefits from government expenditure and aid (including the distribution of investment and jobs).
2. To ensure balance in group access to education at all levels; health services; water and sanitation; housing and consumer subsidies (if relevant). Equality of access in education is particularly important, as this con-

tributes to equity in income earning potential, whereas its absence perpetuates income inequality.

    3. To monitor sources of horizontal inequality arising from the private
sector and introduce policies to correct it where needed.

    The private sector can be an important source of group differentiation.
It is generally a less explosive source politically than an inequitable state
sector, as it is less directly under political control. Nonetheless, in societies
where the private sector forms a major source of group inequality in jobs,
incomes, and assets, horizontal inequality in this sector could be conducive
to conflict; in such a situation it would be necessary to adopt policies to
reduce the horizontal inequality present in the private sector. The situation
in South Africa represents an example where a huge amount of horizontal
inequality stems from private-sector activity. The particular policies to be
followed to deal with private sector sources of horizontal inequality differ
across countries, but may include:

• Policies to ensure balanced participation in education and the acqui-
sition of skills at all levels. This has been an important and effective policy
measure in Malaysia.

• Land reform so as to ensure fair access to land by different groups.
This policy would be relevant only where differential access to land is an
important aspect of horizontal inequality. In El Salvador, differential
landownership was a major source of conflict, and the subsequent land
reform was intended to contribute to a peaceful solution.

• Policies to promote balanced access to industrial assets and employment. This is more difficult to achieve than reform of public-sector policies
and needs to be attempted only where the private sector is a major source of
group inequality—which is generally not the case in many conflict situations in very undeveloped economies. Private-sector firms may be required
to have an equal-opportunities policy; they should be monitored and, where
horizontal inequality is high, may be required to provide a certain proportion of jobs at every level to members of the main groups. Similarly, banks
may be required to spread their lending across groups. Asset redistribution
across groups can be achieved by government purchase of assets and redistribution to disadvantaged groups.

    Although the detailed policy requirements would differ according to
the situation in a particular country, the important recommendation is the
general requirement to follow inclusive policies, offsetting major elements
of horizontal inequality. However, a cautious approach is required, as
heavy-handed corrective action can itself promote conflict. Action to eliminate some privileges in education and employment enjoyed by Sri Lankan

Tamils, for example, was itself among the causes of conflict—one reason for this was the lack of political inclusivity of the Sri Lankan government (see above).

As noted, many governments are pursuing precisely the opposite policies to the inclusive ones recommended here. It is critically important that politically inclusive policies are built into the requirements of the international community in its dealings with conflict-prone countries. At present, they are not—certainly not explicitly. Aid allocation within a country depends on efficiency considerations, and sometimes vertical equity, but not horizontal equity. Pursuing horizontal equity may sometimes conflict with efficiency or even with vertical equity. These are trade-offs that may have to be accepted. In the long term, both growth and poverty would benefit more from the avoidance of conflict than is lost from any short-term output reduction that the new policy might involve. Mostly, there would not be a significant trade-off with poverty reduction, as balanced policies are also likely to be poverty-reducing, and extending education to the deprived would be likely to contribute to economic growth. Malaysia, for example, was remarkably successful in achieving economic growth and poverty reduction as well as horizontal equity through the New Economic Policy, which effectively narrowed the gap in incomes, employment, and assets among the major groups.

The International Monetary Fund and World Bank policy conditionality is blind to these issues, that is, they take no account of horizontal equity in their policy prescriptions, or allow for the possible undermining of the state resulting from cutbacks in government expenditure and powers following their recommendations. As lead institutions, it is essential that they incorporate these considerations into their conditionality, not only with respect to project allocation but also in the policy conditionality applied to government economic interventions and expenditures. This would require a marked change in their programs for conflict-prone countries.

Private Incentives

The policies just sketched were all addressed to the need for inclusivity and group equity. When applied to a situation not yet affected by conflict, these policies, if effective, might be sufficient to eliminate the underlying causes of conflict, although an additional requirement is that there is a sufficiently strong state to avoid violence erupting for private benefit in a near-anarchical situation. In such a context, it may not be necessary to introduce policies to tackle the private incentives to violence of leaders or followers. But when conflict is ongoing, policies tackling the root causes may need to be accompanied by policies encouraging particular individuals involved to stop fighting and enter more peaceful occupations.

The private incentives of leaders of major groups may best be turned around by offering them positions in government. Lower-level leaders may be offered jobs in the state army or civil service—or even money. This proposal may fall on deaf ears for political reasons; as with other policy proposals suggested here, only governments seriously intending to end violence and enhance national unity will follow the recommendation. Yet many postconflict governments have adopted it. For example, upon taking power in Uganda, Museveni aimed to incorporate all the various military forces into a single national army (the National Resistance Army, or NRA) with a balanced ethnic composition.[46] The NRA included not only the various forces that had fought against Obote but also those who had fought with him, as well as later Amin supporters from the West Nile. Soldiers who had served in the Obote army were sent to camps for screening and "political education." The consequence of the policy of incorporation was that the NRA grew from a small, tightly disciplined guerrilla force into one of the largest armies in Africa, comprising more than 100,000 soldiers.

Those who have been active soldiers (the followers) need income-earning employment—money or jobs in works schemes can be offered in exchange for arms or, where appropriate, land or agricultural credit. In some contexts, the offer of a lump sum upon demobilization appears to have been quite effective (e.g., after the Ugandan and Mozambique wars).[47] Such policies can be expensive and need international support. Moreover, they are difficult to apply in less organized conflicts where large numbers move in and out of a conflict and there is no clear demarcation between those who fought in the conflict and those who did not. Improving the income-earning opportunities for the young generally, especially for males, is needed in such contexts. To some extent, this would happen by itself if peace were restored, as farms could again be worked on, and other private-sector activities could resume (though some other war-related activities would cease). But in most cases, there is likely to be an interval when special employment schemes or financial handouts may be needed.

As with the earlier policies, what is appropriate inevitably differs among countries. The general requirement is that these issues are explicitly considered when conflict is ending.

General Development Policies

General analysis as well as some of the econometric evidence suggest a connection between predisposition to conflict and levels and growth of per capita incomes, although the correlation is not strong.[48] Economic growth would be likely to reduce the propensity for conflict, if it narrows horizontal inequalities. Equitable and poverty-reducing growth would normally be likely to reduce horizontal inequality and might make persisting inequalities more tolerable. Hence, policies that succeed in promoting such growth should form part of any propeace policy package. But it should be stressed that the growth must be widely shared. Inequitably distributed growth can reinforce horizontal inequality and thus be conflict-promoting, as in Rwanda.

A great deal of analysis has been devoted to delineating the conditions for widely shared growth. Policies to promote equitable development include the spread of education; measures to increase savings and investment; price and technology policies to encourage labor-intensive technologies; new credit institutions to extend credit to the low-income; measures to encourage the informal sector; land reform and support for small farmers; and international policies to improve market access and terms of trade and reduce debt burdens. Many measures can be designed specifically to reduce horizontal inequality as well as to promote growth and reduce poverty. There is no question that a successful development strategy of this kind would reduce conflict propensity. However, it is difficult to envisage the success of such policies in countries where major structural divisions that bring about major conflict are present. Hence, even though successful development would undoubtedly contribute to conflict prevention, it seems likely that the more specific policies discussed above concerning group differentials and individual incentives will be needed not only in and of themselves but also as preconditions for the success of development more broadly.

The discussion above has referred to "conflict-prone countries" as being the special targets for preventive policies. This implies the need for some definition of "conflict-proneness." Conflict proneness appears to be identified by the following characteristics: serious past conflict at some time over the previous twenty years; evidence of a considerable degree of horizontal inequality; low incomes; and economic stagnation. These are the conditions that predispose to conflict according to most case studies and statistical analyses.[49] The first condition is invariably a serious sign. In addition, the high incidence of conflict among low-income countries suggests that they should be regarded as conflict-prone as a group. Among middle-income countries, sharp horizontal inequalities would put them into the same category.[50] The delineation of "proneness" to violence is important because it would be more effective to focus conflict prevention policies on the subset of most vulnerable countries, as well as to channel aid and/or debt relief to them if necessary. Moreover, special care should be taken to avoid providing resources (in the form of aid or military assistance) that is likely to help finance conflict in such countries. This might seem an obvious point, yet many studies show that international resources have poured into countries on the brink or in the process of conflict.

Conclusion

The search for the underlying causes of civil conflicts is an ongoing one. No definitive answers can be expected, especially since conflicts occur in a huge range of countries and situations. The findings of this chapter must be regarded as tentative. Yet because of the continuing nature of these crises and the heavy human costs they impose, it is important that some action is taken on the basis of current knowledge, without waiting for further confirmation. It is in this spirit that the policy conclusions have been presented above as a set of definitive recommendations.

One conclusion in particular stands out: in every major conflict there is an interaction between economic, political, and cultural factors, with group perceptions and identity (normally historically formed) being enhanced by sharp group differentiation in political participation, economic assets and income, social access, and well-being. Consequently, there needs to be a comprehensive approach, simultaneously tackling political, economic, and social inequalities, as well as addressing cultural perceptions. Tackling only one dimension—for example, focusing just on political inequalities, as is often the case in peace negotiations—will not be sufficient, as continued inequalities in other dimensions are likely to give rise to renewed violence. Key elements of any effective peace-promoting effort must include policies to reduce all major elements of horizontal inequalities. This means incorporating considerations of horizontal equity into policies for public expenditure, employment, education, and social support systems, as well as political participation at all levels. Yet such policies need to be introduced with sensitivity, because the process of correcting the inequalities can give rise to violence from the better-off groups whose privileges are being reduced.

For long-term conflict prevention, then, it is vital that monitoring, avoiding, and (where necessary) correcting major horizontal inequalities in all dimensions becomes an intrinsic aspect of development policy—not just an add-on for countries already suffering conflict. In the long term, this would be at least as important for poverty reduction as the more obvious policies toward poverty reduction currently being proposed, for conflict is one of the major causes of low incomes and poor human development.

Notes

This is a revised version of a paper that was published in *Oxford Development Studies* 28, 3 (October 2000). The ideas in this chapter draw heavily on a QEH/WIDER research project, "The Origins of Humanitarian Emergencies," directed by Wayne Nafziger, Raimo Väyrynen, and this author; see E. W. Nafziger, F. Stewart, and R. Väyrynen, eds., *The Origin of Humanitarian Emergencies: War and Displacement in Developing Countries* (Oxford: Oxford University Press,

2000); and E. W. Nafziger, F. Stewart, and R. Väyrynen, eds., *Weak States and Vulnerable Economies: Humanitarian Emergencies in the Third World* (Oxford: Oxford University Press, 2000). I am grateful for stimulating collaboration with Wayne Nafziger and Raimo Väyrynen. I would like to record my thanks to the editors of this volume for insightful comments on a previous draft, and to Marcia Hartwell for research assistance on Northern Ireland.

1. Among the ten countries with the lowest Human Development Index, Sierra Leone, Niger, Mali, Burundi, Ethiopia, Eritrea, Guinea, and Mozambique have all been subject to civil conflict at some time over the past twenty years.

2. See, for example, the statistical evidence produced by J. Auvinen and E. W. Nafziger, "The Sources of Humanitarian Emergencies," *Journal of Conflict Resolution* 43 (1999): 267–290.

3. F. Stewart and E.K.V. FitzGerald, *War and Underdevelopment: The Economic and Social Consequences of Conflict* (Oxford: Oxford University Press, 2001).

4. UNDP Human Development Report (New York: Oxford University Press, various years); World Bank, *Poverty Reduction and the World Bank in Fiscal 1996 and 1997* (Washington, D.C.: World Bank, 1998).

5. E.K.V FitzGerald, "Global Linkages, Vulnerable Economies, and the Outbreak of Conflict," in *War and Destitution: The Prevention of Humanitarian Emergencies,* eds. E. W. Nafziger and R. Väyrynen (London: Macmillan Press, 2000).

6. See Nafziger, Stewart, and Väyrynen, eds., *The Origin of Humanitarian Emergencies,* and Nafziger, Stewart, and Väyrynen, eds., *Weak States and Vulnerable Economies.*

7. See A. Rangasami, "'Failure of Exchange Entitlements' Theory of Famine: A Response," *Economic and Political Weekly* 20, 41–42 (1985); D. Keen, *The Benefits of Famine: A Political Economy of Famine Relief in Southwestern Sudan, 1983–1989* (Princeton: Princeton University Press, 1994); D. Keen, "The Political Economy of Civil War," in *War and Underdevelopment: The Economic and Social Consequences of Conflict,* eds. F. Stewart and E.K.V. FitzGerald et al. (Oxford: Oxford University Press, 2001); P. Collier and A. Hoeffler, "On Economic Causes of Civil War," *Oxford Economic Papers* 5-0 (1998): 63–573.

8. See, for example, D. Keen, "Sierra Leone: War and Its Functions," in *War and Underdevelopment,* eds. F. Stewart and E.K.V. FitzGerald et al.

9. See J. Alexander, J. McGregor, and T. Ranger, "Ethnicity and the Politics of Conflict: The Case of Matabeleland," in *The Origin of Humanitarian Emergencies,* eds. Nafziger, Stewart, and Väyrynen; D. Turton, "War and Ethnicity: Global Connections and Local Violence in North East Africa and Former Yugoslavia," *Oxford Development Studies* 25 (1997): 77–94; A. Cohen, *Two-Dimensional Man: An Essay on the Anthropology of Power and Symbolism in Complex Society* (Berkeley: University of California Press, 1974); A. D. Smith, "The Nation Invented, Imagined, Reconstructed?" *Millennium: Journal of International Studies* 20 (1991): 353–368.

10. Alexander, McGregor, and Ranger, "Ethnicity and the Politics of Conflict."

11. See Turton, "War and Ethnicity," 84; and A. D. Smith, "The Myth of the 'Modern Nation' and the Myths of Nations," *Ethnic and Racial Studies* 2 (1988): 1–25.

12. Smith has argued that "the [past] acts as a constraint on invention. Though the past can be 'read' in different ways, it is not any past." See Smith, "The Nation

Invented, Imagined, Reconstructed?" 357–358, quoted in Turton, "War and Ethnicity."

13. J. Lonsdale, "Mau-Maus of the Mind: Making Mau-Mau and Remaking Kenya," *Journal of African History* 31 (1990): 393–421.

14. See P. Gaffney, "Burundi: The Long Sombre Shadow of Ethnic Instability," in *Weak States and Vulnerable Economies,* eds. Nafziger, Stewart, and Väyrynen; and P. Uvin, "Rwanda: The Social Roots of Genocide," in *Weak States and Vulnerable Economies,* eds. Nafziger, Stewart, and Väyrynen.

15. Cohen, *Two-Dimensional Man.*

16. See Ted Robert Gurr, *Minorities at Risk: A Global View of Ethnopolitical Conflict* (Washington, D.C.: United States Institute for Peace Press, 1993).

17. See J. Klugman, "Kenya: Economic Decline and Ethnic Politics," in *Weak States and Vulnerable Economies,* eds. Nafziger, Stewart, and Väyrynen.

18. Collier and Hoeffler argue that the desire for personal enrichment is the main motive for conflict ("greed" rather than "need"), and conflict is therefore more prevalent in mineral-rich countries. Collier and Hoeffler, "On the Economic Causes of War."

19. K. Holsti, "The Political Sources of Humanitarian Disasters," in *The Origin of Humanitarian Emergencies,* eds. Nafziger, Stewart, and Väyrynen.

20. Auvinen and Nafziger, "The Sources of Humanitarian Emergencies."

21. "Symbolic systems" are the values, myths, rituals, and ceremonials that are used to organize and unite groups. See Cohen, *Two Dimensional Man.*

22. See J. Fairhead, "The Conflict over Natural and Environmental Resources," in *The Origin of Humanitarian Emergencies,* eds. Nafziger, Stewart, and Väyrynen; W. Reno, "Liberia and Sierra Leone: The Competition for Patronage in Resource-Rich Economies," in *Weak States and Vulnerable Economies,* eds. Nafziger, Stewart, and Väyrynen.

23. M. O'Sullivan, personal communication.

24. Keen, *The Benefits of Famine;* and Keen, "The Political Economy of Civil War."

25. Klugman, "Kenya: Economic Decline and Ethnic Politics," in *Weak States and Vulnerable Economies,* eds. Nafziger, Stewart, and Väyrynen.

26. In Angola, for example, the impoverished government is acquiring finance to fight the rebels by selling licenses for oil drilling.

27. A seven-country study of countries at war showed debt rising rapidly, faster than nonwar countries (see Stewart and FitzGerald, *War and Underdevelopment*).

28. For a decomposition of the Gini of this kind, see J. Fei, G. Ranis, and S. Kuo, "Growth and Family Distribution of Income by Factor Components," *Quarterly Journal of Economics* 92 (1978): 17–53; and for a decomposition of the Theil, see S. Anand, *Inequality and Poverty in Malaysia* (Oxford: Oxford University Press, 1983).

29. See J.-M. Matovu and F. Stewart, "The Social and Economic Consequences of Conflict: A Case Study of Uganda," in *War and Underdevelopment,* eds. Stewart and FitzGerald.

30. I am grateful to research assistance from Marcia Hartwell for information about Northern Ireland.

31. J. Ruane and J. Todd, *The Dynamics of Conflict in Northern Ireland* (Cambridge: Cambridge University Press, 1996): 151.

32. A. C. Hepburn, "Employment and Religion in Belfast, 1901–1951," in *Religion, Education, and Employment: Aspects of Equal Opportunity in Northern*

Ireland, eds. R. J. Cormack and R. D. Osborne (Belfast: Appletree, 1983); and R. J. Cormack and E. P. Rooney, "Religion and Employment in Northern Ireland, 1911–1971," unpublished paper.

33. For example, Gallagher, Osborne, and Cormack, 1994, note that "significant change in the labour market is starting to occur." A. M. Gallagher, R. D. Osborne, and R. J. Cormack, *Fair Shares? Employment, Unemployment, and Economic Status* (Belfast: Fair Employment Commission, 1994): 84. "The increase in the Catholic middle class has involved an expansion into occupations beyond those identified as 'servicing' the Catholic community—teachers, doctors, lawyers and priests. Now Catholics are also substantially represented among accountants and other financial service professionals, middle managers, middle ranking civil servants, architects and planners and university and further education lecturers." Ibid., 83–84.

34. Ruane and Todd, *The Dynamics of Conflict in Northern Ireland,* 177.

35. This legislation was in part a response to a strong popular campaign in the United States to prevent investment in Northern Ireland unless fair employment practices were followed, as summarized in the so-called MacBride principles.

36. According to Ruane and Todd, "Today the British government's commitment to redressing Catholic inequality is on a scale that is historically unprecedented." Ruane and Todd, *The Dynamics of Conflict in Northern Ireland,* 172.

37. This section draws heavily on discussions with and the thesis by D. Sriskandarajah, "The End of Serendipity: Politico-economic Explanations of Ethnic Conflict in Sri Lanka," M. Phil. thesis, Oxford, Queen Elizabeth House, 2000.

38. Indian Tamils in Sri Lanka account for another 5.5 percent.

39. P. Glewwe, "The Distribution of Income in Sri Lanka in 1969–1970 and 1980–1981: A Decomposition Analysis," *Journal of Development Economics* 24 (1986): 255–274.

40. There are other groups within Sri Lanka—including Muslims (7.1 percent of the population)—not included in the analysis here for the sake of simplicity.

41. C. R. de Silva, quoted in Sriskandarajah, "The End of Serendipity," 51.

42. C. Manogoran, *Ethnic Conflict and Reconciliation in Sri Lanka* (Honolulu: University of Hawaii Press, 1987).

43. S. W. Samarasinghe, "Ethnic Representation in Central Government Employment and Sinhala-Tamil Relations in Sri Lanka, 1948–1981," in *From Independence to Statehood: Managing Ethnic Conflict in Five African and Asian States,* eds. R. Goldman and A. Wilson (London: Frances Pinter, 1984).

44. The use of the term "horizontal equity" to mean an acceptable degree of horizontal inequality should not be confused with the concept of "horizontal equity" used in the tax literature—where it means equal tax treatment of people in similar circumstances (see, e.g., A. B. Atkinson, "Horizontal Equity and the Distribution of the Tax Burden," in *The Economics of Taxation,* eds. H. J. Aaron and M. J. Boskin [Washington, D.C.: The Brookings Institution, 1980]).

45. F. Stewart and M. O'Sullivan, "Democracy, Conflict, and Development—Three Cases," in *The Political Economy of Comparative Developments into the 21st Century, Essays in Memory of John Fei,* eds. G. Ranis, S. Hu, and Y. Chu (Cheltenham: Edward Elgar, 1999).

46. D. Mudoola, "Political Transitions Since Amin: A Study in Political Pathology," in *Uganda Now: Between Decay and Development,* eds. H. B. Hansen and M. Twaddle (London: James Currey, 1988).

47. See P. Collier, "Demobilisation and Insecurity: A Study in the Economics

of the Transition from War to Peace," *Journal of International Development* 6 (1994): 343–352; C. Dolan and J. Schafer, "The Reintegration of Ex-combatants in Mozambique: Manica and Zambezia Provinces," Final Report to USAID (Oxford: Refugee Studies Programme, Queen Elizabeth House, 1997).

48. See Auvinen and Nafziger, "The Sources of Humanitarian Emergencies"; and E.K.V. FitzGerald, "Global Linkages, Vulnerable Economies, and the Outbreak of Conflict," in *War and Destitution,* eds. Nafziger and Väyrynen.

49. See Nafziger, Stewart, and Väyrynen, *The Origin of Humanitarian Emergencies*; Auvinen and Nafziger, "The Sources of Humanitarian Emergencies"; Fitzgerald, "Global Linkages, Vulnerable Economies, and the Outbreak of Conflict"; Collier and Hoeffler, "On the Economic Causes of Civil War."

50. This is also the conclusion of Stavenhagen. Writing on ethnic conflict, he concluded: "When regional and social disparities in the distribution of economic resources also reflect differences between identified ethnic groups, then conflicts over social and economic issues readily turn into ethnic conflict." R. Stavenhagen, ed. *Ethnic Conflict and the Nation State* (New York: St. Martin's, 1996): 294. But I believe this holds more widely to any form of differentiation among groups—religious, class, clan—not merely ethnic.

PART 2

Conflict Prevention: The State of the Art

6

Preventive Diplomacy at the United Nations and Beyond

Fen Osler Hampson

The purpose of this chapter is to provide an overview of some of the scholarly and policy literature that emerged especially during the 1990s on preventive diplomacy (PD).[1] The chapter identifies some of the key fault lines in these debates about the definition, range of techniques, and utility/feasibility of PD. The possibilities for strengthening the role of the United Nations in PD are also considered, including the various recommendations for institutional reform and operational effectiveness that are offered in the literature. The survey of the literature in this chapter is by no means exhaustive or in any sense definitive; rather, it focuses on the major works and some of the key findings in the burgeoning literature on PD.

Definition and Instruments

Although there has been renewed interest in PD in recent years, neither the term nor the concept are new. The term was first coined by UN Secretary-General Dag Hammarskjöld when he referred to UN efforts "to keep localized international disputes from provoking larger confrontations between the superpowers."[2] It is arguably the case that much of the United Nations' traditional involvement in peacekeeping was motivated, in part, by a desire to prevent local and regional conflicts from dragging in the two superpowers, which would have greatly increased the risks of escalation.[3] PD obviously also has a basis in international law and the UN goal to "take effective collective measures for the prevention and removal of threats to peace."[4] In the post–Cold War era, however, the evolving interest in PD has been directed at expanding the concept to address a wide variety of different kinds of conflicts (ethnic, civil, intrastate, interstate) from escalating. Within the United Nations and the broader policy community, interest in PD gained momentum with the publication of Boutros Boutros-Ghali's *An Agenda for Peace*.[5] A number of foreign-policy institutes and think tanks as well as blue-ribbon panels like the Carnegie Commission on Preventing Deadly Conflict have also studied the concept in some depth.[6]

In current discussions there continues to be some debate about the scope and relevant instruments of PD. In *Agenda for Peace,* the former Secretary-General defined PD as "action to prevent disputes from arising between the parties, to prevent existing disputes from escalating into conflicts and to limit the spread of the latter when they occur."[7] The instruments of PD were defined rather broadly to include: (1) confidence-building measures such as the exchange of military missions, risk reduction centers, information exchanges, and monitoring of regional arms control agreements; (2) fact-finding "in accordance with the [UN] Charter"; (3) early warning; (4) preventive deployments, that is, inserting armed forces before a crisis develops; and (5) demilitarized zones.[8] Noticeably absent from this list are mediation and negotiation—activities that the former Secretary-General considered to be different from PD and that he argued were instead part of the UN's *peacemaking* functions (i.e., "action to bring hostile parties to agreement through such peaceful means as those foreseen in Chapter VI of the Charter of the United Nations").

A somewhat different reading of the instruments of PD is to be found in the work of scholars like Alexander George and Michael Lund, who subsume mediation and negotiation within the framework of PD. George, for example, suggests that PD is essentially about techniques of conflict avoidance and conflict resolution such as mediation, peacekeeping, peacemaking, confidence- and trust-building measures, and unofficial track-two diplomacy.[9] His view is echoed by the Carnegie Commission's *Final Report on Preventing Deadly Conflict*, where PD is defined as "frontline diplomacy" undertaken by ambassadors, senior foreign office officials, and personal envoys of the UN Secretary-General in a crisis where the threat of violence is high. The Commission suggests that PD may also involve "urgent efforts" through "bilateral, multilateral, and unofficial channels" to "pressure, cajole, arbitrate, mediate, or lend 'good offices' to encourage dialogue and facilitate a nonviolent resolution of the crisis."[10]

Lund defines PD as "action taken in vulnerable places and times to avoid the threat or use of armed force and related forms of coercion by states or groups to settle the political disputes that can arise from the destabilizing effects of economic, social, political, and international change."[11] Like the Carnegie Commission, he agrees that "such action can involve the use of a variety of 'diplomatic' (in the narrow sense) political, military, economic, and other instruments that can be carried out by governments, multilateral organizations, NGOs [nongovernmental organizations], individuals, or the disputants themselves."[12]

Some scholars argue that PD involves diplomatic interventions at a particular point in the so-called conflict life cycle. Bruce Jentleson, for example, distinguishes between (1) developmentalist diplomacy, that is, efforts to address long term societal and international problems that, if allowed to worsen, have the potential to lead to violent conflict; (2) preventive diplomacy involving situations with shorter time frames, "where the likelihood of violent mass conflict is imminent" and the "objectives are to take the necessary diplomatic action within the limited time frame to prevent those crises or wars which seem imminent"; and (3) war diplomacy involving situations where conflict or war has already broken out.[13]

It should also be noted that whereas some scholars and practitioners include coercive diplomacy within the general rubric of PD, others eschew "power-based" approaches in favor of "noncoercive" or "problem-solving" approaches that rely on the rule of law and negotiation.[14] For some, PD also reflects a "short-term problem solving" approach that must be complemented by "long-term structural approaches" that tackle the deep roots, or "causes," of conflict such as poverty, underdevelopment, proliferation of arms, denial of human rights, and the like.[15]

Early Warning Versus Response

There are different views in the literature about where the real challenges of PD lie. Some believe that there is a need to improve methods of gathering information about impending crises and develop better early warning indicators of crises.[16] Others argue that there is usually sufficient warning in most humanitarian crises or situations involving human rights abuses, ethnic conflict, civil strife, or regional conflict.[17] George suggests that "the problem is not a lack of warning but the fact that governments often ignore an incipient crisis or take a passive attitude towards it until it escalates into a deadly struggle or a major catastrophe."[18] In his study of so-called missed opportunities, Jentleson argues that "where opportunities for preventive diplomacy were seized, it was in part due to the timely availability of reliable intelligence and other early warning information. Where opportunities for preventive diplomacy were missed, it was despite early warning availability. All told, and contrary to what is often argued, early warning was not the problem."[19] As Jentleson further notes, the problem with early warning that goes wrong is not the absence of timely information but "flawed analysis" of the likelihood of escalation of conflict and or the risks/costs of inaction.

Even so, the inability to distinguish properly between background "noise" and clear "signals" of impending violence may reflect a combination of two distinct kinds of problems: poor information in terms of both its quality and sources, coupled with weak or deficient analytical capabilities and assessments at the bureaucratic level.

In the context of the UN's early warning capabilities, there have been numerous calls over the years to strengthen the Secretary-General's capacity to monitor global developments in anticipation of potential conflicts. The creation of the Office for Research and Collection of Information in 1987 after the Falklands/Malvinas War was intended to enhance the information-gathering capacities of the United Nations. However, the office was disbanded in 1992 and its functions transferred to the Department of Political Affairs (DPA). DPA desk officers have primary responsibility for gathering and analyzing information. However, as one observer notes, although "DPA has set up an effective framework and its early warning system has become an integral part of the Secretary-General's repertoire of preventive measures . . . the political early warning system has yet to reach its full potential." Other key constraints include personnel reductions and financial difficulties in addition to DPA's need "to act cautiously to avoid arousing the concern among Member States with its activities."[20]

Within the wider UN system, many of the early warning activities are carried out by those bodies concerned with humanitarian, environmental, and natural disaster relief and assistance. The Humanitarian Early Warning System within the Office for the Coordination of Humanitarian Affairs plays a central role in monitoring various socioeconomic and human rights trends. Even so, its monitoring capabilities are limited by resource constraints. In addition, humanitarian and environmental early warning systems within the UN have to be careful not to jeopardize their relationships with governments by becoming involved in political matters and thus limiting their ability to engage in conflict prevention.[21] Some member states are also opposed to early warning systems on the grounds that they violate state sovereignty and Article 2(7) of the UN Charter.

Utility of Preventive Diplomacy

There is a lively and ongoing debate between PD advocates and their critics. Some critics focus on feasibility issues, stressing the rather obvious point that there may be countervailing political pressures against PD interventions (such as public and/or bureaucratic pressures, unwillingness on the part of key decisionmakers to take the requisite risks, etc.).[22] Others contend that PD interventions in situations of intrastate conflict transgress the norms of noninterference, that is, sovereignty, especially within intergovernmental bodies like the United Nations. In addition, PD may require the creation of new, more autonomous kinds of institutions, which is unfeasible in the current fiscal and political climate. Still others argue that PD interventions may, in some circumstances, be quite counterproductive if they freeze the status quo and thwart political change, and that "clear goals . . . and prudent judgments about acceptable costs and risks" are required before undertaking PD or other kinds of conflict prevention.[23] Some are even prepared to argue that third-party interventions of any kind are futile in situations where violent conflict is already occurring; accordingly, the "best" solution is simply to let these conflicts burn themselves out.[24]

Defenders argue that PD is "not just a noble idea, but is a viable real world strategy."[25] Their arguments rest on a combination of factual and counterfactual evidence, much of which is drawn from in-depth, comparative case studies. According to Jentleson, in a number of cases the international community "did have specific and identifiable opportunities to limit, if not prevent, the conflicts. But its statecraft was flawed, inadequate, or even absent."[26] (These cases include Somalia, Rwanda, Chechnya, Nagorno-Karabakh, Croatia-Bosnia, and Congo.) Identifiable PD success stories are Ukraine, the Baltics, North Korea, and initially Congo (Brazzaville). In these so-called successful examples of PD, the cooperative calculus of key actors was influenced by incentives, assurances, and other support provided by international actors.[27] Jentleson stresses that the role of international actors was "not necessarily determinative" but had a "major impact on whether domestic actors [made] a conflict or a cooperative calculation."[28]

Many of these same cases are examined by Lund (although not at the same level of detail as Jentleson). Lund reaches similar conclusions about the possibilities for PD, but he also concludes that there must be a local "audience" for PD, that is, the parties must possess "common interests, which they perceive at risk because of the actions of other parties."[29]

The United Nations itself also faces some unique political difficulties in engaging in PD. As Lilly Sucharipa-Behrmann and Thomas Franck observe: "Preventive measures are handicapped because they seek to pacify, in Sherlock Holmes' terms, 'the dog that didn't bark.' Full fledged crises or armed conflicts generally receive extensive media coverage, which in turn raises public awareness of the crisis and exerts pressure on governments to act. Without this pressure, it is usually difficult to get the Security Council to act."[30]

Timing

As noted by Connie Peck, there are differing views about the appropriate timing of PD interventions. What Peck calls the "late prevention" model is

one under which the United Nations (and presumably other actors and institutions) acts only at the point a dispute is about to erupt into armed conflict.
Under this model early warning is critical, and the UN Security Council is
considered to be the best institution for PD because it has the requisite
leverage to pressure the parties. However, Peck questions this approach to
PD on the grounds that in an escalating conflict it may be too late to really
influence the parties because the pressures to escalate are too intense. Her
view is one that is shared by others in the conflict resolution field.[31]

The early intervention model advocated by Peck favors the creation of
dispute resolution services to UN members that would allow them to com-
ply with their obligations under Chapter VI of the Charter. Accordingly,
"the goal would be to provide skilled third-party assistance through good
offices and mediation as early as possible in a dispute, when the opportunity for dispute resolution is most 'ripe.'"[32]

Much like Peck, Jentleson's comparative case study analysis lends support to early as opposed to late interventions: "As difficult as preventive
diplomacy is, the onset of mass violence transforms the nature of a conflict.
A 'Rubicon' gets crossed, on the other side of which resolution and even
limitation of the conflict become much more difficult."[33] Some of the more
quantitative literature on mediation and negotiation also lends support to
this thesis. Jacob Bercovitch and Jeffrey Langley in their study of ninety-
seven disputes involving 364 mediation attempts find a declining success
rate for mediation as fatalities increase.[34] David Carment and Patrick James
argue that third parties are more likely to achieve definitive rather than
ambiguous outcomes if they intervene early in a conflict rather than in the
middle and that there are diminishing prospects for mediated intervention
over time as conflicts escalate.[35] Roy Licklider also suggests that once civil
wars get going a military solution is more likely to be stable than a negotiated one—an observation that is at best ambiguous because it can be interpreted either way: in favor of early intervention or not at all.[36]

These provisional findings about the relationship between timing and
successful PD, suggestive as they are, should be viewed with some caution.
There may well be other factors affecting escalation/de-escalation processes that are not adequately taken into account either in aggregated data
analyses or individual case studies. Causal connections may be suggestive
but obviously cannot be proven in counterfactual assessments of conflicts
that did escalate where so-called opportunities to prevent them from doing
so were missed. The same is obviously true for conflicts that did not escalate (was PD really the critical intervening variable or do other factors
explain outcomes?).

The very concept of timing is extraordinarily elusive and difficult to
apply with any real precision across a range of cases. This is because different conflicts tend to move along different paths or trajectories, and it is not

at all clear that early intervention means the same thing in different contexts, especially if some conflicts are on a steeper escalation curve than others.

Mediation theory also suggests that we should be attentive to what might be called the "negotiation-concession paradox" in the early stages of a conflict. It is certainly true that there may be more chances for mediation and negotiation at the early stages of a conflict because attitudes and perceptions have not hardened and parties are still willing to talk to each other. However, negotiations at this stage are a relatively low-risk strategy for the disputants because they do not equate negotiations with the need to make concessions.[37] Moreover, negotiated solutions will seem less attractive because parties, having not yet experienced the full costs and limits of what can typically be achieved on the battlefield, may consider violence in support of unilateral goals to be a viable alternative to compromise and politically based solutions.[38]

Coercive Diplomacy

As noted above, there is debate over the range of techniques and instruments that are relevant to PD. Whereas some argue that PD refers to noncoercive diplomatic methods and peaceful means described in Article 33 of the UN Charter (i.e., negotiation, inquiry, mediation), others take a broader view of the techniques and methods that are available. Reflecting on the Bosnian and Rwandan experience, some argue that limited uses of force and the threat to do so can have a useful role to play in conflict prevention.[39] Whether the approach is broad or narrow, there is a considerable degree of eclecticism in the choice of PD techniques. Many studies stress the importance of mixed strategies that combine coercive measures with inducements.[40]

For example, Jentleson's case studies suggest that "sufficiently credible threats and/or earlier and more decisive uses of military force would have made a crucial difference [and] make for very plausible counterfactuals."[41] Carment argues that most PD interventions by third parties have relied on some form of coercive diplomacy.[42] Coercive diplomacy is also seen as being useful in the Taiwan Strait crisis of 1996 and as having some interesting parallels with the Cold War.[43] Similar arguments have been offered about the utility of coercive diplomacy in the negotiation of the Dayton Peace Accords and the negotiated "removal" of the Cédras regime in Haiti although these are not "pure" cases of PD.[44]

When it comes to peacekeeping, many commentators cite the deployment of UN peacekeepers in Macedonia as a successful example of this kind of PD in recent years. Those who have examined the mission in some depth attribute its success to the intensity of the conflict, timing, and the behavior of leaders of the conflicting parties. The Macedonian government chose an accommodating approach to meet minority demands while supporting international involvement. The deployment of UN peacekeepers was swift and took place less than three weeks after the Security Council resolution. There was also extensive cooperation between the United Nations and the Organization for Security and Cooperation in Europe (OSCE). Both organizations shared complementary objectives in the crisis. A broad network of international, regional, and local NGOs also tried to address ethnic tensions at the local and community level, reducing prejudice and working toward ethnic reconciliation.[45]

There is also growing interest in the use of economic sanctions as an instrument of coercive diplomacy as noted in the works of several scholars.[46] Although some favor the use of sanctions, especially targeted sanctions, others argue that sanctions frequently backfire (i.e., buttressing the will to resist) or misfire (i.e., hurting civilians more than governments).[47]

Absent from much of the literature about different PD techniques and the relationship between PD and coercive diplomacy is any kind of sustained analysis on whether some techniques are better suited to certain kinds of conflict situations than others, what the real tradeoffs are in adopting different PD strategies, and whether choosing one/some option(s) forecloses the use of others.

Positive Incentives and Inducements

David Cortright's study examines the role of positive inducements of the economic, political, and security variety in preventing armed conflict and encouraging more cooperative kinds of behavior. He and his coauthors argue that such incentives can be both conditional and nonconditional and go well beyond traditional kinds of reciprocity. A variety of cases including targeted economic assistance programs, aid and development packages, trade agreements, access to advanced technology, and the like is covered by the study. Among the key variables that are stressed are the timing of inducements, sensitivity to the cultural context of conflict, the need to avoid rewarding evil (appeasement), and minimizing moral hazard (via packaged incentives that follow a step-by-step reciprocal process that conditions the delivery of rewards on specific concessions by the recipient).[48] In some instances, the promise to remove sanctions can also serve as a positive kind of inducement, and one of the challenges in any situation is to decide whether to emphasize incentives or sanctions in a particular situation in order to reduce moral hazard.

However, whether international organizations like the UN can sustain a coherent "inducement" strategy remains an open question. Cortright argues that a "major disadvantage of coalitions or international institutions is that sustaining a coherent policy commitment over time is more complex. Especially if the inducement strategy involves security assurances or financial assistance, maintaining the required levels of support among all the participating nations will be difficult."[49] PD will also be affected by the coherence of the objectives (modest as opposed to comprehensive objectives tend to be more desirable), whether one is trying to influence a single actor as opposed to multiple parties, as well as social and political effects within the recipient nation ("external attempts to change policy must be able to influence the political preferences of important actors within the recipient country").[50]

Fact-finding

A number of key studies argue that international organizations that have used fact-finding as their basic tool and sent missions on site can contribute to conflict prevention and resolution. *Fact-finding* is defined "as an investigation that helps international organizations fulfill their duties, in particular in the area of conflict resolution."[51] Fact-finding procedures are typically governed by certain standards and transparency to all of the parties involved. In some instances, lacking the resources of individual states or the United Nations, and in other instances reluctant to use the resources they have, regional organizations have used fact-finding missions to engage in problem-solving and dialogue to shift perceptions and change attitudes among conflict parties.

A prime example of the use of this approach is found in the conflict prevention work of the OSCE's High Commissioner on National Minorities.[52] By maintaining an arms' length relationship with the formal institutions of OSCE, and eschewing the formal language of mediation, the commissioner has been able to gain entry into conflicts in ways that a formal mediation approach could not because it would raise the stakes and limit the flexibility of the parties to make concessions.

Advocates of PD as a form of fact-finding suggest that these activities need to be protected against accusations that result from the inability or unwillingness of the states and societies concerned to settle the conflict. The best protection is to give the parties the floor and allow them to comment officially on their positive and negative evaluations of the missions' findings.[53] The downside of fact-finding approaches to PD, however, is that some situations may require greater leverage to bring the parties to the table and get them to make concessions than the fact-finder can muster on his/her own.

Linking PD with Longer-Term Structural Prevention

There is widespread recognition in the PD literature that the range of activities associated with PD—mediation, diplomacy, fact-finding, preventive peacekeeping deployments, and so on—are only a subset of a much wider range of responses and measures to conflict prevention. Some studies argue that PD initiatives when taken alone and independently of a broader strategy of conflict prevention are likely to fail unless they are linked to measures and actions that tackle the deeper, or "root," causes of conflict. As the report of the Carnegie Commission underscores, "effective preventive strategies rest on three principles: early reaction to signs of trouble; a comprehensive, balanced approach to alleviate the pressures, or risk factors, that trigger violent conflict; and *an extended effort to resolve the underlying root causes of conflict.*"[54] Structural prevention—as distinct from PD—involves measures that address the root causes of violence such as discrimination and economic deprivation, societal stress, military threats and sources of insecurity, and various environmental and resource degradation problems that may contribute to political instability and conflict. Many organizations and actors can contribute to structural prevention, including NGOs, development assistance agencies, educational institutions, religious leaders, the scientific community, the business community, and others. Within the United Nations, the functional agencies that have a critical role to play in structural prevention are the United Nations High Commissioner for Refugees (UNHCR), the United Nations Childrens' Fund (UNICEF), the United Nations Development Programme (UNDP), the World Food Program, the World Health Organization, and the Bretton Woods financial institutions (the World Bank and the International Monetary Fund [IMF]). Linking the efforts and activities of these bodies to a PD strategy that is simultaneously attentive to structural prevention is widely seen as one of the main challenges to creating a culture of prevention within the UN system. As Jan Eliasson and Robert Rydberg argue, "The UN system as a whole must be set in motion. Funds, programs, and specialized agencies place the United Nations in an excellent position to address the root causes of conflict and deal with prevention."[55]

Recommendations for Institutional Reform

Within the PD literature, considerable attention is devoted to the United Nations and to ways of strengthening its role in PD. Jentleson believes that "the UN brings great strengths to preventive diplomacy. One is its unique legitimacy as authorizer of actions in the name of the international community. . . . Second is its network of agencies, which do provide it with significant institutional capacity to help cope with refugee flows, help relieve starvation, and perform other humanitarian tasks."[56] But he sounds a cautionary note about the UN's capacity to undertake successful PD in the area of peacekeeping: "The area in which the limits on UN capacity have perhaps become most evident in recent years, and in which little is likely to change, is in peace operations in situations other than traditional peacekeeping."[57]

Others see an enhanced role for the Security Council and the Secretary-General in PD. The Carnegie Commission's recommendations include a strengthened role for the Secretary-General in PD through the more frequent use of Article 99, greater use of "good offices" to help defuse developing crises, annual contributions by member governments to the Fund for Preventive Actions established by the Norwegian government in 1996, and regular meetings between the Secretary-General and heads of major regional organizations. In addition, the Commission calls for private sector advisory committees and a more activist UN High Commissioner for Human Rights (UNHCHR) to strengthen the UN role in early warning, protection of human rights, and conflict prevention. The Commission also urges the enlargement of the Security Council. Another one of the Commission's key recommendations is a strengthened role for regional organizations in conflict prevention and preventive diplomacy:

> Regional arrangements can be greatly strengthened for preventive purposes. They should establish means, linked to the UN, to monitor circumstances of incipient violence with the regions. They should develop a repertoire of diplomatic, political and economic measures for regional use to help prevent dangerous circumstances. . . . Such a repertoire would include ways to provide advance warning of conflict to organization members and to marshal the necessary logistics, command and control, and other functions that may be necessary to support more assertive efforts authorized by the UN.[58]

In a similar vein, Jüergen Dedring argues that the Security Council is "sufficiently equipped to undertake a variety of preventive measures under the terms of the Charter, specifically Article 34 and 40." However, this requires the "awareness and willingness of the States composing the membership of the Council and of the full UN membership, regarding the realization of the potential for preventive action. . . . Politicians and diplomats must learn to be more daring in the conception of feasible approaches and in the execution of a commonly arrived plan of action."[59]

Not all commentators are as enthusiastic about the Security Council and the Secretary-General's own ability to conduct successful PD. Lund believes that it would be a mistake to situate early warning and PD within UN Headquarters on the grounds that the Secretary-General and his staff are already overworked. Furthermore, the Security Council "finds difficulty in addressing claims and conflicts involving nonofficial parties" and always faces the "ever-present possibility of a veto from one or more of its permanent members."[60] Peck argues that in spite of its mandate for maintaining international peace and security, the Security Council is not well suited to PD. This is because member states do not want to bring their disputes to the Council, relinquish control, or compromise their sovereignty. The Security Council's authority is also largely of a coercive nature and its members are not always seen as being impartial:

> The notion of the Council as a kind of arbiter causes the parties to engage in adversarial debate rather than problem-solving. Mutual recriminations and arguments by each side to convince the Council of the "rightness" of its case may further harden positions and inflame a situation. And when Council members are forced to declare their sympathies, support for one or both sides may widen the situation or encourage the parties.[61]

Peck is also skeptical about the Secretariat's role in PD. Although there was a major restructuring of the Secretariat that was initiated by Boutros-Ghali, "resource shortages and bureaucratic constraints have rendered even these reforms less than adequate to this vital task."[62] In addition, says Peck, the United Nations also suffers from a lack of institutional memory or case histories to deal with recurring problems.

Peck argues for a more decentralized approach to PD that would see the establishment of UN Conflict Prevention and Resolution Centers at the regional level. They would be established under a mandate from the Security Council or the General Assembly and could report regularly to the Council and/or Assembly. These centers "would be staffed by senior professionals with expert knowledge in conflict resolution and sufficient experience and stature to negotiate at the highest levels."[63] Centers would also engage in research and could "systematically analyze the nature and causes of disputes in their region and the factors which lead to their escalation."[64]

Others, including Peck herself in her later work, argue for a greater delegation of responsibility for PD to regional organizations and/or subregional entities and forums.[65] These studies take as their point of departure Chapter VIII of the UN Charter, which explicitly allots a share of the responsibility for the maintenance of international peace and security with regional arrangements or agencies. As Andy Knight observes,

> The founders had a particular vision of how the *division of labor* should take place between the UN system and regional agencies and arrangements; note that there is some ambiguity about whether this refers to formal or institutionalized regional organizations. In the event of the eruption of a local dispute, according to the founders' vision, member-nations of

the UN existing in that particular geographical (regional) location would
be expected, if they were part of a regional arrangement or agency, "to
make every effort to achieve pacific settlement of local disputes through
such regional arrangements . . . before referring them to the Security
Council."[66]

Some would also like to see greater involvement by the broad spectrum
of NGOs involved in human rights, the organization and provision of
humanitarian assistance, and fostering economic and social development
and conflict resolution. They see this "third system" as serving as "the primary link between 'we the peoples' of the UN Charter, states, and the intergovernmental system."[67] The voluntary sector would therefore be more
closely involved in fact-finding missions, informal consultations with the
parties to the conflict, lobbying governments and intergovernmental agencies, and serving as mediators and arbitrators in conflict situations.
However,

> for NGOs to become more effectively involved in preventive diplomacy
> processes, they would need to reconsider their mandates in the light of the
> changing international situation. . . . They could consider forming
> alliances with other NGOs to form networks that are country- or region-
> specific to minimize the duplication of work. Such cooperation could lead
> on to the establishment of clearing houses with a capacity for analysis and
> information targeting of situations relevant to conflict prevention and
> transformation.[68]

In the growing literature on PD there are also specific institutional recommendations that are directed at enhancing specific capacities of the
United Nations (and other bodies) in PD.[69] It should be noted that many of
these analysts underscore the need for a systemwide approach that couples
preventive diplomatic initiatives with the wider institutional and programmatic resources of the United Nations. As Sucharipa-Behrmann and Franck
argue,

> even the finest diplomatic skills deployed by the most influential inter-
> state groups require the support of some "carrots and sticks." The UN
> does have some carrots at its disposal, but these are usually within the
> prerogative of autonomous, programmatic institutions such as the World
> Bank or [UN Development Programme], rather than within the control of
> those involved in a preventive diplomatic initiative. Only a system-wide
> coordinated approach can make these carrots available to support preven-
> tive measures.[70]

Among the success stories in coordination, they point to the World
Bank's mediated solution of the Indus Basin dispute between India and
Pakistan that proposed engineering measures and provided the necessary

financing to increase regional water supplies to both parties, the coordinated response of donors to provide financing to resettle guerrilla fighters in Mozambique, and the coordinated response and role of UNHCHR, UNHCR, UNICEF, IMF, and World Bank in stabilizing the situation in the former Yugoslav Republic of Macedonia.[71]

Operational Lessons

The literature on PD also offers a large number of operational lessons to advance the application of PD principles. The Carnegie Commission, for example, suggests four elements that can contribute to the operational success of PD: (1) lead players (international organizations, states, or individuals); (2) coherent military-political approaches to engagement that address the humanitarian and political aspects of the problem; (3) adequate resources; and (4) advance plans for the restoration of host country authority.[72]

Jentleson argues that successful PD depends upon the following elements: (1) negotiators who gain and keep the trust of the major parties; (2) terms of the negotiation that allow all sides to be able to show their domestic constituencies that there are real gains to be had from cooperation; (3) special envoys and lead diplomats who enjoy credibility with the parties; (4) actions that have "to be taken *early, early, early*" because "one of the strongest, least conditional conclusions we can draw is that the longer you wait, the more there will be to do and the more difficult it will be to do well";[73] (5) sanctions that are an important part of a mixed strategy (comprehensive, decisive, and tightly enforced sanctions work better than partially or incrementally enforced sanctions, although the partial-incremental sanctions with lax enforcement are more common than comprehensive, tightly enforced ones);[74] (6) inducements such as the lure of membership in major international and regional organizations or the threat of expulsion; and (7) political, especially "executive," leadership, which is a key ingredient for effective PD.[75]

Lund concludes his own study by stressing the role of political will: "Preventive diplomacy must come to terms with the lack of national and international political will to act decisively and concertedly in launching and persisting with preventive efforts."[76]

Conclusion

As this brief review has tried to suggest, the body of scholarly and policy literature on PD is impressive and growing. Although earlier studies offered a rather simplistic rendering of the challenges of PD, recent work offers a more sophisticated understanding of the potential strengths and limitations of PD and how to operationalize the concept across a range of institutional settings, including the United Nations. Nonetheless, there remains a degree of disquiet in this literature about the scope of PD, the timing and sequencing of PD interventions, and what constitute appropriate PD instruments or techniques. In spite of the wealth of research, there are no simple lessons that can be taken off the shelf and plugged into official (diplomatic) or unofficial (e.g., NGO) practices and behavior. What lessons there are have to be examined and applied with considerable care.

There are essentially two schools of thought about the UN's own role in PD. Some studies, like the Carnegie Commission report, call for a strengthened role of the Security Council and Office of the Secretary-General in PD. Others believe that the liabilities of the United Nations outweigh its assets, especially in the case of the Security Council. These analysts prefer to see greater involvement by regional organizations in PD and/or advocate the creation of new institutions at the regional level under UN auspices that would have a specialized role to play in conflict resolution and PD.

There is a degree of consensus in the literature. All analysts and commentators agree that PD cannot exist independently from a broader strategy of conflict prevention that addresses the deep-rooted causes of conflict and is informed by coherent and sustainable political objectives. And there is growing appreciation that PD can work only if there is a coordinated systemwide approach in the United Nations that brings the resources of independent programmatic bodies like the World Bank and UNDP into PD initiatives.

Notes

This chapter was initially commissioned by the International Peace Academy (IPA) to serve as a background paper for the Expert Workshop and International Policy Conference under the rubric of IPA's prevention project "From Reaction to Prevention: Opportunities for the UN System in the New Millennium," June 1999–April 2000. The findings of the project and related research are presented in this edited volume.

1. Aside from the works cited below, Rodger A. Payne, "The Limits and Promise of Environmental Conflict Prevention: The Case of the GEF," *Journal of Peace Research* 35, 3 (1998): 363–380, and Fred H. Cate, "Communications, Policy-Making and Humanitarian Crises," in *From Massacres to Genocide: The Media, Public Policy and Humanitarian Crises*, eds. Robert I. Rotberg and Thomas G. Weiss (Washington, D.C.: Brookings Institution, 1996), were also reviewed for the purposes of this chapter.

2. Bruce W. Jentleson, "Preventive Diplomacy and Ethnic Conflict: Possible,

Difficult, Necessary," in *The International Spread of Ethnic Conflict: Fear, Diffusion, and Escalation,* eds. David A. Lake and Donald Rothchild (Princeton: Princeton University Press, 1998), 295.

3. See Luis Drüke, "The United Nations in Conflict Prevention," in *The Art of Conflict Prevention,* eds. Werner Bauwens and Luc Reychler (London: Brassey's, 1994), 40–45; and Michael S. Lund, *Preventing Violent Conflicts* (Washington, D.C.: United States Institute of Peace, 1996), 33.

4. United Nations Charter, Article 1.1. See also Articles 11.3, 33, 34, 35, and 99.

5. Boutros Boutros-Ghali, *An Agenda for Peace: Preventive Diplomacy, Peacemaking, and Peacekeeping.* Report of the Secretary-General pursuant to the statement adopted by the Summit Meeting of the Security Council on January 31, 1992. Reprinted in Adam Roberts and Benedict Kingsbury, eds., *United Nations, Divided World: The UN's Roles in International Relations,* 2nd ed. (Oxford: Oxford University Press, 1993), 468–498.

6. Carnegie Commission on Preventing Deadly Conflict, *Preventing Deadly Conflict: Final Report* (New York: Carnegie Corporation of New York, 1997).

7. Boutros-Ghali, *An Agenda for Peace,* in *United Nations, Divided World,* 475.

8. Ibid., 476–480.

9. Alexander L. George, "Strategies for Preventive Diplomacy and Conflict Resolution: Scholarship for Policy-making," *Cooperation and Conflict* 34, 1 (1999): 10.

10. Carnegie Commission on Preventing Deadly Conflict, *Preventing Deadly Conflict,* 48.

11. Lund, *Preventing Violent Conflicts,* 37.

12. Ibid.

13. Jentleson, "Preventive Diplomacy and Ethnic Conflict: Possible, Difficult, Necessary," 295–296.

14. Connie Peck, *Sustainable Peace: The Role of the UN and Regional Organizations in Preventing Conflict* (Lanham, MD: Rowman and Littlefield, 1998): 22–23.

15. See many of the chapters in this volume. In addition, see ibid.; Carnegie Commission on Preventing Deadly Conflict, *Preventing Deadly Conflict;* and John W. Burton, *Conflict Resolution and Prevention* (New York: St. Martin's, 1999).

16. See Ted Robert Gurr (Chapter 3) and Patricia Cleves, Nat Colletta, and Nicholas Sambanis (Chapter 14) in this volume; and Ted Robert Gurr, "Early Warning Systems: From Surveillance to Assessment to Action," in *Preventive Diplomacy,* ed. Kevin Cahill (New York: Basic Books, 1996).

17. Alexander L. George and Jane E. Holl, *The Warning-Response Problem and Missed Opportunities in Preventive Diplomacy: A Report to the Carnegie Commission on Preventing Deadly Conflict* (New York: Carnegie Corporation of New York, 1997); and George, "Strategies for Preventive Diplomacy and Conflict Resolution."

18. George, "Strategies for Preventive Diplomacy and Conflict Resolution," 11.

19. Bruce W. Jentleson, ed., *Opportunities Missed, Opportunities Seized* (Lanham, MD: Rowman and Littlefield, 2000): 324.

20. Sara Rakita, "Early Warning as a Tool of Conflict Prevention," *New York University Journal of International Law and Politics* 30, 3–4 (1998): 551.

21. Rakita, "Early Warning as a Tool of Conflict Prevention," 552–553.

22. Stephen J. Morrison, "Zaire: Looming Disaster After Preventive Diplomacy," *SAIS Review* 15, 2 (1995): 39–52.

23. Stephen John Stedman, "Alchemy for a New World Order," *Foreign Affairs* 74, 3 (1995): 20.

24. Edward N. Luttwak, "Give War a Chance," *Foreign Affairs* 78, 4 (1999): 36–44; Chaim Kaufman, "Possible and Impossible Solutions to Ethnic Wars," *International Security* 20, 4 (1996): 136–175.

25. Jentleson, ed., *Opportunities Missed, Opportunities Seized*, 319.

26. Ibid., 320.

27. Ibid., 322.

28. Ibid., 323.

29. Lund, *Preventing Violent Conflicts*, 134.

30. Ibid.

31. See, for example, Louis Kriesberg, "Preventing and Resolving Destructive Communal Conflict," in *The International Politics of Ethnic Conflict: Theory and Evidence*, eds. David Carment and Patrick James (Pittsburgh: Pittsburgh University Press, 1997); John Paul Lederach, *Building Peace: Sustainable Reconciliation in Divided Societies* (Washington, D.C.: United States Institute of Peace Press, 1997): 73–85; and Burton, *Conflict Resolution and Prevention*.

32. Connie Peck, "Preventive Diplomacy: A More Effective Approach to International Disputes," *Ecumenical Review* 1, 74 (995): 329.

33. Jentleson, ed., *Opportunities Missed, Opportunities Seized*, 330.

34. Jacob Bercovitch and Jeffrey Langley, "The Nature of the Dispute and the Effectiveness of International Mediation," *Journal of Conflict Resolution* 37, 4 (1993): 670–691.

35. David Carment, "The Ethnic Dimension in World Politics: Theory, Policy, and Early Warning," *Third World Quarterly* 15, 4 (1994): 551–582; David Carment and Patrick James, "Internal Constraints and Ethnic Conflict: Towards a Crisis-based Assessment of Irredentism," *Journal of Conflict Resolution* 39, 1 (1995): 82–109.

36. Roy Licklider, "The Consequences of Negotiated Settlements in Civil Wars, 1945–1993," *American Political Science Review* 89, 3 (1995): 685–687.

37. Thomas Princen, *Intermediaries in International Conflict* (Princeton: Princeton University Press, 1992), 54.

38. I. William Zartman, *Ripe for Resolution: Conflict and Intervention in Africa* (New York: Oxford University Press, 1989); I. William Zartman and Saadia Touval, "International Mediation: Conflict Resolution and Power Politics," *Journal of Social Issues* 41, 2 (1985): 27–45.

39. Andrew J. Goodpaster, *When Diplomacy Is Not Enough: Managing Multinational Military Interventions: A Report to the Carnegie Commission on Preventing Deadly Conflict* (New York: Carnegie Corporation of New York, 1996).

40. David Cortright, *The Price of Peace: Incentives and International Conflict Prevention* (Lanham, MD: Rowman and Littlefield, 1997); Jentleson, ed., *Opportunities Missed, Opportunities Seized*; Lund, *Preventing Violent Conflicts*.

41. Jentleson, ed., *Opportunities Missed, Opportunities Seized*, 342.

42. Carment, "The Ethnic Dimension in World Politics."

43. Cheng-Yi Lin, "The U.S. Factor in the 1958 and 1996 Taiwan Straits Crisis," *Issues and Studies* 32, 12 (1996): 14–32.

44. Richard Holbrooke, "The Road to Sarajevo," in *Herding Cats: Multiparty Mediation in a Complex World*, eds. Chester A. Crocker, Fen Osler Hampson, and

Pamela Aall (Washington, D.C.: United States Institute of Peace Press, 1999), 325–386; Robert A. Pastor, "More and Less Than It Seemed: The Carter-Nunn-Powell Mediation in Haiti," in *Herding Cats*, eds. Crocker, Hampson, and Aall, 505–526.

45. Alice Ackerman, "The Former Yugoslav Republic of Macedonia," *Security Dialogue* 27, 4 (1996): 409–424; Laura L. Miller, "Do Soldiers Hate Peacekeeping? The Case of Preventive Diplomacy Operations in Macedonia," *Armed Forces and Society* 23, 3 (1997): 415–450.

46. Margaret P. Doxey, *International Sanctions in Contemporary Perspective*, 2nd ed. (New York: St. Martin's, 1996). John Stremlau, *Sharpening International Sanctions: Toward a Stronger Role for the United Nations: A Report to the Carnegie Commission on Preventing Deadly Conflict* (New York: Carnegie Corporation of New York, 1996). Robert A. Pape, "Why Economic Sanctions Do Not Work," *International Security* 22, 2 (1997): 90–136. Richard N. Haass, "Sanctioning Madness," *Foreign Affairs* 76, 6 (1997): 74–85.

47. George, "Strategies for Preventive Diplomacy and Conflict Resolution"; John Mueller and Karl Mueller, "Rethinking Sanctions on Iraq," *Foreign Affairs* 78, 3 (1999): 43–53.

48. Cortright, *The Price of Peace*, 278.

49. Ibid., 282.

50. Ibid., 287.

51. Hanne-Margaret Birckenbach, "The Role of Fact-finding in Preventive Diplomacy," *International Journal of Peace Studies* 2, 2 (1997): 21.

52. Diana Chigas with Elizabeth McClintock and Christopher Kamp, "Preventive Diplomacy and the Organization for Security and Cooperation in Europe: Creating Incentives for Dialogue and Cooperation," in *Preventing Conflict in the Post-Communist World*, eds. Abram Chayes and Antonia Handler Chayes (Washington, D.C.: Brookings Institution, 1996): 25–98; P. Terrence Hopmann, *Building Security in Post–Cold War Eurasia: The OSCE and U.S. Foreign Policy: Peaceworks No. 31* (Washington, D.C.: United States Institute of Peace, 1999); Max van der Stoel, "The Role of the OSCE High Commissioner in Conflict Prevention," in *Herding Cats,* eds. Crocker, Hampson, and Aall, 54–84; Foundation on Inter-Ethnic Relations, *The Role of the High Commissioner on National Minorities in OSCE Conflict Prevention* (The Hague: Foundation on Inter-Ethnic Relations, 1997).

53. Birckenbach, "The Role of Fact-finding in Preventive Diplomacy."

54. Carnegie Commission on Preventing Deadly Conflict, *Preventing Deadly Conflict*, xviii (emphasis added).

55. Jan Eliasson and Robert Rydberg, "Preventive Action and Preventive Diplomacy," in *Preventing Violent Conflicts: Past Record and Future Challenges,* ed. Peter Wallensteen (Stockholm: Elanders Gotab for Department of Peace and Conflict Research, Uppsala University, 1998), 44.

56. Jentleson, "Preventive Diplomacy and Ethnic Conflict," 312.

57. Ibid.

58. Carnegie Commission on Preventing Deadly Conflict, *Preventing Deadly Conflict,* xiv.

59. Jüergen Dedring, "The Security Council in Preventive Action," in *Preventing Violent Conflicts,* ed. Wallensteen, 62.

60. Lund, *Preventing Deadly Conflicts*, 174–175.

61. Peck, "Preventive Diplomacy: A More Effective Approach to International Disputes," 330.

62. Ibid.

63. Ibid., 332.

64. Ibid., 333.

65. Peck, *Sustainable Peace;* Andy W. Knight, "Towards a Subsidiarity Model for Peacemaking and Preventive Diplomacy: Making Chapter VIII of the UN Charter Operational," *Third World Quarterly* 17, 1 (1996): 31–52; Julie Chater, "Peacebuilding and Preventive Diplomacy: Australian Initiatives at the United Nations," *Melbourne University Law Review* 20, 1 (1995): 155–163; Simon S.C. Tay with Obood Talib, "The ASEAN Regional Forum: Preparing for Preventive Diplomacy," *Contemporary Southeast Asia* 19, 3 (1997): 252–268; Daljit Singh, "The Politics of Peace: Preventive Diplomacy in ASEAN," *Harvard International Review* 16, 2 (1994): 32–35; Townsend-Gault, "Preventive Diplomacy and Pro-activity in the South China Sea," *Contemporary Southeast Asia* 20, 2 (1998): 171–190.

66. Knight, "Towards a Subsidiarity Model for Peacemaking and Preventive Diplomacy," 45.

67. Kumar Rupesinghe, "Towards a Policy Framework for Preventive Diplomacy," *Security Dialogue* 26, 3 (1995): 113.

68. Ibid., 114.

69. See Margaret Satterthwaite, *New York University Journal of International Law and Politics* 30, 3–4 (1998): 709–791; Paul Martin, "Regional Efforts at Preventive Measures: Four Case Studies on the Development of Conflict-Prevention Capabilities," *New York University Journal of International Law and Politics* 30, 3–4 (1998): 881–937; Alys Brehio, "Good Offices of the Secretary-General as Preventive Measures," *New York University Journal of International Law and Politics* 30, 3–4 (1998): 589–643; Stephen Ostrowski, "Preventive Deployment of Troops as Preventive Measures: Macedonia and Beyond," *New York University Journal of International Law and Politics* 30, 3–4 (1998): 793–880; Rakita, "Early Warning as a Tool of Conflict Prevention"; Sucharipa-Behrmann and Franck, "Preventive Measures."

70. Sucharipa-Behrmann and Franck, "Preventive Measures," 502.

71. Ibid., 503.

72. Carnegie Commission on Preventing Deadly Conflict, *Preventing Deadly Conflict,* xix–xx.

73. Jentleson, *Opportunities Missed, Opportunities Seized,* 337.

74. Ibid., 337.

75. Ibid., 338.

76. Lund, *Preventing Violent Conflict,* 163.

7

From Lessons to Action

Michael S. Lund

Since the early 1990s, a series of new intrastate conflicts, and the human suffering and diplomatic and peacekeeping travails that they cause, swayed more and more leaders and organizations to a novel argument: it might be more humane and cost-effective to try to keep these horrible and costly wars from arising in the first place. In 2001, this idea is no longer novel, at least in certain circles. Numerous intergovernmental and nongovernmental organization (NGO) international conferences and study groups have taken it up in Europe, North America, Africa, and Asia, and several institutes have sponsored policy research on it.[1] Although "conflict prevention" is not a household word, it is now frequently urged in the policy statements of major governments, the United Nations, the European Union, and many regional bodies. As a thematic debate by the UN Security Council in both November 1999 and July 2000, a priority urged in July 2000 by the G-8 Okinawa Summit, and the focus of a report of the UN Secretary-General that was released in June 2001, conflict prevention has never been more salient on the international policy agenda.

The recent interest in the prevention of violent conflicts (i.e., conflict prevention) has also gone beyond exhortation, talk, and research. It is increasingly being practiced through a variety of concrete efforts—usually little publicized and not always explicitly referred to as such—in Eastern Europe, Africa, Latin America, and Asia. In addition, the UN Secretariat, the European Commission, regional intergovernmental bodies (e.g., the Organization for Security and Cooperation in Europe [OSCE] and the Organization for African Unity), and subregional bodies (e.g., the Southern Africa Development Community, the Intergovernmental Authority for Development, and the Economic Community of West African States) have created mechanisms with small units that assign a few staff to look for early warning signs and consider preventive responses.[2] Such mechanisms have been used to respond to threatening situations arising in several countries, with some at least partial successes witnessed in Congo-Brazzaville (1993), Guatemala, Peru, and Venezuela. NGOs have sprouted up that are specifically dedicated to advocacy, analysis, and action in conflict prevention (e.g., the Forum for Early Warning and Early Response and the International Crisis Group), and they are forwarding country situation reports to governmental bodies, often accompanied by prevention policy recommendations.[3] Also noteworthy is the recent recognition that international programs must address the basic causes of conflict through postconflict peacebuilding—indeed, nation-building—activities in order to prevent the reemergence of violence.

Furthermore, the procedures entailed in early warning and identifying and implementing appropriate preventive responses are beginning to be mainstreamed in the regular ongoing operations at the country-mission level of the European Commission, the United Nations, and most major bilateral donor agencies, through the development of practical analytical tools for early warning and preventive policy responses.[4] A series of week-long training workshops held by the UN Staff Training College, begun in January 1999, has since graduated more than 900 desk officers from all major UN agencies, each of whom has been introduced to issues in conflict analysis and the range of possible preventive responses.

This mainstreaming activity stems from the idea, not accepted even in the mid-1990s, that conflict prevention is not a specific policy sector in itself or a single method of intervention. It is an orientation, a potential policy and bureaucratic "culture of prevention," which ideally cuts across, and to some degree pervades, a wide range of major policy sectors and organizations; it is not limited to the domain of diplomacy and conflict resolution (thus the declining usage of the too-narrow term "preventive diplomacy"). It also could include economic development, democracy-building, human rights, military affairs, environment, education, health, agriculture, and so on, as well as commercial activity such as international trade, finance, and natural resource development. It must also involve actors within the affected countries themselves. In sum, it has become accepted that there is a large policy "toolbox" that includes a range of cross-sectoral instruments on which preventive strategy can potentially draw.[5] In this culture of prevention, such sectoral policies are not always carried out in the usual ways, but rather are seen through a "conflict lens" and modified to give them a sensitivity to their impact on conflict and peace.

Indeed, the trendiness of conflict prevention is such that many program activities that were once described as "conflict resolution" or "conflict management" have now been relabeled as "conflict prevention" or one of its synonyms. This ascendancy may reflect genuine diffusion of the prevention idea. But with so much existing activity now being lumped under conflict prevention, there is also a risk it will lose its distinctive value-added meaning.

In particular, the popularization of prevention discourse seems to have led to the remuddling of a vital conceptual distinction—that between proactive efforts that act before significant violence has arisen, and reactive efforts taken after armed conflict has ensued. To keep things straight, a core definition of conflict prevention would read: any structural or intercessory means to keep intrastate or interstate tensions and disputes from escalating into significant violence and use of armed force, to strengthen the capabilities of potential parties to violent conflicts for resolving such disputes peacefully, and to progressively reduce the underlying problems that produce those issues and disputes.[6] To ignore the emphasis on preempting the eruption of violence, and instead define prevention loosely as applicable to any postescalation level in a conflict's hostility, ignores the original practical reason why this idea was raised in the early 1990s, namely, that social tensions and political disputes should be addressed before they spiral into destructive violence, not after. It also ignores the empirical evidence that the initial, largely nonviolent stage of a potentially emerging conflict is qualitatively different from a more escalated or militarized stage, as well as from a postconflict stage when war-ravaged societies have to be put back together.[7]

Despite this residual conceptual confusion, however, the international climate in which conflicts are perceived and discussed has become more accepting, albeit slowly and tacitly, of the normative imperative of engaging early to keep wars from breaking out. As each successive bloody crisis has hit the headlines, less is heard about how they are inevitable tragedies resulting from age-old animosities. Instead, more doubts seem to be publicly voiced that perhaps the calamity could have been avoided, and questions are asked about what went wrong and who is responsible. In 1998, UN Secretary-General Kofi Annan and U.S. president Bill Clinton publicly acknowledged that their respective bureaucracies could have acted earlier to prevent the Rwanda genocide in 1994. Parliamentary official public inquiries have been made in France and Belgium into the roles that their governments may have played in neglecting or worsening that horrendous human calamity. A legal suit has even been brought by some families of victims of the Rwandan genocide against the UN Secretary-General for failing to prevent it. Evidently, the moral and legal stakes are being raised for well-positioned international actors, who now may be held more accountable for purported lapses of duty on their presumed conflict prevention watch. Despite some dramatic failures of prevention, or perhaps because of them, an implicit new international norm may be receiving gradual acceptance: if violent conflicts are not inevitable and can be prevented with reasonable effort, international actors are morally bound to act to do what is possible wherever situations could very likely lead to massive violence.[8]

Stated differently, conflict prevention, although clearly not mature, is no longer in its infancy. It has reached adolescence. Almost a decade has passed since UN Secretary-General Boutros Boutros-Ghali's *An Agenda for Peace* (1992) called for "preventive diplomacy" toward conflicts such as the one brewing in Yugoslavia, and the genocide in Rwanda. It could be debated whether the amount of attention that conflict prevention was getting in the year 2001 is remarkable, or woefully overdue. But it is clear that both the idea and the practice have achieved wide acceptance.

As things now stand, the field of violent conflict prevention must continue to deal with certain basic questions or sets of concerns in order to advance further. These are:

1. *Causation:* what are the various underlying and immediate sources of violent, destructive conflict, and what warning signs indicate its emergence?

2. *Political will:* how can concerned people obtain sufficient political support and resources from publics, governments, and bureaucracies to undertake timely and effective preventive action?

3. *Effectiveness:* what methods of preventive action actually work in various contexts?

4. *Institutionalization:* how can procedures and policies for anticipating and responding to possible conflicts be operationalized in the regular functioning of international governmental organizations and NGOs, and how can separate actions be undertaken in a more concerted way?

Although these questions require further research, consolidation, and refinement, a disproportionate amount of time and timber has been used on the first two.[9] The field is very long on studies of the problem of intrastate conflicts in terms of incidence and the diagnosis and analysis of causes. A great deal of hand-wringing is done about the lack of political will, almost to the exclusion of the other issues. However, the field is very short on the identification and organization of effective preventive policy prescriptions.

To help fill those gaps, the following sections will make a few observations on the issues of conflict causes and political will, respectively, but take up more extensively the questions of:

• *Effectiveness:* identifying several important decisionmaking levels in the international system at which preventive activities are currently underway, and then summarizing some lessons that are being learned about what is effective at one such level; and

• *Institutionalization:* suggesting how to incorporate the lessons being gathered from country-specific decisionmaking and implementation that are being carried out by development agencies, foreign ministries, and multilateral organizations.

Contemporary Conflicts: The Liberal Solution as Problem

An important starting point for understanding the sources of conflicts since the early 1990s is to put them in the perspective of the fundamental global-historical forces that are shaping the post–Cold War phase of state- and nation-building. The intensification of the processes of globalization following the end of the Cold War has brought strong pressures—some from within and some from outside—to remake many developing societies' economies and polities by creating more open markets, enlarging political pluralism and participation, redressing existing social hierarchies, and tolerating unconventional styles of life and belief. The current liberal consensus on these values that prevails among mainly the major Western powers is now also deeply ensconced in their donor agencies and in the UN system, including the World Bank and the International Monetary Fund. They are widely and vigorously promoting market-oriented economic reform, democratization, human rights, rule of law, civil society, and good governance in developing countries.

Although much of this activity is beneficial, it presents a largely ignored policy dilemma for conflict prevention policy. At present, most officials and professionals within these organizations tend to assume that any and all of these liberal values advance peace and prevent conflict ipso facto.[10] The liberal model is most conspicuously being grafted onto societies by international agencies associated with postconflict peace operations, where the destruction of many local institutions has often left an institutional and value vacuum. But the model also drives most international development activities in societies that have not experienced recent conflicts. It is perhaps true that in the long run the basic liberal model for national and international order, once achieved, is the best preventor of inter- and intrastate violent conflict. But in the short run, the shift toward more political and economic openness that liberalism seeks can, and has, contributed to the intrastate instabilities in which violent conflicts have arisen.

Most developing countries are now in one phase or another of evolution from a relatively centralized political order (e.g., autocratic or authoritarian regimes, communist or other one-party states, military governments, executive-dominated clientelist and oligarchical political systems, etc.) to some other, uncertain political order in which power is more devolved and fragmented. Indeed, much of the world may be said in the post–Cold War years to be engaged in World War IV: a global competition between the governing principles of liberalism, on the one hand, and political and economic centralism or patrimonialism, on the other. In some instances, this movement has seen the assertion of desires for more self-determination through autonomy or full independence. In others, it has seen power struggles over control of the existing state.

Many countries experiencing this transition—even those with significant ethnic divisions—have handled the pressures to devolve power more or less peacefully, such as Czechoslovakia, Hungary in its relations with neighbors such as Romania, the former Soviet Union, Macedonia, the Baltic states, Ukraine, and South Africa. But others, apparently with newer and weaker states and political systems, have fallen into violent, destructive conflicts, such as parts of the former Yugoslavia (Croatia, Bosnia, Kosovo), Tajikistan, Rwanda, Burundi, the Democratic Republic of the Congo, Afghanistan, East Timor, and others.[11] In light of the fact that most societies with rearoused ethnicity and its tensions have remained peaceful during this period, it is not ethnic identities, or even their mobilization based on nationalist causes (expressed, for instance, in the desire for self-determination) per se that should be the utmost concern. It is their *violent* expression. The most urgent problem is the inability of some political systems to regulate through peaceful processes the conflicts that are to be expected from the major and sometimes rapid redistribution of political and economic power and the dispersion or dissolution of state authority that has been occurring during this tumultuous period. In this sense, all post–Cold War conflicts, peaceful or otherwise, are not ethnic, self-determination, or Islamic fundamentalist conflicts. They are fundamentally *liberalization conflicts.*

The liberal revolution that is unfolding presents a dilemma for conflict prevention policymakers in the major powers and multilateral organizations. This dilemma has most usually been addressed as the tension between peace and justice in postconflict situations.[12] But it also arises in transitional and thus potential conflict situations to the extent that incumbent regimes have poor records in terms of political justice and human rights. International aid and foreign policies that provide unqualified support for such policy goals as democracy and respect for human and minority rights *alone,* whatever the context—even at the expense of creating serious political and economic uncertainty—can sometimes contribute to the breakdown of a state and help to precipitate violent conflicts as in Croatia, Bosnia, and Burundi.[13] However oppressive of minorities and others the preliberal orders have been under many noxious regimes, they provided in many instances a measure of physical and economic security for large numbers of people. If a rapid or radical shift to a new and highly uncertain order, albeit in the name of social and political justice, brings widespread violence, destruction, and human suffering, the overall price paid in pursuit of progressive change, assuming that it actually follows, is exceedingly high.

The policy implication is that, rather than a one-size-fits-all approach that presses for the same reforms everywhere, individual countries need to be differentiated according to their capacity to absorb disruptive shifts in unregulated power, and consequent instability, without violent conflict. A more balanced, holistic, contextualized approach to fostering desirable liberal change needs to be applied. Clearly, moves toward democratization and other liberal reforms can often be among the adaptive mechanisms that help ensure peaceful transition in particular settings. But the overarching and overriding policy goal should not be simply democracy or human rights or marketization or other such a priori goals, especially at any cost. It should rather be peaceful transition toward ultimately more democratic—or at least legitimate and effective—governments, increasingly more productive economies, and in any case more humane societies. Tailored country-specific policy strategies are needed that at a minimum "do no harm" by taking care in changing vulnerable societies not to inadvertently increase the risks of destructive conflict; and, if possible, "do some good" by deliberately and sensitively fostering peaceful and constructive political conflict and avoiding violent destructive expression of the inevitable clashes between interests during a period of strife. How prevention policies can be more contextualized is pursued further below.

Lack of Will, or Lack of the Way?

The problem of the lack of political will in conflict prevention, and the corollary problem of the lack of resources devoted to it, have been much discussed. Its ubiquity, however, may be based largely on the few highly dramatic instances such as Rwanda and Kosovo, where conflicts had reached a point when violence was imminent or had already broken out, and the international community failed to take the extraordinary measures to deter or stem the escalation that occurred into higher levels of violence. Because some kind of forceful and intrusive action is usually needed at that incipient stage of overt hostilities, international actors find it much more difficult politically to take robust action. Among other things, security risks are higher, the use of coercion is controversial, and conventional arguments can be raised against international intervention. You're damned if you don't, and you're damned if you do. There is no doubt that in these moments lack of political will is a serious obstacle to preventive action.

However, not all recent situations requiring preventive action have necessarily been of this very demanding sort. In most developing countries that are now facing strains over transition issues, the international community is already present in the form of multiple diplomatic missions, development activities, structural adjustment programs, trade and commercial activities, military assistance, and, as we have noted, efforts to promote democracy, human rights, and civil society. In other words, they are already engaged in places that may be in the early stages of potential conflicts. However, most international activities of this sort are being carried out without specific consciousness as to whether they are helping or hurting the larger processes of sociopolitical change without violence. Programs are initiated and resources allocated for many sector-specific reasons, but with little thought as to how such choices might be oriented to preventing violent conflicts or buttressing the peaceful capacities of these societies to navigate the perils of wrenching change. In other words, the policies that are already at work and the resources that are already being spent in developing countries are not yet being effectively mobilized for conflict prevention purposes.

In this light, it will not always be the case that political will for conflict prevention has to be generated in the face of oppressed minorities at peril from raised machetes or the threat of massive human rights violations imposed by police crackdowns or paramilitary squads. Rather, it is a more mundane matter of reorienting support for the requirements of analysis and reengineering the bureaucratic procedures of many existing diplomatic, development, and other programs and routines that are already operating in developing countries, so that they might serve conflict prevention objectives in particular—on an ongoing basis.[14] Neither does the only hope for prevention lie solely in international action; domestic forces for peaceful change often exist as well, within and outside governments, and can be enlisted. Presumably, a significant difference could be made if these multiple multilateral and domestic efforts were each somewhat modified so that their aggregate impact in a given country would begin to be more "conflict-smart" than is currently the case. Such bureaucratic change is not easy. But it does seem to require less political risk and fewer new resources. The issue of political will would be less significant if conflict prevention, like environmental and gender concerns, incrementally became part of the picture.

Prevention Accountability and Effectiveness

Adolescence implies that one is old enough to have taken some individual initiative and to have had some impact on the world. By the same token, adolescents can do damage. But with this might also come an increasing self-awareness that one needs to take responsibility for one's mistakes and to learn from them. Something like this greater accountability is emerging in the conflict prevention field.

Up until the last year or so, a conventional wisdom was that the problem is not early warning but lack of political will to respond. Although sufficient political will is still lacking, of course, now there is also a dawning realization that the problem is not merely getting *some* response to early warnings. It is also getting an *effective* response. It is no longer sufficient merely to take just any preventive action ("Do something, quick!"). Practitioners are increasingly expected to produce tangible results, in both potential- and postconflict situations, that build toward the ultimate goal of sustainable peace.

The new pressure for more effective prevention has been stimulated by evidence that existing international policies and actions inevitably get implicated in the course of conflicts and their outcomes and often can worsen the situation.[15] In addition to the Rwanda debacle and doubts raised over the necessity of the peace enforcement intervention by the North Atlantic Treaty Organization in Kosovo, the interest in more effective preventive action has been building for some time due to developments such as the following:

1. Errors of judgment in prevention decisionmaking, such as conferring diplomatic recognition on Croatia in 1991 without guaranteeing Serb security, and failing to vigorously enforce aid conditionalities regarding human rights abuses in Rwanda in 1993–1994 following the Arusha Peace Accords.

2. The do-no-harm debate has raised the question of whether humanitarian aid can often abet conflicts, which some argued was a consequence of maintaining Hutu Interhamwe militants in the refugee camps of eastern Zaire from 1994 to 1997 after their exodus from Rwanda.

3. Funding agencies and foundations, wondering whether their money is being well-spent, have commissioned program evaluations. The findings in some instances reveal strengths but also serious limitations of frequently used and well-meaning types of initiatives, such as NGO "track-two" diplomacy.[16]

4. Evidence that the unqualified championing of major and rapid reforms in highly polarized societies, such as promoting democracy and minority rights through majoritarian elections, can increase the risks of violent backlash by the losing factions.[17]

Recent prevention failures have involved not only lack of action but also ineffective action. Policy errors have occurred in countries where international actors are already present on the ground carrying out programs, not places where they have yet to arrive. So if prevention failure involves not only acts of omission but also acts of commission, the challenge for the UN, European Union, and other major international actors is not simply taking timely action, although timing is, of course, still crucial. The action taken must also be appropriate to and effective in the country context where it is applied. These actors need to respond to incipient conflict situations more promptly; they also must respond more intelligently. The problem is political will as well as political wisdom.

Specifically, then, how can the agencies, resources, and policies already available to and often present in transitioning countries be applied more effectively for conflict prevention? In essence, the question of conflict prevention effectiveness is, What methods, programs, policies, and actions can achieve peaceful transition—and under what conditions? In response to the growth of conflict prevention activity, several researchers in the early 1990s began to gather policy-relevant lessons from actual prevention experience through various methods of quantitative, case-study, and evaluation research.[18] More recently, donors and other funders are beginning to take an interest in learning lessons and identifying best practices. However, the findings from the accumulating research studies have been scattered and diverse, so they have not been consolidated or disseminated to the locations where they might be applied. Supply and demand have yet to meet in any significant way. But there are lessons on the shelf.

Levels of Preventive Action in the International System

One reason for the gap between existing knowledge and application is the lack of a common frame of reference in which to classify the accumulating findings so they can be linked to relevant decisionmakers, as well as further tested and cumulated by researchers. Without such a framework, the business of deriving and testing lessons from preventive activity is like reading tea leaves or seeing shapes in the clouds on the sky—almost anything can be offered about any facet of the subject. But one way to become more systematic and thus useful is to recognize that governmental and nongovernmental policies that are impacting positively or negatively on conflict prevention and peacebuilding are being carried out at several rather distinct levels: global, regional, national, and local. Examples of potential conflict prevention action at these respective levels include:

- the international criminal court, or international regulation of illicit small arms;
- a regional embargo on arms traffic, or regional economic sanctions;

- a national political debate, or a preventive deployment; and
- a rural village development project.

Because preventive action can take place at all of these differing levels, the question What is effective? also needs to be raised and answered at each of these levels.

Busy practitioners may want researchers to provide them with say, *the* five lessons to be learned in conflict prevention. A few overarching lessons may apply to the world as a whole, such as the one developed in the previous section about the need for balancing change and stability. Although these have heuristic value, they are very general, and some tend toward platitudes that provide little specific guidance ("Act early!" "Study the conflict!" "Consult with those involved on the ground!"). However, there may be several *sets* of such lessons concerning what is effective or ineffective. Various more concrete and specific lessons relate to different regions, individual states, and substate communities in the international system where preventive activity is being carried out, as well as to the sectoral or other units of collective activity that are operating at a given level.

Actually, the practitioners who are potential consumers of these lessons play varied roles at and across different levels of activity. Headquarters-level officials and planners set general policy and oversee agency operations; desk officers monitor specific country-level developments; country-level administrators run programs; and project managers operate activities in local communities. Given their particular stations, practitioners will naturally tend to take an interest in the results of preventive activities that are within their control, and thus in lessons that focus on their particular opportunities for action.

In sum, one reason why relatively little progress has been made in applying the existing experience in conflict prevention is that the lessons have not been codified in a unified classification scheme that indicates where they apply in terms of levels and types of activities. Such a catalog would enable the many differing actors who can influence a conflict situation to find prevention guidance that applies to *them*.

Major Levels of Preventive Action for Lesson-Learning

We can begin to create a lesson-learning framework by charting the terrain of conflict prevention activity. Accordingly, the following list identifies major levels and units of preventive action. These then suggest the corresponding units of analysis about which prevention lessons have been or can be gathered.

1. *International standard-setting: a priori norms, standards, goals, or requirements set for countries globally or regionally.* This level of collective action involves worldwide or regionwide legal and normative principles that define standards regarding human rights, the rule of law, democratic government, environment, and so on. These standards seek to encourage or enforce appropriate institutions and government behavior. They are agreed to mainly by states, written up in international conventions and treaties, and promoted or enforced by international bodies (e.g., OSCE standard-setting, international human rights conventions, the EU Lomé Convention goals for democracy). The standards are not formulated for particular countries that face conflicts at a given moment in time, but adherence to such rules is widely seen as an effective measure of structural conflict prevention—especially before any violent expressions of conflict on such issues are imminent.

2. *Constitutional and territorial governance structures.* These are overall institutional arrangements that can be adopted by states in order to define the prerogatives and relationships of the various parts of their central and local governments: federalism, autonomy, decentralization, parliamentary and presidential systems, and so on. These arrangements tend to persist for long periods of time and are considered to channel political life in ways that can help prevent violent conflicts in certain conditions.

3. *Time-sensitive interventions into specific situations.* There are three subsets. (a) Policy instruments (the "tools" approach): organized roughly on sectoral or functional lines, these are generic types of more short-term preventive interventions or policy tools that can be initiated at the global or national levels and are applied to particular conflicts at particular points and for limited periods of time (e.g., human rights observers, conditional aid, media professionalization, track-two diplomacy, conflict resolution training, preventive deployment, special envoys, etc).[19] Such instruments tend to embody differing kinds of incentives, disincentives, and other means to influence a conflict. They may be carried out in several locations in a conflict arena and usually require several actors at multiple levels to implement them.[20] (b) Multi-instrument engagements: these refer to the combination of programs that a multilateral peace operation or other mission, along with NGOs, has initiated and maintained over a certain period of time with regard to a particular potential or past intrastate conflict. They often apply several kinds of instruments (e.g., political dialogue, police training, electoral assistance, civil society projects, etc.). (c) Individual agencies' programs and projects: some foreign or host governments and multilateral organizations, or their specific agencies, have taken an interest in how their own set of programs and projects in a developing country perform in conflict prevention terms. The unit of analysis may

include single or groups of programs. The smallest unit of collective activity that can be intended explicitly to have its own prevention impacts would be projects (e.g., one or more radio programs developed by a peace radio studio).

Overall, these units of preventive activity compose major parts of a de facto and potential international conflict preventive system, a system that is currently affecting conflicts positively or harmfully in many ways. What is ultimately needed is to improve the overall efficacy of this system, by imbuing more of it with the values and criteria of a "culture of prevention."

Lessons from Country-Level Multi-Instrument Engagements

Some of the lessons being gathered from recent experience in conflict prevention can be illustrated here. In response to the increase in explicitly preventive activity, a number of researchers have looked at cases of intrastate potential or actual violent conflicts in order to identify some of the elements that appear to be associated with the unheralded successes and the more publicized failures (although most outcomes are not simply one or the other). These studies have focused on the multiactor, multi-instrument preventive engagements in situations of potentially violent conflict described above. Table 7.1 pulls together some of the generalizations that are suggested by these case studies. Although based on existing systematic research, the generalizations are preliminary hypotheses that additional case studies need to test further. They are presented in a structured outline in which lessons can be cumulated in an ongoing database, which is currently under development. This database will be tested further and continuously refined, its findings continuously disseminated to those decisionmakers who can make best use of these lessons. Presented in this way, case studies can provide the basis for policy guidelines regarding effective conflict prevention practice for would-be conflict preventors—rules for peaceful revolutionaries.

Institutionalizing Conflict Prevention: Linking Lessons to Standard Operating Procedures

Although lessons are accumulating, they have yet to be significantly recognized, boiled down, and utilized to inform decisionmaking and thus really learned by the very organizations to which they pertain. The lessons gath-

Table 7.1 Key Ingredients of Effective Multi-Instrument Country-Level Preventive Engagements

Recent case-study findings suggest that serious intrastate political tensions and issues will tend to be addressed peacefully, rather than escalate into violence, to the extent that the following ingredients are present:[a]

Features of the Preventive Engagement Itself

When?

1. Timely, early action is taken as tensions are emerging, but before, rather than following, significant use of violence, or immediately after initial outbreaks.

2. Engagement prioritizes the various goals of preventing violence (security, "peace"), managing issue disputes, and transforming overall institutions and societies (e.g., political and social justice)—i.e., "direct" and "structural" prevention—in contextually appropriate mixes and sequences. Such prioritization generally recognizes that when behaviors and actions immediately threaten major loss of life and destruction, they need to be deterred or stopped before more fundamental structures of power and socioeconomic advantage are changed. But also that short-term crisis management needs to be followed by actions that credibly tackle more fundamental issues.

What?

3. Early action is robust, rather than halfhearted and equivocal, and exerts vigorous positive and negative inducements, specifically on the major potentially conflicting parties' leaders and their mobilized rank and file.[b]

4. Early action thus brings an appropriate mix of sufficiently vigorous (conditional) carrots, (unconditional) support, sticks, negotiating "tables," and other modes of influence to bear on the several most important short-term and long term sources of potential conflicts, the key "fronts" in which conflicts are being played out.

5. Early action does not solely promote the cause of the weaker parties to the conflict but also addresses the fears and insecurities of dominant parties.[c]

6. Support and protection is provided to established governing formal institutions of the state, to the extent that they incorporate the leaders of the main contending communities in power-sharing in rough proportion to their distribution in the population, rather than buttressing an exclusionary governmental structure or, alternatively, an antistate political opposition. Responsible autonomous organs of the state and within the security forces are assisted to provide public services professionally. This enables the state to host a process of give-and-take politicking over public policy and constitutional issues and to carry out business for the benefit of the general population.

7. Opportunities for joining regional security alliances and trade cooperation also create an overall climate of support for building liberal peaceful states.[d]

8. Outside formal government, a broad-based "constituency for peace" is built up over time that cuts across the society's main politicized identity groups, one that is not solely interested in politics, is primarily interested in business pursuits, and can generate wealth and thus has a vested interest in political stability and social prosperity.[e]

9. A politically active but independent and cross-cutting civil society is encouraged to unify major identity groups. Peaceful "people power" campaigns are supported through training opposition leaders not only in nonviolent tactics and nonincendiary rhetoric, but also how to exert significant pressure on incumbent leaders to take peaceful, responsible actions or retire from office.

Who?

10. Preventive engagements are implemented by a sufficient number and kind of governmental and nongovernmental actors so as to provide the range of needed instruments (mediation, deterrence, institution-building, etc.) and resources to address the leading sources of the conflict. In the process, these actors form a "critical mass" that visibly symbolizes a significant international commitment to nonviolent change. Rarely can any single actor or action prevent serious violent intrastate conflicts.

11. The engagement is supported politically and in other ways, or at least tolerated and not blocked or undermined, by major *regional* powers and/or major *world* powers.

12. The engagement is generally viewed as legitimate by its being carried out under the aegis of the United Nations or a regional multilateral organization involving the affected states.

How?

13. The early multifaceted action is concerted and consistent among the major external actors, rather than scattered or contradictory.

Features of the Regional, National, and Local Context

Where?

14. Past relations between the politically significant groups have been peaceful in the recent past, rather than violent.

15. Moderate leaders from each of the contending communities are in positions of authority and in regular contact as they carry out the public's business, and they show some progress in carrying out public policies that benefit all communities, including providing for physical security.

16. The following regional actors adjacent or close to the immediate arena of conflict (neighboring states and refugee communities) are neutral to an emerging conflict or actively promote its peaceful resolution, rather than supporting one side or another politically or militarily.

17. The diasporas of the parties to a conflict that reside in major third party countries also support peaceful means of resolution, or at least are not highly mobilized behind their respective countrymen's cause. Thus, they do not aid and abet coercive or violent ways to pursue the conflict and lobby their host governments to take a partisan stance toward the conflict.

Notes

a. This synthesis draws from, among others, Hugh Miall, *The Peacemakers: Peaceful Settlement of Disputes Since 1945* (New York: St. Martin's Press, 1992); Gabriel Munuera, *Preventing Armed Conflict in Europe: Lessons from Recent Experience* (Paris: Institute for Security Studies, June 1994); Susan Woodward, *Balkan Tragedy: Chaos and Dissolution After the Cold War* (Washington, D.C.: Brookings Institution, 1995); Michael S. Lund, *Preventing Violent Conflicts* (Washington, D.C.: United States Institute of Peace, 1996); Peter Wallensteen, ed., *Preventing Violent Conflict: Past Record and Future Challenges* (Uppsala, Sweden: Uppsala University, Department of Peace and Conflict Research, 1998). Lund, Rubin, and Hara, "Learning from Burundi's Failed Democratic Transition, 1993–96: Did International Initiatives Match the Problem?" in *Cases and Strategies of Preventive Action*, Barnett R. Rubin, ed. (New York: Century Foundation Press, 1998); Raimo Väyrynen, et al., *Inventive and Preventive Diplomacy* (Notre Dame, Ind.: Joan Kroc Institute, University of Notre Dame, 1999); Lund, "'Preventive Diplomacy' for Macedonia, 1992–1997: Containment Becomes Nation-Building," and other chapters in Bruce W. Jentleson, ed. *Preventive Diplomacy in the Post–Cold War World: Opportunities Missed, Opportunities Seized and Lessons to Be Learned* (Lanham, Md.: Rowman and Littlefield, 1999); Lund, "Why Are Some Ethnic Disputes Settled Peacefully, While Others Become Violent? Comparing Slovakia, Macedonia, and Kosovo," in *Journeys Through Conflict,* Hayward Alker et. al., eds. (Lanham, Md.: Rowman and Littlefield, 2001). Special note should also be made of an outstanding book being written by Barnett R. Rubin, *The Politics of Preventive Action* (forthcoming, 2002), which includes four case-studies.

b. For example, empirical studies of the antecedents of "genocide" and "politicide" conflicts by Barbara Harff suggest that announcements of possible international preventive interventions that in fact do not happen or are half-hearted and largely symbolic may be interpreted by determined combatants as a go-ahead signal to pursue the conflict with impunity through further oppression or aggression.

c. Where needed to avoid backlash from a threatened but powerful *ancien regime*, such an approach seeks to keep lines out and open to moderates or other persuadable elites, rather than prematurely stamping them as pariahs and giving them no recourse for shifting their loyalties to join the forces of change. It looks for opportunities for quiet "constructive engagement" with existing regime leaders and their cliques, to point out the "handwriting on the wall" and conjure up historic roles for them as national invigorators. This avoids a sentimental or expressive moralistic approach in favor of an instrumental pragmatic approach. It eschews Manichean "good guys" versus "bad guys" campaigns in favor of tactics that address leaders' specific political and economic incentives. If necessary because of the prevailing balance of power, it creates opportunities for amnesty or "soft landings" to avoid existing leaders from digging in their heels.

d. As in Eastern Europe, this may involve offering specific attractive incentives to current or alternative leaders and elites that promise that, if their national policies achieve economic and political reforms, respect minorities, etc., they can hold power by gaining the political support of interest groups and publics who will see benefit from integration.

e. This guideline thus eschews reinforcing or coddling ethnic minority movements that tend to polarize national politics by boycotting a polity's elections and declining other opportunities to participate in and thus leaven mainstream political life. It avoids polarizing the political conflict to dangerous lengths by siding only with political oppositions in "us versus them" struggles and thus keeps international support from being a catalyst that provokes violent backlash, unless it is also prepared to protect the innocent victims of repression.

ered from actual experience at the country and other levels of practice need to be reconnected to the actual routines and established processes of decisionmaking and implementation.

Incorporating the Lessons in Country-Level Strategies

The first thing that is needed is a process of conflict diagnosis, selection of options, and strategy development, implementation, and evaluation that allows the lessons about effective prevention to become integrated into the standard operating procedures of governmental and nongovernmental bureaucracies. Fortunately, as mentioned above, the process of mainstreaming early warning and prevention responses is already beginning among all major multilateral and bilateral development agencies (although less so perhaps among their colleagues in foreign ministries).[21] At headquarters level, the UN Secretariat now operates a Prevention Team that meets regularly to monitor potential trouble spots and recommend appropriate action. At the country level, the United Nations and every other major donor and multilateral organization have established some regular process of drawing up country-specific development assistance plans such as the UN Common Country Assessments and the Development Assistance Framework. But so far, these procedures often are not oriented explicitly to conflict sources or peace capacities.

The ideal steps of such a planning process for the purpose of developing effective country-level prevention strategies are essentially the following:

1. *Conflict analysis, diagnosis ("What is the problem?")*. The principal current need is not so much gaining more reliable knowledge than is already available, but rather synthesizing it in formats that can be readily used by practitioners. This would include:

• Drawing on the voluminous literature that deals with the several structural and immediate causes of conflict, as well as the wealth of early warning signs or indicators of these phenomena, and then synthesizing these into a generic checklist of possible factors to address.
• Including in the list not only negative risks and threats (causes of conflict) evident in the situation, but also the positive opportunities and capacities (causes of peace).
• Applying the generic checklist to the context to identify the country-specific configuration of *needs or problem areas* arising in and across several different sectoral areas (e.g., economic, political, social, etc.).
• Because the causation of violent conflicts is multilayered, suggesting

that violent conflicts are contingent on several ingredients, the diagnosis will generate a particular configuration of underlying and more immediate sources of conflict, as well as peace capacities, that need to be attended to.[22]
• Ranking short-, medium-, and long-term priorities in order to sequence actions in some relation to the risks that have the most potential for destruction.

2. *Identifying possible actions ("What is appropriate to do?")*. This would include:

• Identifying possible entry points, or angles of attack, with regard to each of the identified areas of need. These become program objectives.
• Considering a range of particular means, actions (policy tools, instruments, measures, activities) for meeting country-specific needs by achieving the various objectives. (See lists of possible instruments such as in Appendix 7.1.)
• Avoiding the pitfalls of universal, a priori objectives: democracy, human rights, economic development, justice.
• Screening all those programs that are already operational, including those that are explicitly preventive as well as other sectoral programs, with peace/conflict evaluative criteria in order to assess their likely impacts on worsening conflict or building peace in relation to the particular country needs identified.
• Consulting the lessons of successful prevention from structured case studies such as those discussed above, then using them as a checklist to see what key overall ingredients ideally may need to be in place.

3. *Prior appraisal or prospective evaluation ("What will work in this context?")*. This includes:

• Consulting the existing track record (past performance) of given instruments, drawing on the small but growing research on the impacts of various instruments and the associated conditions that apply peace and conflict impact criteria.
• Screening proposed actions for their likely effectiveness and implementability.

4. *Implementation ("Who does what, and when?")*. This includes:

• Engaging other actors to address the needs you cannot fulfill—regional organizations, governments, NGOs, and other donors.

5. *Monitoring and evaluation, or retrospective evaluation ("What are the results?")*.

6. *Strategy modification or termination ("How can we do better?")*.

Organizing Concerted Strategies: Joint In-Country Planning and Implementation

Some organized process is then needed that conducts the analysis described above in order to apply the lessons from experience in strategies that fit particular potential conflict situations. This process should not be simply bilateral but multilateral. One of the lessons is that multiple actors and their respective policy instruments and political influence are needed to steer any given unstable country toward peaceful progressive change. Thus, to the extent that the country situation is difficult to influence, what is ideally needed is for many actors to join others in collaborative assessments and country-specific conflict prevention strategy development. More effort is needed to link the country desk officers at the headquarters level in the differing agencies. In addition, the respective development staffs in the field could engage informally with each other at the country level in joint analyses of each host country's conflict vulnerabilities and peacebuilding opportunities. Joint inventorying could determine how the mix of instruments that these organizations might already be operating in a country, or that could be introduced, might be modified and amplified to achieve more effective leverage over emerging tensions that could turn destructive. Although not obligatory or coerced, such joint consultation might over time encourage more complementary in-country programs. This is one practical step that could help to spread a culture of prevention.

Major donor agencies are beginning to discuss issues informally through consultations sponsored by the Development Assistance Committee Task Force on Peace, Conflict, and Development of the Organization for Economic Cooperation and Development and the Conflict Prevention and Post-Conflict Reconstruction Network. So far, however, when it comes to operationalizing concerted conflict prevention strategies on the ground, there seems to be little cross-agency consultation even within the same governments or international organizations. Even among the most prevention-oriented organizations there persists an understandable, but ultimately short-sighted, tendency to ask for lessons of effective prevention that are packaged only in terms and forms that are specific to their particular organization's programs and procedures. International NGOs are stepping forward to stimulate country-level exercises in specific sites such as Georgia and Kenya, in the hopes of encouraging donors, the UN, the EU, the OSCE, host governments, and local NGOs to engage in collaborative assessment and response.[23] Ultimately, this convening function might be handled by UN Resident Coordinators or Special Representatives, EU country delegations, or key NGOs, who could take the initiative and act as convenors and facilitators.

Conclusion

Of course, putting more emphasis on examining recent prevention experience to understand what is effective in prevention, and then incorporating these lessons into existing country-level programming procedures, will not by themselves change existing political priorities at the top levels of decisionmaking. But they can build up a basis for sounder policymaking as conflict prevention advocacy increasingly garners more serious and detailed attention at the policy level. In the meantime, knowing that there are plausible and tried methods on the shelf for addressing potentially violent conflict situations may actually help to increase decisionmakers' comfort levels. Possibly, they may feel more confident that they can exercise political will, individually and multilaterally, without taking huge risks.

In any case, better analysis is essential even when more political will exists. Publicity and lobbying do not automatically lead to more effective decisions and policymaking. In fact, the popularization of the awareness of conflicts and of the promise of conflict prevention might sometimes worsen policy decisions, just as responding to public sentiments during humanitarian crisis interventions has in some instances led to unwise choices. More political will needs to be accompanied by solid analysis of the various likely consequences of particular policies in order to inform how various agencies' regularized procedures can apply a range of policy instruments to problems in developing countries.

*   *   *

Appendix 7.1   A "Toolbox" of Some Preventive Instruments

Official and Nonofficial Diplomacy
- mediation
- negotiations
- good offices, consultations
- conciliation
- use of UN Charter Article 99
- "track two" dialogue facilitation
- diplomatic inducements and sanctions
- economic sanctions
- fact-finding missions
- special inquiries, commissions of inquiry
- "friends' groups"
- contact groups

Development
- food security programs
- targeted antipoverty programs
- small enterprise, job creation, and micro-credit projects
- intergroup development projects
- intergroup women's cooperation
- natural resource (e.g., water, land) management projects
- structural adjustment programs
- conditional aid
- land reform
- natural resources regulations
- peace media (radio, TV)
- indigenous dispute resolution mechanisms
- peace commissions

Democratization and Effective Governance
- electoral assistance
- election monitoring
- political party development
- civil society capacity-building
- executive and civil service assistance
- legislature assistance
- constitutional and legislation assistance
- judicial and legal assistance and reform
- local government assistance and reform
- decentralization
- autonomy
- federalism

Security and Human Rights
- preventive deployment, protective forces
- postconflict peacekeepers
- international police
- military reform
- civilian police
- police reform
- human rights monitors
- civilian volunteer "witnesses"
- human rights assistance
- confidence and security building measures
- arms control
- demobilization
- mine clearance

Humanitarian Assistance
- food, medicine, and other relief in conflict areas
- conditional relief aid
- refugee and internally displaced persons assistance
- reintegration programs
- rehabilitation and reconstruction projects
- promulgation of humanitarian law

Justice and Reconciliation
- arbitration
- adjudication
- war crime tribunals
- truth and reconciliation commissions

Notes

This chapter is indebted to many influences, some of which are noted. An earlier version was prepared for the conference "Facing Ethnic Conflicts: Perspectives from Research and Policy-making," Center for Development Research, University of Bonn, December 4–16, 2000. The chapter draws also from Michael Lund and Guenola Rasmoelina, eds., *The Impact of Conflict Prevention Policy: Cases, Measures, Assessments*, Yearbook 2000 of the Conflict Prevention Network (Ebenhausen, Germany: Stiftung Wissenschaft und Politik, Nomos Verlagsgesellschaft, 2000).

1. The first project specifically on conflict prevention (in the sense defined below) may have been the Preventive Diplomacy Initiative at the United States Institute of Peace (USIP) from 1994 to 1995, which grew out of a USIP/U.S. State Department Study Group on Preventive Diplomacy from 1993 to 1994. The topic was subsequently taken up by the Carnegie Commission on Preventing Deadly Conflict, as well as the Center for Preventive Action at the Council on Foreign Relations, from about 1995 to the end of 1999, the Conflict Prevention Network of the Stiftung Wissenschaft und Politik from 1996 to the present, and, most recently, the International Peace Academy.

2. The Association of South East Asian Nations has also addressed the subject informally through the Asian Regional Forum, largely under the rubric of confidence-building.

3. What one book described a decade ago as the "emerging global watch" seems to be gradually taking some form. See Bertie G. Ramcharan, *The International Law and Practice of Early Warning and Preventive Diplomacy: The Emerging Global Watch* (Dordrecht, Netherlands: Martinus Nijhoff, 1991).

4. The recent trends are surveyed in Manuela Leonhardt's chapter in Lund and Rasamoelina, eds., *The Impact of Conflict Prevention Policy*, and in her monograph, *Conflict Impact Assessment of EU Development Cooperation with ACP Countries: A Review of Literature and Practice* (London: International Alert and Saferworld, 2000). An example of such an analytical tool is Michael Lund and Andreas Mehler, *Peacebuilding and Conflict Prevention in Developing Countries* (Ebenhausen, Germany: Stiftung Wissenschaft und Politik, Conflict Prevention Network, 1999), which was prepared for country-desk officers of the European Commission. A primer prepared for development practitioners on conflict and prevention tools is "Preventing and Mitigating Violent Conflicts: A Guide for Practitioners" (Washington, D.C.: Creative Associates International, Inc., 1997; viewable at www.caii-dc.com/ghai).

5. See Appendix 7.1 for an illustrative list of several possible prevention instruments.

6. Accordingly, it includes not only avoiding violence but also the range of more fundamental changes now referred to as "peacebuilding." Prevention can come into play both in places where conflicts have not occurred recently (i.e., prevent vertical escalation), including forestalling the spread of already active hostilities to new sites (i.e., prevent horizontal escalation), and also where recent but terminated violent conflicts could recur (i.e., prevent relapse in postconflict situations).

In short, the essence of conflict prevention is a *stance of responsiveness* to unstable, potentially violent conditions that are unfolding on the ground in particular places at particular times. Thus, despite the earlier use of the term "preventive diplomacy," conflict prevention cannot be restricted to any particular means of intervention or implementing actor, such as diplomats. In principle, it could involve the methods and means of any governmental or nongovernmental policy sector, whether labeled prevention or not (e.g., not only mediation, good offices, and the like but also sanctions, conditional development aid, mediation, structural adjustment, humanitarian assistance, arms control, media, education, preventive military deployment, democratic institution-building, private investment, trade, etc.). Of course, whether any such means are *in fact* conflict preventive (i.e., effective) is not automatic from their mere aims and application but depends on how they are applied and the results they actually obtain. Indeed, some of these tools applied without conflict sensitivity have contributed to violent conflicts.

7. The idea that conflicts typically evolve through a "life cycle," or history, implied in the UN Charter's Chapters VI and VII, is developed more explicitly in Creative Associates International, "Preventing and Mitigating Violent Conflicts." Differing stages of conflict, such as emergence, escalation, deescalation, (re)construction, and reconciliation, have been adopted as an organizing framework by recent textbooks in the conflict field; see, e.g., Louis Kriesberg, *Constructive Conflicts: From Escalation to Resolution* (Lanham, MD: Rowman and Littlefield, 1998); Hugh Miall et al., *Contemporary Conflict Resolution* (Cambridge, U.K.: Polity Press, 1999).

8. Other implications of this new period of accountability are discussed below.

9. These topics are addressed in Chapters 2, 5, 8, and 13 in this volume.

10. This tendency may reflect in part the fact that the outsider organizations that carry out programs in developing countries are bureaucratically structured predominantly in a "stovepipe" fashion along sectoral or functional lines, rather than along more decentralized, geographically focused lines.

11. Still others have postponed resolving these conflicts or evolved peacefully into neoauthoritarian populist quasidemocracies.

12. See, e.g., Pauline H. Baker, "Conflict Resolution Versus Democratic Governance: Divergent Paths to Peace?" in *Managing Global Chaos,* eds., Chester Crocker, Fen Osler Hampson, and Pamela Aall (Washington, D.C.: United States Institute of Peace Press, 1996).

13. One might hypothesize that a certain pattern has characterized the international responses to pregenocide Rwanda, 1993–1994; Burundi, 1993; Kosovo, 1992–1998; East Timor, 1999; and possibly other cases. The international community's sympathetic political championing of an ethnic minority's rights, such as through honoring unofficial referendums and denouncing the human rights violations of their oppressors, may tend to polarize the local political relations further by demonizing the perpetrators and thus help to catalyze violence. The forces of violent backlash in those settings may be encouraged to preempt militarily the impending threat of political change, but the international community is not prepared to deter such moves. Ostensible violence *prevention* can become violence *precipitation,* if well-intentioned advocacy of human rights promotion, provision of humanitarian aid, or other international measures are advanced on behalf of a vulnerable group. However, this can put them at greater risk by tempting the more powerful and better-armed forces of reaction to strike while they can preempt the forces of change because adequate international provision is not made to protect their victims.

14. See Michael S. Lund, "Not Only When, but How: From 'Early Warning' to Rolling Prevention," in *Preventing Violent Conflict: Past Record and Future Challenges,* ed. Peter Wallensteen (Uppsala, Sweden: Uppsala University, Department of Peace and Conflict Research, 1998).

15. See, for example, Peter Uvin, "Summary Report to the DAC Task Force on Peace and Development," (Paris: DAC/OECD), 4.

16. See, for example, Gunnar M. Serbe, Joanna Macrae, and Lennart Wohlgemuth, "NGO's in Conflict—An Evaluation of International Alert" (Bergen, Norway: Chr. Michelson Institute, 1997).

17. See, for example, Ben Reilly, "Voting Is Good, Except When It Guarantees War," *Washington Post*, October 17, 1999, B2.

18. The earliest research of this nature includes Hugh Miall, *The Peacemakers: Peaceful Settlement of Disputes Since 1945* (New York: St. Martin's, 1992); Gabriel Munuera, *Preventing Armed Conflict in Europe: Lessons from Recent Experience* (Paris: Institute for Security Studies, June 1994); and Michael S. Lund, *Preventing Violent Conflicts* (Washington, D.C.: United States Institute of Peace Press, 1996).

19. The UN Charter refers to many diplomatic preventive measures, especially in Chapter VI. Appendix 7.1 lists several other measures.

20. A small but growing field of analysis is evaluating the effectiveness of such instruments. Instruments such as mediation, negotiation, and sanctions have received libraries of attention, although not usually from a prevention perspective. A recent book that probes the prevention value of negotiations is I. William Zartman, ed., *Preventive Negotiations* (Lanham, MD: Rowman and Littlefield, 2001). But very little has been done on the wide range of other possible preventive measures. Work that has begun to do the latter includes David Cortright, ed., *The Price of Peace: The Role of Incentives in International Conflict Prevention* (Lanham, MD: Rowman and Littlefield, 1998); Milton J. Esman, "Can Foreign Aid Moderate Ethnic Conflict?" *Peaceworks* 13 (Washington, D.C.: United States Institute of Peace, March 1998); and Peter Harris and Ben Reilly, eds., *Democracy and Deep-Rooted Conflict: Options for Negotiators* (Stockholm: International Institute for Democracy and Electoral Assistance, 1998). A forthcoming USAID-funded study under the Greater Horn of Africa Peacebuilding Project at Management Systems International, Inc., is evaluating the peace and conflict impacts of peace radio, traditional local-level peace processes, and national "track-two" political dialogues in five countries. Earlier rudimentary efforts to apply various criteria to evaluate the conflict prevention capacities and limits of nineteen diverse prevention policy instruments are found in Creative Associates International, "Preventing and Mitigating Violent Conflicts," and Michael S. Lund, "Impacts of Development Aid as Incentives or Disincentives in Reducing Internal and Inter-state Conflicts: A Review of Findings from Documented Experience," unpublished report to the Development Assistance Committee, Task Force on Peace, Conflict, and Development, 1998. The case studies in Mary B. Anderson, *Do No Harm: How Aid Can Support Peace—Or War* (Boulder: Lynne Rienner Publishers, 1999), and subsequent studies organized and analyzed by Mary Anderson and her associates at Collaborating for Development Associates, Inc., are also very relevant here. Some products are putting instrument assessments into forms that can be used by country-desk officers and other practitioners. See, for example, the brief assessments of election observers, human rights observers, and other instruments in Lund and Mehler, *Peacebuilding and Conflict Prevention in Developing Countries*. A manual of UN "preventive measures" such as fact-finding missions, humanitarian aid, and local community economic development is also being prepared for the Framework Team in the UN Secretariat.

21. For recent developments, see the chapter by Manuela Leonhardt in Lund and Rasmoelina, eds., *The Impact of Conflict Prevention Policy*. Earlier outlines of

the essential steps in developing strategies are found in Lund, *Preventing Violent Conflicts*, chapter 4, and Michael S. Lund, "Developing Conflict Prevention and Peacebuilding Strategies from Recent Experience in Europe," in *Preventing Violent Conflict: Issues from the Baltics and the Caucasus,* eds. G. Bonvicini et al. (Baden-Baden, Germany: Nomos Verlagsgesellschaft, 1998).

22. The likelihood of violent conflict arising in a particular country situation tends to be determined contingently based on whether a number of these factors combine situationally. For example, a recent comparison was made of politically active pairs of contending ethnic groups within a state, one of which had "kingroup" supporters in nearby states. It found that whether their respective disputes escalated into violence or not depended on the degree to which several domestic and international factors, similar to those listed, were present. The factors were: (1) there had been violence or coercion in the past between them; (2) the groups differed in multiple societal and cultural respects and had little everyday interaction; (3) they were highly conscious of their respective identities and organized into separate political movements, parties, or governmental machinery; (4) an uneasy balance of social power existed between them; (5) the dominant government structure permitted little participation by both groups simultaneously (power-sharing), or it was in effect divided between them; (6) the incumbent leaders on at least one side were insecure and accentuated the existing ethnic divisions through provocative statements and policies; and (7) the countries and societies in which the groups lived had limited diplomatic and economic ties or direct engagement in domestic issues by major international bodies. See Michael S. Lund, "Why Are Some Ethnic Conflicts Settled Peacefully, While Others Become Violent? Comparing Slovakia, Macedonia, and Kosovo," in *Journeys Through Conflicts,* eds. Hayward Alker et al. (Lanham, MD: Rowman and Littlefield, forthcoming 2001).

23. See, for example, Andrew Sherriff and Njeri Karuru, "Methodology for Conflict Sensitive Planning for NGO, INGO and Donor Operations in Kenya," unpublished draft (London: International Alert and Centre for Conflict Research, September 2000).

8

Planning Preventive Action: Context, Strategy, and Implementation

John G. Cockell

As the prevention of violent conflict has rapidly gained a position of prominence on the global security policy agenda in recent years, governments and international organizations have pushed for the development of concrete approaches to prevention planning and capacity-building. Within the United Nations system, the rapid expansion of activities that could be understood to have a preventive potential led then–Secretary-General Boutros Boutros-Ghali to call in 1995 for the adoption of wider "preventive action," rather than the outdated "preventive diplomacy."[1] In a sense, this shift has reflected the general trend in conflict analysis toward a greater emphasis on the role of structural causes of conflict and the importance of their early prevention. At earlier phases of escalation, there is a greater range of options available to the UN system and the international community, as well as a sense that the costs of those options will be lower and the chances of success in their application greater.

However, it also remains true that this conceptual development has not been matched by a corresponding willingness by governments to back the prevention agenda. Proactive interventions are often resisted by the regime under scrutiny, and major donors often fail to support (or even mandate) ambitious field operations with the necessary financial and human resources. Moreover, governmental commitment to international norms of state sovereignty and noninterference continue to impede the early and concerted planning of such prevention operations. These political and diplomatic constraints have often reduced attempts at prevention to ad hoc, insufficient, and/or delayed efforts that fail to have significant preventive impact.

Nevertheless, UN Secretary-General Kofi Annan has recently suggest-

ed that a general intergovernmental consensus has emerged that "comprehensive and coherent conflict prevention strategies offer the greatest
potential for promoting lasting peace and . . . sustainable development."[2]
The strategic prevention of multiple causes of conflict, however, clearly
relies upon cross-sectoral coordination of the relevant operational measures. The drive to develop the prevention agenda has contributed to a
heightened focus on both the causal complexity of protracted conflict and
the need for multifaceted operations to address those causes in an integrated manner. As Annan argues, in order to "address complex causes we need
complex, interdisciplinary solutions." He further notes that "implementing
prevention strategies . . . requires cooperation across a broad range of different agencies and departments" and that "cross-sector cooperation . . . is
a prerequisite of successful prevention."[3] Preventive action implies, then,
both the *strategic* and *integrated* application of a range of preventive
measures in protracted conflicts. It should also be understood to be applicable, in various configurations, to all phases of conflict escalation, from
low-intensity societal tensions through to postconflict peacebuilding. The
purpose of this chapter will be to examine the key issues of *causal complexity* and *cross-sectoral implementation* of operational action, as well
as the planning connection between these two points: *preventive action
strategy*.

Context: Targeting Causal Complexity in Conflict

The recent efforts of the United Nations to assess and develop its conflict
prevention practices point to the fact that preventive action planning
requires both early warning analysis as well as options for the implementation of preventive measures. As Jacob Bercovitch argues, the successful
management of conflict demands the development of a coherent plan rather
than ad hoc responses that can not only lead to policy reversals but also
damage the operational credibility of an organization. He concludes:
"Consistent and effective policies require a framework to suggest when the
international community, operating through the United Nations, should
respond to conflict and determine the appropriate responses."[4] Reiterating
the relevance of such a framework approach for governments and donor
agencies, a 1996 policy study on conflict analysis by the government of the
Netherlands stated that analysis should be linked to conflict prevention in a
single process consisting of "the collection of information; its analysis and
evaluation; its dissemination; political decision-making, which would
include an assessment of the validity, practicality, and feasibility of preventive steps; and, finally, preventive action as such."[5] These are the hallmarks

of policy planning, which incorporates the structuring of problems, the application of appropriate analytical tools to solving those problems, and the communication of analysis and recommendations in a format useful to decisionmakers.

A policy framework for producing coherent plans would focus on targeted preventive measures, making their potential impact more effective by applying them through a strategy derived from action-oriented early warning. It is important to note that this calls for preventive action planning to be rooted in a case-based approach to conflict early warning. Absent such an approach, the analysis of conflict can become implicitly framed by pre-existing categories and policy options current within an organization. This can directly compromise the accuracy and objectivity of the analytical results produced.[6] As one practitioner has observed: "If you only have a hammer it is very tempting to see every problem as a nail, rather than developing different tools to deal with different problems."[7] In other words, in contrast to the tendency for external organizations to consider and define preventive responses to conflict on the basis of their institutional mandates, a case-based approach would generate *context-specific strategies* for action, which would in turn shape the formulation and integration of operational measures and their related decisionmaking processes (see Figure 8.1).[8]

A context-specific approach to planning preventive action has some implications for the manner in which the causes of conflict, and their interactive complexity, are interpreted. Most models of conflict causes distinguish between long-term (structural) conditions and more near-term (proximate) events and actions.[9] An emphasis on contextual nuance in conflict formation should incline analysis in the direction of uncovering the underlying structural conditions that produce conflict escalation, rather than on specific events of violence. If the nature of the problem is viewed as the perpetuation of structural conditions of human insecurity, more proactive measures may be planned to begin to address the various sources of that structural violence, as well as to build human security at the societal level. As Raimo Väyrynen has argued, without such strategies aimed at structural transformation, "the operational [i.e., proximate] manipulation of political processes can be futile as the underlying differences in social identities and material interests continue to erode the society."[10] In addition, reactive measures targeted at proximate factors will tend to be ad hoc and make little strategic sense for the long-term management and amelioration of the causes of conflict. The more serious and complex the structural causes, the less likely local and external interventions will be to prevent specific proximate acts from generating heightened potential for violence. One might argue then that preventive action should be oriented toward the strategic

Figure 8.1   Context-Specific Planning Process for Preventive Action

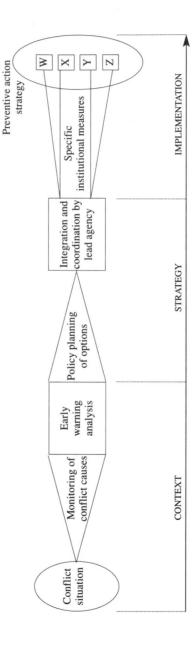

prevention of structural conditions of human insecurity at the heart of protracted social conflict.

However, structural conditions of deprivation may not necessarily lead to violent conflict in and of themselves; rather, it is their exacerbation by proximate events that increases the propensity of the situation toward violence. It is the complex combination of both conditions and events that is of analytical importance. This, in turn, requires an analysis of conflict actors, nested in the consideration of proximate factors that exacerbate the various sectors of structural conditions. Two distinctions are of importance here: the *capacity* of governmental and opposition actors to mobilize for either conflictual or accommodative interaction; and the specific *agendas* that these actors pursue. In terms of actor capacity, context-specific analysis should consider the factors that might determine whether and when violence may be employed: elite organization and means; levels of group cohesion versus internal divisions; levels of in-group/domestic and external support; a moment of opportunity; the actors' mutual perceptions of capacity status; the institutional capacity of the state; and/or governmental closure of political capacity for dialogue and accommodation.[11] What are the perceptions of leaders and elites of the values and issues (e.g., identity, recognition, access) at stake in the conflict? The motivations of these actors to opt for violence over dialogue is also crucial: do they involve group ideology, or even narrow (mis)calculations of greed, power, and/or self-interest?[12] Context-specific (and nested) actor analysis is important in laying the basis for preventive action, because it can allow for later consideration of how issues perceived to be at stake may be reframed as potential bases for peace and reconciliation, as well as what incentives might be required to facilitate such a transformation of perceptions. As such, actor analysis highlights the importance of gaining the cooperative engagement, or "buy-in," of key actors in any future peace process.

It is also common for models of conflict escalation to presume a linear path of development, from latent tensions to high-intensity violence to postconflict stabilization.[13] But the chronologies of internal conflicts in specific cases rarely present such a simple picture. The inherent dynamism of conflict escalation means that situations of low-intensity confrontation and violence may escalate into high-intensity conflict, but only if there is a certain combination of political, social, and economic structural conditions with proximate events/acts by conflict actors. Moreover, certain societies will escalate more rapidly (or slowly) than others due to the mitigating influence of either structural factors such as social norms of nonviolence and consensus-building, proximate events such as conciliatory gestures or unilateral ceasefires, or lack of organization, resources, or perceived opportunity by conflict actors. The point to be made here is that a context-sensitive approach to conflict analysis will examine the dynamics of escalation, from latent conflict through to protracted violence, and seek to identify windows of opportunity for the amelioration of structural conditions as well as the transformation of conflict actors' capacities, perceptions, and agendas. Because conflict dynamics are nonlinear, there are often potential opportunities to preventively deescalate these dynamics by facilitating "mutually enticing opportunities" for conflict actors, instead of presuming the need for a "mutually hurting stalemate."[14]

In spite of the fact that conflict phases do not necessarily proceed in a linear fashion, it is possible to argue that external preventive measures should be adjusted and sequenced to take into account the particular phase of conflict in a given context. This is because, among other reasons, in the absence of effective preventive action at early stages of escalation, the impact of high-intensity violence in conflict dynamics is such that the violence itself becomes a proximate cause of the conflict's protractedness. The actions taken by the conflict actors reinforce mutual perceptions of fear and insecurity, creating a cycle of reciprocal negative images, demonization, exclusionist myths, and dehumanizing ideologies.[15] As losses mount on each side, it becomes more difficult for moderate elites to counsel restraint and de-escalation. Indeed, militant extremists can come to dominate the conflict agenda (e.g., the Liberation Tigers of Tamil Eelam in Sri Lanka, the Harkat-ul-Mujahideen in Kashmir, Hamas in Palestine) and reject all efforts to promote integrative dialogue. The conflict actors can also develop vested economic agendas at this stage, which further exacerbates the protractedness of high-intensity violence.[16] In view of the causal role that high-intensity violence can play on the dynamics of conflict, preventive action strategies are most likely to be successful if applied during either the latent to low-intensity conflict phases or to the de-escalation and postconflict peacebuilding phases. Drawing on case studies such as Somalia, Bosnia, and Chechnya, Bruce Jentleson observes that the outbreak of "mass violence" marks the crossing of a Rubicon, "on the other side of which resolution and even limitation of the conflict become much more difficult."[17]

The most common causes of protracted social conflict may be grouped into sectoral categories to aid the real-time planning of operational action: the breakdown or paralysis of a contested political process; the polarization of social divisions along communal identity (ethnic, religious, tribal) lines; the systematic violation of human rights and endemic personal insecurity; the presence of differential economic underdevelopment, deprivation, and possibly resource scarcity; the militarization of political action and availability of small arms; and the presence of regional and/or international support for one or more conflict actors.[18] But in addition to tracking conflict causes individually as they evolve over time, analysis must also focus on their interaction dynamics. This is to say that as conflict causes grow in salience for the groups and elites in society, they also impact upon each other and mutually influence their further formation and development. For example, the suspension of political access for a group may be the prelude to the imposition of a state of emergency on that particular region. This can exacerbate the group's collective perception of exclusion and may lead to popular demonstrations. Emergency laws can then allow for security forces to crush such demonstrations with impunity, perhaps with gross violations of human rights. The human rights violations, political closure, and communal mobilization may in turn create the fertile conditions for the emergence of antistate militant groups, pushing the conflict toward a higher level of violence. This pattern of escalation has been witnessed in conflicts as diverse as Kosovo and Kashmir, Sri Lanka and Sudan. Disaggregating and relating such key causal factors is a crucial element in context-specific analysis, as that will present the basis for a plan to prevent further escalation of the situation.

Although a single effort to address one or two key causes may have the effect of de-escalating the conflict dynamic, it is much more likely that effective prevention would entail the integrated engagement of all relevant conflict causes. An effective response, in other words, must be *strategic*: engaging all the primary conflict factors in an integrated fashion such that their preventive management results in successful de-escalation, rather than a narrowly focused intervention that leaves certain key causes unresolved.

Strategy: Preventive Measures Options and Integration

Effective preventive action thus requires the strategic coordination and application of multiple measures in order to address the causal complexity of protracted conflict. The capacity within multilateral organizations such as the United Nations to generate strategic plans for conflict prevention has typically, however, been limited. One study has characterized it as "rudimentary" in comparison with military planning, although it notes that the United Nations is no better than most intergovernmental organizations in this respect.[19] This view is shared by the former UN Under-Secretary-General for Political Affairs Marrack Goulding in his 1997 evaluation of the organization's peace and security departments. He recommended that these departments, concerned with the prevention and management of complex political emergencies, evolve an integrated policy planning method to:

- identify situations which could lead to conflict;
- identify among such situations those in which action by the United Nations is desirable, practicable, and reasonably likely to succeed;
- decide what form of action to recommend; and
- monitor how well that action is achieving the desired objectives.[20]

More recently, the final report of the high-level Panel on UN Peace Operations recommends that the UN Secretariat establish a central planning unit to support the decisionmaking of the Executive Committee on Peace and Security (ECPS). This unit (an ECPS Information and Strategic Analysis Secretariat, known by its acronym EISAS) would integrate cross-sectoral analytic capacity with assessments of the potential capacity and utility of the organization to field a peace support operation in a given conflict situation.[21]

The Goulding and Brahimi panel studies suggest that there is a clear imperative for various elements of the UN system to combine their efforts in the prevention of complex conflicts and that this will require improved methods for both interagency headquarters planning and operational coordination in the field. Mechanisms for joint planning and operations should bring together both civil and (where required) military actors and seek to evolve concrete, goal-oriented strategies that will provide clear guidance to those departments and agencies involved in preventive action operations at the field level.[22] In many cases, mandates passed by official bodies such as the Security Council will require the explicit inclusion of such terms of reference. In the planning of preventive strategies, three elements are of particular importance: the specification of concrete *objectives*; the identification of realistic preventive measures *options* to achieve those objectives; and the coordinated *integration* of the chosen measures to ensure comprehensive unity of effort on the ground.

Objectives

Effective strategic planning is based on the identification of explicit operational objectives. Objectives should state a specific outcome that preventive action is intended to achieve in each key causal sector. In addition, an actionable objective is also a realistic one that is derived from the nature of the situation and the position of the conflict actors with regard to external intervention. Context-specific conflict analysis requires that specified objectives derive from the composite analysis of the conflict situation, not from institutional mandates or goals, for example, requiring that elections are held and the intervention withdrawn by a predetermined date, regardless of conditions (see Chapter 15, by Bengt Säve-Söderbergh and Izumi Nakamitsu Lennartsson). This is important because it is likely that some key objectives will not be achievable through the action of one external actor alone, such as the United Nations, but will likely require the involvement of others (e.g., regional organizations, nongovernmental organizations [NGOs], donors) as well. Although specific objectives should be stated that address each of the causes of conflict, as a whole such objectives should reflect the larger outcome of all forms of preventive action: that of enabling *sustainable* peace. A lasting peace cannot be built if continuing structural threats to human security needs have not been addressed.

But defining objectives such that they strategically facilitate the emergence of a sustainable peace requires attention to three related implications in order to ensure that multiple objectives are not defined in a manner that makes them mutually incompatible. First, given that external engagement by international organizations in any conflict situation is going to be of limited duration (diplomatic and financial resources being in perennially short supply), objectives should explicitly anticipate the emergence of a self-supporting peace dynamic. This is related to the point made earlier about actively facilitating the participation (buy-in) of key conflict actors, but it also involves the strategic engagement of all key conflict causes such that local actors and communities see that there is a real opportunity to break out of the cycle of escalation and that basic grievances are going to be addressed in a concrete way.

Second, objectives should clearly address the structural causes that are perceived by the primary conflict actors as central to the conflict dynamic. In some cases, this may mean that achieving a specific objective would require the termination of some existing forms of external intervention in that society (e.g., structural adjustment programs imposed by international financial institutions) that are exacerbating conflict causes.

Finally, in order to promote such an integrative process of de-escalation at the local level, operational objectives should build, wherever possible, on indigenous capacities for conflict management and moderate forms of political and social mobilization. Such objectives can do much to reinforce the local coping strategies of the population. As Jonathan Moore has argued, the recent field experience of the UN suggests that not enough is done to explicitly foster self-sufficiency, to ensure that "those being helped assume the primary responsibility for their recovery."[23] At a minimum, the definition of objectives should take care to avoid goals that may be incompatible with local resources and may indeed undermine them, fostering dependency. The superordinate objective of preventive action is a sustainable, self-supporting peace that enjoys the active involvement of all key conflict actors.

The primary conflict actor in most such situations, however, is the national government of the state concerned, and timely acceptance of external preventive action by governments is still the exception rather than the rule. It is for this important reason that Secretary-General Annan recently put great emphasis on the responsibility of governments to request international assistance for prevention at the early stages of conflict formation. This emphasis both highlights the central role of national governments in the acceptance and implementation of preventive action operations and points to the need for external actors to frame preventive strategies in a manner that promotes long-term capacity-building and institutional reform.[24] Where operational objectives can be set jointly with governmental authorities, this can allow for technical assistance and institution-building, in addition to lowering suspicions that preventive action is contrary to the interests of the state. Such joint capacity-building can also be pursued with nonstate conflict actors, as has been done by the UN Interim Administration Mission in Kosovo (UNMIK). In its successful 1999 effort to dissolve the provisional government of the Kosovo Liberation Army (UÇK), the mission established the various institutions (both central departments and municipal authorities) of the Joint Interim Administrative Structure (JIAS). UNMIK now shares a broad range of administrative processes not only with former UÇK factions but also other moderate Kosovar nationalist and minority parties, and the JIAS process is widely accepted as the template for the transition to autonomous self-administration in Kosovo.

Options

Consistent with the earlier emphasis on context-specific planning, Ismat Kittani argues that it is important not to formulate preventive action so broadly that it captures most of the activities of the organization: "While development, democratisation, and the promotion of human rights are all worthy goals and can contribute to political stability, they do not necessarily constitute preventive action"; Kittani continues: "It is the context and purpose of the activities that matter, that is, whether they are implemented as part of a deliberate strategy to prevent the outbreak of violence."[25] Thus, the test of whether an option will be preventive in practice is the extent to which it strategically addresses a specific conflict cause in the situational context of the larger causal interaction in the conflict dynamics, the phase of the conflict, and the broader strategic requirements of sustainable peace. Some existing development and/or humanitarian assistance programs in conflict-afflicted areas may in fact be shown to be exacerbating conflict causes once a multisectoral, composite analysis of conflict escalation is completed. This highlights the central importance of identifying and analyzing potential options against the objectives set for engaging the various sectoral conflict causes. As the Clingendael Institute in the Netherlands has observed, the "number of options available is dependent on the conflict situation, available policy tools [i.e., measures], the urgency of intervention, and a first rough assessment on expected policy priorities."[26] Conflict prevention is ultimately a political strategy, and options should be focused on the need to engage the various factors that conspire to produce political breakdown and violence. Not all (or even most) programs that fall under the rubrics of development or humanitarian action or human rights will be relevant for preventive action in a specific situation, if this political perspective is kept in mind.

Thus, analyzing options is a key element of the policy planning process, as support for decisionmaking requires that recommendations for action be based on a considered survey of available measures, both from within the organization and from outside it. In the specific context of UN capacity, policy statements on conflict prevention and preventive measures, from Boutros Boutros-Ghali's *An Agenda for Peace* (1992) to Annan's 2001 report on conflict prevention, point to the emergence of six basic categories of UN preventive measures. Three of these are considered to be shorter-term measures directed primarily at *proximate* causes of conflict: preventive peacemaking (including preventive diplomacy); preventive deployment; and preventive humanitarian action. The other three are viewed as longer-term measures designed to address the *structural* causes of conflict: preventive peacebuilding; preventive disarmament; and preventive development.[27] Human rights, as a cross-cutting priority in all areas, would clearly have particular programmatic relevance for preventive deployment, preventive peacebuilding, and preventive development. From these basic categories, a brief, UN-oriented typology and survey of preventive measures options might look like this:[28]

The three components of proximate prevention:

1. *Preventive peacemaking:* this group of measures is directed at preventing the possible collapse of nonviolent modes of conflict resolution through various forms of diplomatic dialogue, contact, and missions. Preventive diplomacy would be one type of peacemaking measure, involving the use of indirect and ad hoc diplomatic contacts with the contending conflict actors (e.g., informal and high-level consultations by the Secretary-General; establishment of contact groups; diplomatic démarches and sanctions). Consultations can also be held with the use of direct, ad hoc missions to the conflict area (e.g., fact-finding missions; familiarization visits; special envoys). Finally, mediation and good offices can be used to prevent the collapse of, or to reestablish, a stable political process and dialogue between conflict actors by providing various forms of direct third-party facilitation (e.g., Special Representatives of the UN Secretary-General

[SRSGs]; dialogue-building through proximity talks or prenegotiation; adjudication of discrete areas in dispute; problem-solving workshops). The good offices of the Secretary-General, in particular, have been the main locus for such peacemaking measures by the United Nations. To that end, the Secretary-General can meet with permanent representatives, foreign ministers, and heads of state; send a personal envoy to initiate talks and/or gather information; engage the help of eminent persons; discuss issues with regional leaders and regional organizations; deploy fact-finding missions; and make private or public appeals.[29]

2. *Preventive deployment:* this group of measures is directed at preventing the threat or potential use of armed force (or to prevent the spread of existing armed conflict to new areas) through preemptive positioning of military/police and/or political/human rights observers. Such deployments can monitor border areas to deter crossborder incursions (e.g., the UN Preventive Deployment in Macedonia [UNPREDEP]), as well as the political situation in high-risk areas (e.g., the UN Mission in the Central African Republic; the Organization for Security and Cooperation in Europe's [OSCE] Kosovo Verification Mission). Other political/human rights deployments could include human rights observer missions, as well as the establishment of political field offices or listening posts (e.g., the UN Peacebuilding Support Office in Bougainville). During open conflict and de-escalation phases, such deployments can supervise the withdrawal of forces and assist in demilitarization and police training (e.g., the UN Transitional Administration Mission in Eastern Slavonia, Baranja, and West Sirmium).[30]

3. *Preventive humanitarian action:* more likely to be applied after the onset of widespread violence, these measures are directed at preventing refugee and/or relief-related humanitarian disasters. Refugee-related measures would attempt to prevent the causes of forced migration (with particular emphasis on support for national protection capacity); they might involve using field offices for advocacy and information dissemination, legal and judicial capacity-building, and/or the proactive provision of protection for internally displaced persons (IDPs) within the country of origin. During postconflict peacebuilding, refugee-related measures could establish provisional reintegration strategies in advance of returns, provide reintegration assistance with community-based initiatives, and/or promote tolerance for diversity through youth education programs. Relief-related measures could focus on the prevention of violations of humanitarian norms by preparing for food security and water management in conflict zones, promoting self-sufficiency with technical cooperation, and using field offices for advocacy and dialogue with local conflict actors (e.g., for humanitarian access to conflict areas).[31] Taking a preventive approach to humanitarian action remains controversial within the relevant UN agencies,

however, and it is fair to say that operational progress in this area is more speculative than actual at the moment.

The three components of structural prevention:

1. *Preventive peacebuilding:* this broad group of measures is focused on the critical objective of preventing threats to core aspects of human security from causing conflict escalation. Measures in this category should thus focus on the sectors of governance, human rights, societal stability, and economic factors.

On *governance,* the objective would be to prevent the paralysis or breakdown of legitimate governance and political processes in the regulation of nonviolent confrontation and conflict between groups.[32] Specific measures could include the promotion of participatory democratic development through programs that would establish regular forums for multiparty dialogue and decentralized power-sharing; technical assistance to reform deficient governance institutions (e.g., constitution, judiciary, police, civil service); the promotion of civil society development and the role of local NGOs in interest aggregation; and the monitoring/supervision of transitional elections and plebiscites.

On *human rights,* the objective would be to prevent the systematic violation of human rights (particularly civil and political rights), as well as to protect and promote respect for human rights in conflict situations. Specific measures could include the use of field missions for monitoring and investigation; technical cooperation for building national capacity in protection and plans of action and for legislative, judicial, and penal reform; promotion of the recognition of group and minority rights; and training in human rights law for the military, police, and judiciary. These sectors lie at the heart of the peacebuilding agenda; in the case of governance, it can be hoped that the United Nations will focus more of its energies on developing the same broad range of measures that it has developed in the human rights sector.

On *societal stability,* the objective would be to prevent the polarization of social relations between different groups within a society (particularly between an ethnic/religious majority and minorities) from leading to political crisis and violence. Specific measures could include the promotion of intercommunity dialogue and cooperation (e.g., in development, reconstruction, education, and social welfare programs); promotion of free media; community-based conflict resolution programs; reintegration programs for former combatants; and promotion of intercommunity recognition through peace and truth/reconciliation commissions.

On *economic factors,* the objective would be to prevent the impact of economic crisis and transition from contributing to political violence and to prevent the escalation of conflict through war economies. Specific measures could include programs to alleviate resource scarcity (e.g., water, land) in unstable regions; closure of market access for militant-controlled resources (e.g., diamonds); economic incentives for demobilization (e.g., youth training and micro-credit schemes); and income-generation programs for returning refugees/IDPs.

2. *Preventive disarmament:* this group of measures is directed at preventing the easy recourse to armed violence by conflict actors by reducing or circumscribing their access to and/or deployment of weaponry. Specific measures could include the promotion of voluntary arms moratoriums; arms embargoes; assistance to national authorities in the prevention of illegal arms trade; establishment of demilitarized zones during conflict; demobilizing child soldiers; the decommissioning and destruction of arms; conversion of military facilities; technical assistance for secure arms storage; and weapons buy-back programs.[33] Demobilization and decommissioning arms, when not guaranteed by a stable peace agreement, often require the direct support of a strong security force (e.g., KFOR, the North Atlantic Treaty Organization [NATO]–led force in Kosovo). The United Nations itself has little in the way of specific measures to compel armed factions to disarm and support the prevention of conflict, where those factions are opposed to prevention as such.

3. *Preventive development:* this group of measures is directed at preventing the emergence of intergroup polarization and hostility within society through the promotion of social norms of tolerance and strategies to manage potential economic inequity and crisis. *Social* measures could include: education programs to promote tolerance and recognition of differences; technical cooperation for human rights education; social welfare and health care programs to address the needs of vulnerable groups (e.g., children, minorities); support for community-based conflict resolution processes (e.g., councils of elders). *Economic* measures could include programs to alleviate poverty in marginalized groups (e.g., ethnic and indigenous minorities); and strategies to address inequitable patterns of economic development and to prevent discrimination (e.g., reforms to improve access to land titles and credit).

In the prioritization of these various types of preventive measures, it is important to make a planning connection back to the causes of protracted conflict in the given situation. As argued above, causes should be viewed in temporal as well as sectoral terms, and that logic is also important in the planning and implementation of the available range of preventive measures. This is to say that specific preventive measures (e.g., fact-finding missions, technical assistance for decentralization) should be targeted and adjusted to address specific key causes of conflict (e.g., political process breakdown, overcentralized governance).

Even though these broad types of preventive measures are all within the operational capacity of the UN system, the organization cannot field all of them with equal effectiveness in every situation. Inevitably, it is stronger in some areas than others: proximate peacemaking (particularly good offices) rather than structural programs to promote democratic governance; military observers rather than robust projection of peace enforcement; technical assistance on human rights and rule of law rather than the provision of interim judicial and penal authorities. In Kosovo and East Timor, the United Nations has called on the provision of regional military capability (in KFOR and the multinational force INTERFET, respectively) to establish a security umbrella for civilian peace support operations. Thus, there are certain preventive measures that the UN can and should look to other organizations to provide, where such organizations are able to apply the necessary resources in a manner consistent with clear comparative advantage. An example here would be the capacity of the OSCE to organize transitional elections in the Balkans, such as the highly successful October 2000 municipal elections in Kosovo.

Within an organization's options analysis, each potential option (or means) for achieving a specific sectoral objective should be assessed for its situational advantages and disadvantages. Again, an option may be advantageous at one phase of conflict escalation, but less so at a later phase. An option that appeared to be successful in an entirely different conflict may be unsuited to the specific situation at hand, even if the two conflicts appear to be at roughly the same phase of escalation. In examining the advantages and disadvantages that attend any potential option, it is also important for there to be some form of risk assessment. This will ascertain the degree to which any particular option is consistent with a corresponding objective, as well as the relative potential for each option to successfully produce the desired outcome. Such risk assessment of options would clearly identify the criteria used in making such an evaluation; it would also look at whether the combination of certain optional measures would undermine or enhance the superordinate objective of sustainable peace. Finally, the projection of scenarios, an important aspect of any planning process, could be carried out at this stage. Potential options for preventive measures should be analyzed in terms of their projected operational outcomes, as well as the net effect that such outcomes would be expected to have on the temporal development of the conflict. Anticipated and worst-case scenarios should be projected on this basis and include some consideration of the possible outcomes of nonengagement by external actors.

Integration

The political, social, economic, human rights, and military measures referred to above are all supported (if not all to the same level of capacity) by extant frameworks for operational planning and implementation within the UN system and in many bilateral donor agencies. But one should not draw the conclusion that most of these existing programs have simply been cast in newly fashionable preventive garb. Apart from the identification of operational objectives and options analysis, the final element in the formulation of preventive strategy is the integration of a range of specific sectoral measures into a coherent and concerted plan of action. As argued above, contextual analysis of the conflict situation is key, for it points to the combination of measures that must be brought together into strategic, and thus genuinely preventive, action. Specific measures must be tailored to address the nature of the situation, particularly the dynamic interaction of the key conflict causes. There are no standard models, in contrast to the impression that generic lists of prevention "tools" might convey.

This means that preventive measures cannot simply be replicated from past cases. Knowing that one particular measure worked at one time tells policymakers little, as it has been abstracted from the important contextual factors in which that success took place. A specific measure P may have worked in conflict X, but only because it was combined with measures Q and R, and only because the conflict was characterized in that phase by the combination of conflict factors $p+q+r$. The simple listing of the successful preventive measure P in conflict X thus strips away this critical contextual information. It leaves practitioners with the false sense that preventive measures can be selected from a generic list of options based on past performance. Such information also tends to elide the reality that measures that worked for one type of organization (e.g., the U.S. Agency for International Development) may well not work for another (e.g., the UN Development Programme [UNDP]) because of differences in mandate and capacity. Finally, some conflict causes may not be amenable to any form of preventive engagement. It should be emphasized that prioritizing engagement with the structural causes of political process breakdown is often central to a targeted prevention strategy.

In integrating a range of specified options for preventive measures, it is thus important for an organization such as the United Nations to determine the required combination of measures for optimal impact. The specific measures, as determined through options analysis, should address the various objectives of the strategy in an accurate and sustainable manner and should also be mutually complementary in their support of a sustainable peace process. Notwithstanding the need for a proactive approach to the prevention of structural causes of conflict, it is also important to note that not all organizations or governmental agencies will be equally suited to engaging structural causes in this manner. This is particularly true where targeted, long-term incentives ("carrots") may be required to engage key conflict actors (e.g., reconstruction programs, economic investment). For example, within the UN system, only the World Bank and UNDP can provide development program funds, which may have to be integrated with the political and military instruments provided by other departments or agencies.[34] Exacerbating the dilemma of evolving a systematic approach, governmental donor agencies often pursue bilateral forms of aid in conflict zones rather than consolidating such support into a single strategy led by a lead organization on the ground, such as the United Nations.

Moreover, proximate causes and the conflict actors responsible for them cannot simply be ignored. Both types of conflict causes should be dealt with in a comprehensive preventive strategy, and it follows that the effective prevention of different types of causes will involve the cooperation of a range of different actors and agencies, from intergovernmental agencies to NGOs. Although some will be best placed to engage conflict actors in the preventive management of proximate causes such as specific policies or acts, others will be better suited to the longer-term amelioration of structural conditions of human insecurity present in the society. Norwegian Minister of Foreign Affairs Thorbjørn Jagland recently called for UN-focused efforts to bring crisis management, humanitarian relief, development, and peacebuilding into a more "integrated approach" to the "root causes" of conflict.[35] Similarly, the SRSG for Macedonia, Henryk Sokalski, noted in 1996 that a "multifunctional approach" to "timely preventive action" was required, as "the challenges involved in its practical application cannot be met by any one instrument in isolation."[36] However, if several different organizations and agencies may be involved (as would often be the case), a lead agency should be identified to provide overall coordination of the prevention strategy. Interagency coordination is very difficult to achieve in practice and yet is one of the most important elements to incorporate into both the planning and implementation of an effective preventive strategy. Successful implementation of an integrated strategy will rely to a great degree on the operational leadership of a lead agency, which should have the necessary mandate and authority to coordinate unity of effort in the field.

Implementing Preventive Action

The final elements in the planning process make the connection between the formulation of integrated preventive action strategies and the translation of such strategies into operational action on the ground. In arguing that most preventive action operations will involve the coordination of several different organizations, the important consideration of comparative advantage arises. Where can each organization, such as the United Nations, contribute successfully to the promotion of a sustainable peace? Where and when does an organization enjoy an operational advantage in certain sectoral roles in comparison with other possible external actors? As Anthony Lake has remarked, international engagement in conflict situations cannot simply amount to a "summons to every possible task."[37]

If the answers to the above questions are not apparent in a particular conflict situation, if no clear options are discernible, it will do little good for an organization to plunge into the conflict's dynamics and risk exacerbation of its causes. Moreover, if key conflict actors are unwilling to entertain a role for an organization, it is very unlikely that that organization will be able to do anything to address the dynamics of the conflict. Although sustained engagement and dialogue with conflict actors can transform their perceptions regarding the desirability of such a role, it remains the case that key actors' rejection of external engagement by the United Nations is one of the primary reasons for the situational inability of the organization to take action on its early warning analysis.[38] In this regard, perhaps the most difficult impediment to preventive action is the continuing tendency of governments to privilege noninterference over intervention in the calculation of state interest. India and Pakistan are perhaps two of the most prominent proponents of this position, which drives the continuing intractability of the conflict over Kashmir. Macedonia, and its preemptive willingness to host the UNPREDEP operation, stands at the positive but exceptional end of the spectrum.

Assessment of organizational comparative advantage has two important elements, both of which are captured by Goulding's concept of *triage*. Triage is an analysis of whether the UN system, in whole or in part, has both the capacity and the opportunity to implement its preferred preventive measures strategically in a given situation. In light of a consolidated options analysis, triage can assess the net potential for UN engagement to be successful and places a priority on those situations that offer the greatest prospects for success. Goulding observes that conflict actors cannot be forced to accept the logic of UN engagement and notes that the United Nations' role should be "to help those who would help themselves." But he also suggests that it is necessary for the organization "to continue to explore ways of providing incentives to encourage parties to accept third party mediation and disincentives to discourage them from declining it."[39] In this effort, the assistance of key governments, multilateral forums (e.g., G-8), and/or ad hoc groups of interested states (e.g., the Contact Group on the former Yugoslavia; groups of "Friends") can play a very important role in promoting ongoing engagement and political will.

If a composite analysis suggests that an opportunity exists for a positive UN-led role, the second aspect of triage is *feasibility*. Feasibility analysis assesses the availability of and constraints upon the organization's political, diplomatic, human, and financial resources in relation to the effect their allocation would have on the calculation of options and risks. In other words, it considers whether such intraorganizational conditions and resources will affect the earlier planning assumptions made concerning available options and assessed risks. From a governmental perspective, this may also be seen as a form of "political cost-benefit analysis" and nested within the broader process of planning potential action.[40] Some organizations may in fact have an advantage over others in taking the lead role in persuading a government to accept a preventive action operation in its territory. Such was the case in the 1999 post-Rambouillet determination that the United Nations would lead the UNMIK operation in Kosovo, as the Federal Republic of Yugoslavia government objected to any lead role for the OSCE.

When the relevant decisionmaking body (such as the ECPS and/or Security Council within the UN system) has approved the recommended strategy, operational implementation entails the coordinated application of all measures to the key causes of conflict, facilitating the conflict actors and the society at large to evolve a sustainable process of de-escalation and stabilization. In this active implementation period, it is important for there to be not only strategic coordination between UN departments and agencies but also the forging of operational partnerships with those regional organizations, NGOs, and other actors that may have greater comparative advantage in addressing certain aspects of the conflict than any single UN department or agency. At the operational level, a lead agency should be deployed in theater as quickly as possible and establish procedures and management bodies for the coordination of all major preventive action components and programs. It is also important for there to be a single, authoritative lead actor to coordinate the prevention strategy and measures with the national government and local nonstate actors (e.g., militias, NGOs). Ideally, a central theater implementation staff would be formed and include representatives of all the major organizations and agencies (including local actors) involved in the implementation process. Finally, operational objectives should be translated into concrete tasks with projected timelines and expected outcomes and agreed criteria laid down to track the progress made in these tasks.[41]

In the Balkans, international attempts to prevent escalation in the breakup of Yugoslavia (1991–1992) and in Kosovo (1997–1998) were largely unsuccessful due to the absence of effective coordination of external actors as well as a clear strategy to address causal complexity with prioritized objectives.[42] However, applying lessons learned from ineffective coordination in Bosnia, UNMIK (established in June 1999) was planned as an interorganizational mission in which United Nations High Commissioner for Refugees, the OSCE, and the European Union all have well-defined roles in addition to those of the United Nations. All four organizations (or UNMIK "pillars") have their operations directly coordinated by the SRSG, as the head of UNMIK. KFOR, though not a part of UNMIK, coordinates much more closely with the mission than the NATO-led Stabilization Force does with the Office of the High Representative in Bosnia. Also, as many evaluations of international assistance in conflict zones have indicated, there is an ongoing need to ensure that all external actors (including bilateral donors) pursue forms of engagement that are mutually complementary and do not overload the absorptive capacity of the conflict actors and their society. As Väyrynen points out, external intervenors and local conflict actors must share a "minimum communality" such that they may "develop conventions" on how different preventive measures should be interpreted and implemented.[43]

But the problem remains that in applying a multisectoral strategy to the prevention of complex conflict causes, approved mandates must also be supported with the requisite levels of budgetary, human, and diplomatic support. Again, the member states of the United Nations often shrink from these implementation needs of the prevention agenda. Effective preventive action should apply the necessary measures to the dynamics of the given conflict, but the likelihood of successful engagement declines markedly if the key measures cannot be executed at the right time or in a complete manner. Governments often fail to contribute promised personnel (e.g., the slow buildup of UNMIK police, hundreds short of its authorized strength eighteen months after its establishment) and/or financial support when needed. As Barnett Rubin notes, action by a multiplicity of external partners "requires more than coordination . . . it requires genuine complementarity in pursuit of common goals."[44] International diplomacy is slowly expanding the idea of a culture of prevention, spurred by the activist policies of governments like Sweden, Norway, and Canada. But support for preventive action still remains more rhetorical than substantive. Although the slow pace of change is reflected within the UN system itself, the primary impediment to proactive engagement in conflict situations remains the reluctance of governments to view prevention in terms of state interest, if not human security. Contrary to common assumptions, this factor impedes timely action more often than the perceived lack of interagency coordination within and outside the United Nations.[45]

This brings us to the question of temporal considerations during implementation: contingency, timing, and sequencing in the application of specific preventive measures. As argued above, the effectiveness of most types of preventive measures will be a function of the phase in which they are applied. This means that in matching specific measures (e.g., technical assistance for reform of state security forces) to key conflict causes (e.g., human rights violations by state security forces), the adjustment of these measures should be contingent upon the characteristics of the particular conflict phase at hand (e.g., low-intensity violence). As Loraleigh Keashley and Ronald Fisher observe:

> A contingency approach to third-party intervention is based on the assessment that social conflict involves a dynamic process in which the objective and subjective elements interact over time as the conflict escalates and de-escalates. Depending on the objective-subjective mix, different interventions will be appropriate at different stages of the conflict.[46]

In a phase of escalating to high-intensity violence, for example, technical assistance may be less effective than efforts to promote the cantonment or withdrawal of security forces from populated areas.

Preventive measures should also be timed in their execution, such that they engage conflict dynamics and actors at the most optimal opportunity, recognizing that to some extent the measures themselves are meant to facilitate and expand such opportunities. This calls for some consideration of whether there would be an optimal point of entry for a specific measure (and if so when), in order to achieve the intended objective. Where such timing is relevant, there should be further assessment of the time required to plan and implement such a measure, as compared to its optimal point of entry.[47] Within the specific phase of escalation characterizing the given conflict, operational objectives may also have to be addressed in a certain sequence. In other words, it may well be the case that one measure (e.g., cantonment of security forces) cannot be secured unless and until another is employed first (e.g., mediated unilateral ceasefire on behalf of opposition militias, moratorium on public demonstrations). The optimal sequencing of measures should thus be determined in advance of their being implemented, particularly where such sequencing considerations involve the coordination of action by more than one organization or agency. In sum, such issues as contingency, timing, and sequencing may be as central to the success of an integrated prevention strategy as the measures themselves. As I. William Zartman notes:

> Often the key to effectiveness is a matter of judging timing in circumstances where both knowledge of appropriate opportunities and the operational ability to seize them remain uncertain. In both prevention and management the window of opportunity is frequently very narrow; situations do not come in standard types and sizes.[48]

Finally, the implementation of preventive action entails the ongoing monitoring and evaluation of the impact of preventive measures on the conflict situation. How have the preventive action operations affected the conjunction of causal factors, as well as the role and position of the conflict actors? Where necessary, such "conflict impact assessments" can act as a basis for the iterative adjustment of the objectives, the specific measures, or of the larger implementation strategy. More broadly, it can be argued that preventive action should be evaluated according to its contribution to the emergence of an "internal democratic peace."[49] With such measures as human rights and election monitoring/technical assistance contributing to the promotion of democratic governance processes (including the principle of internal self-determination), this would emphasize the centrality of assuring the structural solidity of participatory democracy and minority rights in a sustainable peace process. This would be consonant with the irreducibly political nature of preventive action and its necessary focus on the potential breakdown of political processes in divided societies. However, as Rubin observes, external intervenors "who see themselves as . . . aiming to prevent or resolve conflict are themselves part of the political process that generates and reproduces the conflict."[50]

Such holistic attention to the overall sustainable consolidation of democratic institutions thus raises questions of when and how to terminate preventive action operations. Indicators used for tracking conflict causes in early warning analysis can be used here to determine the point at which external engagement has met its specific objectives and may thus be ended. In the event that certain programs, missions, and/or agencies depart, follow-on arrangements for long-term development programs in collaboration with local actors will be important to determine. Such planning should also incorporate, as early as possible, guidelines for the phased transfer (or "nationalization") of program control to the local authorities.

Conclusion

For the effective planning of preventive action operations, organizations such as the United Nations need to take a context-specific approach to the analysis of causes and the coordination of preventive measures. Accordingly, effective preventive action is based upon making explicit planning connections between: (a) the causal dynamics in a given conflict; (b) a concerted strategy to address those dynamics; and (c) the strategic execution of corresponding preventive measures on the ground. At this time, however, a nascent international recognition of the importance of taking strategic approaches to the prevention of conflict is outpacing the concrete willingness of key governments to give effect to the principle with timely and well-resourced preventive action operations. This means that even though the United Nations and other relevant organizations and agencies are improving their ability to plan and coordinate policies and operations, they remain constrained by a lack of diplomatic and budgetary capacity.

This disjuncture calls for innovations in the proactive application of existing resources, as well as an interorganizational commitment to combining various measures into concerted operational coordination on the ground, both between external intervenors and in capacity-building with local actors. More than anything else, perhaps, the growing emphasis on preventive action calls for making these cross-sector interventions *real* in a proactive but practical manner, through the timely application of targeted strategies. Recent international efforts in Macedonia suggest that preventive action *will* increasingly move from rhetoric to policy and substantive operations, and the planning of context-specific strategies holds the possibility that this progress can be made with the interests of those peoples affected by conflict (and perhaps even, in time, of their governments) kept firmly in view. In this endeavor, those advocating a culture of prevention will have to redouble their efforts to ensure that coordination not only occurs across sectors but also fosters an increasing convergence of interests with national governments and local populations in the prevention of protracted conflict and the promotion of sustainable peace.

Notes

This chapter draws upon background research and content development conducted for the joint UN Department of Political Affairs–UN Staff College project on Early Warning and Preventive Measures. For their thoughtful comments on various aspects of the material discussed here, I wish to thank my fellow Design and Development Team members Derek Boothby, George D'Angelo, and Mark Hoffman. Several individuals outside the team also provided invaluable input, particularly Sir Marrack Goulding, Bertie Ramcharan, Andrew Mack, Tapio Kanninen, Udo Janz, Jüergen Dedring, Jehangir Khan, Connie Peck, Andrei Dmitrichev, David Malone, and Fen Hampson. Finally, I would like to express my deep appreciation for all those UN staff who participated in the various workshops and meetings conducted under this project in 1999. I remain, of course, wholly responsible for the content of the chapter itself.

1. The initial formulation of the concept "preventive action" is found in Boutros Boutros-Ghali, "Report of the Secretary-General on the Work of the Organisation," UN Doc. A/50/1, 1995, para. 652.

2. United Nations, "Prevention of Armed Conflict: Report of the Secretary-General," UN Doc. A/55/985-S/2001/574, 2001, para. 160.

3. Kofi A. Annan, "Report of the Secretary-General on the Work of the Organization," UN Doc. A/54/1, 1999, paras. 24–25; United Nations, Joint Inspection Unit, "Strengthening of the United Nations System Capacity for Conflict Prevention," UN Doc. JIU/REP/95/13 (also as Annex to A/50/853, December 22, 1995), para. 156 at 33. As Boutros-Ghali also noted in 1995: "If the United Nations is to play a timely and constructive role in averting or mitigating the destructive

effects of complex crises, the various elements of the Organization must have an early, common understanding of the nature of the problem and the options for preventive action." See Boutros-Ghali, UN Doc. A/50/1, para. 644.

4. Jacob Bercovitch, "The United Nations and the Mediation of International Disputes," in *Past Imperfect, Future UNcertain: The United Nations at Fifty,* ed. Ramesh Thakur (London: Macmillan, 1998), 50.

5. Government of the Netherlands, "Early Warning and Encouraging Co-ordinated Action on Analyses of Violent Conflict Potentials," draft paper submitted for Working Group I, Topic Area IV, Sixth Task Force Meeting (Paris: OECD Development Assistance Committee, Task Force on Conflict, Peace and Development Cooperation, September 1996), 22.

6. As noted in Charles K. Cater and Karin Wermester, "From Reaction to Prevention: Opportunities for the UN System in the New Millennium" (International Policy Conference Report, Regal UN Plaza Hotel, New York: April 13–14, 2000), 5.

7. Cornelis de Rover, a Geneva-based expert on police reform, as cited in Rama Mani, "The Rule of Law or the Rule of Might? Restoring Legal Justice in the Aftermath of Conflict," in *Regeneration of War-Torn Societies,* ed. Michael Pugh (London: Macmillan, 2000), 94.

8. Greg A. Beyer, "Human Rights Monitoring: Lessons Learnt from the Case of the Issaks in Somalia," in *Early Warning and Conflict Resolution*, eds. Kumar Rupesinghe and Michiko Kuroda (London: Macmillan, 1992): 17–18, 23. Figure 8.1 is adapted from his "Situation Specific Decision-Making Process" diagram. Consequently, Beyer argues that in making these connections between early warning, coordination, and implementation of specific measures, "bridges . . . into decision-making processes are vital, if this information is to be used and have an impact on resource allocations" (ibid., 31).

9. See, for example, Ted R. Gurr, "Testing and Using a Model of Communal Conflict for Early Warning," *Journal of Ethno-Development* 4, 1 (1994): 20–24; Barbara Harff, "A Theoretical Model of Genocides and Politicides," *Journal of Ethno-Development* 4, 1 (1994): 25–30; and Alex P. Schmid, "Indicator Development: Issues in Forecasting Conflict Escalation," in *Preventive Measures: Building Risk Assessment and Crisis Early Warning Systems,* eds. John L. Davies and Ted R. Gurr (Lanham, MD: Rowman and Littlefield, 1998), 47–49.

10. Raimo Väyrynen, "Preventing Deadly Conflict: Failures in Iraq, Yugoslavia, and Kosova," paper presented at the fortieth annual convention of the International Studies Association (Washington, D.C., February 1999), 7.

11. A good example of actor analysis applied to structural factors as well is presented in Gurr's risk factors for ethnopolitical conflict: structural group *incentives* for initiating political action (particularly sources of collective grievance), group *capacity* for sustained political action, and potential for coercive versus accommodative *action* by the state. See Ted R. Gurr and Barbara Harff, *Early Warning of Communal Conflicts and Genocide* (Tokyo: United Nations University, 1996): 14–18, 32–36.

12. I wish to thank Adriaan Verheul and Connie Peck for calling these aspects of actor analysis to my attention. See Connie Peck, *The United Nations as a Dispute Settlement System* (The Hague: Kluwer for UNITAR, 1996), 140–141. On economic agendas and their policy implications, see Mats Berdal and David Keen, "Violence and Economic Agendas in Civil Wars," *Millennium: Journal of International Studies* 26, 3 (1997). The importance of actor buy-in and transformation of perceptions means that external attempts to impose a predetermined settlement are highly

unlikely to foster the cooperative engagement of key conflict actors in a stable peace. On conflict transformation, see Raimo Väyrynen, "To Settle or to Transform? Perspectives on the Resolution of National and International Conflicts," in *New Directions in Conflict Theory: Conflict Resolution and Conflict Transformation,* ed. Raimo Väyrynen (London: Sage, 1991), 2–7.

13. See, for example, the CASCON model of Lincoln P. Bloomfield and Allen Moulton, *Managing International Conflict: From Theory to Policy* (New York: St. Martin's, 1997): 99–102; and Schmid, "Indicator Development," 44–46.

14. The concept of "mutually-enticing opportunities" is a modification of I. William Zartman's well-known theory of "mutually-hurting stalemate" that emerged in workshop discussions at the Ditchley Foundation conference "Preventive Diplomacy and Conflict Resolution," December 4–6, 1998. See his own report of the conference, *Preventive Diplomacy and Conflict Resolution,* Ditchley Conference Report No. D98/15 (Ditchley Park, U.K.: Ditchley Foundation, 1999), 3; I. William Zartman, *Ripe for Resolution: Conflict and Intervention in Africa* (Oxford: Oxford University Press, 1985); and I. William Zartman, "Dynamics and Constraints in Negotiations in Internal Conflicts," in *Elusive Peace: Negotiating an End to Civil Wars,* ed. I. William Zartman (Washington, D.C.: Brookings Institution, 1996), 18.

15. Edward E. Azar refers to this proximate cause as the "built-in mechanisms of conflict." See his *The Management of Protracted Social Conflict* (Aldershot, U.K.: Dartmouth, 1990), 15; Hugh Miall, Oliver Ramsbotham, and Tom Woodhouse, *Contemporary Conflict Resolution* (Cambridge: Polity Press, 1999), 75; Morton Deutsch, "Subjective Features of Conflict Resolution: Psychological, Social, and Cultural Influences," in *New Directions in Conflict Theory,* ed. Väyrynen, 48–49: "The conflict . . . is maintained and perpetuated by the commitments and investments given rise to by the malignant conflict process itself."

16. Mats Berdal and David M. Malone, "Introduction," in *Greed and Grievance: Economic Agendas in Civil Wars,* eds. Mats Berdal and David M. Malone, a project of the International Peace Academy (Boulder: Lynne Rienner Publishers, 2000), 1–15; see also David Keen's "Incentives and Disincentives for Violence" in the same volume.

17. Bruce W. Jentleson, "Preventive Diplomacy: Analytical Conclusions and Policy Lessons," in *Opportunities Missed, Opportunities Seized: Preventive Diplomacy in the Post–Cold War World,* ed. Bruce W. Jentleson (Lanham, MD: Rowman and Littlefield, 2000), 330–331.

18. This is comparable to some extent to Azar's structural preconditions, which are the categories of governance, communal stability, needs (including economic), and international linkages (including arms supplies). See Azar, *The Management of Protracted Social Conflict,* 7–11. See also Jüergen Dedring, "Sociopolitical Indicators for Early Warning Purposes," in *Early Warning and Conflict Resolution,* eds. Rupesinghe and Kuroda, 206–211, who points to the following five comparable categories of causal indicators: governance, particularly oppressive, weak, or corrupt government; social unrest and divergence of principles between groups; human rights violations; ethnic polarization, particularly in combination with discrimination; and environment.

19. See Antonia Handler Chayes, Abram Chayes, and George Raach, "Beyond Reform: Restructuring for More Effective Conflict Intervention" (Cambridge: Conflict Management Group Working Paper, November 1996), 26.

20. Sir Marrack Goulding, "Practical Measures to Enhance the United Nations' Effectiveness in the Field of Peace and Security," report submitted to the

UN Secretary-General, New York, June 1997, para. 3.14 at 17. This capacity-building for working-level analysis and planning began in earnest in 1998–1999. The UN Early Warning and Preventive Measures (EWPM) project has since developed an early warning methodology that can serve as a common analytical language for the various UN departments and agencies responsible for the joint planning of preventive action. For further detail, see my "Early Warning Analysis and Policy Planning in UN Preventive Action," in *Conflict Prevention: Path to Peace or Grand Illusion?* eds. David Carment and Albrecht Schnabel (Tokyo: United Nations University Press, 2001).

    21. United Nations, "Report of the Panel on United Nations Peace Operations," UN Doc. A/55/305-S/2000/809, August 21, 2000, paras. 65–74 at 12–13. A very similar recommendation was made in the Goulding report of 1997 (see paras. 12.15–12.18).

    22. One recent study, drawing on operational lessons learned in Bosnia, has advocated the use of integrated Civil-Military Implementation Staff teams at both the strategic (headquarters) and operational (field) levels. See George A. Joulwan and Christopher C. Shoemaker, *Civilian-Military Cooperation in the Prevention of Deadly Conflict* (Washington, D.C.: Carnegie Commission on Preventing Deadly Conflict, December 1998), 20–22.

    23. See Jonathan Moore, *The UN and Complex Emergencies* (Geneva: UNRISD, 1996): 18–19.

    24. United Nations, "Prevention of Armed Conflict," paras. 162–168.

    25. Ismat Kittani, "Preventive Diplomacy and Peacemaking: The UN Experience," in *Peacemaking and Peacekeeping for the New Century*, eds. Olara A. Otunnu and Michael W. Doyle (Lanham, MD: Rowman and Littlefield, 1998), 105.

    26. Luc van de Goor and Suzanne Verstegen, *Conflict Prognosis: A Conflict and Policy Assessment Framework*, vol. 2 (The Hague: Clingendael—Netherlands Institute for International Relations, 2000), 21. This study was commissioned by the Ministry of Foreign Affairs of the Netherlands.

    27. See Boutros Boutros-Ghali, "An Agenda for Peace: Preventive Diplomacy, Peacemaking, and Peace-keeping—Report of the Secretary-General," UN Doc. A/47/277-S/24111, June 17, 1992, paras. 20–22; Boutros Boutros-Ghali, "Supplement to An Agenda for Peace: Position Paper of the Secretary-General," UN Doc. A/50/60-S/1995/1, January 3, 1995, paras. 23–65; Boutros-Ghali, UN Doc. A/50/1, para. 652 at 193; United Nations, "Strengthening of the United Nations System Capacity for Conflict Prevention: Note by the Secretary-General," UN Doc. A/52/184, June 24, 1997, Annex para. 10; United Nations, "Achievement of Effective Prevention Is Testament to Succeeding Generations 'That Ours Had the Will to Save Them from the Scourge of War,'" Press Release SG/SM/6454, February 5, 1998 (Secretary-General's Address on the Final Report of the Carnegie Commission on Preventing Deadly Conflict); Annan, UN Doc. A/54/1, paras. 36–47; United Nations, Security Council, "Role of the Security Council in the Prevention of Armed Conflicts," UN Doc. S/PRST/1999/34, November 30, 1999; and United Nations, "Prevention of Armed Conflict," paras. 61–136. Additional description of four types of measures may also be found in Boutros Boutros-Ghali, "Challenges of Preventive Diplomacy," in *Preventive Diplomacy*, ed. Kevin M. Cahill (New York: Basic Books, 1996), 18–21.

    28. The specific measures here are intended to be illustrative rather than comprehensive. Most are drawn from my larger EWPM project document, *Typology and Survey of Preventive Measures* (Turin, Italy: United Nations Staff College, Early Warning and Preventive Measures Project, May 1999). This is available online at

www.itcilo.it/unscp/ and lists more than 130 different specific preventive measures in these six broad categories.

29. Consultations with senior officers in the Executive Office of the UN Secretary-General (EOSG) and in the UN Department of Political Affairs (DPA), New York, October 1998. See also Cyrus R. Vance and David A. Hamburg, *Pathfinders for Peace: A Report to the UN Secretary-General on the Role of Special Representatives and Personal Envoys* (Washington, D.C.: Carnegie Commission on Preventing Deadly Conflict, 1997).

30. Consultations with senior officers in the Office of the High Commissioner for Human Rights, Department of Peacekeeping Operations (DPKO), and DPA, Geneva and New York, September-October 1998. See also Stephen T. Ostrowski, "Preventive Deployment of Troops as Preventive Measures: Macedonia and Beyond," *New York University Journal of International Law and Politics* 30, 3–4 (1998): 793–880.

31. Consultations with senior officers in UNHCR and OCHA, Geneva and New York, September-October 1998. See also, I. Khan, "Report of the Consultation on Prevention" (Geneva: UNHCR, February 18–20, 1997).

32. The development of new forms of coordinated preventive peacebuilding action on governance could form the basis of closer operational cooperation between DPA and UNDP, whose expanding activities tend to converge around the concept of governance. See also the similar point made in the "Report of the Panel on United Nations Peace Operations," para. 240.

33. Consultations with senior officers in the UN Department of Disarmament Affairs (DDA) and DPA, New York, October 1998. See also Edward J. Laurance, "Small Arms, Light Weapons, and Conflict Prevention: The New Post–Cold War Logic of Disarmament," in *Cases and Strategies for Preventive Action,* ed. Barnett R. Rubin (New York: Century Foundations Press, 1998), 135–167.

34. Lilly R. Sucharipa-Behrmann and Thomas M. Franck, "Preventive Measures," *New York University Journal of International Law and Politics* 30, 3–4 (1998): 502.

35. Thorbjorn Jagland, "Conflict Prevention and the Role of the United Nations," Opening Statement at the thirteenth annual meeting of the Academic Council on the United Nations System, Oslo, June 16, 2000.

36. Henryk J. Sokalski, "Preventive Action: The Need for a Comprehensive Approach," in *Preventive Action in Theory and Practice: The Skopje Papers,* eds. Jeremy Ginifer, Espen Barth Eide, and Carsten Ronnfeldt (Oslo: Norwegian Institute of International Affairs, 1999), 65.

37. Anthony Lake, "After the Wars—What Kind of Peace?" in *After the Wars,* ed. Anthony Lake (New Brunswick, NJ: Transaction for ODC, 1990), 16.

38. Consultations with senior officers in EOSG and in DPA, New York, October 1998.

39. See Goulding, "Practical Measures to Enhance the United Nations' Effectiveness in the Field of Peace and Security," paras. 4.7–4.8; Goulding, "Observation, Triage, and Initial Therapy: The Role of Fact-Finding Missions and Other Techniques," in *Preventive Diplomacy,* ed. Cahill, 144–153.

40. Van de Goor and Verstegen, *Conflict Prognosis,* 84–85.

41. Joulwan and Shoemaker, 38.

42. Väyrynen, "Preventing Deadly Conflict," 16.

43. Ibid., 2.

44. Barnett R. Rubin with Susanna P. Campbell, "Introduction: Experience in Prevention," in *Cases and Strategies for Preventive Action,* ed. Rubin, 17.

45. Comments by former UNMIK Deputy SRSG (for UNHCR) Dennis

MacNamara to BBC World, January 9, 2001. Also interviews with Andrew Mack, Strategic Planning Unit EOSG, and Michael Møller, DPA, New York, November 13, 2000.

46. Loraleigh Keashley and Ronald J. Fisher, "A Contingency Perspective on Conflict Interventions: Theoretical and Practical Considerations," in *Resolving International Conflicts,* ed. Jacob Bercovitch (Boulder: Lynne Rienner Publishers, 1996), 240. See also Ronald J. Fisher, *Interactive Conflict Resolution* (Syracuse: Syracuse University Press, 1997), 163–184; see, for the comparable use of this approach, Louis Kriesberg, "Preventing and Resolving Destructive Communal Conflicts," in *Wars in the Midst of Peace: The International Politics of Ethnic Conflict,* eds. David Carment and Patrick James (Pittsburgh: University of Pittsburgh Press, 1997), 240–246.

47. See Louis Kriesberg, "Introduction: Timing Conditions, Strategies, and Errors," in *Timing the De-escalation of International Conflicts,* eds. Louis Kriesberg and Stuart J. Thorson (Syracuse: Syracuse University Press, 1991): 1–24.

48. Zartman, *Preventive Diplomacy and Conflict Resolution,* 2.

49. Margaret Satterthwaite, "Human Rights Monitoring, Elections Monitoring, and Electoral Assistance as Preventive Measures," *New York University Journal of International Law and Politics* 30, 3–4 (1998): 764.

50. Rubin with Campbell, "Introduction: Experience in Prevention," 18.

9

Reassessing Recent Conflicts: Direct vs. Structural Prevention

Peter Wallensteen

The operational concept of conflict prevention is a post–Cold War novelty. There are earlier references to "preventive diplomacy" as well as to "preventive war" and "preemptive strikes." However, the end of the Cold War laid bare a weak international community faced with a series of crises for which it was ill-prepared. The traumas that ensued have forced collective learning. One lesson is that by observing early warning signs, developing agendas for early action, summoning support, implementing particular measures and sustaining collective action, the chances increase of preventing disastrous escalation and great human suffering. A further lesson is that conflict prevention requires focused attention on the structural factors that have the potential to develop into violent conflict. Conflicts stem from some form of malfunction in a society, and thus preventive measures need to be devised and implemented at a time when that society is *not* directly on the path to war.

Conflict prevention, then, is a matter of anticipating conflicts even prior to the formation of parties with incompatible goals. It involves building societies with little likelihood of violent conflict. In essence, structural prevention is a reform program for states and societies at high risk of violence.

The relationship between the two concepts of direct and structural prevention is, as a consequence, complicated. It might be a matter of sequencing. Direct prevention could come into play when actors and issues have crystallized and conflictual situations have occurred. These direct actions reduce or eliminate violence, without necessarily eliminating the conflict as such or its underlying causes. Structural prevention, conversely, is not immediately tied to the possibility of an armed conflict and involves a longer time perspective. It includes measures such as the promotion of democracy, ethnic integration, international regional cooperation, arms control, and disarmament. However, it is obvious that many of these structural measures could also be undertaken parallel to direct prevention. Thus, it is not always a matter of time-sequencing but also of affecting different parts of a society for different lengths of time.

In this chapter I aim to explore and clarify the relationship between direct and structural conflict prevention. The chapter takes direct prevention as its point of departure, analyzes the measures involved, and then delineates the potential role of structural prevention.

The phrase "conflict prevention" in this chapter is taken to mean a set of constructive actions taken by third parties to avoid the likely threat, use, or diffusion of armed force by primary parties in a political dispute. This is also referred to as "preventive action" or "preventive diplomacy." A broad spectrum of measures is customarily involved, including military action.[1] It is important to note that preventive actions are measures taken by outsiders—third parties—not by the parties themselves. The concept separates preventive action from the moves made by the primary parties as part of their own attempts to deal with or win the conflict. Furthermore, the word "constructive" indicates that these are outsiders that aim to influence the primary parties to change their behavior in favor of de-escalation and resolution. Preventive actions are thus "neutral" or at least "impartial" in their approach to a conflict. This does not exclude the possibility that a third party is closer to one side than the other; what matters is the acceptability by the primary parties of the actions taken.

The current understanding of conflict prevention is somewhat different from related concepts during the Cold War. At that time, prevention was often synonymous with preempting the actions of the other side. For instance, the strategic concerns of the nuclear superpowers were based on preventing the other side from gaining a first-strike capacity. This attitude is also often found in countries under considerable external threat and where there is an absence of a peace process. For instance, Israel's understanding of prevention was for a long time a matter of preempting the other side from initiating a war that would have threatened Israel with encirclement. However, the end of the Cold War—which began not with the fall of the Berlin Wall but earlier, notably with confidence-building measures, nuclear weapons agreements, and a rapprochement on human rights issues—brought a significant shift with regard to the concept of conflict prevention. The détente periods changed the perception of what actions were possible between the two alliances. Similarly, Israel's involvement in the Oslo peace process changed its perceptions to include a more complete set of preventive measures such as preventing terrorism, as well as regional cooperation, mutual confidence-building, and peacemaking. The perspectives in the post–Cold War era have broadened globally as well as locally.

Candidate Cases for Conflict Prevention

In many ways, conflict prevention is difficult to study. It is hard to identify cases for empirical analysis. It is also difficult to evaluate the effects of preventive actions. For instance, how do we know there is an imminent threat that is ripe for preventive action? If there is no crisis at a particular moment in time, do we know that one is likely in the near future? It is no doubt easier to establish that preventive actions have failed and that war has resulted than to show cases of preventive measures that were instrumental in producing a nonwar outcome.

Nonetheless, observers and policymakers can agree that it is possible to locate disputes that had the potential for escalating into violence. Table 9.1 presents an attempt to develop a register of cases of preventive action in the 1990s. By no means exhaustive, it provides a baseline from which to begin a discussion of direct and structural conflict prevention.

The examples in Table 9.1 are candidates for an analysis of conflicts that were contained, at least for a long enough time to claim that preventive action had an impact. The cases are divided into three basic categories of conflict: conflicts *between* states, conflicts *within* states, and conflicts *about* existing states. Table 9.1 contains almost thirty situations from the 1990s in which there is some evidence that preventive actions were taken and in which no serious violence or escalation occurred within a year of those actions. Technically speaking, this means that there was no record—within twelve months of the preventive actions—of an armed conflict being initiated between the main parties resulting in more than 1,000 battle deaths. In other words, some smaller instances of violence may have taken place, but no warlike situations occurred. It is still difficult to determine whether this should be regarded as "success" or not. Nonetheless, it suffices here to note that in the cases listed in Table 9.1 no large-scale conflict followed the preventive actions.

The inclusion of some cases is debatable. For instance, international sanctions were imposed on India and Pakistan following their nuclear tests in 1998. In 1999, a war between the two countries took place in Kashmir. It could be argued that the sanctions were imposed to prevent the development of further nuclear capacity within the two countries, rather than to reduce the danger of armed conflict along their border. It is thus possible that a nuclear, but not a conventional, confrontation was averted. However, this may be an unconvincing argument; if so, the case should be dropped

Table 9.1 Candidates for Conflict Prevention Analysis: Disputes Since the End of the Cold War

Dispute[a]	Incompatibility	Time	Outside Actor	Preventive Action
Interstate disputes				
Yugoslavia-Macedonia	Border unrest	1992–1993	UN	UN peacekeeping
Greece-Macedonia	Recognition	1992–1995	U.S., EU	Negotiations
Eritrea-Yemen	Border dispute	1993–1995	UNSG	ICJ
China-Vietnam	Island dispute	1988	Australia	Diplomacy
Uganda-Rwanda	Border unrest	1993–1994	UN	UN mission
Hungary-Slovakia	Minority issue	1993–1996	U.S., EU	OSCE
Hungary-Slovakia	Dam in border river	1993–1997		ICJ
Hungary-Romania	Minority issues	1993–1996	U.S., EU	Negotiations
Russia-Latvia	Radar installation	1994	Neighbors	Negotiations
Russia-Ukraine	Division of fleet	1992–1997	(U.S.?)	Negotiations
Botswana-Namibia	Border dispute	1995–1996		Arbitration
Greece-Albania	Border dispute	1994–1995	U.S.	Negotiations
Greece-Turkey	Island dispute	1995–1996	U.S.	Negotiations
China-Taiwan	Independence, missiles	1996	U.S.	US fleet
Cyprus-Turkey	Missiles	1997–1998	U.S.	Negotiations
Iran-Afghanistan	Diplomats killed	1998	U.S.	Negotiations
India-Pakistan	Nuclear explosions	1998–1999	U.S., EU	Sanctions

Dispute	Incompatibility	Time	Outside Actor	Preventive Action
Intrastate disputes over government				
Burundi	Government	1994–1997	OAU, UN	Negotiations
Belarus	Government	1996–	EU	Pressure
Albania	Government collapse	1996–1997	(W)EU	Peacekeeping
Zambia	Government	1997	EU	Subtle persuasion
Central African Republic	Government	1997–1999	UN	UN peacekeeping
Lesotho	Government	1998–1999	SADC	SADC peacekeeping
Zimbabwe	Government	2000	UK, region	Talks, sanctions
Yugoslavia	Government	1999–2000	EU	Sanctions
State formation disputes				
Estonia (Russians)	Minority status	1992–	OSCE	Office
Latvia (Russians)	Minority status	1992–	OSCE	Office
Ukraine (Crimea)	Autonomy	1992–1996	?	Elections
Yugoslavia (Montenegro)	Independence/force	1999–2000	NATO, EU	Positioning
Palestine	Independence	1998–1999	U.S., EU	Negotiations

Sources: Boutros Boutros-Ghali, *Unvanquished: A U.S.–UN Saga* (New York: Random House, 1999), 289; Richard Holbrooke, *To End a War* (New York: Modern Library, 1999), 61, 121–127 (Macedonia), 331–332, 367; Zsuzsanna Racsmany, "Conflict Prevention and Early Action in Albania: Too Little, Too Late," in Peter Wallensteen, ed., *Preventing Violent Conflicts: Past Record and Future Challenges* (Uppsala, Sweden: Uppsala University, Department of Peace and Conflict Research, 1998), 101–137; Wohlgemuth in Wallensteen, *Preventing Violent Conflicts*, 87–100; Michael E. Brown and Richard N. Rosecrance, eds., *The Costs of Conflict: Prevention and Cure in the Global Arena* (Lanham, Md.: Carnegie Commission on Preventing Deadly Conflict, Rowman and Littlefield, 1999); UN documentation; Peter Wallensteen and Margareta Sollenberg, "The End of International War? Armed Conflict 1989–1995," *Journal of Peace Research* 33, no. 3 (1996): 353–370; Tyler Felgenhauer, *Ukraine, Russia and the Black Sea Fleet Accords* (Princeton: Princeton University, Woodrow Wilson School of Public and International Affairs, WWS Case Study 2/99); Uppsala University, Sweden, Department of Peace and Conflict Research, Conflict Data Project.

Note: a. Disputes with a likelihood or history of violent conflict, where third parties acted to contain the conflicts and where no major armed conflict was initiated within the following twelve months.

from the list. Similarly, international action in Burundi following the coup and massacres in 1993 can be regarded as preventive, since the genocide in Rwanda half a year later did not spread into Burundi. Avoiding spillover from Rwanda was in fact the goal of international action in Burundi; but it did not end the fighting there, and in 1998 the internal armed conflict in Burundi was recorded as a war.[2] The cases of Russia-Ukraine and Ukraine (Crimea) are also disputable for different reasons, namely, whether there was important outside third-party activity or not. The roles of the United States in the former, and Russia and the Organization for Security and Cooperation in Europe (OSCE) in the latter, remain to be uncovered. Suffice it to say that the cases provide a starting point for an empirically based discussion of conflict prevention.

A first observation is that the list includes more interstate conflicts than we would expect from the fact that armed conflicts since the Cold War were largely internal. In fact, the record of ongoing armed conflict suggests that the numbers of intrastate wars as well as state formation disputes are equally high and, taken together, are about ten times greater than the number of interstate conflicts.[3] This can be understood in two different ways. A positive reading is that there are more instruments in place to handle interstate conflicts and that they are functioning more often and more effectively than might be expected. This could even explain the relatively low number of actual interstate armed conflicts—they are simply solved at the dispute stage. In some instances, direct action was required to bring the parties to acquiesce to the resolution of the dispute by, for instance, the International Court of Justice. However, the existence and effective operation of such institutions points in turn to the utility of structural prevention: by creating institutions for conflict resolution, more conflicts become manageable. A negative reading is that interstate conflicts get more attention and, as a consequence, will see greater preventive effort from outside third parties. There could be many more internal disputes that were on the brink of a serious crisis that were instead handled by local actors or not reported at all. The underreporting of these cases is a serious problem, often a result of diplomatic pressure not to bring attention to them. To remedy this, there is a need to search energetically for cases relating to the prevention of internal conflicts.

The reporting problem can be understood more fully upon closer observation of the second category: intrastate conflicts over governments. These are conflicts that dispute the positions of political power in a country. Much political life is about the control over such posts, and most countries experience a certain amount of tension as a result. Consequently, it is not easy for the outside world to assess which of these are likely to escalate into violence and, thus, when to take preventive action. Furthermore, even if such actions are undertaken, they are not easily reported, and it is not simple to claim success.

This can be illustrated by the case of Zambia in 1997. The situation had to do with tension between the former president of the country, Kenneth Kaunda, and his successor, F.J.T. Chiluba. In 1997, a crisis erupted: shots were fired, and there was an attempted coup against the incumbent government. The European Union undertook low-key diplomatic actions, and the conflict did not escalate into violence. Tension then subsided. Unsurprisingly, the Chiluba government took the credit for having prevented the escalation of tension. Moreover, in a gesture of good relations, international actors did not quarrel with this, particularly since the third parties did not have an interest in undermining the legitimacy of the incumbent government by claiming they had been instrumental in directing its actions. It is possible that many more such cases exist in diplomatic archives.

Caution on the part of outsiders is typical of many internal disputes. Their actions are tailored precisely so as not to attract attention. It is thought that the matter can be handled with the right amount of persuasion. At the same time, few governments will admit that they were persuaded by external actors to pursue particular courses of action. As a whole, this means that there will necessarily be public underreporting of preventive action in internal disputes. What we clearly see in Table 9.1 is that interstate conflicts are likely to attract higher, more public, and more immediate attention compared to intrastate conflicts. This means that direct preventive action is likely to be taken in internal conflicts only when there are some highly visible events that call on the international community to act.

Table 9.1 gives some examples. Interest in Burundi increased after the November 1993 massacres. The situation in Albania was attended to only after the collapse of the pyramid schemes in early 1997. Zimbabwe became internationally interesting in 2000 when European-owned farms were occupied. The internal affairs of Yugoslavia drew more attention following the Kosovo conflict and NATO bombings there in mid-1999. However, these are probably exceptional cases, and a large fraction of internal conflicts is likely to be and remain outside the scope of direct preventive action. Importantly, this provides a window of opportunity for structural prevention, particularly in many internal situations, as such action does not need or receive the same visibility. Rather, structural prevention is an integral part of long-term development strategy, which appears to be less intrusive.

A third general observation is that the category of state formation conflicts is the smallest, although we would expect it to be at least equal in size to the category of intrastate disputes over government. State formation conflicts are cases where the dispute focuses on the status of particular territories (for instance, with groups demanding autonomy, independence, joining neighboring countries). Several other serious cases were brought to a stand-still through cease-fires or other arrangements, such as Nagorno-Karabakh, Abkhazia, and Chechnya. Chechnya illustrates how a conflict, seemingly managed, can quickly escalate into war as a result of a rapid sequence of events. This was the case in the autumn of 1999, and Russia refused to let outside actors interfere. The Chechen conflict suggests that cease-fire agreements and volatile peace agreements need to be constantly monitored for the danger of escalation. It also shows the extreme sensitivity of central governments to international involvement in conflicts, which call into ques-tion the territorial integrity of the state. Again, state formation conflicts are perhaps better suited to long-term structural prevention, rather than direct action that may be unfeasible or too late.

The Palestinian crisis is the most obvious example of a state formation conflict. The situation referred to in Table 9.1 was sparked by Palestinian president Yassir Arafat's unilateral threat to declare independence when the Oslo peace process formally expired on May 4, 1999. In the Palestinian view, this was simply the culmination of the declaration of independence already issued in 1988. From the Israeli perspective, such a declaration would mark the end of the peace process and force Israel to respond accordingly in order to maintain control. The threat of crisis was credible, and escalation into armed confrontation became likely. In an effort to defuse tension, a series of diplomatic and political initiatives were launched. Most important among these were the summit negotiations at Wye Plantation, Maryland, in October 1998. It saw the participation of U.S. president Bill Clinton, Israeli prime minister Benjamin Netanyahu, King Hussein of Jordan, and Chairman Yassir Arafat. An agreement was worked out that endeavored to keep the peace process alive; it subsequently fell apart when the Israeli cabinet split over differing views on its implementa-tion. New elections were set for May 17, 1999. In the meantime, Arafat had managed to extract promises of support from the European Union and had effectively postponed his threat to declare independence. The crisis was one of brinkmanship, one from which Arafat was able to leverage some diplomatic advantages. The event gives an interesting perspective on how international support for conflict prevention, particularly at the highest lev-els, can be used as an opportunity for diplomatic and political accomplish-ment by local actors.

This was, of course, not the end of the story. Incoming Prime Minister Ehud Barak hoped for a peace agreement within a specified and short peri-od of time, offering a new window of opportunity for peace—or so it seemed. Seizing the moment, President Clinton attempted to reach an agreement at the summit meeting at Camp David in the summer of 2000. However, trust and confidence among the parties had apparently been exhausted. In late September 2000 a new Palestinian uprising began. At the time, it looked like the crisis that had been anticipated in 1998 had been successfully prevented. Two years later, however, it appeared that it may only have been postponed. This sheds additional light on the problem of identifying "successful" cases of conflict prevention. Moreover, it indicates that there are limitations regarding what can reasonably be expected from preventive action, particularly in strongly entrenched conflicts.

This does not mean that state formation conflicts are not amenable to preventive action; but it does suggest that once conflict becomes entrenched, the scope for outside impact may be more limited. Returning to Table 9.1, none of the cases in the third category has as long a history of continued and protracted conflict as Palestine. For the Russians in the former Soviet territories, it is a novel experience to be a minority. It is, similarly, a new experience for the majority population to actually take political command in their newfound country. This suggests that there is considerable scope for the international community to have an impact on the dynamics of state formation conflicts and participate in the building of new states in the future. For instance, the OSCE was very important in the Baltic cases of Estonia and Latvia (listed in Table 9.1), operating there, as in many other instances, somewhere in between direct and structural prevention. Conversely, the post-Soviet relationship of Moldova developed quite differently, possibly because of a lack of international involvement. It would be interesting to pursue a comparative analysis of the post-Soviet cases in an effort to shed light on the effectiveness of direct prevention.

Predicting Escalation and Taking Early Action

Interstate armed conflicts are the ones that are the least likely to come as a surprise to the international community. Many of the disputes mentioned in Table 9.1 are familiar to decisionmakers and analysts: unsettled border questions, minorities with "their" majority on the other side of a border, incompatible claims on islands, documented historical grievances. This being the case, it is remarkable that there has been little forward-looking action to find settlements prior to the crises that generate great suffering and attention. In fact, many interstate conflicts are frozen in an uneasy state of affairs. To predict that they are dangerous is not difficult. But to specify more exactly *when* acute danger will arise is more problematic. It may, however, be possible to construct a register of unsolved or contested international situations. A serious preventive strategy could then attempt to act early in these cases, perhaps most usefully with structural preventive measures. By generating cooperation, interlinkages, and dialogue, potential disputes could then, ideally, simply be removed from the list.

It is more difficult to assess which internal conflicts are likely to esca-

late into severe violence and when. Even more difficult is developing effective international preventive action to respond to these conflicts. The main
obstacles are the inability to forecast internal dynamics and the reluctance
to act. It is difficult to determine if the actions of a particular government
toward its opposition will work without causing a major internal crisis. The
government may feel confident that its actions will be effective; but it may
also make serious errors. This uncertainty only compounds the difficulty
that outsiders face in attempting to predict what will happen.

The case of Malaysia in the late 1990s illustrates the complexity of
predicting the escalation of conflict. In September 1998, the deputy prime
minister of Malaysia, Ibrahim Anwar, was removed from power, put in jail,
and accused of sodomy and corruption. This sparked a serious domestic crisis, and the trial that ensued drew considerable international attention. The
fairness of the Malaysian court was brought into question. At a summit
meeting in Kuala Lumpur, U.S. vice president Al Gore expressed support
for the slogan "Reformasi" used by the opponents—a move, effectively, to
warn Malaysia and ask it to be more accommodating to its critics. Instead,
the government, under Dr. Mohamad Mahatir, reacted negatively to what
was seen as domestic interference. He suggested that the West was turning
against Malaysia. In early 1999, Anwar was found guilty on some of the
charges that were brought against him. Despite the fact that Anwar's wife,
running on Anwar's platform, won a seat in parliament, Mahatir's power
remained unbroken, for the time being.

No doubt, this was an unusually sharp internal confrontation by
Malaysian standards. Only some months earlier in neighboring Indonesia,
student protests had led to the overthrow of the Suharto regime. This, compounded by a severe economic crisis and the potential for ethnic cleavages
in Malaysia, may have created the conditions under which escalation into
violence was possible. The situation seemed ripe for early preventive
action. However, the conflict did not escalate. Moreover, international pressure neither improved the position of the opposition nor reduced the level
of confrontation. Instead, the Malaysian government manipulated reactions
by the international community to strengthen its own position in the country. Although this may not be the end of the story, immediate international
attention to the internal affairs of Malaysia subsided.

It is likely that there are many more government crises that do not
escalate into violence and where international action may in fact be counterproductive. The dilemma is that the longer the international community
waits to act, the more difficult it becomes to intervene at all. This makes it
very difficult to judge how outsiders can help to bring about nonviolent
change in authoritarian governments. Southeast Asia at the time of the
financial crisis of 1997–1998 is another example. Regime transition
occurred without violence or international political pressure in Thailand

and Korea in 1997, whereas in Indonesia the transition was accompanied by violence. This suggests that the prior existence of legitimate structures and democratic forces may be a necessary condition for nonviolent change. It is equally possible that a clear conflict prevention strategy may have had an impact. However, there was none. The reluctance of outsiders to intervene in support of change could be explained by the fear of stimulating counterreactions, such as those that were ignited in Malaysia, or even fear of increasing tension. If the outside world supports a particular government, those outsiders risk becoming the target of counterdemonstrations. If it acts to undermine the incumbent government, it risks spurring a military coup. Faced with these unattractive options, the balance will often tilt in favor of nonaction—in essence, a wait-and-see policy.

It is probably true that only a small number of unusually sharp government-opposition confrontations will result in violence and war. A list of potential internal armed conflicts could easily include most countries in the world; but most countries do not experience civil war. To date, the routes from minor tension to large-scale internal war are not sufficiently well identified. Perhaps the most important clue lies in whether there has previously been an internal war.[4] The manner in which the conflict was handled internally and externally is likely to have a strong impact on how the government and the opposition treat new issues. Furthermore, focusing on societies or countries that have experienced internal war and on the use of development cooperation to bridge rather than reinforce old divides can offer insights into the way in which structural prevention could be instrumental in cases at risk of violent conflict.[5]

The difficulties of international involvement in the internal affairs of states are even more acute in state formation conflicts. Not only are these conflicts difficult to detect early; typically, the government in control of the disputed territory actively prevents the international community from becoming involved with the rebel groups when the conflict becomes explicit. As many leaders in outside states face similar threats, they are reluctant to set potential precedents that can turn against them. From the perspective of the government, the establishment of any kind of relations by rebels with outsiders is tantamount to a challenge to its right to rule. For the opposition, the reverse is, of course, true: international action vindicates the "justice" of its struggle. Given these opposing poles, we would expect early action by the international community in state formation conflicts to be rare, at least at the open, diplomatic level. This observation is confirmed by noting that issues such as Tibet in China, Aceh in Indonesia, Corsica in France, Samis in Scandinavia, Montenegro in Yugoslavia, and Native Americans in the United States rarely come up in intergovernmental fora. Little or no international action has been planned in most of these cases. Heavy involvement in Palestine and, remarkably, in Kosovo from 1998 onward can perhaps be understood only from the perspective of the actual or potential regional implications of these conflicts.

The reluctance to act preventively early on in state formation conflicts is particularly tragic from a human rights point of view. State formation conflicts are often based on the manipulation of identity groups that in turn give dissenters an important and highly charged pool from which to recruit. The creation of shared experiences of domination is an additional incentive for escalation. At the same time, these groups are easy targets for repression that does not distinguish between actors and bystanders. In other words, violations of human rights, and at times genocide, may be particularly strong in conflicts involving identity groups.

The cases in Table 9.1 are thus instructive on a variety of different levels. They have been handled at the international level via interstate agreements or through international organizations. In Europe, the OSCE has been more active than, for instance, the United Nations. This could be due to its unintrusive nature, as well as the fact that it does not represent the interests of any particular major power. The UN Commissioner for Human Rights could play a similar role in other conflicts. For state formation conflicts, it is urgent that special tools be developed by the international community both to enhance understanding of the internal dynamics and to prevent the escalation of violence. This is a particularly difficult task and places the onus on structural preventive measures, including strategies such as supporting constitutional guarantees and social integration, as well as reducing political control by some ethnic groups (ethnocracy) in order to enlarge democratic space.

Forms of Preventive Action

Preventive action can be formulated according to a ladder of action with different degrees of engagement by and imposition on the parties.[6] Table 9.1 includes cases where the level of intensity of preventive action varies considerably. It appears, for instance, that most cases are handled through some form of negotiation, involving the international community and/or the primary parties themselves. Negotiation is the form of action that is the least intrusive and thus the most acceptable and still means that the disputes are given international recognition, which in itself can stimulate the parties toward settlement.

In some cases in Table 9.1, conflict prevention involved more comprehensive action. The table shows four examples of major international peace operations. A UN peacekeeping mission, defined as a preventive deployment, was stationed in Macedonia from 1993 to 1999. Another UN mission was sent to the Central African Republic in 1998. A European force under

Italian command was deployed in Albania for some months in 1997, and a force formally under the Southern Africa Development Council was stationed in Lesotho in 1998. These are the largest preventive peace operations to date, unusual not least because they are costly and difficult to administer. Only about one-tenth of all cases of preventive action seem to elicit such strong involvement.

There is also a set of cases where sanctions, of varying degrees of intrusiveness, were applied. It is clear that sanctions were used more frequently in the 1990s than in previous decades combined. However, their efficiency has been hotly debated and remains in doubt.[7] Table 9.1 suggests that they may have a more limited but perhaps more constructive *preventive* role, if used with great care.

There are also cases where preventive action has included taking a firm stand in relation to particular developments. This positioning, which is sometimes coupled with sanctions or diplomatic moves, can be tantamount to international support for a particular solution or position in the conflict. Nonetheless, in most cases it consists of diplomatic efforts to find a political agreement or bringing the issues to the attention of particular dispute resolution mechanisms. The frequent resort to international legal procedures is noteworthy; the OSCE High Commissioner on National Minorities has also played an important role in attending to some crises.

Normally, we think of preventive actions as concrete measures that are taken so that a situation does not deteriorate. There are, of course, also nonactions that can serve the same purpose. An interesting example is the escalation of conflict in Northern Ireland in 1969. The prime minister of the Irish Republic, Jack Lynch, was under strong pressure from his own party and from opinion polls to send Irish troops across the border to protect the Catholic and Republican population in Northern Ireland. According to Ireland's constitution, the north was part of the country, making such action legal from an Irish point of view. Later, Lynch said that the plan, which was seriously entertained, aimed to get a UN peacekeeping force into the conflict. Effectively, the plan had been to deliberately internationalize a state formation conflict. Again, it is difficult to know what *would* have happened. The heading of Lynch's obituary—"A 1969 Decision Not to Invade Ulster . . . Led to a 1998 Peace Agreement"—may be an overstatement of his role in preventing escalation.[8] Lynch acted in the spirit of UN Security Council resolutions in which it is customary to ask parties not to undertake actions that can lead to further deterioration of a situation. It is also likely that Lynch was exposed to pressures not to act—indeed, to make a party refrain from acting may sometimes require as much diplomacy as making a party act. However, one thing is certain: had Irish troops entered Northern Ireland, tensions would have increased considerably on the island.

The Role of Neighbors

An analysis of basic conflicts in the regional context makes clear that neighbors are at risk under certain conditions, from some interstate conflicts but also from intrastate conflicts.[9] Many of the conflict prevention cases noted in Table 9.1 involve actors proximate to ongoing armed conflict, countries that are close to or part of a regional conflict complex. These require serious preventive action. The settlement of the dispute between Greece and Macedonia was seen as regionally stabilizing.[10] Surveying the neighborly relations in the Balkans, it is clear that there were and are many potential dangers. Obvious cases include Montenegro, which is one of the two republics of the Federal Republic of Yugoslavia (FRY), and Macedonia, after the withdrawal of UN troops in February 1999. The heavy presence of NATO troops in Kosovo and the backup facilities in Macedonia may, however, have served a similar function as the UN preventive deployment force, in the interim at least. However, the situation in Montenegro began to elicit international concern. The leadership there opposed the actions taken by Yugoslavian and Serbian authorities in Kosovo in early 1999, but Montenegro was still subject to the international sanctions against the FRY. International efforts since then have aimed to reduce the danger of escalation of conflict between the FRY and Montenegro, although efforts have waned since the fall of the Milosevic regime in Yugoslavia in October 2000. However, the underlying tension remains and the status of Montenegro remains undecided.

Several other conflicts in Table 9.1 were part of broader regional conflict complexes, notably the Uganda-Rwanda dispute that was linked to the ongoing civil war in Rwanda and tensions in Burundi. Nothing has prevented the emergence of a conflict complex in the whole Great Lakes region. In view of the destabilization of the entire region that followed, drawing in the two Congo Republics, it is obvious that only a regional perspective suffices for developing preventive strategies. Another conflict with strong regional connections is the nexus of Cyprus, Greece, and Turkey. This is an area of repeatedly contentious disputes in which acting early has become almost routine. For twenty-five years it has been possible to prevent a renewed war in the eastern Mediterranean. No solution has been found, however, and measures of structural prevention are rare.

Conclusion:
Direct and Structural Conflict Prevention

The analysis of conflict prevention would benefit from an examination of the possibilities of simultaneously using structural and direct approaches.

Both of these are operational and can accomplish different goals. They may appear to be applicable at different points in time, with structural measures designed for early dynamics and direct actions for late phases of conflict. However, this chapter illustrates how structural means can also support direct measures. At the same time, structural action may not be sufficient to prevent crises, and thus the ability to act directly must be maintained and strengthened. In fact, the two have different ambitions: structural action aims to build societies that can absorb and benefit from a certain level of conflict, whereas direct action aims to prevent conflict from becoming destructive. In policymaking, they may have different priorities at different phases of conflict, but each requires the other in order to be truly effective.

It has also been possible to identify a surprisingly large number of cases of preventive action of all types during the last decade. This indicates that without such measures the number of armed conflicts may in fact have been much higher. It also suggests that some preventive actions are taken by parties who may not necessarily see their actions as being preventive but self-motivated.

Finally, although Table 9.1 indicates that interstate conflicts are dominant, this is likely to be largely the result of biased reporting. Nonetheless, it does underline that there are many ways in which the international community acts to reduce the likelihood of armed conflicts *between* states. Identifying and acting upon *internal* conflicts, however, seems underdeveloped at present. As a result, internal conflicts are likely to arrive on the international agenda when they are already highly difficult to disentangle. In particular, structural preventive measures are currently ill-equipped to respond to regional conflict complexes, which means that direct prevention may be the only source of preventive action. During the postconflict peacebuilding phase, structural remedies once again become extremely important, and there are many lessons to be learned for the prevention of conflict through structural measures elsewhere. Strategically, structural prevention offers an important opportunity to promote reforms in society in the direction of reconciliation, democracy, interethnic cooperation, and economic growth—measures that may in themselves be more effective over the long term to prevent the recurrence of violence.

Notes

1. See Kevin M. Cahill, ed., *Preventive Diplomacy: Stopping Wars Before They Start* (New York: Basic Books, 1996); Michael S. Lund, *Preventing Violent Conflicts: A Strategy for Preventive Diplomacy* (Washington, D.C.: United States Institute of Peace Press, 1996); Carnegie Commission on Preventing Deadly Conflict, *Preventing Deadly Conflict: Final Report* (Washington, D.C.: Carnegie Commission on Preventing Deadly Conflict, 1997); Stephen John Stedman,

"Alchemy for a New World Order: Overselling 'Preventive Diplomacy,'" *Foreign Affairs* 73, 3 (1995): 14–20; Peter Wallensteen, ed., *Preventing Violent Conflicts: Past Record and Future Challenges* (Uppsala, Sweden: Uppsala University, Department of Peace and Conflict Research, 1998); OECD/DAC, *Conflict, Peace and Development Co-operation on the Threshold of the 21st Century* (Paris: Development Co-operation Guidelines Series, OECD, 1998); Peter Uvin, *The Influence of Aid in Situations of Violent Conflict* (Paris: OECD/DAC, 1999).

2. See Lennart Wohlgemuth, "Conflict Prevention in Burundi: A Case Study," in Wallensteen, *Preventing Violent Conflicts*, 87–100.

3. Peter Wallensteen and Margareta Sollenberg, "Armed Conflict, 1989–1999," *Journal of Peace Research* 37, 5 (2000): 647–661.

4. See Peter Wallensteen et al., *Conflict Prevention Through Development Co-Operation* (Uppsala, Sweden: Uppsala University, Department of Peace and Conflict Research, 2001).

5. See Mary B. Anderson, *Do No Harm: How Aid Can Support Peace—or War* (Boulder: Lynne Rienner Publishers, 1999).

6. See Jan Eliasson, "Establishing Trust in the Healer: Preventive Diplomacy and the Future of the United Nations," in Cahill, *Preventive Diplomacy*, 318–343.

7. See Peter Wallensteen, *A Century of Economic Sanctions: A Field Revisited* (Uppsala, Sweden: Uppsala Peace Research Papers No. 1, Uppsala University, Department of Peace and Conflict Research, 2000); and David Cortright and George A. Lopez, *The Sanctions Decade,* a project of the International Peace Academy (Boulder: Lynne Rienner Publishers, 2000).

8. *The New York Times*, October 21, 1999.

9. Mats Hammarström, "The Diffusion of Military Conflict: Central and South-East Europe in 1919–1920 and 1991–1992," *Journal of Peace Research* 31, 3 (1994): 263–280.

10. Richard Holbrooke, *To End a War* (New York: Random House, 1998).

10

Deconstructing Prevention: A Systems Approach to Mitigating Violent Conflict

Tobi P. Dress and Gay Rosenblum-Kumar

The scale and speed of social and economic transformation, together with the forces of globalization, have had a profound impact on the character of international conflict. Conflicts in the twenty-first century pose new challenges as countries complete the transition from statist policies and command economies to new forms of democratic governance, free markets, and global interdependence. Traditional approaches to diplomacy and peacebuilding, which typically viewed the nation-state as the fundamental unit in international relations, are increasingly inadequate to deal with the new sources or causes of international conflict. The international community must find new ways to address these evolving needs and challenges.

The shift in the causes and nature of contemporary conflict requires a commensurate shift in analysis and response from the United Nations, other international organizations, governments, nongovernmental organizations (NGOs), and civil society. Recent events underscore the fact that current strategies for conflict prevention and reduction are woefully inadequate. There is a growing consensus among practitioners and scholars alike that international responses to conflict require greater coherence, coordination, and integration, as well as upstream planning and action to transform wartorn societies and to promote coexistence and economic and social development. Yet at virtually all levels—from the local to the global—there is little capacity to meet these challenges.

Increased attention is now being paid to designing new coordination structures and models for conflict preparedness and management. The latest thinking on preventive action has come to embrace a number of disciplines, actors, and levels of engagement but without a clear understanding about the roles different actors can play in conflict prevention and how their respective efforts are best integrated. Accordingly, this chapter recommends a shift in perspective within and outside of the UN system that would entail the development of a "systems approach" to peacebuilding and preventive action. What we mean by this is that although there are many agencies, organizations, mechanisms, and modalities for peacebuilding and conflict prevention within the United Nations and other international organizations, there is no coordinated system for long-term peace planning and preventive action. We suggest that this lack of a systems approach to conflict prevention is one of the primary reasons that every new armed conflict comes as a surprise to the international community and why resources are stretched to the limit in meeting the needs of those who are most vulnerable to violence.

If prevention is framed in a more integrated and comprehensive way, governments and the international community will focus more attention, and consequently a greater share of their budgets and resources, to the long-term aspects of peacebuilding instead of short-term crisis management.

In this chapter we also argue that the United Nations must engage in an internal process of intersectoral and interagency dialogue to better integrate and maximize the capacities of UN agencies, sectors, and departments in structural conflict prevention, peacebuilding, and long-term peace planning. We recommend that key policymakers in international organizations be convened to engage with key officials of leading international conflict resolution networks. The goal of such a dialogue would be to determine infrastructure requirements for long-term peace planning and to assess what roles different organizational actors would assume within this infrastructure and how they could be mutually reinforcing.[1]

This chapter is divided into two sections, one on global and regional capacity-building, the other on the United Nations' role in national capacity-building in conflict management. It briefly reviews the current organizational capacity requirements in an attempt to suggest better ways of making use of existing peacebuilding, peace planning, and conflict prevention capacity and infrastructure. It also suggests ways in which peacebuilding can become part of the operational design of development and governance strategies of the United Nations, international aid agencies, and developing and transitional countries themselves.

Global and Regional Capacity-Building for Conflict Prevention

The concepts of preventive action have broadened substantially as academic research, networks, task forces, and training initiatives have begun to look more deeply into what the United Nations and the international community are achieving in conflict prevention, as well as what still needs to be done.

The Current Peacebuilding and Conflict Prevention Landscape

Structures and frameworks for analysis, cooperation, and implementation have substantially improved within the last decade. But the international community has not yet come to grips with the difficult, yet essential, process of visualizing an entire system of conflict prevention and determining how the numerous elements of that system can work together as a more coherent, integrated whole.[2]

Work currently undertaken by donors and multilaterals and within other international settings creates a critical basis for future action. But it must be accelerated by the provision of greater resources and innovative thinking. It is important to note that the United Nations and several other multilateral agencies have undertaken departmental and interagency initiatives on specific aspects of conflict and its mitigation. The UN Department of Political Affairs (DPA), which serves as the focal point for conflict prevention and postconflict peacebuilding, has undertaken a number of important initiatives, including activities to strengthen DPA's internal preparedness and the creation of a Policy Analysis Unit to facilitate a departmentwide prevention process and outreach throughout the UN system. Especially noteworthy among these efforts are: the UN/Regional Organization meetings on Conflict Prevention that have been convened over recent years to establish stronger working relationships and new modalities for cooperation among the agencies; the DPA/UN Staff College's Early Warning/Preventive Measures training course, which aims to strengthen the professional capabilities of UN staff worldwide to anticipate, respond to, and deter conflict; and the interdepartmental Framework Team for Coordination, an innovative interagency mechanism for joint analysis and policy formulation vis-à-vis preventive measures for specific country situations.

Many other UN agencies (notably, but not exclusively, the Office for the Coordination of Humanitarian Affairs [OCHA], the Office for the High Commissioner for Human Rights, the UN Development Programme [UNDP], the United Nations Children's Fund [UNICEF], the UN High Commissioner for Refugees, the UN Department of Economic and Social Affairs, the War-torn Societies Project, the International Labour Organization, the UN Research Institute for Social Development, United Nations University, the UN Staff College, and the World Bank) are taking measures to reframe their policies and positions in response to conflict, to develop the capacities of staff to address conflict, and to redefine their roles in peacebuilding and prevention planning with new partners. Similarly, other intergovernmental bodies and civil-society networks (such as the

Development Assistance Committee of the Organization for Economic Cooperation and Development [DAC/OECD], Conflict Prevention and Post-Conflict Reconstruction Network, European Platform on Conflict Prevention, West Africa Peace-building Network, Southeast Asia Regional Forum on Peaceful Conflict Resolution and Good Governance, and others) continue to share and advance research and practical information in the field. These networks are somewhat less ad hoc than they have been in the past. But much remains to be done in terms of how they can be mutually reinforcing and work more competently with each other and with the community of nongovernmental organizations (NGOs) in addressing preventive issues.

Current efforts notwithstanding, the United Nations and the international community have yet to achieve an integrated, collaborative long-term strategy for strengthening national, regional, and international capacities to effectively manage conflict. As the UN Secretary-General has said in his Program for United Nations Reform,

> The prevalence of intra-state warfare and multifaceted crises in the present period has added new urgency to the need for a better understanding of their root causes. It is recognized that greater emphasis should be placed on timely and adequate preventive action. The United Nations of the twenty-first century must become increasingly a focus of preventive measures.[3]

The Future of Peacebuilding and Conflict Prevention

There is a real need to look ahead to the kinds of conflicts the United Nations and the international community will confront in the future. It is conceivable that the international community will have to devise new approaches to conflict prevention, conflict management, and peacebuilding. Although UN agencies will continue to work on a case-by-case and country-specific basis, which will always be fundamental to their operations, they will also have to widen their perspectives to encompass a more global and systemwide approach if they are to grasp how the nature of international conflict, as well as the terrain on which they operate, are changing.

The challenge is not just to expand research, allocate more resources, and develop new mechanisms of interagency cooperation; it is to fundamentally reconceptualize the shape of the field of conflict management and prevention. This involves imagining how the world's conflicts will look in future decades and what tools will be required to mitigate them. We may not be able to draw any definitive conclusions or answers to our questions, but we cannot assume that the world will necessarily look the way it does now. A useful place to begin is with an interdisciplinary dialogue about, and an assessment of, the potential dynamics and contours of future conflicts. Some key questions include the following:

- Will the majority of conflicts in the future be predominantly intrastate, as they are now, or will we again see an increase in the incidence of interstate conflict?
- What role will pressures for accountability, devolution of power, and group rights and representation play in future conflicts?
- To what extent will conflicts be fueled by illicit business interests and unregulated movements of small arms—factors that have clearly assumed greater salience in recent years?
- To what extent will conflicts be propelled by civil/political human rights violations, including the exclusion and marginalization of minorities within states, from inequitable access to resources and services, or from ideological or religious cleavages that have not been reconciled?
- To what extent will privatization and globalization efforts, in which vulnerable population segments in developing and transitional economies lose access to employment, security, and adequate social safety nets, contribute to social violence and unrest and the outbreak of armed conflict?

Together with thinking about how international conflicts will evolve in the future, there is a need to think more deeply about how local, national, regional, and international capacities can be harnessed to create venues for dialogue and provide opportunities for community participation in proactive prevention, conflict analysis, dispute resolution, and the mediation not only of disputes and violence but also of conflicting ideas, ideologies, and values. In addition, we also need to explore how the development of the terms and conditions of peace agreements and treaties can make better use of input from involved communities and population sectors, so that they become durable and self-sustaining and contribute to reintegration. From a training perspective, planning for interested governments to have access to training programs for government officials, police, armed forces, teachers, students, religious leaders, and others in mediation, negotiation, conflict assessment, resolution, prevention, and peacebuilding should also be a priority.

These are just a few of the many issues that should be part of a collective approach to prevention, ones that have not been sufficiently aired and debated.[4] The international community is in need of an interdisciplinary, cross-sectoral forum for airing emerging ideas and introducing them into the public debate.

Imagining the Parameters of a System of Peace Planning and Peace Preparedness

In thinking about how to create a systemic foundation for prevention, it is useful to compare the current peacebuilding landscape with global defense and military systems. The functions of the military include war planning,

preparedness, and readiness, as well as situational deployment of personnel, equipment, and weapons to accomplish specific goals. In the process of
preparing for armed conflict, most countries, but especially those that are
adversaries, in effect collude to perpetuate this system. This is not to say
that all wars are well planned, but the global military complex as a system
is planned and supported by national legislation, business, and other vested
interests. Arguably, there should be similar structures and systems in place
to promote peace. However, there is no real counterpart or infrastructure
for peace planning, no coordinated structure for the development of tools
and strategies.

Only systemic thinking can lead to in-depth innovation and change.
One way to think about the issue of conflict and its constant potential to
emerge is to consider the fact that there are a variety of entities with differing or competing interests, including nation-states, governments, regional
organizations, NGOs, associations, religious institutions, and private entities such as multinationals that together form our global geopolitical and
macroeconomic infrastructure. Every interaction among these entities has
the potential for misperception, misunderstanding, and divergent interests
and thus the potential for conflict. Every time violent conflict occurs, the
operation of the system is jarred, and the system has to gear up to manage,
contain, restrain, or ameliorate the conflict so that the entities and actors
can continue to interact and function. Competition among different elements of this system is inevitable. The challenge is to prevent it from
becoming destructive. This is why a systems approach to conflict prevention is so essential and why it is of paramount importance that structures
and venues for dispute resolution are developed to allow the system to
work more effectively.

We must therefore acknowledge the multidisciplinary, multilingual
nature of a *holistic system of prevention*. Looking at the field of conflict
prevention holistically and from a multidisciplinary perspective involves
understanding the relationships between and among the fields of development, governance, human rights, democratization, and conflict prevention.
Both the causes of, and sustainable solutions to, protracted conflict are
closely linked to the disciplines of development, governance, and human
rights. Just as equitable economic progress and social development can
ease competition over resources, sound governance can address underlying
issues out of which conflicts emerge by developing strong and impartial
civil-society institutions, institutions for the rule of law, and structures for
representative governance together with an independent judiciary, an
accountable security sector, and mechanisms for effective civil society participation.

We must also explore the *linkages between conflict, economics, and
poverty*. As Frances Stewart argues (see Chapter 5 in this volume), the rela-

tionship between poverty and conflict is a complex one. Still, there is general agreement that those who are the most impoverished are most vulnerable in conflict and crisis settings. This reinforces the importance of proactive poverty reduction as a significant part of development and conflict prevention policy. It is also a reminder that agencies that have not traditionally worked in the field of conflict prevention must become more fully engaged in conflict prevention efforts than they are now.[5]

Early warning (versus *urgent warning*) and early response should of course be a major component of any system or infrastructure for peace planning, as well as form the basis for predicting future crises and advancing plans and creating tools for response. This type of planning must include broader use of local indicators and much greater input and participation from local actors.[6] It must also include earlier determination of patterns and trends, such as population movements, natural disasters that impoverish certain groups, and sudden changes in the political or macroeconomic landscapes of a country or region. For example, widespread labor strikes may signal broad-based economic dissatisfaction that could potentially lead to violence. When these social and political indicators clearly show a propensity toward social disruption and violence, the warning is no longer early. At this point it is *urgent warning*, not early warning, that warrants an immediate response.

Envisioning Alternative Models

Some models that offer guidance to our understanding of conflict prevention are based upon *methodologies for research and development in the scientific and medical communities*. The models are used to address and search for responses to major scientific and medical concerns such as the outbreak of pandemic diseases.

In devising an approach to addressing such a critical problem, scientists often say that at the outset what is required is for relevant actors to create a forum in which they can collectively look at the problem in a detached way in order to determine whether they are dealing with a large number of independent or isolated random outbreaks of the disease or whether there is a deeper, underlying pattern to these outbreaks that suggests that disease is going to infect large sectors of the population. The answer to this critical question presents not just a clearer picture of the problem but also what needs to be done in terms of response strategies and whether the medical system can cope with the problem within the context of current systems and infrastructure or whether a more radical response is required.

Other alternative models are based on *emergency relief and humanitarian aid*. The UN system, through OCHA, UNDP, UNICEF, together with numerous NGOs and private voluntary organizations (such as the

International Committee of the Red Cross, OXFAM International, and Médecins sans Frontières), have created a network that spans the developing world and deals with the broad spectrum of emergency aid responses and relief to victims of conflict and crisis. They form a humanitarian assistance infrastructure that is, in effect, a partnership between the United Nations, other multilateral actors, bilateral actors, and international, national, and local NGOs. These NGOs have largely been members of two networks, the American Council for Voluntary International Action[7] and PACT.[8] These networks provide information to their members, apprise them of current initiatives and needs, and keep actors in the field connected to each other and to the overall network. A peace planning model based upon these loosely knit types of informational structures in the relief and humanitarian aid arena might be a good way to begin formulating a more coordinated peacebuilding network.

We can also point to models based on the *environmental movement*. Since the Earth Summit in Rio de Janeiro, first held in 1992 with a follow-up session in 1997, myriad ecological and environmental actors and advocates around the globe have coalesced into an extremely potent, high-powered, and well-funded movement. Their methods of interaction are not unlike the relief and development community in that there are numerous organizations, actors, and types of initiatives. But during crises or situations of special need, they generally tend to mobilize quickly to respond to the problem.

The environmental movement is active at virtually all levels, from the local to the transnational, and produces powerful informational tools that are relatively accessible in hard copy and electronic formats. There are numerous North-South and East-West exchange programs that transcend ideological, political, and technological divides in order to share information and advance the objectives of the movement, which are, in general, sound, sustainable ecological and environmental policies and practices worldwide. Although there are many organizations with varied interests and belief systems doing diverse work ranging from global policy initiatives to efforts to save one species, river, or harbor, the movement and its informational network provide something akin to an umbrella under which the work of different independent organizations is harbored. This network allows each organization to be aware of the work of others in the network in a manner that is mutually reinforcing.

It would be a signal achievement if the peacebuilding and dispute resolution community could be brought into a mutually reinforcing, information-sharing relationship of the kind described above. Although environmental organizations typically rely heavily on external sources of funding, and although the groups within the movement are known to have widely divergent views about environmental policy, they have nonetheless found a way to transcend many of these obstacles in order to achieve results that they consider vital to saving the earth and its living resources.

Alternative models might also be based on the field of *natural disaster management*. Destructive conflict often seems random, but it is not. Most eruptions of conflict are usually predictable. In a similar way, many natural disasters, once thought to be entirely random and spontaneous, are now understood to be predictable through an examination and analysis of various confluences of geophysical forces.

Moreover, the impacts of natural calamities, which cannot be averted in themselves, can nonetheless be significantly mitigated through predisaster early warning, coupled with disaster preparedness, planning, and even preidentified postcrisis and exit strategies. Specialists in natural disaster management now argue that becoming familiar with these methodologies, utilizing them, and educating populations about them can dramatically alter the outcomes of natural calamities.[9]

Developing a Worldwide Network of "Neutral Venues" for Dialogue, Conflict Resolution, and Negotiated Mediation

One model for conflict prevention envisions the establishment of a worldwide, linked network of conflict prevention venues.[10] The network would include dispute resolution and dialogue centers for engaging in early dispute anticipation and mitigation, peace planning, and conflict resolution training. This network would also include and build upon existing institutions and networks of NGOs, relevant academic programs, and national, subregional, and regional organs already working in the field to strengthen the impact of their work, create linkages among them, and raise awareness.

These centers or institutions would function both as training grounds and as neutral territorial venues for dialogue, drawing on panels of trained mediators respected in their regions for their capacity for objective analysis and impartiality. They would be available to engage in mediation and other third-party dispute resolution technologies at multiple levels of interaction to reduce intergroup, interethnic, and transborder misunderstandings and tensions. They would provide a venue and resource base for skill-building in mediative processes for government, community, and civil-society representatives, including central and local government public servants across many disciplines and departments, as well as jurists, religious leaders, NGO staff, educators, academics, development practitioners, representatives of the media, and others. They would also function as repositories for the development of local expertise and resource libraries and as training centers for the trainers themselves.

In addition to the need for regional and subregional networks, there is a corresponding requirement to develop them on a national basis, through NGO networks, civil-society groups, or academic institutions, as well as respected government institutions that can be proactively supported by the United Nations. Networks at all levels could share resources, jointly develop and share skills training, and develop collective and mutually useful databases, including databases on early warning and informational tools. This would serve to create working relationships between and among international organizations and institutions with a purview and expertise in conflict prevention and resolution.

A network to address conflict management such as the one described need not require the proliferation or creation of new institutions or structures. Conflict prevention centers or initiatives could be built into the frameworks of existing offices such as national ombudsman offices, offices of development organizations, within relevant ministries, within academic institutions or as part of other national, government, quasi-governmental, academic, NGO, or civil society organizations.

Such neutral venues can also be created as partnerships that bring together divergent perspectives in socially constructive ways. For example, a joint UN/government/civil-society project for capacity-building in conflict prevention has recently been formulated as a partnership for conflict prevention and management in Romania, and it is hoped that it will ultimately become a subregional initiative as well. Supported by the former president of Romania and Romanian administration, it will be implemented through a partnership of national and international NGOs specializing in conflict prevention and management.[11] A similar East-West, university-to-university collaboration will create a conflict resolution training center in the Ukraine.[12] A current UN Department of Economic and Social Affairs/UNDP project is partnering with NGOs in sub-Saharan Africa to design and deliver conflict management training to government officials, as well as their civil society counterparts, through local institutions on the continent.[13] Over time, such networks of programs and venues for conflict prevention and amelioration will dramatically increase the capacity for dialogue, mediated negotiation, conciliation, multiparty facilitation, and tension reduction at the subregional, regional, national, and international levels.

The types of peacebuilding, peace planning, and conflict prevention functions discussed in this chapter, and in the various models described above, are partially aimed at developing the long-term capacities of institutions and societies to discuss and address structural problems and injustices and to understand how the manifestations of these injustices trigger overt violence. They do not presuppose or presume involvement in political peacemaking but rather in the development of structural foundations, networks, and systems that over the long term substantially reduce the outbreak of armed conflict by offering viable nonviolent alternatives.

Strengthening the Capacity of the UN and Its Member States

Managing conflict is one of the primary and enduring responsibilities of all governments and, therefore, one of the preeminent areas in which the UN needs to serve its member states. Starting from this premise, the work of the United Nations, in its myriad forms, must systematically and systemically incorporate conflict awareness dimensions, as well as carefully conceived peace-promoting elements, into its many areas of work. This can be done, in part, by infusing greater conflict sensitivity into development and governance programming, mainstreaming conflict awareness into other disciplines, employing educational tools, disseminating information, and increasing staff awareness and training opportunities. But first and foremost, it starts with a shift in awareness and attitudes that acknowledges the centrality of conflict prevention and transformation as part of the manifold missions of the United Nations.

The United Nations' prevention agenda, in policy and practice, should be expanded well beyond its current set of responses to violence mitigation to include a much broader, clearly articulated constellation of interdisciplinary interventions for the prevention of destructive violence. This can be accomplished, principally, through developing the capacities of states and their civil societies to channel conflict in constructive ways. This approach would aim to: increase government capacities, through specific governance and institution-strengthening modalities; and concurrently expand the United Nations' own capacities to assist member states by infusing all of its work with greater conflict prevention awareness and sensitivity in its formulation, objectives, and impacts, as relevant to many policy areas such as economic and social development, environment, human rights, labor, public health, refugee and internally displaced persons policies.

In addition to the United Nations' currently accepted role in prevention, such an approach would establish and promote a new, impartial, technical role for the United Nations in "prevention" by providing information, advisory services, and technical assistance for capacity-building to assist states in the analysis, development, and implementation of their own national strategies for avoiding destructive conflict. The United Nations could offer interested states a range of support services, including assistance in policy formulation, institutional strengthening, civil service training, educational curriculum development, and other modalities to support and strengthen environments and cultures of constructive conflict management.

Thus, a principal role of the United Nations would be to assist interested member states to proactively strengthen conditions for peace and human security through a combination of normative standard-setting, information dissemination, and capacity-building. Over the long term, such activities would develop national and regional capacities to channel conflicts constructively.

The Operational Challenge

In the early 1990s, Michael Lund said that "prevention is an idea in search of a strategy."[14] Several years later, much has been done to develop a strategy. But the remaining challenge is how to operationalize it.

The representatives of preventive strategy at the United Nations are the General Assembly, the Security Council, and the UN Secretariat, each of which has consistently affirmed that effectiveness requires a concerted multiactor, cross-disciplinary strategy, balancing short-term political exigencies with long-term governance, economic, and social factors.[15] There is growing consensus on the importance of effective prevention and post-conflict peacebuilding strategies as important means for preventing the reemergence of conflict.[16] The General Assembly has also recognized that such a comprehensive approach must fully involve national authorities as well as the UN system, donors, intergovernmental organizations, and NGOs.[17]

Several components of a process to revise the current doctrine on conflict prevention are suggested below. These elements could infuse the structures, policies, and practices of the UN system with new analytical and operational dimensions. Given the current level of policy and practice, the field would benefit greatly from undertaking a collaborative process to legitimate and reframe the concepts of conflict prevention, management, and transformation, set operational standards for their implementation, and promote awareness, understanding, and acceptance among member states.

Growing out of such a collaborative analysis, the next step is to operationalize a technical cooperation approach to conflict prevention and transformation that reconceptualizes the way in which prevention is articulated and implemented within development assistance and makes capacity-building in managing conflict an accepted and major part of development cooperation. A related step is to fully infuse the international community's and the United Nations' own policy and practice with conflict prevention awareness and sensitivity, cutting across the diverse policy areas in which the UN Secretariat and specialized agencies are engaged.

The final challenge is to put these newly developed resources of the

United Nations at the disposal of governments in order to assist member states to develop national capacities to attain these standards and to manage all types of disputes, including economic, social, intergroup, interethnic, as well as environmental, ecological, labor, and others, with their own institutions and resources.

The United Nations could then be available to assist states, upon their request, to analyze their in-country situations and develop their own strategies to improve their capacities in conflict prevention and transformation. These four components are elaborated below.

As for deconstructing conventional understanding in the operational context, UN departments and agencies conceive of conflict prevention along the following parameters:

- *Humanitarian intervention:* undertaking preparedness measures and delivering humanitarian relief for civilian casualties due to complex emergencies.
- *Early warning analysis:* identifying and analyzing potential outbreaks of violence in a three- to twelve-month time frame and advising on the application of a range of short-term preventive, ameliorative, or containment measures.
- *Preventive diplomacy and other diplomatic initiatives:* the application of high-profile or confidential diplomacy, good offices, fact-finding missions, and application of varying degrees of pressure.
- *Peacekeeping operations:* the interposition of peacekeeping forces, with the concurrence of concerned parties, to ensure or enforce a cessation of violence.

In reviewing these general measures, it is clear that conflict prevention is concerned with preventing, reducing, limiting, and eliminating violence. Thus, it is evident that when the United Nations and the international community use the term "conflict prevention," what they really mean is "violence prevention." But where tensions are high and violence is imminent, the above measures, though desirable and necessary, are often insufficient.

A broader, more comprehensive approach to conflict prevention and mitigation must therefore also address structural injustices and develop interventions aimed at poverty alleviation, social empowerment, and reducing horizontal inequality. In addition, conflict resolution skills and institutional capacity that can appropriately manage normal social conflict and competing interests in society may also be required.

Practitioners and policymakers increasingly agree that in its broadest conception, conflict prevention not only aims to achieve the avoidance or cessation of violence encompassing the full conflict continuum but also includes a range of social, economic, and political conditions for sustainable peace. Mainstreaming includes not only developing new projects or adding prevention components to existing interventions; it involves situating prevention at the center of decisionmaking and policymaking, planning, budgeting, and institutional processes and structures. Mainstreaming requires a reorientation of goals, strategies, and actions that promote necessary and constructive changes in organizations, structures, and cultures to create organizational environments infused with awareness of, and commitment to, prevention as a preeminent and overriding goal.[18]

Mainstreaming prevention will require a thorough reassessment of the major policy areas of UN specialized agencies as to how their traditional spheres of work relate to the amelioration of destructive conflict environments. For example, how can the UNDP identify constituencies for peacebuilding and harness their assistance in the formulation of development programs? How can UNICEF's community development initiatives be employed to promote prevention? How does prevention relate to the field of public health and the work of the World Health Organization? How do World Bank projects promoting political and economic reforms ensure sensitivity to the distributional effects of their policies and programs and the consequent conflict-inducing potential? How can technical cooperation strengthen institutions, within and outside of government, to help defuse and obviate traditional types of intrastate conflict? Where is the nexus of conflict prevention with refugee protection and reintegration, as well as with human rights protection and promotion, and how can they be mutually reinforcing? Such organizational introspection requires in-depth, innovative strategic planning together with long-term organizational development strategies.

We must also consider the *technical cooperation approach to conflict transformation, a preeminent part of the United Nations' work.* UN responses to fragile environments and violent conflict would benefit greatly if they were informed by a technical cooperation approach to conflict prevention that enlarges the way in which the currently accepted definition is operationalized. The goal of conflict transformation, to transform negative relationships leading to violence into constructive opportunities for growth, requires a reorientation and expansion of responses.[19] Conflict transformation would promote the successful channelling of conflict into nonviolent outcomes that are inherently sustainable because they are grounded in well-developed capacities (legal, institutional, societal) to manage the conflicts that inevitably arise.

Such a change in approach would have several substantive, positive ramifications. First, the international community's attention to prevention would commence much earlier in the conflict continuum and would target greater intellectual and financial resources for preconflict and potential conflict scenarios. Second, international efforts would systematically address the economic and social dimensions of conflict transformation that can channel potentially destructive conflict away from violence and toward sustainable peace. Finally, as an outgrowth of the above, development cooperation would embrace conflict resolution principles and techniques and become a powerful vehicle for conflict transformation while simultaneously enhancing its poverty eradication and development goals, the need for which is increasingly recognized by many departments and agencies of the United Nations.[20]

In industrialized countries, the existence of conflict resolving and transforming institutions, skills, and knowledge are often accepted as the norm and are infused into the fabric of judicial systems, administrative and regulatory agencies (such as consumer protection agencies, ombudsman institutions, and environmental agencies), human rights protection, and parliamentary proceedings. By and large, these systems and institutions are able to moderate competing interests successfully so that they are assumed to be the basic operating institutions of a well-functioning society. Yet adaptation of such principles and institutions within developing and transitional countries has been minimal, ad hoc, and demonstrably insufficient. Many developing countries that find themselves trapped in cycles of violence do not have the benefit of access to all of these institutional resources. This is an area where the United Nations has an opportunity to act as a conduit of information, promoter of dialogue, and facilitator of change that can assist interested member states to acquire greater competencies in governance-based conflict management.

The dual tasks of channeling conflicting interests and managing diversity in society are key to moving forward and transforming the social, economic, and political affairs of state in developing countries.[21] According to the World Bank, "In diverse societies where inter-group interactions have been uncooperative, the fundamental problem has been a failure to develop political institutions able to accommodate such diversity. . . . This becomes explosive when mass poverty enters the picture."[22] Thus, particularly in developing and transitional countries, the state has a pivotal role to play in the development and maintenance of effective governance structures that can balance competing interests in ways that promote human dignity, foster the rule of law, and support equitable development. The challenge is to use the full conflict mitigating potential of governance policies and institutions to channel and manage conflicts so that societies can find ways to avoid resorting to violence or repression.

If conflict and its prevention were demystified and legitimized in this way, states would see conflict prevention and transformation as something they need *not* because they have failed at a task or as something that assails their sovereignty. Instead, building conflict management capacity could, in fact, be seen to strengthen state sovereignty by developing internal capacities that obviate the need for interference or rescue by the international community.

There is also the need for *infusing awareness and developing skills and capacities.* Conflict resolution tools and techniques can open channels for dialogue to reduce mistrust and hostility. They are confidence-building measures to be used in cooperative negotiation at all levels of problem-solving. These practical working tools can be employed to facilitate communication within and among ministries, agencies, and tiers of government; between government and civil society; and between and among governments. Perhaps most important, conflict resolution and transformation principles and techniques can empower governments and the governed to competently engage with each other in constructive communication and joint problem-solving.

The articulation and acceptance of such an approach toward dealing with conflict would greatly benefit from an intergovernmental process of information-sharing and consensus-building, not unlike that which has taken place in other fields of endeavor, such as environmental protection, human rights, and gender equality. Such a process could establish norms and standards to which national governments can aspire and set their own criteria and objectives. The UN Secretariat could facilitate such a process, at the request of governments, with the aim of (a) gaining clarity and consensus on the use of various methodologies for conflict prevention and transformation; (b) disseminating such information broadly to promote the understanding and use of such principles and practice at local, national, and international levels; and (c) providing technical assistance, upon the request of member states, in developing and implementing programs, much as the UN High Commissioner for Human Rights provides technical assistance in formulating human rights programs and policies.[23]

The application of conflict management techniques by the United Nations to internal issues would also improve its managerial efficiency, problem-solving capacity, and interagency cooperation. The United Nations has long been thwarted by uncoordinated and, at times, competing activities of departments and agencies at UN Headquarters and in the field. A concerted, systemwide initiative to raise awareness, change attitudes, and develop skills in solving conflicts cooperatively would help change key elements in the current institutional culture that contribute to some of the ongoing managerial impasses. It would further expedite cooperation on humanitarian, development, and peacekeeping operations so that the UN could reap the benefit of potential synergies among its branches and the full utilization of its respective strengths.

Developing the UN staff's awareness and skills in conflict management would markedly enhance the impact of development assistance on peacebuilding and related activities. Although conflict resolution tools are

recognized for facilitating political negotiations, it is not as widely understood that progress in social or humanitarian areas is equally hampered by
competing and conflicting interests that can be mitigated by similar tools
and mechanisms. The work of UN staff engaged in development, relief, and
peacekeeping would benefit significantly from understanding and employing cooperative negotiation strategies and collaborative conflict-managing
techniques. Training, information, and resources need to reach staff at UN
Headquarters, regional commissions, specialized agencies, country offices,
and particularly staff preparing for peacekeeping, peacebuilding, and
humanitarian missions so that they can apply these skills to both the substantive content of their work and the internal processes of UN operations.
Such extensive training and awareness-raising among staff would change
the perception of conflict resolution as a remote and discrete concept
applied only to high-level diplomatic efforts into a fully infused characteristic of the work and organizational life of the United Nations.

Building national capacity is another critical component. The pursuit
of enduring peace will not succeed unless issues relating to sociopolitical
structures and dysfunctional governance arrangements are fully addressed.[24] From a governance perspective, capacity in conflict management
needs to focus on institutional and organizational skill-building that can
promote a culture of constructive problem-solving, cooperative negotiation,
dialogue, and dispute resolution throughout society. As an integral part of
an overall governance strategy, such capacity-building would impart to
society as a whole—especially to key actors such as government officials
and their interlocutors—skills to: analyze the structural and proximate
causes of conflict; anticipate potential areas of dispute and develop appropriate responses not only for averting violence but also for promoting
peace; understand and employ dispute resolution principles and practices;
strengthen the institutional capacity for managing diversity and conflicting
interests; and use development tools in ways that mitigate the long-term
structural, as well as proximate, causes of conflict.

There are numerous ways that the United Nations can, at the request of
member states, assist in developing their capacities in conflict prevention
and transformation. Within an expanded conception of prevention, the goal
would naturally embrace not only the prevention of violence but also the
amelioration of conditions that have the potential to lead to violence. For
example, the United Nations could assist national ministries to undertake
conflict transformation assessments for the purpose of analyzing, within
their specific historical and sociopolitical context, existing and potential
causes of destructive conflict, as well as to develop corresponding national
response strategies.

Such processes examine structural issues, relational issues, and potential sources of conflict such as resource equity, identity, and interethnic ten-

sions. The structural component would look at laws, institutions, systems, and practices that by their presence or absence create susceptibility to violent conflict. Relational issues would be dealt with by exploring the level and types of participation in the polity and how groups in society interact with each other. Based on the issues and needs emerging from the analysis, a nationally generated, integrated, conflict transformation strategy would include:

• A strategic plan for incorporating conflict prevention/transformation and preventive peacebuilding into relevant current and future national development policies.

• Wider use of conflict impact assessments on existing and proposed development projects to examine the intended and unintended effects of development activities on tensions that can trigger violent conflict, as well as to seek ways to reorient projects so that negative effects can be transformed into peace-promoting impacts.

• Formulation of appropriate dispute resolution elements that can be infused into existing development activities to ensure that they have a more beneficial impact on the peace and security environment.

• Formulation of new projects to introduce specific dispute resolution mechanisms and activities that can regulate conflict through acceptable channels, such as the creation or strengthening of mediation centers, ombudsman offices, human rights structures, improved judicial mechanisms, and other conflict prevention and resolution modalities.

• Development of awareness-building and educational components that provide training and curriculum development in mediation, negotiation skills, judicial process, human rights, conflict resolution, tolerance, civic education, problem-solving, and bias reduction. This can be implemented through formal and informal education channels, for example, primary training through tertiary levels of education, workplace training, civil service training programs, and the media.

• Review of national legal frameworks with regard to their compatibility with conflict resolution principles, as well as development of a plan to refine laws and regulations to reduce structural impediments that can lead to and exacerbate violence and destructive conflict.

• Review of the status and needs of civil society with the aim of initiating local community activities to develop a more balanced, constructive interface between NGOs, civil society, the religious sector, the private sector, and government.

• Assistance in developing a national multicultural policy orientation that counteracts discrimination and marginalization, promotes development equity (ensuring that development benefits are distributed equitably and perceived as such), and fosters employment equity (including public service hiring according to accepted transparent norms and standards).

• Development of integrated governance capacity-building programs for the public service, legislative branch, judiciary, and security sector, with emphasis on mediation and negotiation skills, tolerance, diversity training, adherence to human rights standards, and ethics and professionalism.

Such a national exercise, which undertakes to analyze economic, social, and other pressures in relation to existing governance and institutional competencies to handle them, and then generates corresponding conflict transformation responses, would produce useful results on two levels. At the field level, the results could provide governments and donors with practical guidance and concrete activities to integrate social-capital building and humanitarian, human rights, governance, and development interventions over the long term in the service of managing and mitigating potentially destructive conflict. On a policy level, it would lend support and credence to strengthening the interlinkages between development, governance, and all of the elements of peacebuilding.

Conclusion

In this chapter we have tried to demonstrate why current responses to conflict have been inadequate thus far and why the case-by-case nature of our collective response remains fragmented and has not coalesced into a global action plan, system, or infrastructure for peace. We believe that responses to conflict are still largely reactive rather than preventive and that postconflict responses are often seen as an isolated series of activities rather than an indefinite process or continuum leading to the creation of enabling environments for peace and stability.

We believe that the United Nations has a greater role to play in the peacebuilding process than is currently recognized and that this role is closely linked with development and governance assistance. In this regard, its first role should be to catalyze a process to develop a consistent, coherent approach to conflict prevention that addresses global and national needs. The role of the United Nations should, in part, be to create frameworks that facilitate the nonviolent mediation of disputes through a global infrastructure for peace planning, by developing the capacities of member states to manage their own conflicts, as well as by infusing UN policies and operations with a central, cross-cutting, overarching focus on conflict prevention throughout its manifold policy areas.

In light of the deficits that characterize the field at present, we have recommended a series of proposals, together with a list of steps that can be taken immediately, in the medium term and long term. They are structural rather than political in nature, closely linked to planning and programming for development cooperation and assistance in governance and national capacity-building.

We have also stressed that most questions about the field of conflict prevention urgently await coherent answers and that the widespread humanitarian tragedies within civil society due to armed conflict will not be ameliorated until policymakers within the international community formulate more coherent, systemic preventive technologies. We hope that this chapter and the others in this volume will serve as catalysts for developing a systems approach to the prevention and mitigation of violent and destructive conflict.

Notes

We wish to acknowledge the editorial insights of Adriana Alberti and Marie-Eve Friedrich in preparation of this chapter. The views expressed herein are those of the authors and do not necessarily reflect the views of the United Nations.

1. See Tobi P. Dress and Gay Rosenblum-Kumar, "Governance in Diverse Societies: Toward Peace and Security in the 21st Century," discussion paper for UNDESA, funded by the Samuel Ruben Foundation, July 1999.

2. Kalypso Nicolaïdis, "International Preventive Action: Developing a Strategic Framework," in *Vigilance and Vengeance, The Role of NGOs in Preventing Ethnic Conflict*, ed. Robert Rotberg (Washington, D.C.: Brookings Institution, 1996), 39.

3. General Assembly, "Renewing the United Nations: A Programme for Reform Report of the Secretary-General," A/51/950, July 14, 1997, para. 110, p. 37.

4. Tobi P. Dress, "Creating a Global Infrastructure for Peace," discussion paper, School of Public Affairs, Baruch College, CUNY, New York, 1996.

5. "Conference Proceedings, High Level Conference on Crisis" (Geneva: United Nations, International Labor Organization, May 2000).

6. Matthias Stiefel, *Rebuilding After War: Lessons from the War-torn Societies Project* (Geneva: War-torn Societies Project, 1999), 27.

7. For more information, see http://www.interaction.org/.

8. For more information, see http://www.pactworld.org/.

9. Patricia Delaney, Working Paper for ILO High-Level Consultation on Crisis and Conflict (Geneva: United Nations, May 2000).

10. See Dress, "Creating a Global Infrastructure for Peace."

11. For further information, see http://esa.un.org/techcoop/flagship.asp?Code=ROM00002.

12. Institute for Conflict Analysis and Resolution, Newsletter, George Mason University, 12.2 (fall 2000): 5–6.

13. For further information, see http://www.unpan.org/technical_highlights-conflictresolutionpage.asp and related sites.

14. Michael Lund with Bruce Jentleson, "Preventive Diplomacy: An Idea in

Search of a Strategy," Discussion Paper for Study Group on Preventive Diplomacy (Washington, D.C.: United States Institute of Peace, November 1993).

15. United Nations: General Assembly, 54th Session, March 27, 2000; "'We the Peoples': The Role of the United Nations in the Twenty-first Century, Report of the Secretary General," A/54/2000; Statement of the President of the Security Council on the situation in Africa, November 30, 1998, S/PRST/1998/35; and Statement of the President of the Security Council on the role of the Security Council in the prevention of armed conflicts, November 30, 1999, S/PRST/1999/34.

16. United Nations, Security Council, *The Role of the United Nations Peacekeeping in Disarmament, Demobilization and Reintegration*, February 11, 2000, S/2000/101.

17. United Nations, General Assembly, 53rd Session, Triennial policy review of operational activities for development of the United Nations System General Assembly, February 25, 1999, A/RES/53/192.

18. United Nations, UN Department of Economic and Social Affairs, Office of the Special Advisor on Gender Issues and the Advancement of Women, internal document on "Gender Mainstreaming: Strategy for Promoting Gender Equality," May 10, 2000.

19. Hizkias Assefa, "Peace and Reconciliation as a Paradigm" (New York: African Peacebuilding and Reconciliation Network, 1999), 4.

20. General Assembly, 53rd Session, Declaration and Programme of Action on a Culture of Peace, October 6, 1999, A/RES/53/243; United Nations, Executive Board of the UNDP and UNPF, "Report of the Administrator Meeting the Challenge: The Role of UNDP in Crisis, Post-conflict and Recovery Situations, 2000–2003", March 20, 2000, DP/2000/18; and General Assembly, Preparatory Committee for the special session of the General Assembly entitled "World Summit for Social Development and Beyond, Promoting Social Integration in Post-conflict Situations," February 24, 2000, A/AC/253/23.

21. Laurie Nathan, "The Four Horsemen of the Apocalypse: The Structural Causes of Crisis and Violence in Africa," *Peace and Change: A Journal of Peace Research* 25, 2 (April 2000): 190.

22. World Bank, "Can Africa Claim the 21st Century?" (Washington, D.C.: World Bank, 2000), 57–58.

23. UNDP/Emergency Response Division, Proceedings, Consultation on Conflict Prevention (New York: United Nations, March 2000).

24. Sam G. Amoo, "The Challenge of Ethnicity and Conflicts in Africa: The Need for a New Paradigm" (New York: UN Emergency Response Division/UNDP, January 1997), 31.

11

Prevention:
Theory and Practice

Edward C. Luck

Since 1990, much of the United Nations community has taken to the challenge of conflict prevention like a duck to water. For the United Nations, an organization accused—sometimes unfairly—of being inept at peacekeeping and irrelevant to peace enforcement, the rediscovery of conflict prevention, one of its founding missions, has been both timely and reassuring. Even friends of the world body had fretted that UN security doctrine, bouncing from crisis to crisis and torn by the divergent demands of different member states, had been "wandering in the void."[1] Yet no one seems to question the desirability of conflict prevention. Also, as the concept of prevention has become more popular, the temptation to cast it in broader, deeper, bolder terms has proven irresistible to many. And as theories of prevention have become ever grander, this chapter argues, the operational and analytical utility of the term—like so many before it—has faded.

The Carnegie Commission on Preventing Deadly Conflict made a useful distinction between operational prevention, that is, steps to employ when confronting an immediate crisis, and structural prevention, which involves measures for dealing with root causes, such as the existence of weapons of mass destruction, underdevelopment, and injustice.[2] This chapter contrasts the policy implications, even the relevance, of these two layers of prevention; and it urges policymakers and policy analysts alike to focus on the operational level. The opening section reviews briefly how the concept of prevention has evolved and grown in recent years and why it has proven so attractive to the UN community. On the surface, there appears to be a propitious fit between the requirements for prevention and the capacities of the organization. The other sections, however, raise a series of conceptual, political, and institutional caveats about whether and how prevention can be translated from the realm of ideas and exhortations to the realm of actions and operations. Based on this analysis, the chapter closes with some modest suggestions for addressing some of these obstacles, so that prevention can take its proper place, alongside peacekeeping and peace enforcement, as one of the United Nations' primary contributions to the maintenance of international peace and security.

Charter Roots and Growing Ambitions

Prevention is hardly a new goal for the United Nations. Its founders had identified conflict prevention as one of its primary purposes, given the failure of the League of Nations to prevent the chain of events that led to World War II.[3] Unlike peacekeeping, prevention was firmly and explicitly embedded by the founders in the UN Charter.[4] Even during the divisive Cold War years, the United Nations' efforts at the peaceful settlement of disputes and at peacekeeping were designed to prevent disputes from escalating into armed conflicts and to prevent small wars from becoming large ones.

With the end of the Cold War, then, it was a logical progression for the Security Council, meeting at the summit level for the first time in 1992, to ask UN Secretary-General Boutros Boutros-Ghali to prepare an analytical report on "the capacity of the United Nations for preventive diplomacy, for peacemaking and for peace-keeping."[5] According to his resulting report, *An Agenda for Peace* (1992), "preventive diplomacy is action to prevent disputes from arising between parties, to prevent existing disputes from escalating into conflicts and to limit the spread of the latter when they occur." Stressing that "preventive diplomacy seeks to resolve disputes before violence breaks out," the Secretary-General suggested that it "requires measures to create confidence; it needs early warning based on information gathering and informal or formal fact-finding; it may also involve preventive deployment and, in some situations, demilitarized zones."[6] It was *not* to be the task of preventive diplomacy, Boutros-Ghali wisely concluded, to try to resolve all of the underlying problems that could contribute to tension and conflict, but rather to track them and to draw the attention of the Security Council in particular and of the member states in general to particularly threatening situations.

Five years later, with the appointment of a new Secretary-General, Kofi Annan, and the release of the Carnegie Commission's study, the notion of prevention took on renewed popularity and much more sweeping proportions. Taking a more structural perspective, the new Secretary-General asserted that "in every diplomatic mission and development project that we pursue, the United Nations is doing the work of prevention."

Calling for the creation of a "culture of prevention" and employing the Commission's categories, he declared that:

> The United Nations operational prevention strategy involves four funda-
> mental activities—early warning, preventive diplomacy, preventive
> deployment and early humanitarian action. The United Nations structural
> prevention strategy involves three additional activities—preventive disar-
> mament, development and peace-building. Guiding and infusing all these
> efforts is the promotion of human rights, democratization and good gover-
> nance as the foundations of peace.[7]

On the operational side, the new list deleted Boutros-Ghali's references to confidence-building, fact-finding, and demilitarized zones, added humanitarian action, and made preventive diplomacy itself a subset of a larger prevention strategy. By including disarmament, development, and peacebuilding on the structural side, as well as humanitarian affairs as an operational measure, Annan managed to label most of the UN system's ongoing work as conflict prevention. Looking ahead, he asserted that "the United Nations of the twenty-first century must become a global center for visionary and effective preventive action."[8]

In an October 1999 speech entitled "Development Is the Best Form of Conflict Prevention," the Secretary-General told the staff of the World Bank that "human security, good governance, equitable development and respect for human rights are interdependent and mutually reinforcing. If war is the worst enemy of development, healthy and balanced development is the best form of conflict prevention."[9] When the Security Council convened the next month to consider the question of conflict prevention, the Secretary-General emphasized the importance of addressing long-term problems of "poverty, repression, and undemocratic government, endemic underdevelopment, weak or non-existent institutions, political and economic discrimination between ethnic and religious communities." He urged member states to "adopt enlightened economic and social policies" and "to prevent conflict by practicing good governance." Acknowledging that this agenda goes well beyond the Security Council's capacities, he suggested roles for the Bretton Woods institutions, the UN Development Programme, the Economic and Social Council (ECOSOC), and the International Court of Justice and called for "much closer co-ordination of policy among them, and also, in many cases, between them and NGOs [nongovernmental organizations] or the private sector."[10]

This extended conception of prevention has proven attractive, if rhetoric is any guide, to an impressive range of member states. One speaker after another, including developed and developing countries, underlined the need for comprehensive and integrated approaches and long-term strategies for getting to root causes when the Security Council met in November 1999

and July 2000 to address prevention.[11] Although China and some developing countries pointed to the importance of acting in accordance with the
Charter and of observing principles of noninterference, sovereignty, and
territorial integrity, they tended, like the Secretary-General, to stress the
utility of a broad strategy that encompassed economic and social development.

These structural dimensions were emphasized in the statement of its
president following the Security Council's November 1999 session. In
echoing the Secretary-General's plea for the building of "a culture of prevention," the Council stressed "the importance of a coordinated international response to economic, social, cultural, or humanitarian problems" and
urged "all United Nations organs and agencies . . . to assist Member States
to eradicate poverty, strengthen development cooperation and assistance
and promote respect for human rights and fundamental freedoms."[12] In a
formulation repeated by the presidential statement following the November
1999 Council session, the July 2000 statement declared that "the Security
Council recognizes that early warning, preventive diplomacy, preventive
deployment, preventive disarmament and post-conflict peacebuilding are
interdependent and complementary components of a comprehensive conflict prevention strategy." It also acknowledged the need for enhanced
cooperation with regional organizations and with ECOSOC. In addition to
reiterating these points, the July 2000 statement included additional elements on confidence- and security-building measures, on the role of
women, on the illicit trade in diamonds and other natural resources, on a
variety of disarmament steps, and on the use of civilian police in peacekeeping operations.[13]

Not to be outdone, the G-8 took up the question of prevention as part
of its 1999–2000 agenda, including it in the July 2000 communiqué from
Okinawa and, at greater length, in a statement from the G-8 foreign ministers' meeting in Miyazaki that same month.[14] The latter document was dou-
bly comprehensive, recommending conflict prevention efforts "at every
stage, from pre-conflict to post-conflict (Chronological Comprehensiveness)" and through "a wide-ranging menu of political, economic and social
policy options . . . (Comprehensiveness in Measures for Conflict Prevention)." They concluded that "conflict prevention is a joint venture involving
all the international community, including other international and regional
organizations, states, business sector, NGOs, and individuals." Although
touching on a variety of issues, the ministers produced more detailed proposals on small arms and light weapons, conflict and development, the
illicit trade in diamonds, children in armed conflict, and international civil
police—all under the heading of "initiatives for conflict prevention."

This chorus of praise for a comprehensive approach to prevention is eminently understandable from a political perspective. For years, advocates of developmental, environmental, social, and humanitarian programs have sought to identify their causes with security (or, more recently, human security), the goal that seemed to attract the most bountiful resources and highest political priority. As the notion of what constitutes an effective prevention strategy expands, in theory so too does the coverage of the security umbrella. As the Secretary-General phrased it in his report entitled "We the Peoples" (known as the Millennium Report), "Every step taken towards reducing poverty and achieving broad-based economic growth is a step towards conflict prevention."[15] To developing countries, this line of reasoning adds one more rationale to efforts to persuade donor countries to raise aid and investment levels. Institutionally, this argument suggests that the restricted and opaque Security Council—as some smaller delegations see it—should not have the last word when it comes to prevention. Many developing countries were no doubt pleased to hear the Security Council conclude that it should open a dialogue on prevention with the less prominent ECOSOC.

Developed countries have ample reasons to want to believe and to embrace this broader conception as well. If there is any truth to the old adage that an ounce of prevention is worth a pound of cure, then the savings for those footing most of the bill for peacekeeping and humanitarian interventions could be substantial. More important, successful prevention could preclude some difficult decisions about whether to become involved in high-risk, low-gain conflicts in the developing world. The general exhortations voiced by the G-8 and the Security Council, moreover, promise few specific actions and contain no binding price tags.

The more comprehensive approach to prevention would also appear to fit the structural profile of the UN system, itself a remarkably broad-based and loosely structured collection of functional, developmental, humanitarian, and security agencies and programs. Between the UN system and the Bretton Woods institutions (World Bank and the International Monetary Fund), there is at least one agency or program to match each of the factors deemed essential to an effective prevention strategy. This more encompassing approach, in other words, has something for everybody. Also, expanding the notion of prevention plays toward the United Nations' areas of presumed comparative advantage and away from those of its comparative disadvantage. At a time when there was much questioning of the United Nations' capacity for undertaking military missions—for example, the Secretary-General had declared in his July 1997 reform report that the world body lacked "the institutional capacity to conduct military enforcement measures under Chapter VII" at that point in its history—it made sense to emphasize nontraditional dimensions of security.[16]

The Dilemma of Comprehensiveness

The core logic underlying a prevention-first strategy is as compelling today as it was almost three generations ago during the planning process that created the United Nations.[17] Whether the all-encompassing manner in which it has been defined by the UN community in the 1990s makes sense, however, is doubtful. The very alacrity with which nations big and small, rich and poor have seized upon the expanded conception of prevention gives some reason for pause. Through the years, the world body, in seeking consensus among its large and diverse membership, stretched a number of important, valid, and simple concepts until much of their initial meaning and operational relevance had been lost. This happened to peacekeeping, a carefully refined technique for dealing with a rather limited range of contingencies and requiring certain well-defined conditions for success, which was repeatedly misapplied during the 1990s as if it was some kind of a miracle cure-all for a broad spectrum of security ills.[18] Rather than developing new concepts and techniques for changing conditions and more demanding security tasks, policy analysts as well as policymakers tried to expand and distort the definition of peacekeeping by suggesting that it could be adapted through a series of generational modifications. The metamorphosis, of course, failed to take, and the results on the ground and in national capitals were enormously destructive in human, political, and conceptual terms.

The stakes may be less dramatic in the case of prevention, yet the dilemma is similar. It appears as if the advocates of prevention have tried to make it be all things to all people; but in the process it could well end up meaning very little to anybody. Prevention and peacekeeping are not the first concepts to get stretched at the United Nations beyond recognition. Through the years, there have been so many attempts in UN fora to expand the scope of the term "human rights" that some of the most ferocious debates are still about its proper meaning. "Development" has gained such wide-ranging connotations that one or two adjectives must precede it before it takes on any specific meaning, and even "sustainable development" has become a catch-all category. "Civil society," a currently popular buzzword, sometimes does and sometimes does not encompass the private sector in UN usage, and top leaders of the world body have even suggested that parliamentarians and local government officials should be included. In recent years, one of the most abused terms has been "reform," used to justify most any change in UN programs, finances, or structures desired by a particular member state or group at any given point in time. Another has been "democratization," which has been employed repeatedly as a rationale for giving a greater voice in the organization to countries with small populations or, in some cases, decidedly undemocratic governments. Yet of all these megaterms, none has assumed the programmatic and definitional proportions of "prevention."

Failing the Power Test

In assessing the power and traction of a new policy concept, three tests would seem apt:

1. Does its acceptance and application compel the organization to make choices and set priorities differently?
2. Are the members of the organization persuaded to alter significantly the pattern and direction of their contributions (whether financial, material, human, or political) to it?
3. Is the organization prepared to undertake substantial operational initiatives or structural innovations to realize the implications and goals of the new policy direction?

At this point, unfortunately, there is little evidence that prevention would pass any of these tests in terms of having made a real difference at the United Nations beyond raising awareness of the benefits of early action in some cases.

By identifying strategies for prevention so closely with the whole range of ongoing UN activities, the expanded approach fails to make the case for new priorities or hard decisions, therefore making little difference under the first test. In fact, at times it seems as if the popularity of prevention is being used as a vehicle for promoting support for the United Nations, rather than vice versa. Making choices among competing priorities is the hardest challenge for a virtually universal, multilateral organization. Such bodies tend to gravitate toward all-encompassing strategies because they justify and support the status quo, taking the wind out of the sails of those pressing for disruptive change and difficult trade-offs. In one issue area after another, UN member states have adopted laundry-list action plans, based on comprehensive, undifferentiated strategies that have not required setting priorities or making choices that might offend one group of member states, agencies, domestic constituencies, or other. The expanded concept of prevention, it seems, is in danger of following this well-worn path toward rhetorical glory and programmatic irrelevance.

For all of their professed enthusiasm for prevention, few member states appear willing to pass the second test. Only a handful have made voluntary contributions toward building UN capacities for preventive action. In July 2000, the Secretary-General ruefully noted that only seven member states had contributed a total of $7.4 million over three years to the UN Trust Fund for Preventive Action, set up with an initial contribution from Norway to assist the organization's capacity for undertaking preventive diplomacy in areas of tension.[19] Neither has there been any rush to increase financial support for the long list of UN system programs and agencies said to be performing essential preventive work. Even the International Atomic Energy Agency, a favorite in Washington, D.C., whose efforts to stem further nuclear proliferation would seem to be vital to prevention, is facing unusually severe cash-flow difficulties as other member states have delayed their payments.[20]

More generally, UN member states remained engaged in a bitter battle over whether and how to revise the assessment scales and spending levels for both peacekeeping and the regular budget, with few volunteers to shoulder a heavier load. It is no doubt true that prevention is a lot cheaper than cure, but as Secretary-General Annan has phrased it, still "there is an endemic paucity of resources for it."[21] The "Report of the Panel on UN Peace Operations" (known as the Brahimi Report after its chair, Lakhdar Brahimi) likewise concluded that an "impediment to effective crisis-preventive action is the gap between verbal postures and financial and political support for prevention."[22] Tellingly, the wide-ranging rosters of priorities agreed by the Security Council and the General Assembly at the September 2000 Millennium Summit made only passing references to prevention and offered no specific ideas, targets, or commitments.[23]

The United Nations' modest response to the third test, relating to operational or structural initiatives, also belies the rhetorical flourishes, judging by the Secretary-General's July 2000 statement to the Security Council, his Millennium Report, and the Brahimi Report. In reporting to the Security Council about what had been done to adapt the world body for its preventive role, the Secretary-General mentioned the establishment of a framework for interdepartmental and interagency cooperation, the designation of the Department of Political Affairs (DPA) as the system's focal point for prevention, and the assembling of a prevention team within DPA to identify situations where the United Nations could usefully take preventive action. He also expressed his intention "to strengthen the information gathering and analysis capacity of the Secretariat."[24] In addition, he praised the Council for banning unlicensed diamonds from Sierra Leone and Angola and for mandating the establishment of an expert panel on the illegal exploitation of natural resources from the Democratic Republic of the Congo.

The Secretary-General's Millennium Report is eloquent on the importance of prevention, yet it fails to make any specific recommendations to the Millennium Summit on the subject.[25] The Brahimi Report, though detailed in its suggestions to improve peacekeeping operations, merely seconds the Secretary-General's appeal for a more integrated approach to prevention and suggests that he might dispatch more fact-finding missions to areas of tension.[26] These would seem to be sensible steps, but they remain hardly commensurate with the grand challenge posed by the Secretary-General of making "conflict prevention the cornerstone of collective security in the twenty-first century."

Apples and Oranges

In policy terms, "operational prevention" embodies the United Nations' traditional emphasis on conflict resolution and dispute settlement. But the concept of prevention becomes vague and unwieldy when structural factors are added. There is no doubt, of course, that conflicts often have a multitude of deeply rooted causes and that the UN system, and other actors, need to keep chipping away at them as persistently as possible. In the long term, one might be able to envision a strategy that incorporates both levels sequentially and/or through distinct mechanisms. Yet it has been counterproductive to try to mix apples and oranges, or specific crises and generic goals, as part of a single overarching strategy. Their time lines, for one thing, are just too different. Exhortations to good government may make a difference over time, but the task of instilling or rebuilding a civil society is neither a sure nor quick enterprise, especially when the impetus comes from outside the country. It may be inconvenient, but unfortunately the most pressing challenges to preventive action happen to arise where bad governments reign, governmental authority has collapsed altogether, or territory is in dispute. These are the places, in other words, where time is in short supply and where the United Nations, regional organizations, and member states need to anticipate better, to respond quicker, and to act in a more, not less, targeted way.

The programmatic content and implications of "structural prevention" have yet to be defined. Would it be either feasible or desirable, for example, to try to place all or most of the world's development, humanitarian, and human rights programs into an integrated conflict prevention framework? The Brahimi Report praises the UN Task Force on Peace and Security for urging development and humanitarian agencies to view their work "through a 'conflict prevention lens' and make long-term prevention a key focus of their work."[27] But the report is silent on what this would mean in terms of adjustments in existing practices and priorities, or on what would become of other "lenses" or perspectives mandated at earlier points. These groups have their own purposes, orientations, and constituencies that long predate the current rage for prevention.

Likewise, the Carnegie Commission failed to recommend any new pro-

gram directions or innovations for the United Nations in the realm of structural prevention, making it sound more like a slogan than a policy choice.
Sensibly, it called instead for further progress in realizing the work programs laid out in the series of agenda-setting reports by Secretary-General
Boutros-Ghali: *An Agenda for Peace* (1992), the *Supplement to an Agenda
for Peace* (1995), *An Agenda for Development* (1995), and *An Agenda for
Democratization* (1996).[28] On top of all this—not to mention the various
lists of high ambitions produced by the General Assembly and ECOSOC—
another agenda for structural prevention would be more than a little super-
fluous.

On the one hand, it is probably worth reminding people that the diverse
development, human rights, and humanitarian programs of the UN system
have made and will continue to make a long-term contribution to laying the
foundation for structural prevention. They were doing the work of structural prevention long before the term was coined. On the other hand, such a
descriptive observation should not be confused with a prescriptive call for
reorienting their programs or for reallocating resources so that areas of high
tension command even more of the inadequate pool of resources available
for such purposes. One cannot safely assume that the aggregate level of
development assistance or of private investment will expand just because a
conflict prevention label is attached. The G-8 Miyazaki initiative for conflict prevention, for instance, includes lots of ways that development assistance can bolster long-term prevention, but it is silent on the prospects for
adding any new funds for this purpose. If the pool fails to grow, should
countries practicing tolerance, austerity, and good governance be penalized
for good behavior by having international resources diverted to less responsible places? Should the emergency needs of conflict prevention be allowed
to overrule the long-term development needs of the growing parts of the
world that show signs of becoming more, not less, stable?

There is some circularity to the structural-level arguments, as well, for
they project a near-perfect world of harmony, tolerance, good government,
equity, prosperity, disarmament, and respect for international law in which
there would be little need for prevention in the first place. Put simply, the
highly touted culture of prevention appears to be designed to turn bad
actors into good while eliminating any incentive for violence or disruption
of an idyllic world order. These are ennobling objectives, but they are dubi-
ous guides to policymaking. At no point in human history has it been possible to completely suppress those ugly instincts and characteristics—intoler-
ance, malevolence, prejudice, ignorance, avarice, jealousy, fear,
competition, demagogy, domination—that have fueled one conflict after
another. As long as some players refuse to play by the rules, international
organizations and member states will have ample opportunities for employing the kinds of crisis intervention and conflict resolution techniques

encompassed by the original notion of prevention and practiced by the United Nations and others for the past half-century.

The prevention mantra fits admirably well with the United Nations' political culture in that both emphasize impartiality, neutrality, and an aversion to coercion or violence. But does this affinity fit so well with the realities of economic and military power and of international and regional geopolitics? Would Saddam Hussein, Slobodan Milosevic, Foday Sankoh, or Osama bin Laden have been satisfied if the world had made more progress toward the high-minded goals associated with structural prevention? Would terrorists, transnational criminals, and those seeking weapons of mass destruction be impressed? Does the expansive version of prevention tell us what a durable framework for peace would look like in the Middle East or South Asia, or how we would persuade all sides not only that the end is right but that we also know a secure path to get there?

From a generic perspective, then, prevention looks impressive. But if it is to be relevant and helpful in individual cases, it needs to be tied to carefully tailored political processes that address the specific issues in dispute. As Pakistan, one of the few dissenting voices in the July 2000 Security Council debate, underlined, the failure of the Council statement to mention political disputes as one of the causes of conflict was itself a cause of some concern.[29] Dispute resolution usually requires outside actors—sometimes including the United Nations—to get their hands dirty in the unpleasant and ambiguous complexities of local and regional politics, perhaps even to take sides at some points. A universal theory cannot, by itself, offer a realistic alternative. Even the best preventive strategy will leave plenty of room for old-fashioned political give-and-take and for the creative management of carrots and sticks by those actors, usually member states, that have the power and will to make a difference. By affecting the calculations and choices of the parties to the conflict, these actors may be able to give life to the good intentions of international institutions and of prevention theory.

Institutional Impediments

On first glance, as noted above, the broad-based character of the UN system would seem to be a good match for an expanded notion of prevention. When the Bretton Woods institutions are added, all of the pieces would seem to be in place or could be created with a bit of jury-rigging here and there.[30] Although superficially attractive, the diffuse and scattered nature of the UN system could pose a considerable barrier to the effective implementation of a structural prevention strategy. As Secretary-General Annan has acknowledged,

> Effective action would often require joint action by many different organs
> and agencies, just as it requires joint action by different government
> departments within Member States. These different agencies often have
> separate agendas and, in the past, have not been used to thinking—let
> alone working—together. This is now improving, but there is still scope
> for much closer co-ordination of policy among them, and also, in many
> cases, between them and NGOs or the private sector.[31]

Coordination problems are as old as the United Nations itself. In his landmark 1969 "capacity" study, Robert Jackson complained that in the development area alone the UN "machine" had evolved into "probably the most complex organization in the world" with "about thirty separate governing bodies," yet "at the headquarters level, there is no real 'Headpiece'—no central co-ordinating organization—which could exercise effective control."[32] Urging greater coordination and more centralized control over agency budgets, he warned that there would be enormous opposition to change, as "that battle was fought when I was at Lake Success in the early days and the supporters of the sectoral approach won the day."[33]

The fact that the Secretary-General is still compelled to flag these same coordination problems testifies to how stubborn and resistant to repeated reform efforts these barriers to integrated planning and action have proven to be. They cannot be wished away, for they are endemic to the very structure and organizing principles that were agreed upon at the United Nations' founding and, to some extent, written into its Charter. The founders were quite taken with the functionalist theories of David Mitrany, who argued that political cooperation among nations could be built up over time through joint work on a variety of functional projects of mutual interest.[34] To ensure that the good work of the various specialized agencies would not be politicized or unduly tainted by the sometimes divisive politics of the principal UN intergovernmental organs, Western officials were especially keen on maintaining their autonomy within the UN system. The Bretton Woods institutions and the specialized agencies, therefore, were given their own charters, intergovernmental governing bodies, financing mechanisms, and leaderships.[35] As the number of agencies within the UN system—not to mention regional, subregional, and global intergovernmental bodies outside of the United Nations, as well as nongovernmental or mixed organizations—has grown, so have their constituencies within and among member states. The task of trying to foster a sense of unity within this expanding institutional constellation, consequently, has become that much more daunting.

It is a considerable irony that the same political dynamics, noted earlier, that compel broader conceptions of policy issues at the United Nations also work to ensure that the system remains structurally unable to implement properly such cross-cutting interagency strategies. This perversity is particularly apparent in issue areas, such as prevention, that necessarily involve an integration of effort between the development and humanitarian side of the house and the security side. Under the UN Charter, the Security Council has no authority to handle budgetary or personnel matters, to set programmatic priorities, or to dictate what any of the agencies or programs should do. According to Article 25, member states "agree to accept and carry out the decisions of the Security Council in accordance with the present Charter," but the Charter is silent on whether the agencies or Bretton Woods institutions have such an obligation.

Although results vary from place to place, crisis to crisis, and agency to agency, a reasonable degree of coordination of effort is sometimes achieved on the ground among the pieces of the UN family despite the barriers described above. Sometimes the Secretary-General or his representatives in the field are persuasive with their partners. At times, key states that are members of all of the major institutions act to ensure that they work together toward common objectives. The personal chemistry between Kofi Annan and the heads of the Bretton Woods institutions and of most agencies appears relatively good. But that has not always been the case, and the prospects for coordination are far too dependent on personalities.

The bottom line is that there are no guarantees and few institutional incentives to facilitate the achievement of any particular overarching goal or theme (and prevention is only the latest in a long list of systemwide mandates). The voluminous tracts on prevention, moreover, provide few insights and even fewer formulas for overcoming the institutional barriers to cooperation. The articulation of ever-wider approaches to prevention, in fact, makes the requirements and standards for coordination that much more demanding. On an operational level, then, prevention is primarily a matter for the Security Council, Secretary-General, key member states, and, where available, regional bodies, with early warning and analytical support from others as attainable. This is usually a doable proposition. The more that questions of economic and social development and of good governance enter the equation, however, the less feasible it becomes to translate lofty theories into a systemwide integration of effort.

Policy Directions

The conceptual dilemmas and institutional impediments flagged above should not be read as casting doubt on the validity and urgency of developing more effective capacities for preventive action. But they do suggest the following:

- Advocates would do well to tone down their rhetoric and to adopt a more candid, searching, and analytical approach to understanding the existing obstacles to effective implementation.
- Likewise, the policymakers, in the United Nations and in member-state governments, should focus on practical steps that can be achieved relatively soon to improve UN performance in operational prevention.
- Member states should accept that some fact-finding and monitoring efforts will be intrusive, as the sources of so many conflicts, whether of the intrastate, transnational, or interstate variety, arise within national territory.
- For the Secretary-General and/or the Security Council to be in a position to make well-informed judgments about local disputes and incipient conflicts, they will need to have access to information that is sensitive in terms of content and sources and that is sometimes potentially embarrassing to individual member states. The Secretariat will need to develop better procedures for handling such information on a fully confidential basis. Some member states will need to develop thicker skins; some will need to learn to be more forthcoming and less selective in sharing such information with the Secretary-General and the Security Council.
- As it has begun to do in cases involving the illicit trade in African diamonds, the Security Council will need to engage in naming-and-shaming tactics from time to time, something that will no doubt prove harder to do when major powers or Council members are involved. And as others have urged and it affirmed in July 2000, the Council should maintain its recent hands-on practice of undertaking fact-finding and diplomatic missions to areas of tension as needed.
- With the growing recognition of the importance of economic, resource, and financial factors both in fueling and potentially curbing conflict, greater attention needs to be directed toward involving the Bretton Woods institutions, regional banks and funds, and, where feasible and appropriate, the private sector in prevention strategies.
- Given the striking gap between rhetoric and action in this field, member states need to demonstrate that they are not ambivalent about strengthening UN capacity for undertaking timely and effective preventive measures. The July 2000 Council statement "recognizes the importance of adequate, stable and predictable resources for preventive action" and "encourages Member States to contribute" to the Trust Fund for Preventive Action. This would be a good place to start. More fundamentally, for all of the calls for closer coordination and greater integration of effort among the parts of the UN system and with the Bretton Woods institutions, member states should make a much more concerted effort, beginning in their national capitals, to ensure that this happens.

There are, no doubt, many other things that could be done to make the United Nations a more proficient instrument for prevention. Two deserve further mention here: early warning and peace enforcement.

No issue has been more inextricably linked to prevention than early warning. Through the years, there have been dozens of proposals for ensuring that the United Nations has mechanisms in place to detect signs of potential trouble and to transmit that information to the Security Council in a timely, accurate, and compelling manner. Many of these suggestions have called for greater receptivity to input from UN agencies and field missions and from nongovernmental groups, as well as for more transparency in the informal deliberations of the Security Council. Most of the proposals have urged more frequent use of the Secretary-General's powers under Article 99 to "bring to the attention of the Security Council any matter which in his opinion may threaten the maintenance of international peace and security." There has been limited progress on both fronts, with the Council employing the Arria formula for consultations with nongovernmental groups with growing frequency and with the Council's July 2000 statement on prevention issuing a virtual invitation to the Secretary-General to make fuller use of Article 99.

These are encouraging developments, and though the provision of timely information may be a necessary condition for prevention, it surely is not a sufficient one. How the information is assessed is equally important, and then how (and whether) member states choose to act on it is, of course, critical. Information, even from reliable sources, may be ambiguous or even misleading. It is frequently manipulated for political purposes. And it often is a poor predictor of future events. Some areas have faced seemingly dire crises for many years, yet local and international actors have managed to keep tensions just below the boiling point. Information, in other words, is not a substitute for judgment, although the latter works best when it is well informed. People, and nations, are selective listeners, usually absorbing what they want to hear or what fits their preconceptions. Surely one of the most intensive fact-finding efforts ever undertaken by the world body was the operation of the UN Special Commission in Iraq, which sought to uncover Baghdad's plans and preparations for acquiring weapons of mass destruction following the Gulf War. Yet even permanent members of the Security Council often chose to read the results of the monitoring in starkly different ways.

Determining whether a threat to international peace and security exists—and, if so, how imminent it is and how dangerous it is likely to become—is a highly political matter. At times, as in Rwanda, key members of the Council may be reluctant to recognize the truth or to see it publicized because they do not want to act. Knowing that violence is about to erupt is not equivalent to having an effective and politically acceptable remedy at hand. At other times, the UN assessment of the situation may clash with that of national intelligence findings or with the preferences of influential constituencies within important national capitals. If information indeed equals power, then member states that have highly developed sources for attaining information may not be eager to see their advantage diluted by the development of an independent UN capacity for gathering, assessing, and disseminating it among the membership as a whole. Small states, for their part, tend to be suspicious of UN efforts to develop intelligence or intervention capabilities, which could threaten their sovereignty and over which they would have little control. And given the highly political and sometimes divided nature of the world body, each member state or group of states could well have reason to question the accuracy and objectivity of UN-produced information and assessments from time to time.

Given these concerns and caveats, as well as others relating to costs, personnel, and turf, progress toward creating a UN early warning and threat assessment capacity has been agonizingly slow despite repeated initiatives. But there has been some modest movement in recent years. The prevention function logically has been assigned to the DPA, where much of the organization's regional expertise presides. Its Under-Secretary-General chairs the Executive Committee on Peace and Security (ECPS), which in turn has developed the interagency Framework for Coordination. These steps define an obvious locus for developing an institutional center for information, early warning, and analysis relating to prevention, and possibly to peacekeeping, enforcement, and weapons proliferation as well. The Brahimi Report has offered one useful model of how this might be done, calling for the creation of an ECPS Information and Strategic Analysis Secretariat that would report jointly to the Under-Secretaries-General for Political Affairs and for Peacekeeping Operations.[36] An earlier model, aimed at providing analytical services to all fifteen members of the Security Council, was offered by the International Task Force on the Enforcement of UN Security Council Resolutions, convened by the United Nations Association of the USA, chaired by Lord Carrington and cochaired by Moeen Qureshi.[37]

Despite some distinct elements, both proposals stress the need for a high-quality, professional, and interdisciplinary unit, one that earns the respect of member states through its competence and objectivity rather than its political correctness. Although both acknowledge the utility of enlisting some top-flight outside experts, as well as drawing on the existing Secretariat, neither provides a clear plan for gaining the input of civil society or for developing effective working relationships with regional and subregional bodies. These dimensions could use some creative thinking, perhaps beginning with lessons-learned case studies about whether nongovernmental and regional or subregional entities did provide or might have provided timely and accurate early warning in specific crises. How to route such inputs into the Council's deliberations in a useful and responsible manner also could benefit from further reflection. For example, in some cases citizen monitoring of weapons developments and deployments might enhance transparency and build confidence, especially if carried out on a transnational basis, although in other situations such efforts could conceivably fuel tensions instead.

Early warning matters, of course, to the extent that it prompts effective and timely action. This equation raises the troubling question of who has the will, capacity, and legal authority to conduct peace enforcement when the Security Council decides that such action is required to deter or limit threats to international peace and security, or to respond to aggression. Enforcement is the missing link in the UN approach to peace and security, as well as the Achilles' heel of global prevention strategies. As noted above, the Secretary-General and the Brahimi Report have asserted that military enforcement is a matter to be taken up by others, as the world body is not in that business at this point in its history. Neither has acknowledged that this assertion, and the facts that underlay it, could well undermine the credibility of the United Nations as a tool for prevention in a range of situations. This may not be a great liability when dealing with the chaotic collapse of local and national governments, when no one seems to be in charge or accountable for their actions. Yet the lack of even a pretense of a military response capability is bound to weaken prospects for deterring bad actors— whether national or subnational—from undertaking horrific or highly destabilizing actions. And these cases, involving deliberate actions or provocations, whether by states, armed groups, or terrorists, are the ones that most threaten international peace and security.

As is said so often in UN circles, ad hoc tribunals and an international criminal court can help to ensure that those who engage in terrible abuses will no longer enjoy impunity. Fair enough, but at the same time, the core requirement—courts or no courts—remains a capacity to enforce the decisions of the Security Council, as well as the findings of the tribunals or the court themselves. Likewise, the proposals by the Carnegie Commission and many others for preventive deployments and for rapid reaction forces would only be credible if they were backed up by larger military contingents and/or greater firepower should they be seriously challenged.[38] In that regard, the oft-cited success of the UN Preventive Deployment Force in Macedonia was no doubt due more to the fact that the forces deployed along the border with Serbia happened to be American than that they were part of a UN mission. As both the Carrington-Qureshi and Brahimi Reports have emphasized, military enforcement and complex peacekeeping, respectively, require the Security Council to shift from best-case to worst-case planning, to clarify mandates, and to provide ample forces and robust rules of engagement.[39] "When the United Nations does send its forces to uphold the peace," argued the Brahimi Report, "they must be prepared to confront the lingering forces of war and violence, with the ability to defeat them. . . . No amount of good intentions can substitute for the fundamental ability to project credible force."[40]

From a military perspective, these points appear almost self-evident, but they have proven distinctly uncomfortable for many at the United Nations, including member states as well as the Secretariat. As this author has discussed elsewhere, the political culture of the world body is deeply ambivalent about undertaking enforcement measures, whether through military or economic means.[41] This discomfort level, moreover, appears to be rising, along with growing divisions in the Security Council. In fact, it would appear that one of the attractions of prevention strategies has been that they promise to do away with the enforcement dilemma. But to suggest that if prevention works then enforcement would not be needed is to offer a false promise. To the extent that current theorizing and posturing about prevention downplay the powerful linkages among prevention, deterrence, credibility, and enforcement, they ring hollow.

Conclusion

Now that they have embraced prevention with such enthusiasm, the Secretary-General and member states need to take a more discriminating approach that emphasizes operational prevention as an immediate policy option while recognizing the long-term importance of structural factors. As a first step, member states should commit themselves to a much larger investment in the practical tools the UN system needs to become a more effective instrument for both prevention and enforcement at the operational level. As the Secretary-General has reminded them on numerous occasions, peace also has a price. At the same time, those advocating a central place for prevention in UN security strategies should address the kinds of dilemmas and challenges raised in this chapter more directly and candidly. Otherwise, much of the power and value of the concept could be lost, and prevention will fail to make the transition from an attractive slogan to a compelling set of policy choices.

Notes

1. John Gerard Ruggie, "Wandering in the Void: Charting the UN's New Strategic Role," *Foreign Affairs* 2, 5 (November/December 1993): 6–31. For a more recent critique by a UN-appointed panel of the organization's failure to update its

peacekeeping doctrine to meet changing conditions, see "Report of the Panel on United Nations Peace Operations" (hereafter referred to as the Brahimi Report), A/55/305, August 21, 2000, especially paras. 17–28.

2. Carnegie Commission on Preventing Deadly Conflict, *Preventing Deadly Conflict: Final Report* (New York: Carnegie Corporation of New York, 1997), 37.

3. For the role of prevention in the planning process during World War II, see Townsend Hoopes and Douglas Brinkley, *FDR and the Creation of the UN* (New Haven: Yale University Press, 1997), 111; and Ruth B. Russell, *A History of the United Nations Charter: The Role of the United States 1940–1945* (Washington, D.C.: Brookings Institution, 1958), 458. At the 1945 founding conference in San Francisco, the proposed references in the UN Charter to prevention stirred little discussion, much less dissent. Ibid., 655–656.

4. See Charter of the United Nations, Articles 1 (paragraph 1), 2 (5), 5, 39, 40, 50, 55, 65, and 99. The UN Charter does not include the term "preventive diplomacy," which has been employed frequently by UN officials and scholars in recent years. This chapter will primarily use the terms "preventive action" and "preventive measures," in order to be consistent with the UN Charter as well as to suggest the wide spectrum of policy instruments that have been utilized for preventive purposes.

5. Statement by the President of the Security Council, S/23500, January 31, 1992.

6. Report of the UN Secretary-General, "An Agenda for Peace: Preventive Diplomacy, Peacemaking and Peace-keeping," A/47/277, June 17, 1992, paras. 20, 21, and 23.

7. Address by the Secretary-General, Forum on the Final Report of the Carnegie Commission on Preventing Deadly Conflict, "The Centrality of the United Nations to Prevention and the Centrality of Prevention to the United Nations," Press Release SG/SM/6454, February 5, 1998. For similar statements by the Secretary-General, see the text of a message by the Secretary-General for the opening of an Inter-Parliamentary Union Conference, "The Importance of Conflict Prevention," SG/SM/6514, April 3, 1998, and the address by the Secretary-General at Rice University, "The Challenge of Conflict Prevention," SG/SM/6535, April 23, 1998.

8. Ibid.

9. Address by the Secretary-General, "Development Is the Best Form of Prevention," First United Nations Lecture (Washington, D.C.: World Bank, October 19, 1999); "The Question of Intervention: Statements by the Secretary-General" (United Nations: Department of Public Information, 1999), 47–55.

10. Address by the Secretary-General to the Security Council, "The Role of the Security Council in the Prevention of Armed Conflict," Press Release SG/SM/7238, November 29, 1999.

11. Security Council debates on the prevention of armed conflict, Press Releases SC/6759, November 29, 1999, SC/6761, November 30, 1999, and SC/6892, July 20, 2000.

12. Statement by the President of the Security Council, S/PRST/1999/34, November 30, 1999.

13. Statement by the President of the Security Council, S/PRST/2000/25, July 20, 2000.

14. G-8 Communiqué, Okinawa, Japan, July 23, 2000, and G-8 Miyazaki Initiatives for Conflict Prevention, G-8 Foreign Ministers' Meeting, Miyazaki, Japan, July 13, 2000.

15. Report of the Secretary-General, "'We the Peoples': The Role of the United Nations in the 21st Century" (United Nations: Department of Public Information, 2000), 45.

16. Report of the Secretary-General, "Renewing the United Nations: A Programme for Reform," A/51/950, July 14, 1997, para. 107. The August 2000 Brahimi Report flatly declared that "the United Nations does not wage war" (para. 53).

17. The case for such a strategy was argued by this author in "Making Peace," *Foreign Policy* 89 (winter 1992–1993): 137–155.

18. The Brahimi panel, in its August 2000 report, reaches a similar assessment of the experience of the 1990s, but its conclusion is not to more clearly distinguish between peacekeeping and peace enforcement missions, as this author would prefer, but rather to clarify the tasks required by Security Council mandates and to provide better intelligence, more robust rules of engagement, and stronger and better pre-pared forces for "complex peace operations." Brahimi Report, paras. 15–28 and 48–75. On these points, also see the Final Report of the International Task Force on the Enforcement of UN Security Council Resolutions, "Words to Deeds: Strengthening the UN's Enforcement Capabilities" (New York: United Nations Association of the USA, 1997).

19. UN Press Release SC/6892.

20. William Drodziak, "UN Atomic Agency Is Threatened by Financial Crisis; U.S. Dues Arrears Could Force Cutbacks, Arms Monitor Says," *Washington Post*, August 8, 2000.

21. UN Press Release SG/SM/7238 (SC/6760), November 29, 1999.

22. Brahimi Report, para. 33.

23. United Nations Millennium Declaration, A/Res/55/2, September 18, 2000, paras. 9b and 28b; S/Res/1318, September 7, 2000, IIa and VIIb.

24. UN Press Release SC/6892, July 20, 2000.

25. "'We the Peoples,'" 44–46 and 77–80.

26. Brahimi Report, para. 34.

27. Brahimi Report, para. 30.

28. Carnegie Commission on Preventing Deadly Conflict, 142–145.

29. UN Press Release SC/6892, July 20, 2000.

30. Although technically considered by some to be specialized agencies of the UN system, in practice the Bretton Woods institutions have acted as autonomous bodies, and they do not report to the General Assembly.

31. UN Press Release SG/SM/7238, November 29, 1999.

32. Sir Robert G.A. Jackson, *A Study of the Capacity of the United Nations Development System*, vol. 1 (Geneva: United Nations, 1969), iii.

33. Ibid., vi. The United Nations had not even reached its third birthday when the U.S. Senate in 1948 issued its first report lamenting the lack of "central program planning" in the UN system, the "overlapping and duplication of effort," and the "proliferation of bodies" caused by "weak coordination among the agencies and within national governments." William S. White, "U.N. Expenditures Called Excessive," *New York Times*, July 10, 1948, as discussed in Edward C. Luck, *Mixed Messages: American Politics and International Organization, 1919–1999* (Washington, D.C.: Brookings Institution Press, 1999), 202–203.

34. Luck, *Mixed Messages*, 208–209, 305–306, and 361.

35. Articles 57, 58, 63, and 64 of the UN Charter define the relationship between the specialized agencies and the central United Nations. Under Article 58, the United Nations can make "recommendations" to the agencies about coordinat-

ing policies and activities, but it has no power to compel them to implement decisions emanating from UN headquarters in New York.

36. Brahimi Report, paras. 65–75.
37. "Words to Deeds," 16–21.
38. Carnegie Commission on Preventing Deadly Conflict, 65–67.
39. "Words to Deeds," 29–41, and the Brahimi Report, 1, 3, 9–12.
40. Brahimi Report, viii and 1.
41. Edward C. Luck, "The Enforcement of Humanitarian Norms and the Politics of Ambivalence," in *Civilians in War*, ed. Simon Chesterman, a project of the International Peace Academy (Boulder: Lynne Rienner Publishers, 2001).

PART 3

Comparative Advantages:
Practitioner Perspectives
Beyond the United Nations

12

The Role of Research and Policy Analysis

Maureen O'Neil and Necla Tschirgi

As the chapters in this book amply demonstrate, conflict prevention is now firmly established on the international agenda.[1] It has been embraced by the United Nations system and given special prominence by UN Secretary-General Kofi Annan, who has argued that "the United Nations of the twenty-first century must become increasingly a focus of preventive measures."[2] It has forcefully been inserted into the G-8 Ministerial discussions. It is incorporated into the Organization for Economic Cooperation and Development (OECD) Development Assistance Committee Task Force's Guidelines for Conflict, Peace, and Development Co-operation.[3] It is part of the operational work of the Conflict Prevention and Post-Conflict Reconstruction Network (CPR),[4] and it has been adopted, with varying levels of commitment, by national governments, regional organizations, and international nongovernmental organizations (NGOs).[5]

There are multiple reasons for the emergence of a "culture of prevention" in the early 1990s. In a nutshell, it is a belated recognition on the part of the international community of the horrendous costs and consequences of violent conflicts in areas of the world that were not considered as major security concerns during the Cold War. Once the main threat to international security was reduced with the end of the Cold War, the United Nations and other international agencies were at long last able to turn their attention to addressing other security issues outside the shadow of superpower confrontation. What became evident to policymakers is that the great majority of violent conflicts of the post–Cold War era are intrastate and have significant effects on human security. Moreover, in a rapidly globalizing world, these localized violent conflicts can no longer be contained within their borders. From refugee movements to arms smuggling, from criminal financial transactions to pandemics, local conflicts present new security threats with far-reaching repercussions. In addition, as a result of the global revolution in information and communication technologies, even distant conflicts are able to claim the world's attention.

As the international community started to pay closer attention to an expanded security agenda, its ability to protect peace was sorely tested in such diverse places as Somalia, Rwanda, and Bosnia. Beyond the moral imperative to respond, even belatedly, to the worst cases of violence involving humanitarian and human rights disasters, the international system found itself ill-equipped to address intrastate or local conflicts. Inevitably, two sets of questions gained particular prominence: What are the causes, dynamics, and consequences of violent conflicts in the 1990s? and What are the appropriate strategies (both at the policy and operational levels) to deal with conflicts before they turn violent?

The answers to these questions were neither obvious nor readily available, leading the policy community to turn to experts, researchers, and policy analysts for insights. As decisionmakers struggled to respond to each crisis on an ad hoc basis, the research and policy analysis community faced an equally difficult task. For almost fifty years, academics and researchers had basically addressed the twin issues of international security and intrastate affairs separately. Yet with the spillover of intrastate conflicts into the international arena—in the form of humanitarian crises or regional security threats—experts and researchers were called upon to explain the links between local conflicts and their related international dimensions.

Two streams of research converged to influence the international community's growing involvement in intrastate conflicts in the 1990s. On the one hand, the academic community responded to the profound shifts in the international system by undertaking a rigorous, lively, and sometimes fanciful rethinking of the new security, peace, and developmental challenges of the post–Cold War era. From micro-level studies of identity-based conflicts to macro-level analyses of the new contours of international security in a globalized world, the academic literature underwent a rejuvenation by freeing itself of the established paradigms of the Cold War. Simultaneously, the policy community (including the UN system, international and regional organizations, and donor governments) commissioned a large body of research on the multiple dimensions of the new security agenda and appropriate strategies for dealing with local conflicts at the national, regional, and global levels. The interest in conflict prevention thus emerged at the intersection of theory and practice.

This chapter aims to examine the contributions of researchers, experts, and policy analysts in informing and influencing the conflict prevention agenda. The analysis attempts several interrelated tasks. In the first instance, it provides an overview of the substantive knowledge base of conflict prevention and peacebuilding.[6] Observing that conflict prevention requires a special mix of theoretical insights and practical strategies that can be used by multiple actors, the chapter then examines selected institutional arrangements and mechanisms that were created in the 1990s to bridge the traditional gap between knowledge producers and users, as well as between theorists, policy analysts, and practitioners. In conclusion, the chapter contains useful insights about how and why these new mechanisms might herald the creation of new models of partnership involving diverse stakeholders with a common commitment to conflict prevention and peacebuilding.

Given this volume's interest in conflict prevention as a global concern, the chapter focuses primarily on research and analysis of direct interest to the United Nations as well as to key national, regional, and international actors. As a result, the chapter does not cover the academic or policy research undertaken in developing countries—except in cases where such research is linked to international policy and action or is part of a global network. This is not meant to minimize the importance of local or country-level research and perspectives. On the contrary, one of the starting points of this chapter is the recognition that conflicts in the 1990s were predominantly domestic or local in nature, even though the impetus for conflict prevention has largely come from the international community. Thus, if the new agenda for conflict prevention and peacebuilding has any chance of success, it needs to integrate a solid understanding of conflict dynamics at the local, national, and regional levels with appropriate strategies for action by national, regional, and international actors. The approach taken here allows not only an examination of the necessary knowledge base for conflict prevention but also the identification of innovative ways of combining research, analysis, advocacy, and action that can link the efforts of diverse actors.

The Knowledge Base of Conflict Prevention

The international conflict prevention agenda lies at the intersection of conflict theory and preventive action. Drawing its insights from conflict analysis, it is solidly rooted in liberal internationalism, which seeks to bring pragmatic, workable, and timely policy prescriptions to reform the international system.[7] In reviewing its knowledge base, it is therefore useful to map out the main streams of work that feed into the conflict prevention agenda, to highlight ongoing debates within the field, and to identify important gaps that require further research and analysis.

The knowledge base of conflict prevention is as rich as it is diverse.

Nonetheless, it is useful to distinguish between two main streams of work that have contributed in significant, albeit different, ways to conflict prevention. The first encompasses the academic literature generated by scholars, area specialists, and other experts that is primarily housed in universities or independent research institutes; the second includes the targeted policy research and evaluation studies undertaken or commissioned by a variety of international actors. This is not to argue that the two streams exist in isolation or are mutually exclusive. However, it is to distinguish between research that is primarily curiosity-based, supply-driven, and designed to further knowledge, and research that is need-based, demand-driven, and designed to advance policy, advocacy, or action. As discussed in the next section, the boundaries between these two types of research have become quite porous in the area of conflict prevention—with significant implications for nurturing new models of collaboration between researchers, scholars, donors, policymakers, and practitioners.

The academic literature bearing on conflict comes from various disciplines and area studies and consists of the theoretical works on peace, conflict, and development as well as the rich array of historical and empirical case studies. Adding to the collective insights on conflict of such distinct fields as political science, psychology, sociology, economics, international relations, law, human rights, peace and conflict studies, and development studies, there has been a proliferation of new research on different aspects of intrastate conflict in the post–Cold War era, as well as the range of military, diplomatic, humanitarian, human rights, economic, political, and legal instruments that have been employed for conflict resolution, peacemaking, and peacebuilding.[8] Not surprisingly, much of this new research is based in Western/Northern universities and institutions and reflects external perspectives on local conflicts. The reasons for the paucity of social science research in developing countries and impediments to effective cross-fertilization of perspectives among social science communities in developing and developed countries deserve separate attention that go beyond the aims of this chapter.[9] However, it is worth noting that the new research on peacebuilding is generally internationalist in orientation and multidisciplinary in nature and seeks to link intrastate conflicts to other international issues such trade, aid, debt, governance, human rights, development assistance, globalization, regional integration, arms regimes, crime, and refugees.[10]

In the best tradition of social science research, however, this large body of literature is predominantly explanatory and diagnostic rather than prescriptive. Given the diversity of theoretical and analytical approaches employed by social scientists, much of the academic research is also open-ended, subject to ongoing interpretation, and not directly linked to immediate policy concerns. For example, there is an impressive body of research on the causes and dynamics of civil wars, conflict analysis, conflict resolution and mediation, and peacemaking. However, there is continuing debate about the causal relationship between such factors as ethnicity, poverty, inequality, and conflict. Recognized experts disagree strongly about what mix of systemic, institutional, or conjunctural factors cause conflicts in different contexts, as well as what the preconditions are for peacebuilding. Recent academic research on early warning has sought to systematize the relevant information on early signs of conflict (such as human rights, security indicators, economic accelerators, or political triggers) that can serve to alert the policy community to the probability of impending conflict.[11] However, the academic community has, for the most part, been relatively reticent to become involved in identifying and proposing relevant early response options.

Similarly, the academic literature is rich with research on the structural sources of conflict at the national, regional, and international levels. There is, for example, growing evidence indicating that the process of democratization in authoritarian regimes often leads to instability and conflict. Yet parallel research demonstrates that historically democratic institutions have effectively served as instruments of conflict resolution and management. Unless they are specifically brought together to generate contingent generalizations, these two strands of research provide little guidance to policymakers on the compatibility of democracy and peacebuilding in concrete contexts or under differing circumstances. In the same vein, the links between conflict, population growth, and environmental degradation/natural resource scarcity remain highly controversial. As social scientists know all too well, establishing causality and attributing responsibility for historical outcomes to concrete actions stretch the boundaries of social science methodologies. Thus, more often than not, research findings from academic research are either at a high level of generalization that falls short of providing guidelines for preventive action or are too context-specific to allow general lessons to be drawn. Yet conflict prevention requires preemptive action informed by an appropriate mix of contingent generalizations drawn from historical precedents and probable hypotheses. The supreme paradox of conflict prevention is, of course, that it erases proof of its success.

The built-in limitations of social science methodologies have not, however, prevented the generation of a recent body of applied, policy-oriented, and operations research, mainly at the request or initiation of governments, donor agencies, foundations, and other national or international actors who have embraced the conflict prevention agenda and need analytical and operational tools to devise appropriate preventive strategies. The breadth of this body of research is quite impressive. Even a cursory review reveals a wealth of research (both geographic and thematic) on conflict and actor analysis, risk analysis, conflict mapping, sectoral analyses, and issue-specific studies.[12] In addition, there is a growing body of evaluation studies on the multitude of policy/programming strategies and tools that have recently been employed for conflict prevention.[13] Unlike academic research, which is often long-term and not particularly time-sensitive, much of the policy-oriented and applied research tends to betray the short time frames, pressing priorities, and narrow institutional mandates of its sponsors. As a result, even though there is a proliferation of applied research projects, many of these are quite narrowly focused, noncumulative, agency-specific, and largely inaccessible to the broader academic and research communities.

Like recent academic research on peacebuilding, much of the commissioned research as well as the large number of evaluation studies referred to above have been undertaken by Western and Northern researchers and consultants and predominantly reflect Western/Northern perspectives—despite the fact that they deal primarily with non-Western countries facing violent conflicts. With few exceptions, researchers and analysts from war-prone, war-torn, or postwar countries have not independently embraced the conflict prevention or peacebuilding agenda, although some are increasingly working with international networks or serving as consultants on international projects.[14]

On the positive side, the great diversity and range of internationally driven and policy-oriented research has served to create the cumulative knowledge base to start moving from a particularistic and impressionistic analysis of individual case studies or discrete evaluation exercises of recent peacebuilding experiences to a compilation of what is increasingly called "best practices" and "lessons learned."[15] Whether it is in the area of Truth Commissions, electoral assistance, demobilization, disarmament and reintegration, the role of regional organizations, or economic sanctions, researchers are increasingly able to draw upon a large body of policy experiments or experiences based on concrete case studies. Simultaneously, on the basis of a growing understanding of the consequences of not acting preventively, researchers are developing new methodologies and approaches to plan, monitor, and evaluate appropriate interventions. For example, two such approaches, so-called do no harm and peace and conflict impact assessments, are designed to sensitize development and/or foreign policy actors to integrate conflict prevention into their regular policies and programs.[16] In short, increasingly there is a wealth of policy and practice upon which to start building a more systematic knowledge base on what works and what does not work in conflict prevention.

Yet if conflict prevention is to sustain itself as a policy field capable of generating robust strategies and policy options, the insights from academic and applied research will need, increasingly, to be merged. There are two areas where these can most productively come together. The first consists of comparative case studies of countries with similar historical trajectories but variable experiences with violent conflict; the second involves a comparative analysis of the variable outcomes of similar preventive strategies. Both require a systematic examination of short-term policy interventions in light of theoretical and comparative work in order to identify insights that might be promising for future action.[17] In fact, several current research projects of special relevance for conflict prevention effectively employ both academic and applied research. Two prominent examples in the area of the political economy of peacebuilding include the Economic Agendas in Civil Wars Project undertaken by the International Peace Academy, and the Economics of Civil Wars, Violence, and Crime Project launched by the Development Economics Research Group of the World Bank.[18]

Despite heightened research interest in conflict prevention, there is a healthy body of opinion that is skeptical of the feasibility of conflict prevention or the broader peacebuilding agenda.[19] Even its supporters are divided among themselves as to what type of information, knowledge, and analysis would best serve conflict prevention. For example, some point to the need for more reliable, timely, and locally grounded information for better decisionmaking. Others forcefully argue that the shortcomings of conflict prevention derive more from political and operational factors rather than any lack of relevant information and analysis.[20] This debate is partially reflected in the number and range of databases that are available to researchers and policymakers such as the State Failure website, the Minorities at Risk Project, and the Global Events Data Base at the University of Maryland; the Country Indicators for Foreign Policy Project of the Norman Paterson School of International Affairs at Carleton University; and the Reliefweb of UN Office for the Coordination of Humanitarian Affairs and Refworld of the UN High Commission for Refugees. Many of these databases are designed to provide empirical, historical, and comparative data along various dimensions of the new security agenda.

However, databases are only as good as the use to which they are put. For example, eschewing existing databases, the UN Secretariat recently launched a web-based documentation project with Harvard University's Center for Population and Development Studies. This new resource is tailored for use by policymakers, in particular, but not only in the UN Department of Political Affairs (DPA), the designated focal point for conflict prevention at the United Nations. The objective is twofold: first, to provide DPA with efficient online access to existing research; second, to facilitate the exchange of ideas on preventing and managing conflict. The novelty of the initiative lies in that it allows users within DPA to put in requests for information on a specific topic. Moreover, the site provides a forum for electronic conferencing with password-protected and, if warranted, anonymous participation. The material posted on the site relates to a diverse range of topics, including conflict prevention, preventive diplomacy, peacebuilding, security and development, causes of conflicts, and human security. The site also provides a selected and guided system of links with other relevant websites, arranged according to topic and source, with a description and evaluation of their interest and utility. In conjunction with the website, a newsgroup is being developed whereby selected members of the UN system will receive regular information on new resources and a short summary of important materials placed on the website.[21] Although this new database is primarily addressed to the needs of the UN system, it remains to be seen how, and with what degree of effectiveness, it will be used by its target group.[22]

The above review demonstrates that there is a solid and growing body of knowledge to help inform and influence the conflict prevention agenda. Yet as indicated above, the availability of knowledge is itself no guarantee of its effective use. There is a longstanding debate about the inevitable chasm between researchers and policymakers, and over the years numerous mechanisms have been created to bridge the chasm with varying degrees of success.[23] Conflict prevention stands out as a particularly difficult policy area because of its activist and interventionist orientation, its urgency and time-sensitivity, the complexity and diversity of its knowledge base, and the multiplicity of its stakeholders. Thus, conflict prevention requires an even stronger infrastructure linking researchers to policy analysts, decisionmakers, diplomats, governmental and NGO representatives in the field, and other key actors in real time. There are numerous specialized institutions and intermediary organizations (such as foreign policy institutes, think tanks, consulting firms, and advisory or advocacy groups) who serve to bring research to the attention of the policy community; however, in most cases these institutions are themselves not linked to the policy process.[24] More recently, the conflict prevention agenda has given rise to a number of new mechanisms or networks that are specifically designed to generate research and analysis through the active participation of a unique mix of academics, researchers, diplomats, eminent personalities, field practitioners, advocates, and activists. The following section focuses on several such innovations by which research, policy analysis, advocacy, policy development, and practice are linked in more organic ways to bridge the gap between knowledge, policy, and practice in the area of conflict prevention.

New Mechanisms for Linking
Research, Policy, and Action in Conflict Prevention

The models described below are quite different from each other, as they are from the earlier generation of policy think tanks or research institutes.[25] In a way, they represent the multiple research-based roles and capacities that are required by the international community to address the conflict prevention agenda effectively. Some mechanisms, like the Carnegie Commission on Preventing Deadly Conflict (CCPDC), are primarily concerned with generating and establishing a knowledge base to launch a new agenda and create a platform for debate. Others, like the International Institute for Democracy and Electoral Assistance (International IDEA), draw upon existing knowledge in order to develop and codify evolving international norms and to provide specific knowledge-based tools for policymakers and practitioners. Still others, like the International Crisis Group (ICG), are interested in generating field-based research and analysis for advocacy. Meanwhile, some networks, including the Peace Implementation Network (PIN) at the Fafo Institute for Applied Social Science as well as the Conflict Prevention Network (CPN), serve to provide targeted research and analysis to improve the operational and policy work of their key stakeholders. Finally, there are new institutional arrangements, like the Forum on Early Warning and Early Response (FEWER), that link local networks and their international counterparts to create the necessary knowledge chain for multilevel policy development, programming, and training. Despite their different roles and capacities, what seems to unite these mechanisms is their contributions to conflict prevention as an explicit area of global concern, their participatory approaches to research generation and utilization, and their appeal to multiple constituencies ranging from the UN system to international and regional organizations, national governments, and the nongovernmental community. The following review is neither comprehensive nor exhaustive but is intended to provide a small sample of innovations in this field by highlighting, without assessing, the unique approach and mandate of each initiative.

Carnegie Commission on Preventing Deadly Conflict

Arguably the single most important research and policy analysis enterprise that influenced the conflict prevention agenda was the Carnegie Commission on Preventing Deadly Conflict. Created and funded by the Carnegie Corporation of New York in May 1994, the CCPDC set out to examine the threat of intergroup violence to world peace and to advance new ideas for the prevention and resolution of deadly conflict.[26] Cochaired by David Hamburg (president emeritus of the Carnegie Corporation and an eminent scholar) and Cyrus Vance (former U.S. secretary of state and UN Special Representative of the Secretary-General), the Commission consisted of sixteen eminent international leaders, and scholars with a long experience in diplomacy, conflict prevention, and resolution. The CCPDC was assisted in its work by an advisory council, expert consultants, and experienced practitioners.

The Commission examined the principal causes of ethnic, nationalist, and religious conflicts within and between states and the circumstances that foster or deter their outbreak. It sought to identify the requirements for an effective system for preventing mass violence. It further looked at the strengths and weaknesses of various international entities in conflict prevention and how international organizations could contribute to developing an effective international system of nonviolent problem-solving.

Over its four-year life span, the Commission generated an impressive body of research and analysis in the form of books, discussion papers, reports, and webcast conferences by engaging some of the most prominent and knowledgeable researchers in different fields. Alongside its massive research outputs, CCPDC produced educational materials, including curricula for university, secondary school, and summer school programs. The products of the Commission's work were distributed and disseminated to multiple audiences through mostly conventional methods, including printed materials, seminars, and workshops. However, making use of recent technology, the Commission also made these materials available through its website and a CD-ROM.

Given its impressive pedigree and composition, the Commission played a key role in drawing attention to the urgency of the prevention agenda and in making a compelling case for the creation of a culture of prevention. By bringing together researchers and influential personalities with a track record in foreign policy, diplomacy, and international affairs, the Commission took research from its academic environment and projected it into the global arena for discussion, policy development, and action. However, there was no built-in mechanism at the creation of the Commission to ensure that the research it commissioned and supported fed directly into the political or policy process except through the informal networks in which the Commission's eminent members and researchers participated. This distinguishes the Commission from other models described below, as well as subsequent international commissions such as the Independent Commission on Kosovo and the International Commission on Intervention and State Sovereignty that have since been established to address aspects of the new international peace and security agenda through research and analysis.[27]

Forum on Early Warning and Early Response

Unlike CCPDC, which was created and funded by a private U.S. foundation, the Forum on Early Warning and Early Response emerged as a global coalition of organizations seeking to provide early warning of violent conflicts and inform peacebuilding efforts by identifying early response options. FEWER is a network supported by multiple donors and is solidly grounded in the work of its member organizations. FEWER members come from Africa, Asia, Eurasia, South America, and North America and include NGOs, academic institutions, think tanks, and intergovernmental agencies. As a network, FEWER seeks to enhance the work of its members by facilitating coordination and avoiding duplication of existing efforts on the basis of a common agenda. Based in the United Kingdom, the FEWER Secretariat serves as a coordinating and outreach hub for the network. Since its creation in 1996, FEWER has produced research and analysis on various international crises. These include (a) early warning, including the prediction of the outbreak and escalation of conflicts in the Democratic Republic of Congo and the ensuing regional war; the Chechen crisis; and the violence in Guinea Conakry; (b) early response, elaborating strategies for conflict prevention in Javakheti (Georgia) and Guinea Conakry and a survey of the conflict prevention capacities of key actors in the Caucasus; and (c) research, including the development of practice-based methods and systems for early warning, processes for planning integrated responses to early warning, and a methodology for impact assessment. Specifically, FEWER has developed conflict and peace indicators for the Caucasus and Great Lakes regions, as well as indicators for small-arms flows.[28]

FEWER is an example of a policy-oriented global network that relies on research and analysis as the centerpiece of its work. The distinguishing features of FEWER are its commitment to link local level information and analysis (early warning) to multilevel policy development and preventive action (early response). FEWER targets its periodic research reports and analyses to multiple agencies, including the United Nations, regional organizations, governmental and donor representatives, and other international actors. FEWER's country or regional reports not only provide locally grounded analyses of current conditions but also identify appropriate preventive strategies for diverse actors in light of the available analyses. Based on its fieldwork and growing understanding of the broader international context for conflict prevention, FEWER is currently developing new training tools and methodologies that are designed for its multiple constituencies. Inevitably, FEWER's long-term success will depend on its ability to serve and strengthen that constituency and to demonstrate the effectiveness of its work in practice.

International Crisis Group

The International Crisis Group is another organization, created in 1995 in the wake of the humanitarian crises of the early 1990s, with the explicit purpose of providing an independent source of information, analysis, and ideas on crises and emerging conflicts to alert senior government officials and the media to upcoming threats to peace and security and to offer options for preventive action. ICG's approach to conflict prevention consists of three interrelated activities: field research and analysis, publication and dissemination, and advocacy. Based in Brussels, in close proximity to the North Atlantic Treaty Organization headquarters and other European decisionmakers, ICG also maintains an office in Washington, D.C., and has field staff stationed in regions of the world it covers. In 2000, these included the Balkans (mainly the former Yugoslavia, Albania, and Macedonia), Africa (Central Africa and Algeria), and Asia (Indonesia, East Timor, and Cambodia). Unlike FEWER, ICG does not have formal links with local organizations or institutes, although it draws heavily on local perspectives by deploying knowledgeable staff in its field offices.

The ICG has a board composed of influential and eminent personalities, including diplomats, journalists, and policymakers from around the world, to reach out to the broader international policy community. Its first chairman was the former U.S. senator George Mitchell; its current chairman is Martti Ahtisaari, the former president of Finland. Unlike traditional think tanks and policy institutes, the ICG is international both in its composition and its target audiences. Its current president, Gareth Evans, who served as Australian foreign minister from 1988 to 1996, explains:

> There has long been a need for fresh thinking, and new ways of communicating that thinking, if governments are to become better—as they must—in dealing with crises and preventing and containing deadly conflict. ICG responds to that need. It's not just a matter of being on the ground in potential trouble spots, producing high quality analysis. It's also a matter of producing for decision-makers, and those that influence them, well focussed, well targeted and highly practical policy prescriptions. And it's a matter of vigorous and effective advocacy of those prescriptions, mobilizing support for their implementation.[29]

Peace Implementation Network

In contrast to the ICG, which was specifically created to serve conflict prevention, the Peace Implementation Network was launched in early 1998 as a project of the Programme for International Co-operation and Conflict Resolution of the Fafo Institute for Applied Social Science in Oslo, Norway. The conceptual framework for PIN rests on the recognition that conflict prevention and conflict resolution, to be effective, require an appropriate mix of practical and theoretical insights. With contemporary conflicts requiring the efforts of a diverse range of policymakers and practitioners, PIN aims to tap into their experiences in order to promote both institutional and cross-institutional learning for organizations involved in international efforts to build peace or implement peace agreements.

Chaired by Norwegian diplomat Terje Roed-Larson and supported by several donor governments and private foundations, PIN has positioned itself to undertake and support research on selected aspects of the international conflict prevention agenda through the mechanism of PIN Forums. Each one aims to facilitate discussion of the policies and practices of implementing peace agreements from a comparative "lessons-learned" perspective. PIN Forums are designed to be empirically driven and involve donors, implementers, and recipients in an ongoing dialogue based on operational experience. PIN's comparative advantage lies in its ability to engage practitioners. By providing a venue for the exchange of lessons learned among the participants, each PIN Forum seeks to promote best practices and the possibility of organizational learning by convening key people and institutions with a special interest in a given topic. To date, PIN Forums have focused on the role of UN Special Representatives of the Secretary-General in shaping the UN role in peace implementation; public-sector finance in postconflict situations; and small-arms and light weapons disarmament.[30]

Conflict Prevention Network

Unlike the previous mechanisms discussed above, which target a diverse international audience, the Conflict Prevention Network was created as a special project to provide the European Union (EU) institutions with policy-relevant research, analysis, and recommendations. Led by the German Stiftung Wissenschaft und Politik, CPN is a network of academic institutions, NGOs, and independent experts who work together to provide the EU system with analytical and operational tools to advance the European Union's conflict prevention agenda.[31] Drawing insights from the large body of academic literature, CPN has generated numerous briefing papers, reports, and other publications that have contributed in important ways to a better understanding of the limits and potential for conflict prevention. Two recent publications by CPN include *The Impact of Conflict Prevention Policy: Cases, Measures, Assessments* (2000) and *Peace-Building and Conflict Prevention in Developing Countries: A Practical Guide* (1999). The former consists of a multidisciplinary discussion of what constitutes effective conflict prevention based on both theoretical and empirical insights alongside several evaluative or analytical reports on concrete case studies. The latter study is intended for European Commission country-desk officers, sectoral units, and in-country representatives. It is a step-by-step guide on both EU policies on conflict prevention and ways of identifying, implementing, and measuring appropriate conflict prevention strategies. Although it is still premature to know the effectiveness of these tools in improving EU policies and practices in conflict prevention, CPN's model of bringing together multiple institutions and independent experts to tailor a conflict prevention methodology and strategy based on academic research as well as policy guidelines deserves attention.

European Platform for Conflict Prevention and Transformation

The European Platform for Conflict Prevention and Transformation is a network of European NGOs involved in the prevention and/or resolution of violent conflicts in the international arena. Its mission is to facilitate the exchange of information and experience among participating organizations, as well as to stimulate cooperation and synergy. The European Platform was an outgrowth of the European Conference on Conflict Prevention held in Amsterdam in February 1997. The Amsterdam meeting issued an appeal for an effective EU approach to preventing conflict and outlined key advocacy issues for NGOs. It stressed the need for participation by a range of actors, including NGOs, and urged coalition-building among NGOs and with national governments and European institutions. Linking national platforms for conflict prevention in various European countries, the European Platform seeks to build support for conflict prevention in general, and for relevant policy initiatives at EU level in particular, through research and educational activities, media work, and networking both within Europe and internationally. The publications of the European Platform, including its "Conflict Prevention Newsletter" and its directories of conflict prevention institutions and activities, constitute important contributions to the expansion and dissemination of information, analysis, and resources on conflict prevention.[32]

International Institute for Democracy and Electoral Assistance

Another important initiative that seeks to combine research and advocacy at the international level, one that is discussed in more depth by its Secretary-General Bengt Säve-Söderbergh and Chef de Cabinet Izumi Nakamitsu Lennartsson in this volume (see Chapter 15), is the International Institute for Democracy and Electoral Assistance. Although it is only indirectly engaged in conflict prevention, International IDEA represents a new institutional model that can enhance the conflict prevention agenda. Created in 1995 by fourteen countries and involving several international NGOs as members, International IDEA is a multilateral institution committed to promoting and advancing sustainable democracy and electoral processes worldwide. Global in membership and scope, International IDEA provides a forum for discussions and action among individuals and organizations involved in democracy promotion. To date, International IDEA's major contribution to conflict prevention is its examination of democracy as an instrument of conflict management and resolution. In a major study entitled *Democracy and Deep-Rooted Conflict: Options for Negotiators*, International IDEA broke new ground in identifying the range of democratic options available to peace negotiators in constructing the institutional framework of countries emerging from violent conflicts. Written by local and international experts and experienced negotiators, and designed as a practical guide with case studies, factsheets, and examples, the study provides an extensive overview of democratic levers such as power-sharing formulas, questions of federalism and autonomy, options for minority rights, and constitutional safeguards. Its in-depth case studies constitute a rich laboratory of comparative experiences.

Based on this pioneering work, and the work of in-house or external experts, International IDEA has established itself as a valuable resource at the intersection between democracy and conflict studies. International IDEA staff are increasingly called upon to provide advice and guidance to national governments, international organizations, and donor-agency representatives. As a multilateral institution committed to democracy promotion, International IDEA thus serves to help advance its own mandate by expanding the knowledge base on the utility of democratic institutions for conflict management, by providing national and international policymakers with viable options for the provision of electoral assistance, and by supporting legal and institutional reform as part of the broader conflict prevention agenda.[33]

Conclusion

The impetus for the creation of the new policy research mechanisms and networks described above clearly came from the complexity and multidimensional nature of the problem they set out to address. Peacebuilding and conflict prevention do not lend themselves to unidisciplinary, single-actor, or unitrack approaches. As the Carnegie Commission report put it eloquently: "We have come to the conclusion that the prevention of deadly conflict is, over the long term, too hard—intellectually, technically, and politically—to be the responsibility of any single institution or government, no matter how powerful. Strengths must be pooled, burdens shared, and labor divided among actors."[34] Because contemporary conflicts involve a volatile mix of local, national, regional, and international actors to sustain themselves, conflict prevention requires the efforts of multiple and diverse institutions to have impact. Yet without a common agenda and interlocking efforts, it is difficult to see how conflict prevention can succeed at either the national or international levels.

Indeed, there is increasing recognition that conflict prevention and peacebuilding are global concerns and stand to benefit from new approaches and mechanisms allowing the development of appropriate global policies and corresponding institutional arrangements to address them in their diversity and complexity. The peacebuilding research and policy networks described in this chapter in some ways correspond to the global public policy networks in other global issue areas, ranging from the environment to human rights. These peacebuilding or conflict prevention networks are, in most cases, multiactor, multistakeholder arrangements encompassing a mix of research, policy analysis, advocacy, and action. They generally enjoy support from multiple sources of funding, often including bilateral and multilateral donors. Whether self-directed or commissioned, their research and analysis are independent and in the public domain. Thus they can be characterized as a new generation of intermediary organizations, seeking to close the gap between knowledge producers and knowledge users, between theory and practice, and between policymakers and practitioners. They generally have influential and international boards of advisers or governing bodies that are designed to feed the networks' research and analysis into multiple constituencies, including governmental as well as nongovernmental agencies, the media, and educational institutions.

This chapter has not attempted to assess the body of knowledge generated by the new research and policy analysis mechanisms described above. Neither has it tried to assess the impact of this research. Those tasks need to be undertaken separately. However, it can reasonably be concluded that the efforts covered above have collectively begun to contribute to the creation of a critical mass of knowledge supporting the case for conflict prevention as an area for global policy and action. Coming from different perspectives and experiences, the variety of mechanisms identified here have started to generate policy analyses and policy recommendations that are increasingly being adopted or implemented by a variety of international or national actors. They therefore are instrumental in creating a knowledge and policy base of best practices and lessons learned of interest to the academic and the policy communities.

Going beyond the single-issue focus of traditional advocacy networks, the conflict prevention networks described above also serve to draw attention to the interlocking policy areas that have a direct impact on conflict prevention. Thus, issues related to debt, trade, arms control, and development assistance are now solidly part of the conflict prevention agenda. Similarly, there is renewed interest in the global systemic factors, alongside the local, national, and regional factors, that exacerbate or help mitigate conflicts.

The creation and multiplication of various international networks and mechanisms in conflict prevention were undoubtedly facilitated by the recent advances in the new information and communications technologies

(ICTs). Although ICTs have also been effectively appropriated as instruments of conflict generation, there is growing evidence that ICTs are instrumental in drawing international attention to the costs and consequences of violent conflicts, as well as in allowing rapid sharing of information, analyses, experiences, and strategies for conflict prevention. It is difficult to imagine that the International Campaign to Ban Landmines or the campaign to establish the International Criminal Court could have been as effective without their ability to mobilize support quickly and globally. Similarly, the range and scope of FEWER's work would be greatly diminished without its ability to draw upon the input of its member organizations in a timely and reliable manner.

Despite the tremendous advances in ICTs, however, one outstanding challenge that global conflict prevention policy and research networks face is their ability to incorporate locally and nationally based research and analysis. Much of the conflict prevention literature (both academic and policy-oriented) is still heavily Northern-based and Northern-centric. Notwithstanding exceptions like FEWER, the global research and policy analysis communities are dominated by Western scholars and experts, and there are serious constraints that inhibit bringing in Southern perspectives, knowledge, and analysis. On one level, with the increasing participation of prominent Southern diplomats, policymakers, and researchers in the new policy networks, there is increased opportunity for broadening the geographic base of policy discussions and options. However, there is a more serious problem that arises from the relative power of Southern and Northern academic, policy, and NGO communities: if conflict prevention is a global concern requiring appropriate policies, the development of these policies needs to go beyond the confines of small "research and policy elites" and engage the participation of the relevant national as well as transnational social forces, including governments, nongovernmental actors, and the private sector. In short, conflict prevention demands going beyond technical and elitist strategies to be able to address violent conflicts that are based in longstanding, deep-rooted local and national cleavages. Yet the research and policy infrastructure, especially in countries facing violent conflicts, is woefully weak, and developing country researchers face considerable difficulties in gaining access to and engaging effectively with global networks.

The policy analyses and recommendations generated by the networks surveyed in this volume collectively aim at influencing the "international community"—a nebulous concept that obscures the fact that under the current international system international decisions and actions are still products of national processes, requiring decisionmaking at the national level. For experts and analysts to be able to influence international policy, they must be able to influence their national governments and national actors.

Governments vary considerably in their permeability and their desire to participate with outsiders in their political process and decisionmaking. It is, therefore, crucial for advocates of conflict prevention to design strategies that are targeted at multiple audiences (both governmental and nongovernmental) in different countries. It is here that the value of multiactor, multistakeholder networks becomes even more important.

In addition to broadening the bases of analysis and diagnosis, global research-based networks offer an avenue for influencing individual governments through multilateral advocacy and action. But to be effective, collective analysis and action need to be communicated to different national audiences in their own idioms. Unfortunately, much of the global research and analysis in conflict prevention is in English. For example, the impressive body of knowledge generated by the Carnegie Commission is almost entirely in English, even though much of it has direct relevance for policymakers as well as key publics around the world. However, the critical decisions that affect war and peace are often taken at the local, national, and regional levels—using discourses, media, and rationales that often go counter to system-centric perspectives. Thus, one of the biggest challenges confronting the global research and analysis community in the area of conflict prevention is to strengthen local capacities for research and analysis. The active involvement of local researchers and analysts will not only enhance the quality of the knowledge base for conflict prevention but also help create domestic constituencies for advancing the conflict prevention agenda.

This chapter highlights the multiple contributions of research and policy analysis to the efforts of governments, international and regional organizations, nongovernmental organizations, and institutions that are actively involved in formulating, designing, and implementing conflict prevention doctrines, strategies, and actions. The key conclusion is that most contemporary conflicts are local or localized in nature, but they can be neither understood nor effectively addressed unless preventive strategies are closely articulated with and respond to multilevel analysis ranging from the local to the global. Conflict prevention is thus a global concern. Many of the methodological and institutional innovations described above have already begun to prepare the ground for multilevel analysis and action. However, they are still at the early steps of what remains a steep learning curve.

Notes

1. This chapter is partially based on the experiences of the authors with peacebuilding research supported by the International Development Research

Centre (IDRC) of Canada. IDRC is a research donor agency which primarily supports research and analysis in the developing countries. However, IDRC is also committed to strengthening knowledge networks that bridge the gap between local and global development concerns, between theory and practice, and between researchers and policymakers.

2. United Nations, "Renewing the United Nations: A Programme for Reform," A/51/950, July 14, 1997.

3. See "DAC Guidelines on Conflict, Peace and Development Co-Operation" (Paris: OECD, 1997).

4. The Conflict Prevention and Post-Conflict Reconstruction Network is an informal network of bilateral and multilateral donors that has been meeting regularly since October 1997 to share knowledge and experience in best practices in peacebuilding. See http://wbln0018.worldbank.org/ESSD/pc1.nsf/Home?OpenView.

5. For a useful review of various donors' initiatives in conflict prevention, see Mauela Leonhardt, "Improving Capacities and Procedures for Formulating and Implementing Effective Conflict Prevention Strategies—An Overview of Recent Donor Initiatives," in *The Impact of Conflict Prevention Policy: Cases, Measures and Assessments. SWP-Conflict Prevention Network Yearbook 1999/2000*, eds. Michael Lund and Guenola Rasmoelina (Baden-Baden: Nomos Verlagsgesellshaft, 2000).

6. In this chapter, the terms "conflict prevention" and "peacebuilding" are used interchangeably. Conflict prevention includes policies, instruments, or activities that keep conflicts from escalating into significant violence, strengthen the capacities to resolve conflicts peacefully, and address the root causes of conflicts. Peacebuilding involves creating the conditions needed to manage or transform conflicts, either before or after they break out into violence. Effective peacebuilding addresses the underlying conditions that lead to violent conflict, thereby eliminating the need for discrete conflict prevention measures.

7. Although his article deals with postconflict peacebuilding rather than conflict prevention, Roland Paris provides an excellent critique of liberal internationalism and its limits. Paris rightly notes that the international community's interest in peacebuilding is a natural extension of its commitment to promote economic and political liberalism internationally. See Roland Paris, "Peacebuilding and the Limits of Liberal Internationalism," *International Security* 222, 2 (fall 1997): 54–89. Similarly, it is difficult to divorce the international conflict prevention agenda from its liberal ideological aspirations. Interestingly, even its critics take issue with the international conflict prevention agenda primarily on practical rather than normative grounds by focusing on the limitations of the social engineering tools and strategies adopted by international agencies in the 1990s. The absence of powerful normative (as opposed to realist) arguments against liberal internationalism at the end of the Cold War deserves to be the subject of another article. One prominent exception is the work of Johan Galtung and his colleagues within the context of the TRANSCEND approach, which involves an integrated approach to conflict transformation through diagnosis, prognosis, and therapy. More information about TRANSCEND is available at its website: http://www.transcend.org.

8. There are numerous bibliographies that document the ever-expanding scope and boundaries of the conflict prevention agenda. A useful starting point is Carnegie Commission on Preventing Deadly Conflict, *Preventing Deadly Conflict: Final Report* (Washington, D.C.: Carnegie Commission on Preventing Deadly Conflict, 1997), and related research by the Commission.

9. Three interrelated features of social science research in developing coun-

294	PRACTITIONER PERSPECTIVES BEYOND THE UN

tries have a bearing on this discussion. Given the political, academic, and financial constraints within which they work, social scientists in developing countries tend to focus primarily on issues of immediate concern to their own societies and are unlikely to undertake comparative research involving other societies; multidisciplinarity in the social sciences is still relatively weak, which militates against collaborative research; and there are limited opportunities for policy-relevant research.

10. What distinguishes conflict prevention from earlier work on conflict mediation or conflict resolution is that it goes beyond the realm of the factual to the realm of the probable. Thus, instead of problem-solving, it involves problem-forecasting. Theoretically, then, its boundaries are limitless—encouraging elaborate and multivariate modeling that defies empirical verification.

11. For a useful overview of the vocabulary of early warning and conflict prevention, see Alex P. Schmid, "Thesaurus and Glossary of Early Warning and Conflict Prevention Terms" (Leiden, Germany: Erasmus University, 2000).

12. International Alert and Saferworld, two international NGOs based in the United Kingdom, have contributed to this literature both by producing relevant research and by compiling useful bibliographies. For two such bibliographies, see Manuela Leonhardt, "Conflict Impact Assessment of EU Development Co-operation with ACP Countries: A Review of Literature and Practice" (London: International Alert and Saferworld, 2000); and Andrew Sherriff and Eeva Vaskio "Development/Humanitarian NGOs and Conflict: A Bibliography and Listing of Web Sources" (London: International Alert, 2000).

13. Ibid. Also see the bibliography in Andreas Mehler and Claude Ribaux, *Crisis Prevention and Conflict Management in Technical Cooperation: An Overview of National and International Debate* (Wiesbaden, Germany: GTZ, 2000).

14. Although there are many examples of collaboration between international researchers and their counterparts in conflict-prone or conflict-torn regions, one project deserves special mention. The War-torn Societies Project (WSP) is an experimental applied research project that was initiated by the United Nations Research Institute for Social Development and the Programme for Strategic and International Studies of the Geneva Institute of International Studies. WSP developed a methodology for participatory action research at the macro level that it implemented in four countries (Eritrea, Mozambique, Guatemala, and Somalia) in full partnership with local researchers. For more information about WSP and its research outputs, see its website: http://www.wsp-international.org.

15. For a thoughtful review of how best to draw upon this growing body of knowledge, see Michael Lund, "Improving Conflict Prevention by Learning from Experience: Issues, Approaches, and Results," in *The Impact of Conflict Prevention Policy,* eds. Lund and Rasamoelina.

16. Both these approaches are designed to assist the international development community to improve its programming in light of new perspectives on conflict prevention. For further documentation on the first of these approaches, see Mary B. Anderson, *Do No Harm: How Aid Can Support Peace—or War* (Boulder: Lynne Rienner Publishers, 1999), as well as the Collaborative for Development Action at http://www.cdainc.com. For PCIA, see Leonhardt, "Conflict Impact Assessment"; and the website of IDRC's PCIA Unit at http://www.bellanet.org/pcia.

17. See Michael Lund, "Not Only When to Act, but How: From Early Warning to Rolling Prevention," in *Preventing Violent Conflicts: Past Record and Future Challenges,* ed. Peter Wallensteen (Uppsala, Sweden: Department of Peace and Conflict Research, 1998).

18. See Mats Berdal and David M. Malone, eds., *Greed and Grievance: Economic Agendas in Civil Wars,* a project of the International Peace Academy (Boulder: Lynne Rienner Publishers, 2000), as well as IPA's website at http://www.ipacademy.org. For the work of Paul Collier and colleagues at the World Bank, see http://www.worldbank.org/research/conflict/crime.htm.

19. See, for example, Charles Philippe David, "Genèse et Developpement de la Consolidation de la Paix: Dimensions Conceptuelles et Empiriques," in *Repensé la consolidation de la paix: fondements, intervenants et rapprochements* (Montréal: UQAM, Téléglobe Raoul-Dandurand, October 1998).

20. Although this debate has its counterparts among academics, its most vocal advocates are in the policy community. The international community's failure to respond in a timely fashion to repeated warning signs of the coming genocide in Rwanda is a tragic example of the futility of early warning information in the absence of political will.

21. In order to assist the United Nations with country-specific and functional expertise necessary to conduct effect preventive activities, a small center, the Conflict Prevention and Peace Forum (CPPF), was created, formally independent of the United Nations, with donor support in November 2000. CPPF identifies academic and other expertise on specific potential crises and makes it available to UN staff pondering the organization's options. It works alongside the IPA's broader prevention program, aimed at overcoming the challenge of operationalizing prevention at the United Nations.

22. For this evolving source, see http://www.preventconflict.org.

23. For a quick overview of this debate, see David Glover, "Policy Researchers and Policy Makers: Never the Twain Shall Meet," available online at http://www.idrc.ca/books/reports/01focus.html. In addition, the Center for International Cooperation at New York University and the International Peace Academy organized a seminar in September 1999 that focused specifically on the relationship between knowledge producers and users in the field of conflict prevention and peacebuilding. For an interesting report of that conference, see "Knowledge for What?" available online at http://www.cic.nyu.edu/seminars/aid/KnowledgeWhat.html.

24. For a list of organizations, universities, and research institutes working on conflict prevention, see the 1998 edition of *Prevention and Management of Violent Conflict: An International Directory,* published by the European Platform for Conflict Prevention and Transformation.

25. The analysis in this section has been greatly influenced by the new literature on global public goods and global public policy networks. In specific, please see the works by Inge Kaul et al. and Wolfgang Reinicke and Francis Deng included in the Selected Bibliography. It can be argued that conflict prevention and peacebuilding are emerging global public goods, requiring the establishment of appropriate mechanisms for global public policies and strategies. However, space limitations have precluded an explicit pursuit of this line of inquiry in this chapter.

26. See http://www.ccpdc.org.

27. For the work of the Independent International Commission on Kosovo, see http://www.kosovocommission.org. For the work of the International Commission on Intervention and State Sovereignty, see http://www.iciss.gc.ca.

28. See http://www.fewer.org.

29. See http://www.crisisweb.org.

30. See http://www.fafo.no/piccr/pin/index.html.

31. See http://www.swp-berlin.org/cpn.

32. See http://www.euconflict.org.
33. See http://www.idea.int.
34. See Carnegie Commission on Preventing Deadly Conflict, *Preventing Deadly Conflict: Final Report.*

13

Development and Conflict: New Approaches in the United Kingdom

Mukesh Kapila and Karin Wermester

Until recently, development actors have had very little direct engagement in conflict and security issues.[1] However, the increased salience of intrastate war and the concomitant focus on the plight of civilians in post–Cold War conflicts have served to bring the formerly separate worlds of development, and peace and security, together. It has become conventional wisdom that violent conflict is likely to continue unabated in the world's poorest countries without a renewed and persistent commitment to the elimination of poverty and the promotion of *sustainable* development that includes addressing the underlying sources of conflict. As a result, it is also now accepted that development actors have a crucial role to play in the prevention of violent conflict.

In the United Kingdom, this new focus on development and security has led to organizational innovation in an effort to join-up the government and adopt an interdepartmental, holistic approach to conflict prevention. However, significant challenges still plague the overall donor community, including the UK government. Beyond measures needed to improve donor response, the effective promotion of lasting peace through sustainable development requires humility in the face of past failures and current inadequacies and a degree of honesty and realism regarding what development strategies can achieve in the immediate period. Development assistance is necessarily an exercise in much needed, and often neglected, *structural prevention* that addresses the root causes of conflict. In particular, it requires focused attention on the sources of insecurity and the factors underlying grievance and exclusion, on the economic incentives that fuel violence, and, from the aid perspective, on the linkages between humanitarian assistance and postconflict recovery and peacebuilding.

Donor Response: From Reaction to Prevention?

All societies experience conflict. It is a normal component of individual and group interaction and can even be the motor for necessary social progress. However, some societies are more likely than others to experience *violent* conflict, the destructiveness of which often imposes significant suffering on civilian populations and poses a major barrier to development.[2] Which underlying factors create the conditions in which violent conflict is more, or less, likely to erupt?

Poverty Reduction: Necessary but Not Sufficient for Peace

Classic liberal economic theory suggests that prosperity and peace are causally linked—by promoting the former, we can achieve the latter. The assumption is that a natural harmony of interests is created from unimpeded free trade and economic growth.[3] By extension, war between states is discounted as too costly as a result of the gains from increased cooperation and free trade in an era increasingly characterized by complex interdependence—the political and economic linkages of globalization.[4] Political factors have also increasingly contributed to interstate peace. Empirical evidence and systematic research both suggest that participatory, substantive democracies are unlikely to go to war with one another for normative, institutional, and interest-based reasons.[5] Thus, a cursory look at theories relating to the causes of peace suggests that countries tend to be less vulnerable to violent conflict where political systems are more inclusive and economic opportunities and benefits are more available to the wider population.

However, the applicability of these insights for development actors may be limited. The first obstacle is that *transitions* to both capitalism and democracy have been shown to be extremely volatile and subject to reversals.[6] Moreover, the consolidation of each process takes a protracted period of time, and the end result can take many different forms.[7] The second important snag is that both classic economic liberalism and democratic peace theory are based on analysis of the incidence of *interstate* war.

But it is *intrastate* wars that seem increasingly to preoccupy policymakers,[8] and these pose significant new challenges relating to peace implementation, state reconstruction, preventing the recurrence of conflict, and more.[9] Empirical evidence suggests that poverty is a key variable affecting the incidence of intrastate conflict: twenty-four out of forty of the poorest countries of the world were either in the midst of armed conflict or recently emerging from it at the end of the 1990s.[10] Systematic research indicates, however, that "neither poverty alone nor worsening economic trends predictably produce acute conflict."[11] Instead, as Joan Nelson points out, international financial institutions' structural adjustment programs no doubt contributed to the reduction of poverty but, as a result, may have also inadvertently *contributed* to the eruption of violent conflict.[12] This suggests that it is not merely pervasive poverty (which exists in many countries that do not experience violent conflict) that causes war, but rather that poverty exacerbates the numerous factors that interact to cause violent conflict. Thus, even though it may be *necessary* for development actors to focus on poverty reduction in order to promote sustainable peace, this approach may not be *sufficient* to prevent conflict.

As Anne-Marie Gardner shows in her contribution to this volume (see Chapter 2), there appear to be four underlying factors that create conditions for the eruption of violent conflict: insecurity, often linked to weak or collapsed state institutions; inequality, or discrimination across recognized groups in society; private incentives that influence the behavior of both leaders and the masses; and perceptions, which are often used instrumentally to foment violent conflict through the manipulation of group histories and myth-making. These four factors are further mediated through a wide array of intervening variables that interact over different periods of time and relate to the particularities of the local context.

Given the complex pathology of intrastate conflicts, development actors need to deploy a range of targeted and interlinked country-specific strategies under the umbrella of poverty reduction to address the sources of conflict in a given society. As with other types of conflict prevention, development strategies need to address the affected society's political capacity to manage conflict without violence. In particular, as Frances Stewart argues in this volume (see Chapter 5), development actors have a crucial role to play in "correcting horizontal inequality along the relevant dimensions . . . [which requires the promotion of] inclusive government, politically, economically, and socially."[13]

Development Assistance During the Cold War

The practice of international development assistance emerged only recently, in the wake of World War II and decolonization. During the Cold War, however, superpower rivalry quickly distorted the purpose of aid from the promotion of development to the advancement of narrow foreign policy goals that were defined primarily by high-stakes security interests.[14] In terms of political, economic, and virtual progress for the developing world, the Cold War was a period of "deep freeze." The role of many aid actors within donor governments was largely subordinate to national security interests, and they had little or no ability to voice opinions or weigh considerations regarding the disbursement of aid for developmental goals.

The end of the Cold War, followed by the collapse of the Soviet Union in 1991, brought about sudden and rapid change in the international system.

In Eastern Europe, the collapse of Soviet tutelage called for a readjustment to the realities of a competitive capitalist system. In Africa and elsewhere, Western donors' support for authoritarian regimes waned as the geostrategic necessity of maintaining them as allies dissipated. Inevitably, in many parts of the world localized conflict began to emerge, or reemerge, as groups contested the national organization of political, economic, and social mechanisms.

Consequently, the 1990s and early 2000s have been a period of multiple transition: between various states of peace and war, between authoritarian and democratic regimes, and between socialism and capitalism. Often, and importantly, these transitions have been characterized by setbacks and reversals. These problems have called for an increasingly active role on the part of development actors, in conjunction with multilateral development institutions and numerous nonstate actors, to create development strategies that promote real relief and long-term sustainability while also channeling disagreement and competition into a constructive and nonviolent direction. The challenge has been to accomplish this task at a time during which members of the international donor community, preoccupied with domestic budget constraints of their own, have largely lost the political will to sustain meaningful investment in foreign aid.

Development Assistance in the 1990s

If the Cold War still conditioned donor response at the beginning of the 1990s, conceptual clarification and empirical reality provided the impetus for its reevaluation at the end of that decade. During the first part of the decade, development assistance was dominated by what might be termed a "category-driven" approach; at the end of the decade, the donor community started moving toward a more "context-driven" approach.[15]

In the early 1990s, development assistance programs attempted to address the political, economic, and social aspects of transition within the confines of what the donor community could—or was willing—to provide. This category-driven approach saw development actors respond as best they could with what little they had available. Predictably, the demand for aid far exceeded the supply. As a result, humanitarian crises that were sparked by conflict or natural disasters began to emerge and recur, partly as a consequence of the failures of previous development assistance to create the conditions for self-sustainable local development.[16] This quickly served to turn development actors into firefighters: responding where necessity dictated with short-term emergency relief.[17]

The problem was twofold. First, domestic budget constraints forced development actors to respond to, rather than preempt, the developmental requirements of much of the world.[18] The perceived "crowding out" of development assistance from national budgets seemed to be confirmed by statistical evidence that indicated that in the 1990s the amount of official development assistance (ODA) spent by industrialized countries on emergency aid had quintupled in comparison to the early 1980s, whereas overall development assistance budgets decreased significantly.[19] Second, insufficient attention to the unintended consequences of development assistance created conditions ripe for the perpetuation, or reemergence, of conflict. Efforts to alleviate poverty, which often placed a premium on economic growth to the detriment of broader social and political developmental processes, were frequently part of the problem. Likewise, evidence also began to emerge that the infusion of aid sometimes served to empower belligerent groups and/or create competition between those that benefit from assistance and those that do not.[20] As Peter Uvin notes, "All aid, at all times, creates incentives and disincentives, for peace or war, regardless of whether these effects are deliberate, recognized or not, before, during or after war."[21]

In light of these events, and late in the decade, the donor community began seriously to rethink its strategies and approaches to development and conflict. Three interrelated factors in particular have contributed to this shift. First, there has been a greater understanding of the social, political, and economic causes and consequences of intrastate violent conflict. Second, despite serious efforts on the part of development actors to improve the efficiency of aid, recent evaluation reports have revealed that previous development assistance programs were successful neither at promoting development nor at preventing conflict. Third, conceptual shifts and policy reevaluations have coincided more generally with the rise of social/liberal governments across the European Union at the end of the decade—thereby increasing the potential for higher spending and greater attention to long-term strategies for sustainable development and self-sustaining peace.

By the end of the decade, then, a context-driven approach to development assistance began to take hold in the donor community. A major turning point was an important report, published in May 1997 by the Development Assistance Committee (DAC) of the OECD, outlining the principles and goals of donor action in conflict, peace, and development.[22] The newly elected UK government and the newly created Department for International Development (DFID) were major contributors to this work. The new approach is based on a long-term, proactive view of sustainable development. Instead of providing one-size-fits-all country assistance programs, it focuses on assessing the particular developmental needs of partner nations and offers country-specific programs and projects. It is based on the fundamental notion that the promotion of sustainable development and the promotion of self-sustaining peace requires addressing factors that contribute to conflict, including—but not limited to—the reduction of poverty. Since this approach may have many dimensions and requires a focus on complex sociopolitical processes, it necessitates "a high degree of political judgement to be effective."[23] Consequently, development actors are becoming more than mere "cash cows" and are developing their own independent capacity and policies to determine whether, and how, ODA should be dispersed.[24]

Development and Conflict Prevention: The Case of the United Kingdom

Although conflict prevention has for some time been a much expressed aspiration, the policies and practices of different government departments often pulled in opposing directions. More recently, conflict prevention has become an overarching goal with political commitment from the highest levels that expects all government departments—foreign affairs, trade, defense, treasury, and development—to work *together*. As a result, the Department for International Development, the Foreign and Commonwealth Office (FCO), the Ministry of Defense (MoD), and Her Majesty's Treasury are "pooling their sovereignty" (and resources) through a voluntary and partial devolution of their autonomy in an effort to maximize the overall impact of the United Kingdom on conflict prevention. This has challenged established bureaucratic mind-sets to allow organizational innovation and the adoption of a context-driven approach to development assistance.

Under the rubric of endeavoring to lift 1 billion people out of abject poverty by 2015, DFID has introduced a conflict reduction policy that has as its goals: the building of political and social institutions that ensure the equitable representation of different interest groups; the promotion of human rights; and the resolution of disputes and grievances without recourse to violence in partner countries. This involves tackling poor governance, corrupt or dysfunctional political and legal institutions, and weak civil societies through the creation of economic and political structures that address the sources of group inequality and marginalization. Importantly, these efforts remain centrally committed to the goal of improving the social and economic welfare of the poorest individuals.

The United Kingdom's approach is based on the assumption that *all* societies experience conflict—both violent and nonviolent, in the industrialized as in the developing world—and have a "conflict career" that is nonlinear and prone to eruptions of violence at different moments. The conflict career can map directly onto the expected so-called development trajectory, identifying those factors in the conflict cycle that predispose a country toward stability or breakdown and assessing developmental needs accordingly. In 1998, DFID established its well-resourced Conflict and Humanitarian Affairs Department as the administrative expression of its move toward the integration of conflict and development objectives.[25] As part of this move, DFID assistance strategies in vulnerable countries and communities are increasingly subject to conflict appraisals. Conflict appraisals involve an analysis of the population groups likely to be affected by external assistance; an assessment of the causes, triggers, intensity, and trends of open or latent conflict; and an identification of the interventions that are at once most feasible and most likely to make a positive contribution in terms of both development and peace.[26]

In this new approach, it is not acceptable to develop and implement a strategy in isolation, as there is much greater awareness of interdependent factors and the potential for inadvertent consequences. Thus, the United Kingdom has begun to develop a new series of tools in order to ensure the coherence and complementarity of interrelated policies. This has led, for example, to the deployment of joint-missions between DFID, MoD, and the FCO concerning Sierra Leone. The government also introduced an Africa Conflict Prevention Initiative, led by DFID, and a Global Conflict Prevention Initiative, led by the FCO, which seek to systematize joint collaboration between government departments on conflict prevention and reduction. The initiatives provide a mechanism for joint programming and a substantial pool of resources that can be harnessed quickly in the service of conflict prevention. They became formally active in spring 2001. Moreover, in December 2000 the UK government renounced its right to interest payments on bilateral debts owed by all the heavily indebted poor countries. For the dozen or so conflict-affected countries in this group, the debt interest payments will now accrue in a special fund to be used for poverty reduction programs. The United Kingdom has called on other industrialized countries to do the same.

In addition, DFID has developed several specific and new strategies under the umbrella of poverty reduction that seek to address the barriers to development in recipient countries and to prevent the outbreak of violence. These strategies seek to address the sources of insecurity, grievance, and exclusion; the political economy of conflict; and the strategic linkages between humanitarian assistance and postconflict peacebuilding policies. Each of these topics will be addressed below.

Security and Insecurity

Insecurity is one of the main causes of conflict and prevents development in many of the world's poorest countries. The focus of the United Kingdom is on two main factors that contribute to insecurity in much of the developing world: the first is an unreformed security sector; the second is a repressive (and often kleptocratic) state that perpetuates insecurity in order to remain in power.[27]

Unreformed security sectors fail to provide responsible and accountable mechanisms to protect the state, communities, and individuals within the state, thereby contributing to basic and often widespread physical insecurity.[28] This has direct, negative effects on development through inappropriate military spending that diverts resources away from the promotion of economic growth and can deter foreign investment. Moreover, an unreformed security sector can fail to prevent, and sometimes causes, violent conflict, which exacerbates poverty and stunts development.

For this reason, security sector reform (SSR) is a key component of the United Kingdom's development agenda. However, the boundaries for legitimate development involvement in the security sector are extremely important. SSR does not seek to replicate the military assistance packages that characterized great power aid during the Cold War.[29] Instead, the United Kingdom places great importance on maintaining government-wide consensus on the rationale of security sector reform as a *development issue*. It is for this reason that UK involvement in this domain emphasizes primary support for legitimate national civilian authorities to reorient or reform their security systems.

The focus is on both processes and goals: establishing an appropriate level of military expenditure that does not hinder development but enables a country to guarantee a secure environment; and increasing the enforcement capacity of security forces by rendering them more democratic, more accountable, and more transparent. For instance, DFID financed a consulting project in Tanzania that reviewed the issues and options for retrenchment and early retirement of the defense forces in an effort to reduce large wage bills; provided support for mine clearance in Cambodia; and initiated an emergency demobilization project in Sierra Leone in July 1998 that, in light of the re-escalation of hostilities there, was being reviewed, strengthened, and broadened to include participation by several other donors interested in collaborating on the project.

Addressing the sources of insecurity also requires dealing with repressive regimes. For the international community, this poses a dilemma: should these regimes be "let in," promoting change through positive incentives such as conditional admittance to regional organizations, or should they be isolated, using disincentives such as economic sanctions until they acquiesce to evolving norms of statehood? Although recognizing that in certain circumstances targeted or "smart" sanctions are necessary, in most cases reducing insecurity for civilians in these countries is better served by international engagement. However, too often in the past sanctions regimes have suffered from poor design, loose commitment from member states, inadequate monitoring, and lax enforcement.[30] Thus, the United Kingdom now works increasingly with other donor governments to deploy economic sanctions only for exceptional cases that are based on clear objectives and supported by effective arrangements for implementation and enforcement by all states, including allowance for humanitarian exemptions. An important aspect of this is a new interdepartmental committee, including DFID, that vets all new sanctions proposals.

The Political Economy of Conflict

The processes of globalization create both incentives and disincentives for peace. On the positive side, increased economic integration and cooperation has the potential to reduce the likelihood of armed conflict. However, as William Reno notes, in a globalized world civil wars are increasingly characterized by "economic motivations that are specifically related to the intensification of transnational commerce in recent decades."[31] The global trade in both small arms and light weapons, and drugs and diamonds in the hands of illicit actors, has led to the emergence of war economies, where the revenues from illicit trade allow parties to the conflict to perpetuate war while amassing great fortunes on the side.[32] Moreover, the potential gains from war could be an incentive to instigate violence. According to Paul Collier, "It is the feasibility of predation [which is primarily, but not only, a function of the level of dependence on primary commodity export] which determines the risk of conflict."[33]

One of the main challenges is a limited understanding of—or a lack of systematic efforts to try to understand—the channels and linkages of international trade that facilitate the movement of goods, many of which are illegitimately bought, sold, or appropriated by belligerent groups. In response, donors may need to face tough decisions regarding the role of their own resource extraction and financial sectors. Moreover, successful efforts to curb the dimensions of globalization that can facilitate violent conflict also require a concerted effort among governments and with multinational corporations. Individual state donors rarely possess the resources needed to create the incentives and disincentives for moving belligerent behavior toward peace unless they act as part of a unified strategy. Furthermore, international trade regimes such as the World Trade Organization, and regional trading blocs, such as the Southern Africa Development Community, have until now paid little or no attention to the regulation of financial and trade flows that facilitate conflict. These multilateral mechanisms, nonetheless, do have the potential to provide a forum in which states can begin to address these issues.

The UK policy on curbing the political and economic sources of conflict is based on attempting to deprive protagonists of the opportunities in which they are able to derive economic gain from provoking and/or prolonging violent conflict. The strategy involves working at the international level to build the capacity of law enforcement institutions to tackle illegal trade, particularly in diamonds and drugs. This includes sharing intelligence with other sympathetic governments on international criminal activities. In addition, the United Kingdom is working on an international certification scheme that would prohibit trade in diamonds from conflict regions and assist with capacity-building measures so that source countries can better regulate the mining and export of diamonds.

The United Kingdom is also focusing its efforts on measures that seek to reduce the supply and demand for small arms and light weapons. This includes promoting international cooperation in multilateral fora, for example, support for the UN 2001 conference on small arms and contributions to developing a European Union code of conduct on arms exports. In addition, the United Kingdom plans to assist poor countries to reduce the proliferation of small arms; encourage responsible behavior by suppliers of arms (including arms-brokering agents in the United Kingdom); and eliminate the threat from landmines (by promoting the universal adoption of the Ottawa Convention on Anti-Personnel Landmines; improving the capacity of international organizations working in this area; and helping develop better clearance technologies).

The support and commitment of the business community are crucial. Because of the weight of resources they can bring to bear in a given country and their role as a motor of the economic dimensions of globalization, multinational corporations are very important partners in the promotion of sustainable peace. This has not always been the case. In the pursuit of profit, violent conflict typically entered the radar screen of foreign direct investment decisions only if it had the potential to decrease profit margins. Thus, corporate involvement has, like development assistance at times in the past, weighed heavily (whether through indifference or involvement) on local political dynamics—and often contributed to the factors that cause or perpetuate conflict.

However, the tide is beginning to change. Corporations are starting to realize that investments in politically sensitive regions are, in fact, bad for business—a lesson De Beers has apparently internalized operationally since November 1999.[34] The United Kingdom has sought to capitalize on this shift by placing businesses and their activities in conflict-prone regions among its most important priorities. This includes encouraging multinational corporations to behave responsibly in conflict situations and, where feasible, contribute to conflict resolution. In addition, UK policy seeks to foster public-private partnerships, an exercise that will initially focus on raising awareness through research, networking, advocacy, and lobbying. It also involves facilitating consultation among business, host governments, and local communities through establishing regional and country-based roundtables. The goal is to mainstream conflict prevention into the business agenda in a similar manner that environmental issues have now become an integral consideration for corporate decisionmakers.

Linking Postconflict Phases

The number of actors in the fields of humanitarian assistance and peace-building is large and growing. This proliferation has led to significant diffi-culties relating to duplication, turf battles, and a lack of coordination. The emergence of a gap between emergency relief and postconflict peacebuild-ing has only compounded these problems because, typically, different actors, strategies, and tools are deployed in each phase. The problems relat-ing to the immediate and postconflict phases urgently require mechanisms for strategic coordination that can capitalize on the comparative advantages of humanitarian and postconflict agencies and ensure coherence.[35]

The delivery of humanitarian assistance has elicited controversy since the precipitous expansion of its role in the 1990s. Accusations have been made that it helps warring parties by feeding fighters rather than intended beneficiaries, thereby perpetuating war economies and prolonging the dura-tion of conflict. Emergency response is no panacea. The political conse-quences of humanitarian assistance can pose genuine moral dilemmas regarding whether or not to intervene at all. Nonetheless, donors have a moral responsibility to help those in need in such circumstances. What is needed is an approach that, in the words of Mary Anderson, does no harm along the way.[36] However, the political aspect of emergency assistance begins, and ends, with that choice: once the decision has been made to respond to a given crisis, the United Kingdom is dedicated to the impartial delivery of aid to all vulnerable noncombatant populations.

To this end, the United Kingdom launched its New Humanitarianism policy in 1998. The approach is based on needs assessment, participation, "ground rules" for action (which includes adopting "smart aid" in order to prevent the diversion of humanitarian goods and collusion with unconstitu-tional armed groups), promoting human rights, and furthering human digni-ty. In February 1999, the United Kingdom launched the Conflict Reduction and Humanitarian Assistance policy, which seeks to bridge the infamous gap between relief and development by marrying humanitarian strategies with longer-term peacebuilding goals. This has led humanitarian aid into new domains and projects such as emergency education and radio outreach, as witnessed in Afghanistan and Kosovo. In addition, recognizing that the most effective emergency response is provided from within the affected communities themselves, the United Kingdom has developed partnerships with the Red Cross movement (the International Committee of the Red

Cross and International Federation of Red Cross and Red Crescent societies). At the same time, DFID has expanded its own operational capability to respond directly and rapidly to emergencies, and recently the emergency response team was expanded to include health, social, management, and logistics expertise.

With respect to postconflict peacebuilding, in addition to the rapidly deployable forces that the United Kingdom makes available for UN peacekeeping and a commitment to improving the capacity of regional organizations, the United Kingdom plans to work more systematically with other donors and with multilateral institutions (especially the international financial institutions) in postconflict peacebuilding. In particular, this effort seeks to improve the planning of postconflict recovery programs in order to reduce delays and foster stronger coordination in the international system; to provide increased support for postconflict reconstruction and peacebuilding, including demobilization and demilitarization programs; and to help to build inclusive political institutions. Recognizing that justice and reconciliation are particularly important elements of sustainable peace, and that they have an important role to play in deterring the potential for resumed conflict, the United Kingdom also plans to support the work of the soon to be established International Criminal Court to ensure that those guilty of war crimes and crimes against humanity are brought to justice.

The United Nations (UN) has an important role to play with respect to the strategic coordination of multiple actors in postconflict settings.[37] However, the requirements of development and humanitarian assistance, in addition to peacekeeping and conflict resolution efforts, have placed high demands on the United Nations, leaving it overstretched in its ability to respond to crises, let alone plan in advance. The United Kingdom has strongly endorsed the recommendations of the "Report of the Panel on UN Peace Operations" (the Brahimi Report) to help strengthen the peacekeeping and peacebuilding capacity of the United Nations, but while debate continues among most UN member states, the United Kingdom has moved on to provide immediate practical help through targeted initiatives backed by multiyear funds, for example, research and policy development projects abroad and the promotion of better training and skills (including policy capacity) for UN officials by supporting the UN Staff College Training Center in Turin, Italy, and the International Peace Academy in New York.[38]

The United Kingdom also supports stronger interagency arrangements for planning, implementation, and coordination that includes developing working partnerships with UN agencies such as the Office for the Coordination of Humanitarian Affairs, the Office of the High Commission for Human Rights, the United Nations Children's Fund, the World Food Program, and the UN High Commission for Refugees; the United Kingdom also seeks to improve the performance of in-country UN peacemaking and peacebuilding missions, especially the efforts of Special Representatives to the Secretary-General.[39] Finally, an important task in the future will be to involve development actors in the routine negotiation and drafting of peace agreements. This should go far to redress one of the primary reasons that peace agreements fail to be sustained, for until now unrealistic politically driven promises on reconstruction and recovery have been made without consulting development experts. An early test of this policy is the intense UK efforts that are going into peacemaking and peacebuilding in Sierra Leone.

The role of regional organizations is also important in the prevention of conflict. Often, they are better placed for earlier action than the United Nations. Accordingly, the United Kingdom encourages regional approaches to conflict resolution and works toward enabling regional organizations to build confidence and the trust of their members to resolve disputes peacefully. In particular, the United Kingdom plans to continue working closely with the OSCE in its various conflict prevention roles and is helping to develop and shape a conflict prevention capacity within the framework of the European Union's Common Foreign and Security Policy. The United Kingdom is also investing substantial resources in capacity building in the Organization for African Unity's Early Warning System.

Thus, the United Kingdom is seeking to adopt a holistic approach to development and conflict that attempts to address the previous shortcomings of fragmented approaches. Organizational changes, new tools, and innovative strategies adopted by DFID are directed toward working more closely with the diplomatic, political, military, financial, and trade resources available from other British government departments.

Managing Opportunities and Constraints

Nonetheless, significant hurdles urgently need to be addressed if development actors genuinely want to be serious about preventing violent conflict and live up to the expectations generated by their rhetoric. In particular, five constraints, and several concomitant opportunities, face state development actors: political, organizational, legislative, professional, and research.

Political

Before donors can embark on a serious policy of conflict prevention through the promotion of sustainable development, they need the commitment and strategies with which to act effectively. One of the problems is that the media thrives on crises. In contrast, conflict prevention is difficult to recognize, because when it is successful, nothing dramatic happens.

However, there really are no more excuses. Donors have a moral imperative to help eliminate poverty, inequality, and conflict around the world. As Michael Brown and Richard Rosecrance persuasively demonstrated in a comparative analysis, the costs incurred (directly and indirectly) by outside powers as a result of conflict are significantly higher than the costs of prevention.[40] In addition, while the budgets of all sectors of government are vulnerable to public pressure, opinion polls indicate that the public in donor countries *expect* their government to relieve poverty and provide humanitarian assistance, although they are suspicious of the potential misuses of aid.[41] However, David Shearer has argued convincingly that relief aid in particular has had little impact on the course of civil wars—in itself a critique of the small magnitude of aid in comparison to other economic incentives and actors, but at the same time a refutation of the cursory claim that aid has too often ended up in the hands of perpetrators fueling violence.[42] His argument underlies two more fundamental problems behind reticent political support for aid: a failure on behalf of political decisionmakers in donor countries to perceive that conflict prevention *around the world* is fundamentally within their economic and security interests; and poor efforts on behalf of donor governments to inform and articulate current policy and assessments of these to their public.

The beginning of the twenty-first century presents an ideal opportunity to place the prevention of conflict at the top of the political agenda of donor countries. Moving from a culture of reaction to one of prevention is, however, a long-term process and requires sustained commitment on the part of donors. Donors and recipients (including local actors) need to do more to highlight the preventive goals and outcomes of a variety of programs and projects and together need to design more of them. Active lobbying and public pressure regarding the promotion, and increasingly the protection, of human rights has helped to focus attention on individuals and communities. In the peace and security world, this widespread commitment to human rights has been instrumental in shifting the focus from conflict resolution to conflict prevention. In addition, UN Secretary-General Kofi Annan, widely perceived to have a high degree of moral authority and long a champion of human rights, has and continues to play an important role in the creation of a "conflict prevention norm" at the international level.[43] To this end, Secretary-General Annan has called on member states and the UN system as a whole to give "prevention . . . primacy, in all our work,"[44] not least in the implementation of recommendations from the Brahimi Report.[45] The UN Security Council is also increasingly devoting thematic discussions to the prevention of conflict.[46] Perhaps most important for the donor world, recent G-8 meetings have focused on conflict prevention in which the heads of government of the richest countries in the world have reiterated their "determination to make prevention of armed conflict a high priority issue in coming years."[47]

Organizational

Once donor states have made the commitment to make conflict prevention a priority, the next problem is largely organizational. However, this is neither a small nor an easy task. With the rising number of political and quasi-political actors working in peace, security, and development, the increasingly complex linkages between issues, and the proliferation of institutions and fora where these forces interact and counteract, governments often contribute to a sterile cacophony with inconsistent and even contradictory policies.

The elaboration of guidelines for self-evaluation in the form of codes of conduct for donor behavior similar to those recently established for the delivery of humanitarian assistance could be a useful mechanism to counterbalance this tendency.[48] Perhaps some "Rules Regarding the Exercise of Influence" could establish ground rules for the delivery of development assistance more broadly. Such guidelines, developed in collaboration with donors and recipients, would allay legitimate concerns from recipients regarding the purposes of intrusive and far-reaching development programs. By providing trust and mutual understanding, such rules could help to ensure that recipients are, from the outset, stakeholders in the development process. To ensure that these principles are abided by, an International Observatory of Donor Behavior could be created to point out lapses, inconsistencies, and otherwise unacceptable donor behavior. Ideally, the Observatory would also be entirely financially independent from the governments and institutions that it monitors. Indeed, past experience has shown that civil-society groups can play a crucial role in influencing governments and businesses into changing their behavior.[49]

In addition, lax evaluation models have in the past contributed to donor laziness regarding needed organizational changes. Until recently, peer group–led review processes in the donor world consisted of mutual legitimation of each other's programs, with little independent input and critical analysis. Such a procedure only contributed to the lack of accountability and responsibility in international assistance policies. Evaluation is an integral part of learning from past mistakes in addition to successes and for doing better in the future. It requires transparency, timeliness, independence, and benchmarks that are set within broader parameters of both time and the specific sociopolitical context. Important areas of concentration for the future evaluation of development assistance include moving away from narrowly defined cycles of project monitoring and evaluation toward a broader perspective of sectors, themes, and country programs. In addition, domestic evaluation capacity in developing countries, which is now slowly emerging, can play an important role in enhancing the development of participatory, democratic political processes.[50]

Legislative

For many donor governments, the challenge for effective development assistance is not only political and organizational but also legislative. The political desire to institute change and the commitment to adopt more coherent systems of policymaking and implementation require changes that can be hampered by rigid internal legislative processes. Effective donors require a political culture of calculated risk-taking and the possibility to capitalize, quickly and easily, on opportunities to promote sustainable development. Indeed, as Judith Randel and Tony German note, "Development cooperation policies which are not backed up by ministers with enough political clout, or which are fragmented between different government departments, stand little chance of achieving coherent, efficient aid programmes."[51]

At first glance, some legislative systems appear to be more flexible than others. For instance, the United Kingdom is fortunate in having very flexible legislative processes that permit a relatively easy adoption of administrative and spending changes, in addition to the rapid disbursement of resources by government departments. In contrast, some other governments are severely restricted by legislation or legislative processes that are more prescriptive and constraining on how money can be spent for foreign assistance. Still, there is a danger that parliamentary systems, which have few mechanisms for checks and balances, could easily lead to inconsistent policies between departments and from one government to the next. More focus is needed on an effective, positive role for donor parliaments in this respect. Recipient parliaments also require assistance in evaluating offers of aid, as has been obvious in Haiti since 1996.[52]

Professional

Another problem that plagues the donor world is a lack of professionalism regarding the giving of aid. First, parts of the donor world are notoriously characterized by empty rhetoric and misleading commitments. For instance, aid pledges are often marred by double-counting aid that was previously promised or already delivered or by pledging large amounts that cannot be delivered in a realistic time frame and that are subject to stringent (often unhelpful) requirements.[53] Second, the delivery of development assistance, including emergency aid, demands technically skilled staff with intimate knowledge of the context into which resources are delivered and the capability to conduct an intelligent analysis of local dynamics. Unfortunately, this technical skill is often not matched by political sense, or vice versa. Moreover, in crisis situations difficult work conditions result in high staff turnover and few qualified replacements.

The UN Staff Training College in Turin could provide a model on which to build an "International System of Accreditation and Training" for development workers at all levels. This would help build the capacity of donors by creating a pool of qualified personnel for all types and levels of development assistance work.

Research

The relationship between policymakers and the academic community is not always optimal. Academics often have limited regard for the dynamics of political decisionmaking and provide lengthy and complex analyses that are difficult to translate into policy, whereas policymakers need timely and practical solutions. Policymakers, meanwhile, have a tendency to reject critical thinking, particularly if it appears counterintuitive or, more immediately, if it points out a need to make significant changes in policy.

From the perspective of donor policymakers, some key issues need further clarification. For researchers, arguably more and more conflicts are caused nowadays by greed rather than grievance. What donors need, however, is a systematic analysis of what has been titled "economic agendas in civil wars." What can be the role of development and humanitarian assistance when the resources available to protagonists of conflict so clearly dwarf those available to donors? In particular, it would be useful to see more analysis of the interests and preferences of competing elites, as well as thoughtful recommendations as to how these can be redirected toward peace through the use of incentives and disincentives.

Second, donors would benefit from a better analysis of the complex interlinkages between countries, regions, and international actors. A particularly useful starting point would be an examination of the role of international financial and trade regimes in preventing, and sometimes facilitating, violent conflict.

Third, although donors are getting better at postconflict peacebuilding activities, including humanitarian assistance (thanks not least to burgeoning research on the subject), a greater understanding is required regarding the period *before* the outbreak of violence. Can donors provide "immunization" to conflict? Is a focus on addressing the structural causes of poverty and inequality enough, and are donors beginning to do it right? Further analysis of the causes of *peace* and what can be learned from these attempts at conflict prevention might prove particularly useful.

And finally, but not least, useful research for donors could include renewed attention to organizational politics and decisionmaking. Overbureaucratization, duplication, complicated financing channels, and poor information flows are significant and, in many cases, likely intractable challenges. Nonetheless, research could usefully focus on a greater understanding of how government and other bureaucracies function and how organizational behavior can be motivated to change so as to remove impediments to effective action. The attendant risk to this is that organizational changes will stimulate organizational conflict—necessary sometimes for change to happen. Such research could thus include analysis of incentives for stronger coordination and cooperation among government departments, donors, international organizations, and nongovernment actors.

Conclusion

A broad consensus has been achieved that the promotion of sustainable development and the promotion of sustainable peace are closely connected. However, although sustainable development is necessary for long-term peace, it is not sufficient. Many donor governments continue to provide development assistance that pays insufficient attention to the needs of partner countries, particularly in relation to specific factors that can contribute to conflict. Instead, structural prevention requires, at the local level, the participation of key local stakeholders in the elaboration and implementation of development strategies. In addition, it is of paramount importance to ensure the coherence and complementarity of policy across issue areas and institutions at national and international levels. And perhaps most important of all, it requires the adoption of a new approach to development assistance that includes specific strategies aimed at defusing violence and addressing the root sources of conflict. This depends on, but also goes beyond, poverty reduction. Some real advances have been made in the last few years. However, the effects are likely to be tangible only after a long-term, sustained commitment on behalf of the entire international community.

Notes

Karin Wermester would like to thank friends and colleagues for their comments on earlier drafts: Charles K. Cater for his immensely valuable suggestions and editing, in addition to Karen Ballentine, Elizabeth M. Cousens, Bruce D. Jones, Leila Kazemi, and Denis Maslov.
    1. The term "development actors" refers, in this chapter, to the agents and institutions within donor governments with responsibility for the disbursement of aid, and the promotion of development. Notably, this chapter does not directly

address the role of intergovernmental development actors or nongovernmental development actors.

2. The term "development" is notoriously difficult to define. The authors posit that development is a continual yet uneven process that *all* societies undergo daily and that has political, economic, and social dimensions. In addition, we note that attention to the process itself may be more important than defining a particular predetermined end goal for development.

3. See Richard Cobden, *The Political Writings of Richard Cobden*, 4th ed. (New York: Kraus, 1969).

4. See Robert Keohane and Joseph Nye, *Power and Interdependence: World Politics in Transition* (Boston: Little, Brown, 1977).

5. See Michael E. Brown, Sean M. Lynn-Jones, and Stephen E. Miller, eds., *Debating the Democratic Peace* (Cambridge: Cambridge University Press, 1996).

6. See Stephen Haggard and Robert R. Kaufman, *The Political Economy of Democratic Transitions* (Princeton: Princeton University Press, 1995); and Adam Przeworski, *Democracy and the Market: Political and Economic Reforms in Eastern Europe and Latin America* (Cambridge: M.I.T. Press, 1991).

7. See Fareed Zakaria, "The Rise of Illiberal Democracy," in *The New Shape of World Politics* rev. ed. (New York: Foreign Affairs Agenda, W. W. Norton, 1999), 242.

8. Although interestingly, as Anne-Marie Gardner notes in this volume (see Chapter 2), the incidence of intrastate war was actually on the decline for most of the 1990s, with a slight increase recorded by some in 1998.

9. The problems relating to the postconflict stage of intrastate wars are particularly acute, especially since Paul Collier notes that there is a 40 percent chance of further conflict immediately after the end of hostilities. See his "Economic Causes of Civil Conflict and their Implications for Policy" (Washington, D.C.: Development Research Group, World Bank, June 15, 2000), 6.

10. DFID Annual Report 2000, available at http://www.dfid.gov.uk/public/news/d_report1.html.

11. Joan Nelson, "Poverty, Inequality, and Conflict in Developing Countries" (New York: Project on World Security, Rockefeller Brothers Fund, 1998), 5.

12. See, for instance, John Stremlau and Francisco R. Sagasti, *Preventing Deadly Conflict: Does the World Bank Have a Role?* (Report for the Carnegie Commission on Preventing Deadly Conflict, June 1998), 17, where they admit (Sagasti as the former chief of strategic planning and senior adviser at the World Bank) that "in some cases . . . the Bank's prescriptions for economic reform may rather have contributed to local tensions and even deadly conflict, even though the Bank's net contribution to global economic growth and peaceful cooperation has undoubtedly been positive." Susan Woodward, in a much more devastating critique, argued that structural adjustment programmes during the 1980s played a major role in creating the conditions that caused the disintegration of Yugoslavia and the wars in Bosnia and Croatia in the past decade. See her *Balkan Tragedy: Chaos and Dissolution after the Cold-War* (Washington, D.C.: Brookings Institution, 1995). Nonetheless, and in fairness, the World Bank has made attempts in the late 1990s to address these problems, notably with the creation of the Post-Conflict Unit in 1997 and the development of a new Operational Policy on Development Assistance and Conflict, 1999–2000. See Chapter 14.

13. The term "horizontal inequality" refers to inequality among groups, as opposed to "vertical inequality," which measures inequality among individuals. See Frances Stewart, Chapter 5 in this volume.

14. See David A. Baldwin, *Economic Statecraft* (Princeton: Princeton University Press, 1985), chap. 10. Economic assistance was used primarily to support governments in countries allied with, or friendly to, the donor government and often took the form of military assistance. The major donor countries during the Cold War were, unsurprisingly, the United States and the Soviet Union. France, the United Kingdom, the Federal Republic of Germany, the German Democratic Republic, and China were also important donors during the Cold War. See also "Supporting Security Sector Reform: Review of the Role of External Actors— Annex 4: Discussion Paper no. 2" (London: International Symposium Report on Security Sector Reform and Military Expenditure, September 15–17, 2000).

15. This distinction is analogous to Elizabeth Cousens's characterization of the international approach to peacebuilding, a term coined by Secretary-General Boutros Boutros-Ghali in his 1992 *An Agenda for Peace*, as "deductive" (category-driven) and "inductive" (context-driven): "Broadly speaking, peacebuilding has been approached along what could be seen as two axes that circumscribe its possibilities. One describes the peacebuilding tools and capacities available to the organized international community; the other describes the particular conflict in question, its nature, intensity, depth of social support, and so on. These different approaches can usefully be considered as 'deductive,' where the content of peacebuilding is deduced from the existing capacities and mandates of international agencies and organizations, versus 'inductive,' where the content of peacebuilding is determined by the particular matrix of needs and capacities in individual cases." Elizabeth Cousens and Chetan Kumar with Karin Wermester, eds., *Peacebuilding as Politics: Cultivating Peace in Fragile Societies* (Boulder: Lynne Rienner Publishers, 2000), 5.

16. Part of the problem is due to the fact that it was only in the late 1990s that development actors, and in particular the DAC, began to focus on developing a foundation for assessing the impact of aid over the long term within a comparable broad-based assessment framework.

17. The main components of emergency assistance include the provision of food aid to those displaced by the crisis; the promotion (and, at times, protection) of the legal rights of civilians; and the provision of emergency medical services. For an excellent comprehensive review of the economic, social, and political roots of humanitarian emergencies, see E. Wayne Nafziger, Frances Stewart, and Raimo Väyrynen, eds., *War, Hunger and Displacement: The Origins of Humanitarian Emergencies*, vols. 1 and 2 (Oxford: Oxford University Press, 2000).

18. The United Nations recommends that donor countries maintain levels of development assistance at a minimum of 0.7 percent of gross domestic product. However, spending on aid has decreased steadily over the years, and in the post–Cold War period it has plummeted. Although a few Scandinavian saints maintained spending at just under 1 percent of gross national product (GNP) on overseas development assistance during the 1990s, many donor countries fell below the paltry level of 0.5 percent. Note that these figures represent net funding to developing countries. A very small percentage of overseas assistance is also spent on "other countries." See "World Aid Flows—Net Official Development Assistance to Developing Countries, and Official Assistance to Other Countries" (DFID Annual Report, Annex 17, May 2000).

19. Annual aggregates for emergency aid peaked at approximately U.S.$7 billion (which actually represents only 0.03 percent of worldwide GNP) in 1994 and have since leveled off at U.S.$3–4 billion. See Shepard Forman and Rita Parhad, "Paying for Essentials: Resources for Humanitarian Assistance," *Journal of Humanitarian Assistance*, available online at http://www.jha.ac.

20. Criticism has been particularly geared toward the failures of humanitarian assistance. For an analysis of humanitarian assistance and review of some of the critiques, see *Famine in Sudan, 1998: The Human Rights Causes* (New York: Human Rights Watch, 1999); and John Prendergast, *Crisis Response: Humanitarian Band-Aids in Sudan and Somalia* (London: Pluto Press, 1997).

21. Peter Uvin, "The Influence of Aid in Situations of Violent Conflict" (Paris: DAC Informal Task Force on Conflict, Peace, and Development Cooperation, September 1999), 4.

22. "Conflict, Peace, and Development Co-operation on the Threshold of the 21st Century" (Paris: DAC, OECD, Policy Statement, May 1997).

23. Ibid., 14.

24. Note that this more explicitly political approach to development assistance (in terms of internal decisionmaking, the governance components of development programs, and an understanding of the political consequences of aid itself) is accompanied by a shift in the post–Cold War era in whom the most important donors are. In terms of percentage of GNP at the end of the 1990s, they are: Denmark, Luxembourg, The Netherlands, Norway, and Sweden. Although in real figures this may not carry great weight, it gives them significant moral power, which can also be used in agenda-setting and decisionmaking, and allays, to a certain degree, neo-Marxist critiques of a revival of neoimperialism. See, for the exact figures, "World Aid Flows—Net Official Development Assistance to Developing Countries, and Official Assistance to Other Countries," *DFID Annual Report* (May 2000), Annex 17.

25. "The Politics of Coherence: The UK's Approach to Linking Political and Humanitarian Responses to Complex Political Emergencies" (London: Overseas Development Institute Humanitarian Policy Group, HPG Key Sheet 1 [draft], 2000), 2.

26. The UK approach is analogous to what is often referred to as Peace and Conflict Impact Assessment (PCIA). See, for instance, Kenneth Bush, "A Measure of Peace: Peace and Conflict Impact Assessment (PCIA) of Development Projects in Conflict Zones," Working Paper no. 1 (Ottawa: IDRC, 1998). The Canadian government is beginning to incorporate such assessments as an integral part of its Peacebuilding Initiative that is a joint effort between the department of Foreign Affairs and International Trade and the International Development Agency. Sweden, like the United Kingdom, announced in 1997 that the development aid department would be submitted to an analysis to ensure that implementation would not increase the risk of violence or human rights violations. The Norwegians and the Dutch have also made efforts to introduce a more coherent, holistic approach to conflict prevention.

27. See, for example, Michael G. Schatzberg, *The Dialectics of Oppression in Zaire* (Bloomington: Indiana University Press, 1988).

28. The World Bank recently produced a major report that records discussions with some 20,000 poor people from more than 200 communities in twenty-three countries. One of the major findings of the report is that poor people feel an enormous sense of demoralization and vulnerability in the face of the power of the elite and state institutions, in particular security institutions such as the military, judiciary, and police. See Deepa Narayan with Raj Patel, Kai Schafft, Anne Rademacher, and Sarah Koch-Schulte, *Voices of the Poor: Can Anyone Hear Us?* (New York: Oxford University Press for the World Bank, 2000).

29. Realistically, many donors continue to provide military assistance along the path set during the Cold War—that is, assistance with explicitly nondevelopmental goals and in which there is a clear separation between military and develop-

ment components. Plan Colombia, whose primary goal is to stem the flow of illicit cocaine and heroine into the United States, is a prime example. The United States has pledged $1.6 billion in assistance to Colombia for the implementation of Plan Colombia. First, USAID is mentioned as the implementing agency only for part of the $93 million attributed to "improving governing capacity and respect for human rights." Second, a full $600 million is pledged for the "expansion of counter-narcotics operations into southern Colombia," which, the report only notes, "includes important humanitarian assistance and development components." And finally, almost two-thirds ($1.036 billion) of the assistance pledged is dedicated to the provision of security sector instruments and tools—as opposed to training and reform. See U.S. State Department, "United States Support for Colombia—Fact Sheet Release by the Bureau of Western Hemisphere Affairs," March 28, 2000.

30. David Cortright and George A. Lopez, *The Sanctions Decade: Assessing UN Strategies in the 1990s*, a project of the International Peace Academy (Boulder: Lynne Rienner Publishers, 2000), 221.

31. See his chapter entitled "Incentives and Disincentives for Violence" in *Greed and Grievance: Economic Agendas in Civil Wars,* eds. Mats Berdal and David M. Malone (Boulder: Lynne Rienner Publishers, 2000), 8.

32. Media attention to the ongoing and particularly brutal conflicts in Sierra Leone and Angola has focused on the role of "blood diamonds" in fueling the war there. In Colombia, the illicit drug trade is thought to be a defining factor of the FARC and right-wing militia's combat. Similar examples can be found in countries as diverse as Cambodia, Bosnia, and the Democratic Republic of Congo. See Berdal and Malone, eds., *Greed and Grievance*, 5.

33. Paul Collier, "Economic Causes of Civil Conflict and Their Implications for Policy" (Washington, D.C.: Development Research Group, World Bank, June 15, 2000), 4.

34. As Alan Cowell notes, De Beers has actually turned the controversy over diamonds largely to its advantage: "Turning necessity into a virtue with the same skill it has used for decades to promote diamonds as glittery icons of love and beauty, it recast and began promoting itself as the squeaky-clean crusader for guarantees across the industry that 'conflict diamonds'—as they are also called—be kept out of the world of luxury goods." See "The Controversy over Diamonds Made into Virtue by De Beers," *New York Times*, August 22, 2000, A1.

35. For a good case study on this issue, see Georgios Kostakos, "Division of Labor Among International Organizations: The Bosnian Experience," *Global Governance* 4, 4 (October-December 1998): 461–484.

36. See Mary Anderson, *Do No Harm: How Aid Can Support Peace—or War* (Boulder: Lynne Rienner Publishers, 1999).

37. The United Nations has recently experimented with two types of coordination mechanisms in a response to this challenge. According to Bruce D. Jones, experience with Strategic Frameworks, essayed in Afghanistan and Sierra Leone, indicates that efforts to be inclusive can lead to a cumbersome, heavy-handed coordination structure. The Integrated Missions approach under way in Kosovo involves the UN Special Representative to the Secretary-General taking the lead on a joint structure composed of various responsible organizations and seems to be more effective for early postcrisis phases. However, one of the main problems with UN efforts to coordinate actors in the field is a proliferation of coordination mechanisms that have resulted in overlapping, unclear, and excessively complicated coordination structures, none of which clearly relates to another. See Bruce D. Jones, "The Challenge of Strategic Coordination," in Stephen John Stedman, Donald

Rothchild, and Elizabeth Cousens, eds., *Ending Civil Wars: The Implementation of Peace Agreements,* a project of the International Peace Academy (Boulder: Lynne Rienner Publishers, forthcoming 2002); and James Busumtwi-Sam, Alexander Costy, and Bruce D. Jones, "International Engagement in Peacebuilding in Africa," unpublished manuscript, July 2000.

38. See "Report of the Panel on UN Peace Operations" (the Brahimi Report), A/55/305–S/2000/809, an independent expert report led by Ambassador Lakhdar Brahimi.

39. See Rick Hooper and Mark Taylor, "Command from the Saddle: Managing United Nations Peace-building Missions, Recommendations Report of the Forum on the Special Representative of the Secretary-General: Shaping the UN's Role in Peace Implementation." *Fafo Report 266* (Oslo, Norway: Fafo Institute for Applied Social Science, 1999).

40. The costs of conflict to outside powers identified by Brown and Rosecrance include those related to the influx of refugees (mainly in neighboring states); direct economic and opportunity costs; military costs; and instability costs relating to the mobilization of ethnic groups at home, drug trafficking, and opportunistic wars of intervention. See Michael E. Brown and Richard N. Rosecrance, eds., *The Costs of Conflict: Prevention and Cure in the Global Arena* (Lanham, MD: Carnegie Commission on Preventing Deadly Conflict, Rowman and Littlefield Publishers, 1999).

41. See Judith Randel and Tony German, eds., *The Reality of Aid: An Independent Review of International Aid, 1996* (The Reality of Aid Management Group [Eurostep and ICVA]) (London: Earthscan Publications, 1996), 25.

42. See his "Aiding or Abetting? Humanitarian Aid and Its Economic Role in Civil Wars," in *Greed and Grievance,* eds. Berdal and Malone, 198–203.

43. Charles K. Cater and Karin Wermester, "From Reaction to Prevention: Opportunities for the UN System in the New Millennium" (International Policy Conference Report of the International Peace Academy, UN Regal Plaza Hotel, New York, April 13–14, 2000).

44. Press Release SG/SM/7491, SC/6893, July 20, 2000.

45. See A/55/305-S/2000/809, August 21, 2000, for the Brahimi Report, and A/55/502, October 20, 2000, on implementation of the Brahimi Report's recommendations.

46. See S/PRST/1999/34, November 30, 1999, and S/PRST/200/25, July 20, 2000.

47. See Kyushu-Okinawa Summit Meeting 2000, "G-8 Miyazaki Initiatives for Conflict Prevention" (Tokyo: Government of Japan).

48. See, for instance, "The Code of Conduct for the International Red Cross and Red Crescent Movement and NGOs in Disaster Relief," prepared jointly by the International Federation of the Red Cross and the ICRC 9 (see http://www.redcross.org); and the more detailed Sphere Project: Humanitarian Charter and Minimum Standards in Disaster Response (see http://www.sphereproject.org).

49. An example of this was the Global Witness campaign that brought the "conflict diamonds" issue into the spotlight. See http://www.oneworld.org/globalwitness.

50. See the DAC/OECD Working Party on Aid Evaluation, "Review of the DAC Principles for Evaluation of Development Assistance" (Paris: DAC/OECD, 1998).

51. See Randel and German, *The Reality of Aid,* 219. They have a chart that maps the political responsibility for OECD aid, but it is rapidly becoming out of

date as many aid actors develop and implement changes relating to the responsibility of decisionmaking regarding ODA.

52. In Haiti, particularly from 1997 to 1999, much multilateral assistance requiring legislative approval was held hostage to a struggle between the executive and parliament, with shocking consequences for Haiti's fragile economy. See Richard Chacón, "In Crisis, Haiti Feels US Chill," *Boston Globe*, October 2, 2000; and Don Bohning, "OAS Trying to Break Haiti Impasse," *Miami Herald*, October 9, 2000.

53. See Shepard Forman and Stewart Patrick, eds., *Good Intentions: Pledges of Aid for Post-Conflict Recovery*, for the Center on International Cooperation Studies in Multilateralism (Boulder: Lynne Rienner Publishers, 2000).

14

Addressing Conflict: Emerging Policy at the World Bank

Patricia Cleves, Nat Colletta, and Nicholas Sambanis

Large-scale political violence—especially civil wars—take place almost exclusively in the developing world, and there is a high degree of correlation between high poverty levels and civil war occurrence. Political violence is a major reason for the broadening chasm between economically developed and developing countries. The majority of young people in poor countries are now being socialized in systems created by war or other significant political repression; these systems give rise to greater poverty and inequality, which in turn increases crime and violence. As a result, we have witnessed the tripling of homicides in sub-Saharan Africa in the 1980s, and during the 1990s we saw an explosion of civil wars, during which civilian war-related deaths as a percentage of all war-related deaths increased to 90 percent (as opposed to only 50 percent in the eighteenth century). In the 1990s, violence created approximately 13 million refugees and 38 million internally displaced persons worldwide, resulting in enormous social and economic costs that have been borne disproportionately by the developing world.[1] Thus, it has become increasingly clear that without developing a greater understanding of the causes and consequences of conflict—and concomitant policies to address them—large-scale political and criminal violence threatens to relegate several countries and regions of the developing world into a perpetual trap of poverty and slow or negative growth.

For the World Bank, the problem became increasingly clear in the early 1990s: civil wars, in Africa in particular, began to pose a significant challenge to the World Bank's traditional approach to development. With military expenditures crowding out social and productive expenditures and the emergence of failed or collapsing states from Somalia to the Democratic Republic of the Congo (DRC), the Bank soon realized that it could no longer continue to conduct business as usual. In 1992, the Bank for the first time supported the demobilization and reintegration of former combatants in Uganda. This was a watershed investment and led to involvement in other related war-to-peace transition activities, ranging from the social and economic reintegration of refugees and internally displaced persons to demining and governance reforms. Driven by financial and economic issues relating primarily to excessive public expenditures, the Bank soon found itself addressing problems relating to divided societies and weakened governance and consequently accenting the social and governance dimensions of state failure. This new cognizance of the negative implications of war for development led the World Bank to create a Post-Conflict Unit (PCU) in 1997 to deal explicitly with postconflict issues as well as countries, and to launch a related research program in the Development Economics Research Group (DECRG) in February 1999 with the aim of advancing understanding of the causes and consequences of large-scale political violence and designing strategies to manage post-conflict transitions.

World Bank Operations in Conflict-Affected and Postconflict Countries

The Bank now operates in more than thirty-eight countries in support of a number of peacebuilding activities, ranging from demobilization and reintegration of combatants to refugee reintegration and justice reform (see Table 14.1 for a representative sample of Bank activities in conflict-affected countries). In addition, it is developing new policies and instruments with which to guide Bank involvement in conflict-affected countries.

New Operational Policy: Conflict and Development Cooperation

One such policy, the Operational Policy (OP) on Conflict and Development Cooperation, was approved by the Bank's Board of Executive Directors in December 2000. The OP ensued in part from evaluations of the Bank's operations in several postconflict countries, including Bosnia-Herzegovina, El Salvador, and Rwanda, and has been formulated in consultation with partner and donor governments, civil society/NGOs, the United Nations, and the private sector. The purpose of the OP is to commit the Bank to a more vigorous approach to countries at risk of conflict, in conflict, and those showing signs of recovery or that are in the postconflict phase. The policy is designed to maintain engagement in such countries and provide a flexible, responsive strategy to guide its operations. This represents a sig-

Table 14. 1   Representative World Bank Activities in Conflict-Affected Countries

Country	Bank's Activities
Albania	Two Post-Conflict Fund (PCF) grants totaling U.S.$1.5 million for emergency activities in education and social/health services for Albanian and Kosovar populations during the refugee crisis, for use mainly in Northern Albania. The first grant closed on June 30, 2000. The second grant is currently under implementation.
Algeria	The Bank's lending program has rapidly adjusted to government requests, including the Earthquake Emergency Reconstruction project (U.S.$83 million), a Telecommunications TA (U.S.$9 million), and a Privatization Learning and Innovation Loan (LIL) (U.S.$5 million), all of which were approved by the Board in June. High-level missions from the Bank have provided an opportunity to renew the basis for Bank relations with Algeria. A program of work was agreed for the next 12–18 months, essentially based on support for rural and local community-based development; infrastructure sectors (energy and mining, transportation, telecommunications); technical assistance for strengthening institutional capacity; and discussion seminars on socioeconomic and sector priorities.
Azerbaijan	A pilot reconstruction program, in part supported by an International Development Association (IDA) credit, continues in a small section of war-damaged territory under Azeri control. The Social Fund for the Development of Internally Displaced Persons (SFDI) has been established with U.S.$10 million in IDA funds to support self-reliance of IDPs. This is the first Social Fund supported by the Bank that primarily targets conflict-displaced populations.
Bosnia	The Board endorsed the Country Assistance Strategy (CAS) on May 18, 2000, and approved the Pilot Emergency Labor Redeployment Project in June. This project will facilitate the reintegration of discharged soldiers into civilian life. A proposal to the PCF for a second year of funding for the Community Based Mental Health Services in Middle Bosnia is currently under review.
Burundi	In May 2000, a Bank-IMF team began working with the government in preparing an Interim Poverty Reduction Strategy Paper (I-PRSP), and in July the National Strategy for Growth and Poverty Reduction was launched with a workshop opened by President Pierre Buyoya, who took the opportunity to make an appeal for international debt relief. Civil society played an active role during the workshop, and the national as well as the international press widely covered the event. The participatory methods introduced in the Bank's BURSAP II project are proving successful in promoting community participation in local rehabilitation programs. The Emergency Economic Recovery Credit, of which 40 percent has already been disbursed, is helping to stabilize the economy and has led to a narrower gap between the official and parallel exchange rates.
Cambodia	Ongoing IDA work with other donors to assist the government with implementation of a pilot Demobilization and Reintegration for Ex-combatants Program and preparation of a full Demobilization Program.

(continues)

Table 14.1   continued

Country	Bank's Activities
Colombia	The government's National Development Plan defines the social, economic, and institutional components of the peace and development initiative with the purpose of promoting development in rural areas with low state presence and high levels of violent conflict. To finance the incremental funding requirements generated by the peace process, the government is using its own funds as well as seeking financing from multilateral and bilateral sources, including the Bank. The National Development Plan is being developed in a participatory manner, and its main objective is the building of social capital and local capacity. Key areas for investment would be those that improve productivity, human capital, and infrastructure. Projects such as the Productive Partnerships for Peace and the second phase of the Magdalena Medio Regional Development Project would build upon the lessons learned from the current Bank-supported Magdalena Medio and Peasant Enterprise Zones Projects. The sustainable development plan for the ecoregion Sierra Nevada de Santa Marta, which is an ecosystem of global significance as well as a conflict-affected region, will be supported by a Learning and Innovation Loan (LIL) and a Global Environmental Facility grant expected to be approved later this year. The Bank is also actively promoting dialogue with civil society to build consensus on a peace and development agenda.
Congo-Brazzaville	The country has successfully negotiated a postconflict program with the IMF. A Bank-led multiagency, postconflict emergency assessment mission visited Congo in April–May 2000. A Transitional Support Strategy (TSS) was submitted to the Board for discussion on December 19, 2000. The TSS sketches out options to deal with the arrears issue. At a donors conference in Paris on October 5–6, 2000, donors expressed strong interest in helping to consolidate the peace process, promote democratization of political life and inclusiveness, and improve economic management.
Croatia	A $1.09 million PCF grant was approved on July 10, 2000, for the Refugee Return and Regional Development Project. A World Bank mission visited Croatia from September 25 to October 4, 2000, to assess the project area, objectives, components, and implementing mechanism. The project will cover the area Zadar-Gracac-Knin-Sibenik and will help in the reintegration of Serb returnees and Bosnian Croat settlers through two main activities: (1) Regional Development Vision; and (2) Social and Economic Recovery Fund. The Regional Development Vision will strengthen the regional planning capacity, through upgrading of territorial management skills, enabling this area to better attract investment. The Social and Economic Recovery Fund will pilot a number of microprojects through grants for producers' groups in rural and urban areas and for community-based social services aimed at vulnerable groups of different ethnic background.
Democratic Republic of the Congo (DRC)	A multiagency multidonor mission relaunched dialogue with the DRC in November 1999, and a Bank-IMF mission in February 2000 followed up on specific macroeconomic issues. A Bank mission visited Kinshasa in June 2000 to continue to assemble the building blocks for the Bank's Interim Strategy. The series of three missions have permitted exchanges by the government with the Bank, the Fund, and the African Development Bank (AfDB) on key policy issues. Since the February mission,

Country	Bank's Activities
Democratic Republic of the Congo (DRC) (continued)	work has been ongoing by the IMF, the Bank, the AfDB, and the government on the debt stock–taking exercise. This will lay the groundwork toward stabilizing arrears, which is a preliminary step for any resumption of lending by IDA, the IMF, and the AfDB, as well as for eventual participation in the HIPC initiative. An Interim Strategy is expected to be submitted to the Bank's Board during the third quarter of financial year 2001. Progress continues on using a PCF grant to prepare a program that supports the demobilization and reintegration of the vulnerable groups that currently serve in the armed forces, including child soldiers.
Djibouti	A peace agreement was signed in 1994. The full reintegration of the former combatants is taking place, supported by a LIL Credit approved in financial year 1999. A CAS is expected to be presented to the Board in mid–financial year 2001.
East Timor	Pledges to the Trust Fund for East Timor (TFET) have risen from U.S.$146 million pledged at the Tokyo conference in December 1999 to U.S.$166.4 million as of October 1, 2000. Contribution agreements covering $100 million of these pledges have been signed, and cash and promissory notes have been received totaling U.S.$94 million.
Federal Republic of Yugoslavia/Kosovo	In early October, the new authorities requested that the Bank field a mission to begin discussion on economic needs and priorities and start efforts necessary to establish relations with the international financial institutions (IFIs). While membership in the World Bank Group may take some time—given in particular large arrears owed to the International Bank for Reconstruction and Development (IBRD)—a strategy for possible assistance is under preparation. This is likely to focus, inter alia, on an economic recovery program and investment needs as well as donor coordination in the near term. In Kosovo, implementation continues of PCF funded Community Development Fund and social sector budget support. Plans are under way for countrywide social and institutional assessment. A TSS progress report is also under preparation.
FYR-Macedonia	Macedonia has received a PCF grant of U.S.$2 million for education activities and interethnic dialogue. The first phase of the grant (U.S.$1.0 million) is fully disbursed. Implementation of the second phase of the grant (U.S.$1.0 million) began in the spring of 2000.
Georgia	A working group has been established by government and donors, with the participation of the Bank, to develop a strategy for enhancing self-reliance of internally displaced persons from conflicts in Abkhazia and Ossetia. The Georgia Self-Reliance Fund (GSRF) has been established to finance pilot programs and analytical work to develop sustainable solutions to IDP living situations. The GSRF is now active with a $300,000 PCF Grant. Commitments to the Fund have been made by UNDP ($200,000), UNHCR ($150,000), and USAID ($300,000).
Guatemala	Transition to the new government has been completed successfully; the government fully supports the peace agenda. The Bank continues to provide support to key socioeconomic activities and indigenous people's issues. Several high-level meetings took place between the government

(continues)

Table 14.1   continued

Country	Bank's Activities
Guatemala (continued)	and the Bank; the Bank proposed to streamline the safety-net system and make the social funds more efficient with a view to strengthening their contribution to the implementation of peace programs. The Bank regularly participates in meetings of the UN interagency group monitoring the socioeconomic and indigenous peoples issues.
Guinea-Bissau	The U.S.$25 million IDA postconflict credit to support the government's National Reconciliation and Reconstruction Program, approved by the Board on May 16, 2000, was declared effective on June 28, 2000. A joint Bank-IMF PRSP mission was fielded in June/July 2000 to (1) review the authorities' draft Interim Poverty Reduction Strategy; and (2) discuss HIPC issues.
Lebanon	Following the Israeli withdrawal, immediate reconstruction efforts are under way in the south. The government is seeking donor support both for immediate needs and for longer-term development efforts. The first donor meeting was held on July 26, 2000. Elections were held on September 8, 2000, and a new government has been elected.
Philippines	Support to postconflict reconstruction for Mindanao is under way through several ongoing operations, in particular the Special Zone for Peace and Development (SZOPAD) Social Fund and the Mindanao Rural Development Project (MRDP). Implementation has been delayed in some areas due to security concerns.
Rwanda	Human Resources Development and Water Supply projects were signed in August 2000 and are awaiting effectiveness. An interim PRSP is scheduled for December 21, 2000, which could lead to Rwanda potentially reaching its decision point under the enhanced HIPC Initiative by end of calendar year 2000. President Kagame met with President Wolfensohn on September 11, 2000, and restated his commitment to peace in the region. The reform program remains on track.
Sierra Leone	Demobilization, Demilitarization, and Reintegration (DDR) Program has been the subject of a review report called for by the key stakeholders (funded through the Multi-Donor Trust Fund) and was reviewed by key stakeholders to design the next phase of the DDR. The government obtained donor backing and financial support for key budget programs. The second tranche of the Economic Rehabilitation and Recovery Credit was disbursed in October 2000. The government has taken the initiative and has prepared a draft Interim PRSP. The Fund has recently disbursed the second tranche under its postconflict assistance program, and discussions are ongoing for a program under the PRGF.
Somalia	Funding of expanded Watching Brief through PCF grant approved in February 2000 and is under implementation by the International Federation of the Red Cross and Red Crescent Societies (IFRC).
Sri Lanka	The violent conflict continues in the North and East. The Bank has submitted a report to the government on the comprehensive district and sectoral stakeholder consultations organized for developing the Framework for Relief, Reconciliation, and Rehabilitation. Four interministerial working groups incorporated findings in policy recommendations to the government in November 2000.

Country	Bank's Activities
Sudan	PCF grant was recently approved for an expanded Watching Brief in key social areas and how these have been affected by the combined effect of war, natural disasters, and economic disruption. Studies will examine the situation with respect to poverty, access to social services, IDPs, and vulnerability. Selected aspects of this work will be carried out in partnership with UNICEF and UNDP offices in Khartoum. Other nonlending work is under way on agricultural sector reforms, including the Gezira Irrigation Scheme and the Nile Basin Initiative as well as macroeconomic analysis.
West Bank/Gaza	The Bank and donors have made great efforts since the Oslo Accords to support the peace process by assisting in comprehensive reconstruction, starting with the Holst Fund. Donors have disbursed some U.S.$2.8 billion in support of these efforts. A report, submitted to a meeting of all major donors in Lisbon in June 2000 summarized the gains made. The recent outbreak of violence, as well as the accompanying closures of the West Bank/Gaza-Israeli border, threaten to undermine these gains. Should the violence and border closures continue for a sustained period, there will likely be a rapid increase in poverty, and the gains made on the economic and institutional front will be further undermined. Although efforts continue at the political level to bring an end to the current situation, the donors are working actively to minimize the impact. Projects with longer-term objectives continue, albeit at a reduced pace. Work in the Bank's office in West Bank/Gaza continues, and the staff remains able to supervise and monitor project progress.

nificant transformation for the World Bank toward active engagement in conflict situations.

Innovative Operational Instruments

As a complement to new such policy initiatives, the World Bank has developed innovative operational instruments to lead its projects in conflict-affected countries. In countries where there is no Bank portfolio due to security conditions, a Watching Brief process is now initiated. The Watching Brief positions the Bank to monitor the political and economic situation in the country, maintain its knowledge base, and develop strategies and partnerships *en attente*, enabling the Bank to reengage rapidly once conditions permit. Currently, Watching Briefs are being carried out in Somalia, Sudan, and Afghanistan.

To help support the transition to peace and prepare a stable foundation for sustainable development in countries or areas emerging from conflict, the Bank now prepares a Transitional Support Strategy (TSS). A TSS is an interim strategy for short- to medium-term Bank engagement in a country emerging from conflict. Given limited capacity and resources, and the urgent need to reinforce fragile commitments to peace, priorities for assistance under a TSS may differ from those for application in a normal development environment. For example, a TSS may focus on activities that promote reconciliation, reinforce the capacity of refugees, demobilize soldiers and other war-affected populations (particularly women and children) to quickly return to a semblance of normality and self-sufficiency, and support the establishment of stable, functioning public institutions.

In Burundi for example, the TSS recognizes the need to support the peace process and to tackle the worst manifestations of poverty through early development assistance. Special care is being taken not to contribute to possible sources of conflict. The main areas of focus are, first, *promoting governance and "ownership"* through participation in rehabilitation and reconciliation. This entails supporting a participatory approach to rehabilitating villages damaged or destroyed by the conflict. Second, *creating labor intensive employment* to rehabilitate infrastructure and restart private sector activity. It will also provide a vehicle for reintegration of demobilized members of militia and the army. And third, *restoring key imports and social services* that will facilitate private sector recovery and provide resources for poverty alleviation through operating funds for the rehabilitated infrastructure in health, education, agriculture, and resettlement. TSSs are also currently under way in Kosovo, East Timor, Sierra Leone, and Congo-Brazzaville, among others. Similar strategies are under preparation for the DRC and Liberia.

New Focus: Community-Level Activities

In an effort to identify strategic areas of intervention that can mitigate violent conflict and/or lessen its consequences and, if possible, help *prevent* the eruption of violent conflict, the Bank is increasingly focusing its efforts on community development in the midst of ongoing conflict. An example of Bank involvement in this area is its support for the Magdalena Medio Project in Colombia. This project is promoting local development activities by bringing together different stakeholders from a wide spectrum of political positions and building consensus regarding the identification of priorities. The project is laying the foundation not only for sustainable development in the area but also for trust and eventually reconciliation.

Building on this experience, several projects are currently under way to address the legacy of conflict at the community levels. In the context of working to bridge the gap between relief and development, the Bank seeks in particular to address the needs of internally displaced persons by providing development assistance to communities that have war-affected populations. Experience in Rwanda, Angola, Cambodia, Kosovo, and East Timor, among others, has shown that community reintegration is a successful vehicle capable of providing social and economic reintegration of displaced persons while at the same time laying the foundation for longer-term development. Similarly, postconflict reconstruction and national reconciliation is possible if special efforts are made to reach out to conflict-affected communities and social groups in order to build an environment of partnerships and mutual trust.

For instance, the Community Development and Reintegration Project in Rwanda demonstrates that community reintegration and development takes place most effectively through a process of government decentralization and community participation in the identification of measures to assist returnees and other vulnerable groups. In Angola, the Post-Conflict Recovery Program established a project to support war-affected rural communities in their efforts to reintegrate displaced peoples and revitalize community-level economic and social activities.

In East Timor, the Community Empowerment and Local Governance Project is not only empowering "elected" community development committees (which are required to be 50 percent female) to set priorities and allocate funds to community subprojects that address the range of issues from social infrastructure rehabilitation to agricultural productivity; it is also instilling a sense of inclusive, democratic decisionmaking and accountability. In addition, the Bank coordinated an international joint assessment mission in October/November 1999 and cochaired with the United Nations Transitional Administration in East Timor a donor coordination meeting in December in order to establish the country's comprehensive financing needs. For the first time, these needs combined humanitarian, reconstruction, and development assistance. To accommodate this, in February 2000 the World Bank Board of Executives endorsed an amendment to the Trust Fund for East Timor (TFET) to enable donor contributions to be accepted to finance development and reconstruction activities. A total of $147 million has been pledged for the TFET, which the World Bank will administer. The grant agreement for the first major reconstruction activity under the TFET, the $22 million Community Empowerment and Reconstruction Project, was signed by World Bank president James Wolfensohn in Dili on February 21, 2000.

The stability and security of individuals is also an extremely important aspect of community development. Within the parameters of the Bank's mandate, support is provided for the efforts of member countries to achieve these conditions, as well as measures that reduce the incentives and opportunities for violence, enabling at the same time governments and civil society to develop peaceful channels for resolving disputes and managing conflict. In this context, the Bank supports demobilization and reintegration programs of former combatants in countries such as Cambodia, South Africa, Uganda, Mozambique, and Guinea-Bissau. In addition, Bank-supported demining programs have taken place in Bosnia, Croatia, and Slovenia.

Partnerships

Over the past year, the Bank has substantially strengthened its collaboration with stakeholders, not least through increased collaboration in the coordination of emergency humanitarian relief among the UN departments and agencies and other humanitarian actors. As part of this effort, the Bank has taken steps to establish greater working relations with UN departments and agencies. The Bank now participates in several fora, including the Inter-Agency Standing Committee and the United Nations Framework Team for Conflict Analysis, and it cross-trains staff (i.e., sends Bank staff to UN training programs and receives UN staff for Bank training programs). Cooperation agreements have also been signed with the UN High Commission for Refugees (UNHCR) and the International Committee of the Red Cross. The Bank also participates in the Conflict Prevention and Post-Conflict Reconstruction Network, which includes more than thirty government departments, international organizations, and NGOs working on issues related to conflict and development. Under the lead of the Bank, a joint website is being developed as an information gateway on issues pertaining to transition from violent conflict to sustainable peace and development.[2]

Under the Brookings Initiative that was launched in January 1999 in an effort to bridge the gap between emergency relief and development, the Bank, UNHCR, and the UN Development Programme (UNDP) undertook a joint high-level mission to Sierra Leone, Liberia, and Guinea in February 2000. The joint mission sought to strengthen operational partnerships between security, humanitarian assistance, and early reconstruction and development and focused on socioeconomic recovery, key governance challenges, and the subregional/crossborder dimension, identifying priority areas for additional funding. The Bank and the government of the United Kingdom then jointly chaired a meeting in March 2000 in London that aimed to mobilize additional resources in order to address the priorities identified during the joint mission. The deterioration of the situation has put the implementation of activities there on hold for now.

Specific Financial Mechanisms

The Bank has also designed a specific grant mechanism, the Post-Conflict Fund (PCF), to finance activities that support transitions to peace. The PCF is a multidonor trust fund administered by the PCU, which provides grants to partner agencies to carry out critical early interventions in conflict-affected countries. Typically, this involves conflict analysis and preventive measures, needs assessments, and planning and piloting of priority reconstruction projects. The fund has been in operation since January 1998 and has made some sixty-five grants amounting to $21 million to twenty-seven conflict-affected countries. Priority is given to proposals focusing on the restoration of lives and livelihoods, especially the rehabilitation of vulnerable groups such as displaced families, child soldiers, widows, and so on. For example, in East Timor, a grant of $1 million enabled the Bank to respond to a request from the United Nations to coordinate the joint assessment mission. In Kosovo a further $1 million grant was used to establish the Community Development Fund, while in Liberia, Somalia, and Sudan grants have facilitated analysis and pilot activities in anticipation of future Bank engagement. The PCF became a trust fund at the beginning of financial year 2000. It is financed through net proceeds of the Bank and bilateral contributions. It has already received more than $4 million in pledges, enabling donor contributions to complement core Bank funding.

Finally, with regard to debt and arrears clearance, the Bank is now working closely with the IMF on the modification of the heavily indebted poor countries program to reduce debt and increase the net flow of capital to heavily indebted *postconflict* countries. A modification of performance indicators, using the framework in this chapter and taking into account the special circumstances and needs of such countries, is currently under way.

Research and Development at the Bank

In addition to its operational work in conflict-affected countries, the Bank is also undertaking new analytical work on conflict with a view to finding innovative ways to answer three fundamental questions: (1) What factors increase the risk of large-scale public violence, terrorism, and crime? (2) What policies are effective in reducing these risks? And (3) How should policymaking in postconflict societies and high-violence societies differ from policymaking in more peaceful societies?

The following sections present the main components of the Bank's ongoing research and policy development efforts to establish a set of conflict indicators to inform lending and other operations in conflict-affected countries that will seek to assess: the risk of conflict in a given country; the intensity and escalation potential of ongoing conflict; and the likelihood that a conflict will not recur. A fourth set of indicators, currently in development, will seek to measure the impact of the Bank's portfolio on the risk of violent conflict in a given country.

Conflict Indicators Project

One of the main thrusts of the Bank's policy research on conflict is the Conflict Indicators Project that is being developed jointly by the DECRG and the PCU. The project seeks to develop four sets of conflict indicators that will help country teams to assess conflict-proneness, and thereby help design informed and appropriate response(s) to the economic, social, and institutional needs of the conflict-affected country, better monitor the performance of these countries, and provide guidance regarding the Bank's fund allocations to these countries.[3] The project builds on the PCU's previous work on conflict indicators and postconflict reconstruction and integrates that work with the findings of DECRG's The Economics of Civil Wars research project and new research and analysis. The results will be linked to the OP on Conflict and Development and will seek to identify best practices to be incorporated into the good practices document currently under preparation in the Bank. The project's methodology and its operational utility is outlined below.

Research Framework

One of the lessons that has emerged from the Bank's operational experience in conflict-affected countries is that they present a unique mix of political-economic and social challenges that complicate the Bank's development objectives there (see Table 14.2). Although recognizing that policy cannot always modify the course of conflict, it is possible to identify those factors affecting conflict that are susceptible to policy management so that carefully designed programs may reduce their negative impact. Among the several possible root causes of conflict, policy cannot influence fixed effects such as geography or the natural resource endowment. However, most of the factors that cause war are the products of human agency and/or institutional failure, and *are* susceptible to policy management. We hypothesize, on the basis of insights gleaned from the Economics of Civil War project, that a conflict escalates and becomes violent when it has access to organizational capital (financing), human capital (armed groups and individuals), social capital (lack of trust and social norms supporting violence), and physical capital (weapons). Policies to reduce the risk of violent conflict should therefore target these four types of capital. Our research seeks to facilitate and help move forward conflict-pertinent policy design by identifying priority areas and discussing possible ways to reduce the overall likelihood of violence.

Beyond analyzing the risk of war outbreak, we also consider the dynamics of postconflict societies. Experience suggests that transition processes can easily fail and lead a country back to war. Although some postwar countries have had a sustainable transition process toward peace (e.g., Mozambique), others have slipped back into violence after reaching a plateau in their transition process (e.g., Sierra Leone).

Four types of conflict indicators are currently in development: (1) a set of *at-risk* indicators to identify conflict-prone countries before large-scale

Table 14.2   Type of Analyses, Bank Objectives, and Tools

Type of Analyses	Bank Objectives	Tools[a]
Countries at Risk (Potential outbreak of violent conflict in a country or parts of it)	To assess the country's proneness to conflict and to design conflict-sensitive portfolios that can help mitigate and/or address root causes of conflict.	At-risk indicators
Countries in Conflict (Extended periods of violent conflict in a country or parts of it)	To design conflict-sensitive portfolio in those countries where the Bank is active to mitigate conflicts and/or support activities toward conflict resolution.	Conflict-intensity indicators
Countries in Transition from War to Peace and Reconstruction (Negotiated settlement has been agreed; formal end to hostilities)	To identify proneness to the re-emergence of conflict and to design a portfolio that can help address underlying causes and mitigate possible outbreaks of conflict. To address the legacy of violent conflicts, e.g., displacement, militarization, weak governance, etc. To assess the country's transition to peace following peace settlements or political agreements.	Performance indicators
All Countries (Portfolio analysis)	To ensure that Banks' programs do not exacerbate conflict, and address and mitigate potential root causes of conflict.	Peace and conflict impact assessment

Note: a. Reality in conflict countries will show an overlapping of analyses and stages, but for operational purposes we have distinguished different tools for different stages and analyses. However, countries at risk, countries in conflict, and countries in transition all have underlying causes of violent conflict that will be measured by the at-risk indicators.

violent conflict actually occurs; (2) a set of *conflict intensity* indicators, to assess the extent and escalation potential of ongoing conflicts;[4] and (3) a set of *performance* indicators, to measure the likelihood of postconflict countries' successful peacebuilding and economic development. A fourth set of indicators on conflict impact assessment will also be developed in time to assess the impact of Bank programs on the likelihood of conflict.[5]

These four sets of indicators correspond to two broad categories of determinants of violent conflict: the underlying root causes, that is, the historical and structural determinants that lead to a breakdown of the state and to the outbreak of violent conflict; and the conflict-induced risks that pertain to postconflict countries, that is, the legacy of violent conflicts such as the excessive militarization of society, the displacement of population, and the destruction of physical, social, and human capital for development.[6]

Research Design

We begin by identifying four substantive areas of analysis that, based on current research, we believe are relevant in designing economic, social, and institutional policies for conflict-affected countries: *security*, *governance*, *social cohesion*, and *economic recovery*. Identifying these areas helps organize the most salient country-specific determinants of conflict and are thus the general categories we have adopted for each set of conflict indicators.[7]

Our project then operationalizes a set of conflict indicators in two steps: First, by using available data sources, we have coded each quantifiable indicator for the period 1960–1999 for at-risk indicators[8] and for the period 1945–1999 for intensity and performance indicators;[9] second, by applying these data and indicators, we have estimated empirical models of initial war risk and postconflict risk, and we have used the results of these models to classify countries in risk categories.

1. *Identifying conflict stages:* the assessment of overall conflict risk is based on, first, using a set of quantifiable indicators within the context of statistical models developed by DECRG to estimate (a) the probability of civil war outbreak; and (b) the probability of war recurrence for each country in our database.[10] These probability estimates can then be used to classify countries according to stages of conflict risk.[11] These can then be used to assist country teams to develop a Conflict Index (see Appendix 14.1), which could be consulted in designing economic and lending policy in conflict-affected countries. The estimates are offered as benchmarks against which country teams can (by re-estimating our models with more current data in future years) assess changes in their countries' estimated conflict risk.[12] Because the benchmark probability estimates constitute sensitive internal information, they will be used with similar Bank-generated economic policy indicators and will not be publicly available.

2. *Ordering and weighting indicators:* using our research to date, we suggest broad guidelines to assist country teams to rank the different sets of indicators (and corresponding substantive areas) in order of importance to their country while assessing their country's conflict risk. One way to achieve that is to decompose the impact of each group of indicators on the overall probability estimate. Country teams may wish to deviate from these models by adding or subtracting indicators and by considering qualitative indicators to supplement the quantitative indicators used in our analysis. In

such a case, country teams would take the lead in determining the indicator weights that they feel best reflect the socioeconomic and political context of their countries.[13] An important issue of particular relevance to postconflict countries is that the weighting of conflict indicators changes over time. Experience suggests that as a country successfully moves away from a transition stage to peace, the importance of economic recovery increases relative to the need for security. However, during the unstable transition period, security continues to be as paramount as in an active conflict situation. Thus, we suggest that the postconflict (or performance) indicators discussed below should be considered particularly relevant during the transition to peace phase (up to five years); and as the country moves further away from the conflict period, the at-risk indicators should be applied to measure conflict risk.

3. *Combining quantitative with qualitative conflict indicators:* there is no simple or straightforward approach to combine quantitative with qualitative conflict indicators at this stage of the project. The main sources of difficulty are the following: (a) Although historical data are available for the quantitative indicators used in statistical analysis (see the Appendixes), no such data are available for the qualitative indicators; (b) given the lack of data for qualitative indicators, we cannot integrate these indicators in the quantitative models to assess their relative impact on conflict risk; and (c) if qualitative indicators are coded on an intensity scale by Bank country teams, these evaluations may be largely influenced by and reflect some of the attributes of the quantitative indicators used in our analysis, which would create measurement and reliability problems in the analysis.

All these problems are surmountable, although not at this early stage of our project. We should also say that some of the quantitative indicators used to make risk assessments are in fact reflections of qualitative variables—such as the degree of ethnic fragmentation, the level of democracy, and the extent of national reconciliation in postconflict societies. This has been done by using indicators that we believe are good proxies for these qualitative variables. At the same time, there are more qualitative variables that are important but for which we have been unable to find existing measurable proxies. In view of this difficulty, we propose to further integrate these variables in our analysis in subsequent years.

For the time being, country teams could obtain measures for these qualitative indicators and use them in an informed though necessarily ad hoc manner to fine-tune the risk measures that we have produced. Thus, if a country is placed in a given risk category on the basis of quantitative analysis, the country team could argue the need to reclassify that country in a different risk category on the basis of qualitative indicators that they have coded. We plan to design surveys and distribute them to country teams to help them identify the best indicators of conflict risk in their country.[14] Over time, this process could generate an important source of data for conflict analysis and could quantify many hard-to-measure variables such as governance and perceptions of fear and trust.

It is also important to note that even though sophisticated quantitative models are useful, they need to be tempered and subject to interpretation by an effort to tap and organize existing indigenous knowledge in order to better understand patterns, trends, and risks. More participatory field-based assessment using the traditional anthropological methods of key informant and group consultation along with participant observation is essential to enriching the explanatory and predictive power of quantitative measures. Currently, such efforts at the Bank are under way to make poverty assessments much more participatory and could usefully inform practice on this in the future in relation to conflict and risk analysis.

Core Conflict Indicators: At-Risk Indicators

The following list of at-risk indicators could be used in developing a Conflict Index for all countries that have not yet experienced war.[15]

1. *Security:* size of ethnic diasporas; arms trade; human rights violations; length of peacetime since last war; length of time since last war.[16]

2. *Social cohesion:* geographic concentration; population size; ethnolinguistic fractionalization index; ethnic dominance; levels of trust and association.

3. *Economic performance:* economic growth; per capita income; secondary education;[17] dependency on primary commodities and natural resources.[18]

4. *Governance:* democracy level; legal and institutional framework;[19] corruption.

In designing a Country Assistance Strategy and the Poverty Reduction Strategy Paper, Bank country teams would benefit from being able to assess the country's conflict-proneness. Countries that are at high risk of large-scale political violence (civil war) should be watched carefully, and specially designed economic assistance should be delivered to those countries to reduce the risk of large-scale violence.[20] At-risk indicators allow us to classify countries in four zones according to their relative conflict-proneness: high risk, medium risk, low risk, and no risk. These four risk zones are relevant to countries that have *not* experienced conflict (i.e., the indicators point to risk of conflict outbreak). Two other classes of countries are also of interest: those that are currently experiencing conflict and those emerging from conflict in postconflict transition. Once countries in transition become sufficiently normalized, they can be considered among the countries that have not experienced war, and at-risk indicators can be applied.

On the basis of the research framework and design depicted schematically above, we estimated the relative influence of key variables on the probability of observing an outbreak of civil war in any given five-year period based on a model developed by Paul Collier and Anke Hoeffler (see Appendix 14.3).

The model and estimations allow a classification of countries according to their current risk of conflict on the basis of the four categories identified above: high risk, medium risk, low risk, and no risk.[21] Note that the model estimates civil war initiation, so if a country had been at war since the preceding period, no estimate is available for that country. For internal use at the Bank, we have classified countries in three risk categories according to their conflict risk: negligible risk (category 0), low risk (category 1) and medium risk (category 2).

It is also possible to use the Collier-Hoeffler model to gauge the relative importance among at-risk indicators—security, social cohesion, economic performance, and governance—for a given country. Overall, the model suggests that economic and security variables are more significant with respect to their impact on the risk of civil war outbreak than political and social cohesion variables, suggesting in turn that policies to reduce the risk of civil war ought to give greater weight to these variables. Nonetheless, country teams would be responsible for the ultimate weighting of these indicators and for the selection of the indicators that best fit their country.

At this early stage of the implementation of the Conflict Indicators Project, all countries are currently being monitored using at-risk indicators.[22] However, if this scale of monitoring generates too high an administrative burden, then countries that have experienced a civil war in the past ten years will be monitored. An alternative threshold would be to monitor all countries that have experienced civil war since 1945. Both of these thresholds are consistent with DECRG research, which suggests that civil wars have the highest probability of recurrence within the first ten years and that countries that have experienced one civil war in the last forty years are much more likely to experience another civil war than are countries that have always been at peace.

Core Conflict Indicators: Conflict Intensity

Using the tools described above with reference to at-risk indicators—that is, a combination of quantitative and qualitative research that builds in on-the-ground, practical experience—we can also attempt to assess the intensity and escalation potential of ongoing conflicts. The statistical analysis used to assess conflict intensity and possible war duration is based on different models than the analysis used to estimate the likelihood of conflict initiation. Here the goals are to assess ongoing conflict in terms of lives lost, economic activity disrupted, and area affected by conflict.

We use the following set of indicators to measure escalation/ intensity[23]:

1. *Security:* unilateral foreign military intervention; arms trade; area covered by landmines; human rights violations; per capita deaths and displacements; changes in conscription rates or changes in military spending.[24]

2. *Social cohesion:* ethnolinguistic fractionalization; number of factions; social inequality; ethnic dominance; levels of trust and association.

3. *Economic performance:* economic growth; per capita income; area affected by conflict; natural resources dependency.

4. *Governance:* legal and institutional framework; levels of democracy; neighborhood effects; transparency and corruption.

Once a civil war has been initiated in a given country, country teams can start monitoring the country (with the help of Watching Briefs) and then code and update the indicators listed above. Currently, DECRG has compiled a database to code initial and historical values for all the quantitative indicators. After the first year of the war, country teams can update the data set and thereby monitor progress or deterioration in conditions on the ground. That analysis can lead to a classification of conflict countries according to a conflict index. Since the focus of this chapter is on initial risk and post-conflict risk, we will not go into detail on the coding of intensity variables.[25] Generally, all the variables listed under the substantive category of security are also relevant for intensity.

Initial findings indicate that the following correlations, and possibly relationships, exist and are highly significant for the formulation of policy response: very low and very high levels of ethnolinguistic fractionalization decrease conflict intensity (and especially duration), whereas ethnically dominated and polarized societies are more prone to conflict escalation; greater economic growth and per capita income reduce intensity and a greater land area affected by conflict increases intensity; human rights violations and increasing political oppression increase conflict intensity; and more democratic neighboring countries can reduce the intensity of conflict.[26]

Core Conflict Indicators: Performance

For those countries that have experienced violent conflict, we need to adapt our analytical framework to measure the likelihood that conflict will end without recurring and that a process toward peaceful development will be established. To this end, the Conflict Indicators Project is seeking to develop performance indicators that will assess, essentially, the success of peacebuilding in a given country. Some of the indicators are similar to at-risk indicators that seek to measure the risk of conflict recurrence on the basis of remaining underlying root causes of the conflict. These are complemented by indicators that we have identified that measure the inherited risks of conflict due to the legacy of conflict.

The following indicators were chosen:[27]

1. *Security:* signing of peace agreements; multilateral peace enforcement operations;[28] demobilization, disarmament, and reintegration; policing and arms control; demining; crime rate; type of war (ethnic/religious).[29]

2. *Social cohesion:* reconciliation efforts among the parties to the war; number of factions; programs for war-affected population; social programs (health and education); trust and association.

3. *Economic performance:* per capita income; economic growth; natural resource dependence; trade policy and safe environment for investment; external debt management.

4. *Governance:* democratization level;[30] corruption; legal and institutional framework; multilateral institutional assistance and reconstruction efforts.

Using these performance indicators, it is possible to identify stages of postconflict transition, which can then be used to measure the probability of peacebuilding success after the conflict.[31]

This can be done following the comparative statistics exercise based on the model of peacebuilding developed in Michael Doyle and Nicholas Sambanis (2000). Each of the independent variables in their model could be considered a conflict indicator, and it is possible to explore how changes in these variables would influence the overall probability of peacebuilding success (see Appendix 14.4 for policy-relevant findings from the Doyle-Sambanis model). The figures in Appendix 14.4 display simulations based on this core model and demonstrate how policy might be used to increase the probability of success given different combinations of underlying conditions. Based on such an exercise, we at the Bank can begin to classify all countries in one of three categories as follows: risk category 0 (i.e., negligible risk of peacebuilding failure); risk category 1 (low risk of peacebuilding failure); and risk category 2 (medium risk of peacebuilding failure), analogous to those for the at-risk indicators.[32] The higher the probability of peacebuilding success, the lower the risk of peacebuilding failure.[33] This kind of assessment will complement other Bank initiatives and will be built into Bank instruments to measure success in the transition of countries emerging from war and to restructure portfolios to avoid the exacerbation or recurrence of conflict.[34]

In further refinements of this work, we plan to integrate the data sets used for the at-risk indicators (Hoeffler and Sambanis, 2000) with the Doyle and Sambanis (2000) data set used for the performance indicators. This would allow us to make predictions of initial conflict risk and post-conflict risk using some of the same variables and the same data set. Currently, the data sets and models are different.

Our estimates could be used as benchmarks against which subsequent progress can be assessed and can also be helpful in identifying potential good performers when deciding International Development Association (IDA) allocations for postconflict countries. In the immediate, several findings emerge from these early statistical exercises.

First, changes in important independent variables (each of which could be considered a conflict indicator) were found to influence the overall probability of peacebuilding success. In addition, Doyle and Sambanis (2000) found that peacebuilding success is not only much more likely if hostility levels are shallow but also that the rate of increase in the probability of success rises faster as local capacities rise. A high level of development does appear to make a reconciled peace easier, especially if the two sides have avoided the worst forms of mutual violence. Furthermore, the probability of success is remarkably higher if a multidimensional peacekeeping operation (PKO) is used and if the parties have signed a peace agreement: at high levels of local capacity, the probability of success when there is a peace treaty and a PKO is extremely high. The difference is also great at low levels of economic development, where a peace treaty and PKO substitute for the lack of local capacities. The differential impact of a PKO and a peace treaty is maximized at middle levels of local capacities.

Doyle and Sambanis (2000) argue that the greater the amount of international assistance, the greater the country's level of economic development, and the lower the level of hostility and damage caused by the war, the higher the probability that peacebuilding will be successful. Knowing the probability of peacebuilding success facilitates the process of deciding initial allocations of IDA funds to postconflict countries based on our assessment of where these funds might have the greatest positive impact (i.e., which countries are least likely to revert to war in the next five years). This does not mean that the bulk of international assistance should go only to certain countries that perform well on prescribed macroeconomic policies, or only to countries with lower hostility and damage because it will necessarily work better under those conditions. However, it does imply that there is a certain threshold of state effectiveness and legitimacy, below which it is difficult to leverage international assistance to promote peacebuilding. In short, where the local actors are reaping greater benefits from the pursuit of war rather than peace (e.g., diamonds, arms and youth mobilization for political control and profit by warlords in West Africa), it is difficult to see how international aid can abate the conflict. Other means of promoting the transition to peace and stability will have to be sought. Herein comes the need for effective peacekeeping and enforcement.

Table 14.3 summarizes the core indicators mentioned above by conflict stage and substantive area.

Core Conflict Indicators: Peace and Conflict Impact Assessment

During the second stage of the Conflict Indicators Project, we will complete our conflict analysis with a fourth set of indicators that applies both to countries that have experienced violent conflict and to those that have not and that measures the impact of the Bank's portfolio on the risk of violent conflict in a given country. The methodological complexity of adequately evaluating the Bank's impact on a country's conflict-proneness is considerable, and most existing assessment frameworks are micro-oriented, whereas a macro perspective is more suited to the purposes of this project. Furthermore, to accurately measure the Bank's impact, we need to establish a counterfactual (i.e., the country's conflict-proneness in the absence of Bank activity). It is against such a counterfactual that we can measure the Bank's impact. This set of indicators will be very useful in portfolio management and assessing the impact of the Bank's project. The development of peace and conflict impact assessment indicators will begin after the initial presentation of the project in June 2000.[35]

Conclusion

The World Bank is committed to assisting other international organizations in developing a better understanding of the determinants of civil violence and in helping to anticipate and prevent such violence. Conflict-pertinent research and operational work has been woven into several aspects of the Bank's development assistance strategies and country operations. The Bank's research department has taken the lead in a large, multiyear, multinational project that will produce some of the best data and research available on conflict. This will help advance the level of scholarship on conflict issues and improve international policy in preventing or managing conflict.

Table 14.3 Core Indicators for Conflict Analysis

Areas	At Risk	Conflict Intensity	Performance
Security	Size and support of ethnic diasporas Arms trade Human rights violations Length of time since last war	Unilateral foreign military interventions Arms control Human rights violations; per capita death and displacement Area covered by landmines Changes in conscription rates or military spending	Peace agreement; multilateral peace enforcement operations Policing, arms control, demining Crime rate (especially changes from prewar levels) Demobilization, disarmament, and reintegration Type of war (was war over identity issues?)
Social cohesion	Ethnolinguistic fractionalization Geographic concentration of population Population size Ethnic dominance Trust and association[a]	Ethnolinguistic fractionalization Number of factions Social inequality Ethnic dominance Trust and association[a]	Reconciliation efforts between the parties to the war Number of factions Programs for war-affected population Social programs: health and education Trust and association[a]
Economic performance	Economic growth Income per capita Secondary education Dependency of primary commodities and natural resources	Economic growth Income per capita Area affected by conflict Dependency on natural resources and primary commodities	Economic growth Income per capita Trade policy and safe environment for investment Dependency on natural resources and primary commodities External debt management
Governance	Democracy level Corruption Legal and institutional framework	Democracy level Corruption Legal and institutional framework	Democracy level Corruption Legal and institutional framework Reconstruction efforts Assistance from international multilateral institutions

Note: a. Trust and association will be incorporated into the analysis once there is available data.

Appendix 14.1:
Constructing a Conflict Index—
Preliminary Guidelines

Country teams may wish to develop a conflict index to use in assessing conflict risk in their countries. A first step is to distinguish between countries that have not yet experienced conflict (category A) and countries that have experienced conflict (category B). The Conflict Index will estimate the risk of conflict in both of these categories of countries. The index could be composed of a set of indicators that correspond to the four substantive areas mentioned in the text: security, governance, social cohesion, and economic condition. The indicators identified in the main body of the text could be used to assess the contribution of each of these areas to overall risk. Substantive areas may have contributions of varying importance to initial risk of violent conflict as opposed to postconflict risk, and there may be differences across countries as well. Country teams will use their extensive country knowledge to assign weights to each of these indicators/substantive areas for their countries.

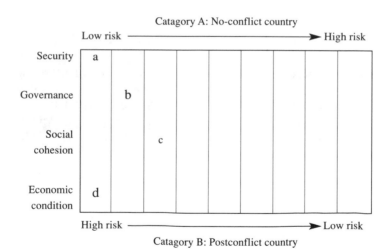

Consider the following example of how the weighting process might work: let country X be a no-conflict country. The conflict index would be composed of at risk indicators and would allow us to determine the conflict stage/zone for country X—i.e., is it a high risk or low risk country? Let *a* rep-

resent the indicator(s) corresponding to security; *b* the indicators corresponding to governance; *c* the indicators corresponding to social cohesion; and *d*
the indicators corresponding to economic conditions. The combined effect of
the position of indicators *a-d* in the plane and the relative (font) size of indicators *a-d* would determine overall risk. In our example, our country has a
level of social cohesion that suggests a high risk of conflict, but the relative
contribution of social cohesion indicators to the overall risk of conflict is
small for this country, as indicated by the relative small font size of indicator
c. The country's security and economic conditions reduce the country's risk-
proneness, and economic conditions have a high degree of influence on the
overall risk index. Finally, the country's governance variables contribute
highly to conflict risk. The overall risk index could be determined by aggre-
gating the relative risk generated by each of the four substantive areas, taking
into consideration the relative importance of each area. PCIA indicators
could be included either as a fifth substantive area or they can be considered
implicitly embedded in each of the other four substantive areas. Country
teams should weigh each substantive area's influence on the overall conflict
risk. A given country's overall risk could be determined by any number of
combinations of the risk associated with each substantive category.

Appendix 14.2:
Regional Frequency of Violent Conflict

Below we present some basic data on the frequency of violent conflict jux-
taposed to: the level of democracy (DEM); the degree of ethnolinguistic
fractionalization (ELF); and the per capita real income (RGDP) in each of
five major regions of the world: sub-Saharan Africa (SSA), Middle East
and North Africa (MENA), Latin America and the Caribbean (LAC), Asia,
and Europe and North America (EUR/NA).

The AT WAR variable denotes the frequency of five-year periods at
any time between 1960 and 1999, during which a country was at war. DEM
refers to the democracy score (one of our indicators) developed by Jaggers
and Gurr (1998) and available through the Polity 98 dataset. Increasing values of the index denote higher degree of democracy. ELF is an index of ethnolinguistic fractionalization, measuring the probability that any two people drawn from different ethnic groups in the same country will speak the
same language. Increasing values of the index denote a higher degree of
ethnolinguistic fractionalization. RGDP is PPP-adjusted per capita index.
The Summers and Heston dataset is used for most countries up to 1992, and
projections beyond 1992 are made using World Bank data on GDP growth
for the period up to 1998.

Regional Comparisons, 1960–1998

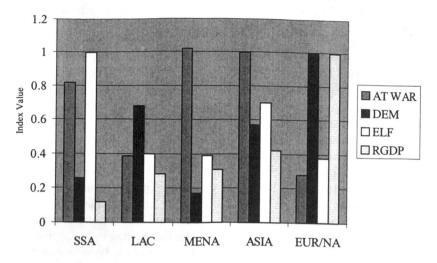

These data help us put in comparative perspective the problems of violent conflict, poverty, and lack of political freedom in these large regions of the world.

Appendix 14.3:
Probability of Civil War Occurrence

Collier and Hoeffler (2000) estimate a logistic regression of initial war risk, using 665 observations (country five-year periods). Observations (country-years) during which war is ongoing (having started in a preceding period) are dropped, as the estimates refer to the probability of an outbreak of civil war in any five-year period. For details on definitions used (e.g., for the definition of civil war used by the authors) and for more information on the estimation method and a presentation and discussion of statistical results, we refer you to Collier and Hoeffler (2000). The estimates presented in this appendix were provided by Anke Hoeffler and are based on the core regression model estimated in Collier and Hoeffler (2000).

The authors estimate the probability of a civil war occurrence in any five-year period based on the following independent (proxy) variables in a model that causally links these variables to the onset of violence: secondary education rates for males; primary exports; economic growth; population size; ethnic fractionalization and ethnic dominance; geography variables (forest coverage, geographical dispersion); and months at peace (starting from last war or from the end of World War II if the country did not experience any civil wars). These variables are measurable proxies for concepts that allow the authors to compute the probability of violence as a function of the opportunity cost and benefit of violence.

The estimated model has a pseudo-R2 of 30 percent and most variables are statistically significant. The results of the estimations are presented in Collier and Hoeffler's paper (the reader should refer to them for details, robustness, and specification tests). These categories reflect quartile ranges of the estimated probabilities of civil war occurrence in the Collier-Hoeffler (2000) model. The estimated probability ranges from a minimum of near 0 to a maximum of nearly .05.

The table below presents this information. We use the Collier-Hoeffler model by plugging in values for the core variables that vary by 50 percent (going from the bottom 25 percent of the range for each variable to the top 25 percent of the range for the variable). We vary one variable at a time and keep other variables constant at their medians. The coefficient estimates from the core regression are used to simulate the change in the probability of war outbreak as a result of changes in the regressors. By comparing the change in the mean estimated probability in column 2 across the different rows, one can gauge the relative impact of same-level changes in each of the core independent variables. Not all at risk indicators can be worked into the Collier-Hoeffler model.

Relative Influence of Key Variables on the Probability of Civil War Outbreak

Change in Independent Variables[a]	Mean Estimate of Change in the War Probability	95% Confidence Interval of Estimate	
Primary exports/GDP	.050	.020	.099
Population size	.031	.012	.061
Secondary education (males)	−.024	−.059	−.005
Ethnic dominance	.023	.004	.053
Geographic dispersion	−.017	−.040	−.005
Length of peacetime	−.016	−.039	−.005
Ethnic fractionalization	−.011	−.028	−.001
GDP growth rate	−.009	−.024	−.001
Democracy	−.006	−.024	.012

Note: a. The range for each variable is from the 25th to the 75th percentile.

Annual changes in these estimated probabilities could serve as indicators of the country's progress toward peaceful development and could also be used to develop thresholds to either add or remove countries from the Bank's Country Monitoring List. The Bank has initiated a series of

Quarterly Monitoring Reports (QMRs) on Conflict-Affected Countries. The data currently available to DECRG on political institutions and conflict variables have annual frequency and would therefore allow only annual updates to these quantitative indicators. However, further analysis would allow for the addition of an *at risk* section to the current QMRs.

Furthermore, the model's residuals can be used to identify high-risk countries that have not yet experienced violent conflict. These countries could be monitored more carefully than the rest, and we should strive to understand how they have escaped conflict. DECRG is currently planning a series of case studies of conflict countries to go deeper into specific non-quantifiable processes that affect conflict-proneness. These case studies will allow us to refine our conflict indicators in later stages of this project.

*   *   *

Appendix 14.4 Cases of Internal War and Peacebuilding Outcomes Since 1944

Country	Start	End	Lenient PB	Strict PB	Country	Start	End	Lenient PB	Strict PB
Afghanistan	78	92	Failure	Failure	Congo/Zaire	96	97	Failure	Failure
Afghanistan	93		Failure	Failure	Costa Rica	48	48	Success	Success
Algeria	62	63	Success	Failure	Cuba	58	59	Failure	Failure
Algeria	92	97	Failure	Failure	Cyprus	63	64	Failure	Failure
Angola	75	91	Failure	Failure	Cyprus	74	74	Failure	Failure
Angola	92		Success	Success	Djibouti	91	95	Success	Success
Argentina	55	55	Success	Success	Dominican Rep.	65	65	Success	Success
Azerbaijan	88	96	Failure	Failure	El Salvador	79	92	Success	Success
Bangladesh	73	94	Success	Success	Ethiopia/Eritrea	74	91	Success	Success
Bolivia	52	52	Success	Success	Ethiopia/Ogaden	77	85	Failure	Failure
Burma	48	51	Failure	Failure	Ethiopia	74	91	Success	Success
Burma	68	82	Failure	Failure	Georgia/Abkhazia	91	93	Failure	Failure
Burma	83	95	Failure	Failure	Georgia/Ossetia	92	94	Failure	Failure
Burundi	65	69	Failure	Failure	Greece	44	49	Success	Success
Burundi	72	73	Success	Success	Guatemala	54	54	Success	Success
Burundi	88	88	Failure	Failure	Guatemala	66	72	Failure	Failure
Burundi	91		Failure	Failure	Guatemala	74	94	Success	Success
Cambodia	70	75	Failure	Failure	Haiti	91	94	Failure	Failure
Cambodia	79	91	Success	Success	Haiti	95	96	Success	Success
Central Africa	95	97	Success	Success	India/Partition	46	48	Success	Success
Chad	65	79	Failure	Failure	India/Kashmir	65	65	Failure	Failure
Chad	80	94	Success	Success	India/Kashmir	89	94	Failure	Failure
China/Taiwan	47	47	Failure	Failure	India/Sikh	84	94	Success	Success
China/Tibet	50	51	Failure	Failure	Indonesia/Mol.	50	50	Failure	Failure
China	67	68	Failure	Failure	Indonesia/Dar.	53	53	Failure	Failure
Colombia	48	62	Success	Success	Indonesia	56	60	Success	Failure
Colombia	78		Failure	Failure	Indonesia/E. Timor	75	82	Failure	Failure
Congo Brazzaville	92	96	Failure	Failure	Indonesia	86	86	Success	Failure
Congo/Zaire	60	65	Failure	Failure	Iran/Revolution	78	79	Failure	Failure
Congo/Kisangani	67	67	Success	Failure	Iran	81	82	Failure	Failure
Congo/Shabba[a]	75	79	Failure	Failure	Iraq/Shammar	59	59	Failure	Failure

Country	Start	End	Lenient PB	Strict PB
Iraq/Kurds	61	75	Failure	Failure
Iraq/Kurds	88	94	Failure	Failure
Iraq/Shiites	91	94	Failure	Failure
Israel/Palestine[a]	47	97	Success	Success
Jordan	71	71	Success	Failure
Kenya[a]	91	93	Failure	Failure
Korea	50	53	Success	Failure
Laos	60	75	Failure	Failure
Lebanon	58	58	Success	Success
Lebanon	75	78	Failure	Failure
Lebanon	82	92	Failure	Failure
Liberia	89	92	Failure	Failure
Liberia	93	96	Failure	Failure
Malaysia	48	59	Success	Success
Mali	90	95	Success	Success
Mexico[a]	92	94	Success	Success
Moldova	92	94	Failure	Failure
Mor./W.Sahara	75	89	Failure	Failure
Mozambique	79	92	Success	Success
Namibia[a]	65	89	Success	Success
Nicaragua	78	79	Failure	Failure
Nicaragua	81	89	Success	Success
Nigeria	67	70	Success	Success
Nigeria	80	84	Failure	Failure
Northern	68	94	Success	Success
Pakistan/Bangld.	71	71	Success	Success
Pakistan/Blch.	73	77	Failure	Failure
Papua N.Guinea	88	91	Failure	Failure
Paraguay	47	47	Success	Success
Peru[a]	80	96	Failure	Failure
Philippines	50	52	Success	Success

Country	Start	End	Lenient PB	Strict PB
Philippines	72	96	Failure	Failure
Philippines	72	92	Failure	Failure
Romania	89	89	Success	Success
Russia/Chechny	94	96	Failure	Failure
Rwanda	63	64	Failure	Failure
Rwanda	90	94	Success	Success
Sierra Leone	91	96	Failure	Failure
Somalia	88	91	Failure	Failure
Somalia	92		Failure	Failure
South Africa[a]	76	94	Success	Success
Sri Lanka/JVP	71	71	Success	Success
Sri Lanka/Tamil	83		Failure	Failure
Sri Lanka/JVP	87	89	Success	Success
Sudan	63	72	Success	Success
Sudan	83		Failure	Failure
Tajikistan	92	94	Failure	Failure
Thailand[a]	67	85	Success	Success
Turkey	84		Failure	Failure
Uganda	66	66	Success	Success
Uganda	78	79	Failure	Failure
Uganda	80	86	Failure	Failure
Vietnam, Rep.	60	75	Success	Success
Yemen	48	48	Success	Success
Yemen	94	94	Success	Success
Yemen, North	62	69	Success	Success
Yemen, South	86	87	Success	Success
Yug./Bosnia	92	95	Failure	Failure
Yug./Croatia	91	91	Failure	Failure
Yug./Croatia	95	95	Success	Success
Zimbabwe	72	80	Failure	Failure
Zimbabwe	84	84	Success	Success

Note: a. These are cases that may not have caused 1,000 deaths for every year of the war, but they have produced 1,000 deaths in at least one year during the war. In total, there are seventy-one failures and fifty-three successes of lenient peacebuilding (PB) and eighty-one failures and forty-three successes of strict peacebuilding. The sources for this table are listed in Appendix A of Doyle and Sambanis, "International Peacebuilding."

Predictors of the Probability of Peacebuilding Success

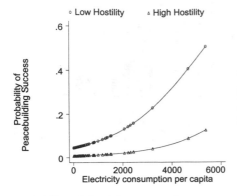

A. Effect of electricity consumption per capita for low and high hostility

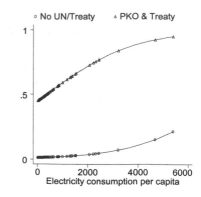

B. Effect of electricity consumption with and without a peacekeeping operation and treaty

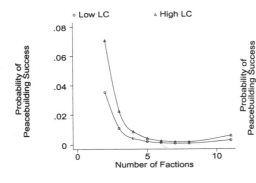

C. Effect of number of factions for low and high local capacity (proxied by electricity consumption per capita and primary commodity exports as percent of GDP)

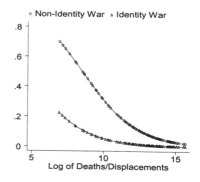

D. Effect of the log of deaths and natural displacements for identity and nonidentity war (ethnic or religious)

Note: Low and high hostility are defined by the proxy variables used in the regression models. "High hostility" includes cases in the top quartile of the range for the variable log of deaths and displacements (LOGDEAD) and "low hostility" includes cases in the bottom quartile. PKO stands for peacekeeping operation (either traditional or multidimensional). "Low local capacities (LC)" includes cases in the bottom quartile of electricity consumption per capita and the top quartile of primary commodity exports as percent of GDP. "High local capacities" are defined in exactly the opposite manner. Identity wars are ethnic and religious wars. Nonidentity wars are ideology-driven revolutions, loot-driven wars, or other nonethnic, nonreligious wars.

Effects of International Capacities on the Probability of Peacebuilding Success in Hypothetical Easy and Difficult Cases of Post–Civil War Transition

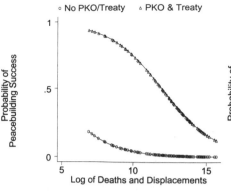

A. Effect of the log of deaths and displacements in a hypothetical difficult case with and without a peacekeeping operation and a treaty

B. Effect of electricity consumption per capita in a hypothetical difficult case with and without a peacekeeping operation and a treaty

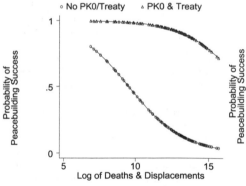

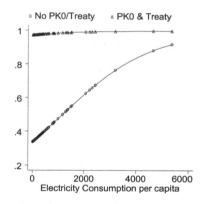

C. Effect of the log of deaths and displacements in a hypothetical easy case with and without a peacekeeping operation and a treaty

D. Effect of electricity consumption per capita in a hypothetical easy case with and without a peacekeeping operation and a treaty

Notes: See Doyle and Sambanis, "International Peacebuilding," model A parameter estimates for the construction of easy and difficult cases. For a difficult case, we set all regressors with a negative coefficient to the value for the 75th percentile of their range and the regressors with positive coefficients at the value defining the 25th percentile of their range. We do the opposite for an easy case. If we allow local capacity variables to vary (e.g., electricity consumption per capita), then we focus on hostility variables to create hypothetical easy and difficult cases. We keep the following variables at their median: war duration, number of factions, and decade. Low local capacities imply electricity consumption per capita at their 25th percentile and primary exports as a percentage of GDP at their 75th percentile. High local capacities imply the opposite. This setup allows us to study the effect of international capacities—peacekeeping operations in conjunction with a treaty—on the probability of peacebuilding success under different combinations of levels of hostility and local capacity.

These tables and figures are drawn from Michael W. Doyle and Nicholas Sambanis, "International Peacebuilding: A Theoretical and Quantitative Analysis," *American Political Science Review* 94, 4 (December 2000).

Notes

1. See the World Bank website, http://www.worldbank.org.
2. See http://wbln0018.worldbank.org/ESSD/pc1.nsf/Home?OpenView.
3. The research project currently uses the country as its unit of analysis. Although it is often the case that one or more regions in the same country are affected by conflict in varying degrees and that level of complexity is not fully captured by country-level data and analysis, complexity was forsaken in return for a "cleaner" classification of each country into one of four categories in the war-to-peace transition. Nonetheless, we recognize that the classification may not apply directly to any one region of a given country. It is possible that a country may be experiencing conflict in some regions, it may be in postconflict transition in other regions, and may have no conflict in its remaining regions. These regional experiences are currently aggregated to classify the country in a risk category but should be taken into consideration when designing the Bank's portfolio in any given country. In further refinements, attempts will be made to develop a more disaggregated analysis, using regional data and looking at regional strategies for Bank activities.
4. The conflict intensity indicators are closely linked to the initial at-risk indicators but will include additional elements, which may not be equally important for initial risk of conflict.
5. The Bank's economic programs should not exacerbate conflict. The methodology and research activity that is required to develop, measure, and test impact assessment indicators is quite different from that used to develop the first three sets of indicators, and for this reason it is relegated to a later phase of our project.
6. Our main source in identifying indicators in both these categories—root causes and conflict-induced causes—is DECRG's work on causes of civil war and determinants of postconflict peacebuilding PCUs and country teams' operational experience in these areas.
7. By "country-specific," we mean that the list does not include external shocks.
8. The source for the data set is Anke Hoeffler and Nicholas Sambanis (2000). Two versions of the data set are currently available. One is a panel data set with five-year frequency and the other (with fewer variables) is a panel with annual frequency. Both cover the period 1960–1999. These have been used in several of the DECRG papers on conflict and will soon be posted online at the DECRG website for the Economics of Civil Wars project: http://www.worldbank.org/research/conflict.
9. Quantifiable indicators are measured given available data from Bank and other sources and are used in the statistical analyses of violent conflict currently conducted by DECRG. The research output of DECRG is our main source for the quantitative indicators of initial war risk, conflict intensity, and postconflict performance. It is not possible to present the wealth of findings and insights that this research has produced, and we will refer interested readers to the relevant literature that can be accessed online at: http://www.worldbank.org/research/conflict/papers.htm. We should note that the choice of indicators is theoretically informed and is based on models that try to capture the causal mechanisms that determine conflict patterns.
10. We focus on civil wars among other forms of political violence and crime because it is the most destructive in both material and other terms. It is also a phenomenon that has been the focus of systematic study and it often includes other

forms of violence such as pogroms, genocides, and coups. We define a "civil war" as an armed conflict that has (1) caused more than 1,000 deaths; (2) challenged the sovereignty of an internationally recognized state; (3) occurred within the recognized boundaries of that state; (4) involved the state as one of the principal combatants; (5) included rebels with the ability to mount an organized opposition; and (6) involved parties concerned with the prospect of living together in the same political unit after the end of the war. This definition is nearly identical to standard definitions; see J. David Singer and Melvin Small, *Correlates of War Project: International and Civil War Data, 1816–1992* (Ann Arbor, Mich.: ICPSR, 1994); J. David Singer and Melvin Small, *Resort to Arms* (Beverly Hills, CA: Sage Publications, 1982); and Roy Licklider, "The Consequences of Negotiated Settlements in Civil Wars, 1945–1993," *American Political Science Review* 89 (September 1995). However, unlike them, our coding of wars does not presume 1,000 deaths per year but rather uses the 1,000 deaths as the threshold for a single year during the war and as a minimum level for the entire war. This allows us to capture less severe forms of violence that may persist in between outbreaks of large-scale violence where more than 1,000 deaths are counted.

11. Using proxy variables/indicators from each substantive area, we can measure a country's conflict risk and classify that country in a risk category along a peace-conflict continuum. We are fully cognizant that countries fall in and out of peace and conflict, thus the "continuum" is merely a heuristic device and does not reflect our belief in any set order of transition. Moreover, differing areas of countries like Colombia may at the same time be in conflict, prone to conflict, and emerging from conflict.

12. We should note that at present available data and existing analytical work constrain us to using two different types of data sets and estimation methods to assess initial conflict risk and post-conflict risk (see note 9). In subsequent refinements of this work, we aim to unify all available data resources so that our risk estimates can be derived from a single data-set using a single model.

13. A ranking of quantitative indicators is implicit in the statistical results presented, as determined by the coefficients for each variable (indicator) used.

14. These indicators could be coded as either Yes/No (binary) variables or as categorical variables measured on a 1–5 intensity scale.

15. The rationale for selecting these indicators is explained in Paul Collier and Anke Hoeffler, "Greed and Grievance," World Bank Working Paper No. 2355 (May 2000). The reader should refer to that paper for a conceptual discussion and empirical evidence regarding the significance of these indicators. The governance indicators are selected on the basis of work conducted by the Post-Conflict Unit. The sources for the governance indicators are Patricia Cleves, PCU internal document; Nicholas Sambanis, "Partition as a Solution to Ethnic War: An Empirical Critique of the Theoretical Literature," *World Politics* 52 (July 2000); and Nicholas Sambanis, "Civil War: Do Ethnic and Non-Ethnic Wars Have the Same Causes?" *Journal of Conflict Resolution* (forthcoming, 2001). Additional works referenced in the works listed above are also of relevance in the identification and measurement of our indicators.

16. Ethnic dominance increases the risk of initial war occurrence, as does the size of ethnic diasporas. Peacetime (length of time since last war) reduces the risk of civil war.

17. Local capacity variables, such as income and education, reduce the risk of civil war. Education is particularly significant in that it has a double effect: it increases the opportunity cost of violence for educated people; and classroom

instruction occupies young men who might otherwise be available to participate in political violence if idle (see Collier and Hoeffler, "Greed and Grievance," for a fuller discussion).

18. Greater dependence on natural resources increases the risk of civil war, as does population size. Ethnolinguistic fractionalization (at very high or low values) reduces the risk of war. Dependence on natural resources is a social cohesion proxy rather than a proxy for economic conditions because it is a determinant of the ease of financing a rebel organization through looting natural resources (see the Collier-Hoeffler model).

19. The more open and democratic a government, the less likely it is to generate political grievance in groups that have the capacity and popular support necessary to mount a violent opposition to the government.

20. We will first focus on intrastate violence and, at a later stage, expand our analysis to also include interstate violence.

21. Although data is not always available for all the countries in the data set, we do classify most countries in one of four broad categories of initial war risk.

22. Although we can monitor 161 countries for which we have sufficient data, our conflict analysis should be focused on the countries with the highest degree of conflict risk. In these countries, policies designed to reduce conflict risk are likely to have a relatively greater impact.

23. The sources and rationale for selecting these indicators are Paul Collier, Anke Hoeffler, and Mans Soderbom, "On the Duration of Civil War," World Bank Working Paper (February 1999); Ibrahim A. Elbadawi and Nicholas Sambanis, "External Intervention and the Duration of Civil Wars," World Bank Working Paper No. 2433 (September 2000). The reader should refer to these papers for a discussion and empirical evidence on the relevance of these indicators. The governance indicators are selected on the basis of work conducted by the Post-Conflict Unit. Governance indicators are very important in determining conflict intensity and escalation potential because improvements in governance indicators will clearly denote a reduction in conflict intensity.

24. On the impact of external interventions of prolonging war, see Elbadawi and Sambanis, "External Intervention and the Duration of Civil Wars."

25. See ibid.; Collier, Hoeffler, and Soderbom, "On the Duration of Civil War"; and Sambanis, "Civil Wars: Do Ethnic and Non-Ethnic Wars Have the Same Causes?" The relationships between measures of intensity and conflict escalation summarized above are based on these works and the broader literature on civil war referenced therein.

26. However, this effect depends largely on the type of war; see Sambanis, "Partition as a Solution to Ethnic War."

27. The sources and rationale for our selection of indicators are Michael W. Doyle and Nicholas Sambanis, "International Peacebuilding: A Theoretical and Quantitative Analysis," *American Political Science Review* 94 (December 2000); and Paul Collier, "Policy for Post-conflict Societies: Reducing the Risks of Renewed Conflict," World Bank Working Paper (March 2000).

28. These are indicators of war-related hostility and the international community's ability to enforce peace, respectively. These variables measure the degree of difficulty in advancing to peace in the security area. The greater war-related hostility, the lower the likelihood of a successful peace process. Further, in many cases low-level armed conflict persists after the formal end of the war, and monitoring levels of violence in the transition period can help identify those cases that are at greater risk of war recurrence.

29. These are indicators of the level of national reconciliation and ability to coordinate a peace settlement. The more factions during the war, the lower the degree of reconciliation. Ethnic wars tend to have a higher likelihood of recurrence. Clearly defined peace treaties facilitate and circumscribe the peace process.

30. The better and more inclusive and democratic the governance of the country, the less likely is war recurrence.

31. Here we focus on postconflict countries, and we assess the short-to-medium term (two to ten years). Beyond ten years, our analytical models estimated with currently available data lose predictive capacity.

32. The Doyle-Sambanis (2000) postconflict data set includes 124 cases of civil war since 1945, and the results are based on logistic regressions. The model estimates the probability of peacebuilding success two and five years after the end of the war. Most of the cases in this data set are historical cases, i.e., we can obviously only make predictions on the likelihood of peacebuilding success for countries currently at war. But these predictions utilize the information provided by historical cases in the data set. Our estimates of the probability of peacebuilding success take into consideration each country's level of economic development, the hostility levels generated by the war, and the amount of international assistance (mainly political and military) available to each country.

33. Please note that even though the model used has relatively high classification success (i.e., it correctly predicts about 90 percent of the cases), in some instances the predictions will actually be wrong. The input of the country teams will be a balancing factor that will provide a stronger contextual basis for the conflict risk classification of each country. The historical examples provided may be of use in considering the postwar economic performance of these countries.

34. The Bank is developing a set of postconflict performance indicators as part of a more comprehensive framework to determine the allocation of IDA funds to post-conflict countries. World Bank, "Draft Proposal: Determining IDA Allocations and Monitoring Progress in Countries Affected by Conflict" (2000).

35. Briefly, an adequate framework for estimating the contribution of Bank programs should do the following: (1) adjust for initial conditions faced by the countries in question and changing exogenous nonprogram factors; (2) explicitly consider policy reactions and hence the endogeneity of policy instruments; (3) avoid the "sample selectivity" bias that results from the nonrandomness of the decision to undertake policy reforms (this complication arises because relative to other nonreforming countries, those countries that decide to undertake reforms and that are likely to need World Bank programs may be more susceptible to conflict regardless of whether or not they take such programs); and (4) adjust the micro-focused methodologies used to assess program impact to the macro-level focus of this project that analyzes conflict risk at the national level. Overall, analyzing the impact of the World Bank's program would require specifying and estimating a simultaneous equations system, as well as fairly intensive work on developing the required indicators and their determinants.

15

Electoral Assistance and Democratization

Bengt Säve-Söderbergh and
Izumi Nakamitsu Lennartsson

A striking characteristic of violent conflicts in the post–Cold War era, a majority of which occur within states, is their sheer persistence and complexity. Violent conflicts derive from root causes that often involve a combination of identity-based and emotionally charged factors and underlying perceptions of political, economic, and social injustice. Such sources of conflict, which are often embedded in societies that have a long history of recurrent disputes, offer many opportunities for political leaders to exploit and manipulate ethnicity and division between groups and thereby increase the potential for conflict, especially violent conflict.

Furthermore, traditional prevention and crisis management strategies, based on reactive responses to early warning signals and composed largely of late interventions, have become increasingly impotent in the face of the wave of conflicts witnessed in the 1990s. Short-term, often last-minute, efforts at "preventive diplomacy," or even the deployment of military force, cannot in and of themselves prevent violent conflict. What is necessary is a more comprehensive, integrated, and long-term preventive strategy that addresses the root causes of conflicts rather than offering a superficial quick fix to the immediate crisis.

Efforts to support democratization and capacity-building for democratic institutions should be placed at the center of such new preventive strategies. Democratic institutions and processes, in which various groups are represented, can help manage competing interests by encouraging political compromises, thereby minimizing the risk that disputes will escalate into violence. Electoral assistance should be considered by the international community as an entry point for longer-term democratization assistance, rather than the prevailing misperception that elections are an easy exit strategy. In and of themselves elections are an important component of democratic governance, but they can mask the existence of what Fareed Zakaria described in 1997 as an "illiberal" democracy if they are not accompanied by an underlying democratization *process*.[1]

Although the usefulness of democratic institutions and processes in preventing violent conflict is increasingly recognized, many scholars also point out the dangers involved in democratic transition. Edward Mansfield and Jack Snyder, for instance, have pointed out the dangerous connection between democratization and nationalism.[2] This obviously does not mean that democracy leads to war. Instead, as Mansfield and Snyder argue, various challenges that can surface during transition, such as problems related to weakening central government or the malfunctioning of newly installed democratic political processes, could lead to war if left unaddressed or improperly addressed. Carol Skalnik Leff has also argued that "a democratizing system and consolidated democracy operate with substantially different resources for problem solving," an "understandably destabilizing" condition in which there are insufficient institutionalized mechanisms for conflict resolutions.[3] As a result, careful planning of external intervention is required in order to ensure that the potentially destabilizing factors are mitigated. Critical decisions that tend to be externally driven in the postconflict phase, such as when to hold elections, may potentially have a negative impact on the entire course of democratic transition.

Precisely because of the potential caveats involved, many argue for carefully crafted, balanced, and long-term democratization strategies. Nicholas Sambanis, who examined 125 civil wars, argues that because of the dangers of democratization "international policy aimed at preventing war recurrence should promote institution building and socio-economic development before war occurs in the first place, rather than supporting partition after war occurs."[4] He further argues for an empirically derived strategy for resolving ethnic wars and that "action by the international community . . . must promote democracy as its number one conflict-prevention strategy."[5]

This chapter attempts to examine the importance of democratic institutions and processes in managing conflict and to demonstrate the usefulness of democratization assistance as an instrument for the prevention of violent conflict. In addition, it makes some suggestions for incorporating support for democratization in conflict prevention strategies.

Root Causes and Structural Sources of Contemporary Violent Conflict

In examining the causes of conflict post facto in Bosnia, Rwanda, and more recently in Kosovo, it appears that too much focus may have been placed on the importance of ethnic or religious factors. However, almost all conflicts have complex root causes of a political and economic nature. These root causes—from human rights violations of a particular ethnic group to economic inequality between different groups, from disputes over the control of resources to political power-sharing—are easily manipulated and dressed up as endemic ethnic differences by political leaders. In fact, ethnicity, religion, and other identity-based factors do not always function as a negative force. Often, they play an important role in enriching and consolidating the well-being of communities. However, ethnic differences can be exploited by leaders for political gain by fuelling perceptions of fear and/or political, economic, and social inequality among groups. Broadly, three main areas of dispute appear to dovetail with identity-related issues.[6]

First, various *economic factors* provide fertile ground for the eruption of violent conflict along ethnic and other identity lines. These include social problems that can result from the transition from a communist to a free-market system, or conflict over the control of natural resources. In many parts of Africa, the latter is often tied to a long history of divide and rule perpetrated by former colonial administrations. Deliberate economic policies that discriminate in favor of or against certain population groups are another set of root causes of conflict, as are the perceptions of economic insecurity that can accompany rapid and large-scale immigration movements into a particular region or country. Second, *cultural factors* often play an important role in aggravating the potential risk for violence. The denial or restriction of minority rights, such as language or religious freedoms, is a classic example. Third, *claims for self-rule* or different constitutional arrangements by ethnic groups, including demands for secession, autonomy, or federalism, could also become a potential cause of violent conflict.

In most situations where any of these potential causes do result in a violent conflict, there is usually an important *structural source* of conflict that can be identified: the lack of a political system that can adequately address these issues as part of a domestic political agenda and manage disputes peacefully through dialogue, negotiation, and compromise. In other words, the lack of democratic culture, processes, and institutions is a fundamental source of contemporary conflict. It is therefore evident that the overarching challenge of peacebuilding and nation-building is to construct a sustainable political order that fosters an environment in which the root causes of conflict can be addressed by national actors. It is of paramount importance that process-oriented, longer-term assistance strategies to democratization be fully integrated into new prevention strategies, alongside the strengthening of early warning systems, international intervention (both diplomatic and political), appropriate military deployment, and development cooperation.

Emerging Linkage Between Peace, Development, and Democratization: The Reality of UN Missions

Contrary to the common perception that democratization assistance is taboo for the United Nations (UN), the organization has in fact been obliged to tackle governance issues in many places despite its lack of a clear policy framework to guide action in this area. Following the UN peacekeeping operation in Namibia, established to ensure the early independence of Namibia through free and fair elections, one of the first major attempts by the United Nations to directly address democracy-related questions was the UN Transitional Administration for Cambodia (UNTAC) in 1992–1993. UNTAC was the first truly multifaceted UN peace mission, where a variety of civilian tasks, including refugee repatriation, the restoration of human rights and law and order, rehabilitation and reconstruction, as well as the organization and monitoring of elections were addressed alongside and in coordination with the military component of the mission. However, UNTAC was also a classic UN failure from the point of view of prevention, a failure that became manifest with the intragovernment coup in July 1997 by Hun Sen following the UN-sponsored elections in 1993. It is now widely agreed that an oversimplified approach to democracy contributed to this failure: for UNTAC, the holding of elections was a goal in itself in addition to a de facto exit strategy. As a result, the more important question of strengthening democracy and transforming the postelection political culture into a democratic one was left unaddressed and the fragile institutions left unconsolidated and largely unsupported. The elections were organized for the people of Cambodia, but democracy was not deepened together with the people.

Since Cambodia and following the United Nations' excruciating experiences in Somalia and in Bosnia with the UN Protection Force, some important evolutions in UN peace missions have occurred.

First, the United Nations continues to be required to tackle an extremely complex set of issues during peacekeeping or peacebuilding missions, and the list is only growing. They include: resolving humanitarian problems; restoring respect for human rights; establishing and maintaining security and stability; disarming, demobilizing, and reintegrating former combatants; providing and restoring law and order and the judiciary; promoting reconciliation; holding elections and providing broader support for democratization; supporting institutional capacity-building; and planning and initiating reconstruction and development. Slowly, it appears that UN member states are beginning to recognize the importance of civilian tasks and how they relate to the military components of a mandate. In this context, it is noteworthy indeed that in many UN peace missions from the mid- to late 1990s, the need for broader democratization support has been recognized—sometimes implicitly out of operational necessity, and sometimes even explicitly. Notably, the Security Council resolutions that established the United Nations Interim Administration in Kosovo (UNMIK) and the United Nations Transitional Administration in East Timor explicitly refer to the importance of democratic government and institutions within the respective mission mandates.[7]

Second, UN peace missions have become structurally more complex and operate with an increasing number of organizations on the ground. The participation of several UN and non-UN actors—regional organizations, military alliances outside the UN framework, international and local non-governmental organizations (NGOs), and international and regional financial institutions—acting under the umbrella of a UN Security Council mandate has become common. This is perhaps a natural evolution given the increasingly complex and wide-ranging tasks in both the military and civilian fields, but it has consequently rendered coherent and integrated strategy formulation and coordinated responses more difficult. Moreover, it is interesting to note that partner organizations working alongside the United Nations or within the UN peace mission framework are increasingly tasked with the provision of democratization support. This was the case for the Organization for Security and Cooperation in Europe (OSCE) in Bosnia (alongside the UN Mission in Bosnia, UNMIB) and in Kosovo (within UNMIK).

Third, several lower-profile UN political offices have been created and directly designated to undertake peacebuilding and preventive activities. These include the UN Peacebuilding Support Offices in Liberia and in Guinea-Bissau, the UN office in Tajikistan, and the UN Political Office in Bougainville. Interestingly, these political missions are normally established by an executive decision of the Secretary-General with flexible mandates, as opposed to the peacekeeping missions, which are created by Security Council resolution based on a mandate that represents the compromise of fifteen member states.[8] These offices normally provide assistance relating directly to the consolidation of peace and democracy, including electoral matters, national reconciliation, or capacity-building for key institutions. They also work closely with the UN Resident Co-ordinators normally appointed by the United Nations Development Programme and therefore may have closer links with "good governance" assistance designed to promote democratic practices.

A connected but broader question relates to whether it is appropriate for the Security Council to deal with these types of issues. Although a holistic and comprehensive consideration of various issues related to UN operations is necessary for the formulation of mission strategy, the current structure of the Security Council is clearly inappropriate due to limited membership, uneven representation, and skewed decisionmaking processes.

The global organization needs to undertake serious reform—both of its decisionmaking bodies such as the Security Council and General Assembly, as well as of the Secretariat—to face the realities of today's world.

The evolution of UN missions just described clearly demonstrates the reality and requirements of complex peacebuilding and prevention, in which the linkage between peace, development, and democracy can no longer be ignored. This linkage is particularly important at the operational level with respect to conflict prevention. On the one hand, it provides a broad framework within which the United Nations could address root causes of conflict. On the other hand, it highlights the importance of development cooperation in an era marked by declining levels of official development assistance. There is an emerging consensus that democracy, which serves to ensure participation, accountability, and transparency, is the best form of governance to fight poverty and achieve development. Sustainable human development, in turn, provides the best prevention of and solution to humanitarian catastrophe and violent conflict.[9]

Successive studies have emphasized the importance of an integrated approach for UN peace operations, which may involve various components from security to political measures, from humanitarian aid to development assistance, from restoring human rights to rebuilding the judiciary, from preparing and holding elections to creating and assisting democratic institutions, in a manner and timing that suits the particular situation. Studies also demonstrate the importance of civilian and political capacity, especially in view of the military dominance in many current peace missions. The same integrated approach should be taken in the formulation of strategies for conflict prevention. A wide range of issues related to the potential causes of violent conflict, including those relating to governance, should be addressed via long-term prevention strategies that are coupled with improved mechanisms and modalities for preventive action. The lack of democratic governance is one of the fundamental structural sources of contemporary violent conflict; consequently, effective prevention requires effective democratization.

Key Challenges of Democratization
Assistance in Conflict Prevention

Although democratization assistance is increasingly becoming an integral part of UN operations, concerted efforts to formulate a clearer policy framework and approach are now necessary. First and foremost, this should be based on an understanding of the importance of democratization assistance for conflict prevention. In addition, the United Nations needs to modify its approach to electoral and democratization support on the following three issues: (1) elections are not a quick-fix solution after which can begin a rapid exit; (2) the current technical approach to democratization should be modified to include a more holistic and comprehensive approach to electoral and democracy assistance; and (3) the United Nations needs to articulate more comprehensively the various democratic transformations that shape societies at different levels.

These three challenges are closely related to the dangers of democratic transition described by Mansfield, Snyder, and others. The shortsighted policy of rushing into elections without previously establishing functioning institutions and a broad consensus on democratic reform processes and culture, based on the misunderstanding that democracy assistance ought simply to ensure periodic elections, could have a negative, destabilizing impact on the overall consolidation of peace. What purpose can elections serve for peace if the voting exercise simply brings about a tyranny of the majority, as Smith Hempstone observes, in a deeply divided postconflict society? What democracy should aim to bring to a postconflict society is not only majority rule but also the guaranteed rights of minorities, a liberal constitution, transparency, accountability and due process, the rule of law, and a political culture of tolerance and compromise.

Strategies for democratization assistance therefore ought to focus on installing a political environment that is conducive to meaningful elections. This requires a deeper understanding of the wide range of political and social transformations that take place over the long term and at different levels. This does not mean that the United Nations itself needs to engage in assisting these transformations, rather that it should learn to work more closely and effectively with international and local civil society actors and organizations that seek democracy and peace.

There Is No Quick Fix

In postconflict situations, elections should aim to achieve two objectives. On the one hand, the installation of a legitimate government is crucial where there is a political vacuum at the state level in the aftermath of violent conflict. On the other hand, it contributes to the consolidation of peace by promoting democratic practices. The timing of elections ought to be planned with these two important objectives in mind.

Elections, if held prematurely, without broadly based political parties and an understanding of the longer-term requirements of democracy, may simply prolong conflict through different means. They can, in this way, heighten the risk that violence will recur. The holding of elections often fails to create a political environment conducive to compromise, as they generally preserve the main parties to the conflict, particularly those at the extreme fringes. The result of premature elections can thus be more devastating than if elections had been postponed until some basic elements of a pluralistic party system and a functioning state had been established. The international community has witnessed the failure of premature elections in the past. The 1992 elections in Angola, held without a constitution suitable for a power-sharing arrangement drove one party back to the battlefield, rather than installing a power-sharing government. The 1993 elections in Burundi mobilized groups along ethnic lines and acted as a catalyst for genocide instead of serving the intended purpose of achieving peaceful coexistence and a power-sharing government. Many criticized the timing of the post-Dayton 1996 elections as premature, and indeed the main parties based their campaign almost exclusively on nationalistic and ethnic sentiments rather than on political issues in the spirit of reaching a compromise.

An interesting comparison can be made between these examples and the international community's subsequent approach to elections in Kosovo. Despite the clear demands in 1999 by Albanians in Kosovo for early general elections, UNMIK chose to hold the municipal elections first, taking "a strategy aimed at building democracy from the ground up."[10] Results of the municipal elections on October 28, 2000, were encouraging. Contrary to earlier predictions, the moderate Democratic League of Kosovo, led by Ibrahim Rugova, won some 58 percent of the votes while the radical Party of Democratic Kosovo of the former commander of the Kosovo Liberation Army, Hashim Thaci, secured only about 25 percent of votes.

The tendency of the international community to push for premature elections is often caused by the fact that elections are seen as a quick-fix solution and the clearest indicator of success of international interventions, particularly in postconflict situations. Often, the international community sees the holding of elections as an exit strategy, when in fact they should be considered an entry point for longer-term engagement in the process of democratization. However, elections can be only one step among many toward the consolidation of substantive democracy.

From a Technical Approach to a Holistic Approach

Despite the changing environment in which the linkages between peace, development, and democracy are recognized, democratization assistance continues to be seen with suspicion by host governments and remains a contentious and divisive issue among UN member states. As a result, the United Nations tends to adopt a very technical approach to electoral matters. However, for elections to be a truly meaningful step in the democratization process, mere technical assistance on the logistics of election-holding is not sufficient. In fact, most technical problems relate to underlying political issues. The problems related to electoral lists and the preparation of electoral laws are typical examples of issues that are fundamentally political in nature. Elections are a meaningful political event, and adopting a strictly technical approach may favor, de facto, a certain political option. Similarly, an overly technical approach to electoral observation, without taking into account the local political background and dynamics, may risk creating merely the façade of democracy, especially when elections are then declared free and fair by international observers.

Elections should take place in conditions of basic security, with political will and commitment by all parties to democratic election procedures, a level playing field, and access to information by independent media. However, the international donor community may in fact be promoting the phenomenon of electoral democracy or "electoracy" in a number of transitional societies by letting "many strongmen pass as democrats who try to keep up just enough of the formalities."[11] In many countries where multiparty elections are held regularly, there is no level playing field for political parties, and therefore opposition parties have little influence in the political scene. Certifying election results in those situations on the basis of short-term election monitoring or observation can instead have a negative impact on the development of substantive democracy.

Understanding Various Democratic Transformations

Democratic transformations occur at various levels and components of society and are not limited to the government level. Rather, democratic transformation must be understood as one facet of nation-building.[12]

Nation-building is the construction of a peaceful and democratic society on the basis of democratic civic culture, which includes safeguarding the rights and freedoms and the security and integrity of citizens, restoring social capital by increasing citizen participation, guaranteeing equal citizenship for all (including minorities and returning refugees), and addressing socioeconomic problems. Although elections are important, it is likewise crucial to support the transformation of various components and levels of the society in question. The often elitist approach adopted by the United Nations and other international organizations, based on a narrow notion of politics, must be broadened to cover other significant political changes, especially at the community level. Transformations at the community level are rarely linear, and yet they often have a significant and long-lasting impact on the functioning of democracy in the entire country.

In practice, this means that democracy assistance needs to take into account the diversity of political institutions, cultures, and logics through which democratic processes may be supported, as well as the empowerment of various civil society actors so that a democratic culture can take root at all levels of society.[13] Economic and social development programs should take this perspective into consideration, ensuring minimal economic security for communities and building the capacity of various democratic political institutions responsible for managing competing interests among citizens.

This does not necessarily mean that the United Nations should be involved in promoting democratic social transformations itself. In fact, the type of social transformations required for democratization can be undertaken only by local actors within their own society. It is, however, extremely important for UN democratization efforts to complement the efforts of local actors. Premature elections that can bring extremists into power, for example, can obstruct the empowerment of moderate forces within civil society. The United Nations should shift from working mainly with government officials and broaden its partnerships to include various civil society actors, especially local ones, in order to benefit from the wealth of information and political analysis they can offer. This is also important to forestall undue dependence on external actors, which only prolongs, unnecessarily in this case, the duration of UN missions.

Designing and Supporting Democratic Institutions as Conflict Management Instruments

A fundamental characteristic of democratic institutions and processes is that they serve as a forum where national stakeholders—or potential parties to conflict—can discuss and negotiate their competing interests peacefully. Democratic institutions include a range of mechanisms and instruments, such as constitutional arrangements regulating the structures for power-sharing, various types of human rights instruments, and protection measures for minorities. In this chapter, three sets of democratic institutions—electoral systems, political parties, and institutions designed to promote reconciliation—are briefly examined as examples of useful conflict management instruments.

Electoral Systems and Conflict Management

The importance of an electoral system as a mechanism for shaping political competition remains underappreciated, despite the fact that an electoral system is an important conflict management instrument.[14] Various studies on past elections held in divided societies suggest that an appropriately designed electoral system can help create a more accommodating political environment, whereas an inappropriate system can considerably harm the process of conflict resolution in a pluralistic state. Depending on the type of electoral system, the same number of votes cast can, for instance, produce a coalition government or a single-party majority. The electoral system also has a major impact on the number and relative size of political parties in parliament, as well as the internal cohesion and discipline of parties. It also influences their political behavior by encouraging or discouraging tendencies toward cooperation and accommodation between political parties in the legislature. This is indeed a crucial factor in conflict management in ethnically divided societies, especially in the process of consolidating peace.

Among the many options, the first-past-the-post system (FPTP) is the world's most commonly used electoral system for its simplicity. As in the cases of the United States, the United Kingdom, and Canada, FPTP gives a clear-cut choice for voters between two main parties, thereby creating a stable and strong single-party government with a broadly based political party rather than a potentially unstable, weak coalition government. Under this system, the winning candidate is the one who wins the most votes, but not necessarily an absolute majority of the votes. A winner can in fact be elected under this system with less than 20 percent of the votes. Disadvantages of FPTP include, therefore, an increased possibility that minorities and women could be excluded from fair representation, leaving a large number of wasted votes. It also encourages the development of political parties based on ethnicity, clan, or region, as political parties under FPTP do not have to appeal to voters outside their original support base.[15]

List proportional representation systems (list PR) are the most common type of proportional representational systems and are widely used in continental Europe, Latin America, and southern Africa. It requires each party to present a list of candidates to the electorate, and parties receive seats in proportion to their overall share of the national vote count. Winning candidates are then decided from the list in accordance with their respective position on the candidate list. List PR is an essential component of the constitutional engineering package known as "consociationalism," which enables a power-sharing agreement within government between ethnic, religious, or linguistic groups of a divided society. Consociationalism is based on four basic principles: grand coalition in the executive branch; proportionality of groups; segmental autonomy where appropriate; and the possibility of a minority veto on most vital issues—which altogether ensure inclusive and multiethnic government. Successful examples of this system include Belgium, the Netherlands, Austria, and Switzerland. The experience of the list PR system in post-Dayton Bosnia, however, demonstrates that it alone does not encourage an accommodative political environment. In Bosnia, groups are represented in parliament proportionally, but political parties normally do not behave accommodatingly on ethnic issues, as they can rely exclusively on their own ethnic votes to win seats in parliament.[16]

Under the alternative vote system (AV), used in Australia and a few other South Pacific islands, voters rank the candidates in order of their preferred choice, thereby enabling voters to express their preferences between candidates rather than only their preferred first choice. The winner is required to win an absolute majority of the votes under this system. If no candidate gains an absolute majority based on first choices, then ballots are examined for their second preferences. This system forces candidates to reach out to voters beyond their core ethnic group, thereby creating incentives for political parties to adopt centrist policies that appeal to broad segments of a divided society. Kingsley de Silva argues that the AV-like system adopted in Sri Lanka since 1978 for presidential elections has had important implications for ethnic relations in the country, as candidates are aware that the second-preference votes may have a decisive impact on election results.[17] The winning presidential candidate would normally have to be backed by minority ethnic parties as a second preference, and thus he/she has little incentive to run on an antiethnic campaign. Ben Reilly compared the results of elections held in Papua New Guinea under FPTP and AV.[18] He argues in support of the thesis presented by Donald Horowitz that AV promotes accommodative political behavior to a greater degree than FPTP.[19] One of the problems of AV is that because of its relative complexity it requires a reasonable degree of literacy to be used effectively. Moreover, the results, compared to proportional systems, are disproportionate, and it may not be as effective as desired when adopted in deeply divided societies where ethnic groups are concentrated in particular geographic regions.

The single transferable vote system (STV) can be considered a mixture of list PR and AV that aims to maximize proportionality and accommodation. Although its use to date in divided societies is somewhat limited and inconclusive, STV was used in the first postsettlement elections in Northern Ireland in 1997. Under this system, a significant number of Catholics and Protestants used their preferences to transfer votes across group lines for the first time.[20]

There are other strategies that explicitly recognize the presence of various communal groups. They include reserving seats for ethnic, linguistic, or other minorities, as in the cases of Jordan (for Christians and Circassians), India (for scheduled tribes and castes), Pakistan (for non-Muslims), and others.

In summary, four specific types of electoral systems may be particularly suited to the promotion of an accommodative political environment (see Table 15.1). They are usually designed as part of overall constitutional engineering packages, in which the electoral system is one component. Some systems place primary importance on the need to achieve representation and proportionality, whereas others address the issue of accommodation and moderation by offering electoral incentives to politicians to look for votes among other groups rather than relying on supporters only from

Table 15.1   Types of Electoral Systems

	List Proportional Representation (PR)	Alternative Vote (AV)	Single Transferable Vote (STV)	Communal Rolls, Party Bloc Vote
Description	Proportional representation elections that lead to an inclusive legislature that includes all significant groups. Under a full consociational package, each group is represented in cabinet in proportion to their electoral support, and minority interests are protected through segmental autonomy and mutual vetoes.	Majority system with in-built incentives for interethnic party appeals. To maximize electoral prospects, parties need to cultivate the second-preference votes from groups other than their own. There is a centripetal spin to the system where elite are encouraged to gravitate to the moderate multiethnic center. In ethnically mixed districts, majority threshold leads to strong incentives to gain support from other groups.	The electoral system delivers proportional results but also encourages politicians to appeal to the votes of members from other groups via secondary preferences. This can result in inclusive power sharing between all significant political forces, but also in incentives for politicians to reach out to other groups for preference support.	System explicitly recognizes communal groups to give them (relatively fixed) institutional representation. Competition for power between ethnic groups is defused because the ratio of ethnic groups is fixed in advance. Electors must therefore make their voting choice on the basis of criteria other than ethnicity.
Examples	Switzerland, the Netherlands, South Africa 1994	Papua New Guinea 1964–1975, Fiji 1997	Estonia 1990, Northern Ireland 1998	Lebanon, Singapore, Mauritius

their own group. It is therefore important that those designing the electoral system, normally the local actors, carefully prioritize the necessary criteria at the outset, so that particular electoral needs in a given political context are best addressed.

Whichever system a divided society adopts, the ideal qualities of electoral institutions in a transitional democracy can generally be characterized as being inclusive, simple for voters to understand, transparent, and fair in their results by achieving proportionality, minimizing areas of conflict, and resulting in grand or even oversized coalition governments.[21]

Support for Political Parties

Political parties are essential elements of a democracy. In postconflict situations, particularly from the conflict prevention perspective, supporting political parties is based on two principles. First, the former armed groups (parties to conflict) must be transformed into legitimate political parties and be included in the political system of the country. In Cambodia, it is clear that the absence of the Khmer Rouge from the political party system in the 1993 elections was a fatal mistake. More positive experiences were witnessed in El Salvador in 1992 and in Mozambique in 1994, where former rebel groups were successfully transformed into legitimate parties and participated in the multiparty elections.

However, there is another, more complex task, especially in ethnically divided postconflict societies, that involves the promotion of political parties that are broad-based and policy- and program-driven rather than being driven by narrowly personalized interests or ethnic factions. The five elections held in Bosnia and Herzegovina from 1996 to 2000 present an interesting case in point.

It is now commonly agreed that the 1996 general elections, held in a war-torn Bosnia that had no tradition of democracy and where political parties were far from democratic and formed almost exclusively on the basis of ethnicity, were a failure. As the OSCE admitted in its report after the elections, the election campaign was totally dominated by nationalistic propaganda perpetrated by media controlled by the three main ethnic parties in the Bosniac-Croat Federation and Republika Srpska. The election results, which were nevertheless certified by the OSCE despite these flaws, returned to political office the extreme nationalists who had started and led the war. The three subsequent elections—the 1997 municipal elections, the 1997 special elections of the Republika Srpska, and the 1998 general elections—all showed similar patterns of domination by nationalist parties. However, positive changes were observed in the municipal elections in April 2000; two moderate opposition parties, the Party for Bosnia and Herzegovina and the Social Democratic Party, gained significant electoral support in the Bosniac Federation areas. In the Croat-dominated Federation areas, the lower voter turnout was believed to be a signal of electoral dissatisfaction with the ruling ultranationalist Croatian Democratic Union. It was hoped that a number of Bosnian Croat moderates would then emerge, in light of the positive developments in Croatia that followed. In Republika Srpska, the nationalist Serbian Democratic Party still won in forty-nine of sixty-one municipalities, but there were also indications that moderate voices were increasingly being heard by voters and that moderate politician Mladen Ivanic from the Party of Democratic Progress was becoming the most popular Bosnian Serb politician.

This positive shift is attributed to various factors, but preelection actions by both the High Commissioner on National Minorities and the OSCE no doubt contributed to it. The OSCE banned a number of ultranationalist politicians from the elections and notified political parties that extremist rhetoric during the election campaign would result in being banned from the elections. It also removed a number of candidates from electoral lists by strictly implementing the eligibility criteria set out in the new provisions of the draft election law.[22] An intense media campaign, "Vote for Change," was also organized by the OSCE, enforcing strict rules on local media in Bosnia.

As the case of Bosnia demonstrates, in this type of postconflict situation, the international community must deploy innovative means to strengthen the voices of moderate political parties committed to liberal democracy. Such measures should include making effective use of reconstruction aid to create incentives for moderate, nonethnic-based policies and to encourage opposition parties by making tangible improvements in the living conditions of the general population where extremists continue to manipulate ethnic factors. Following such moves, international support could be reallocated to municipalities that have elected moderate leaders, which many observers in Bosnia recommended after the 2000 elections.[23] Obviously, this must be executed delicately so as not to create the image of moderate parties and leaders as agents of external interests. For instance, as an electoral campaign tactic, Slobodan Milosevic would frequently blame the opposition for compromising Serbian national interests, manipulating the nationalistic sentiments that were only aggravated by the economic sanctions regime and the bombing campaign by the North Atlantic Treaty Organization. Support for independent media, particularly television, is also crucial in aiding the development of a moderate political environment.

As demonstrated above, innovative support for broad-based political parties requires sensitive, often controversial, but well-balanced political judgment. On the one hand, democratic values have to take root within the given country. On the other hand, international donors can help foster a political and economic environment that is conducive to such democratic values. The appropriate methodology for this type of international assistance, however, remains under development, which makes it difficult to reach a consensus regarding how best to approach support for political parties in postconflict societies at the global level. In the interim, initiatives at the regional level, as in the case of the OSCE in Bosnia, may be better placed to act.

Promoting Reconciliation After Conflict

Ethnic tolerance, peaceful coexistence, and eventual reconciliation are the keys to sustainable peace and the prevention of violent conflict. Too many examples of the recurrence of violent conflict engendered by a lack of adequate reconciliation following the previous outbreak of violence litter the track record of the 1990s—from the former Yugoslavia, to the Great Lakes region of Central Africa, to Sierra Leone, to name only a few. The primary reason for seeking truth, justice, and reconciliation should be to build a peaceful future. Reconciliation processes should be designed to establish a common history for the community that experienced conflict and/or gross human rights violations and to prevent the manipulation of the past as a seed for renewed conflict.

Arguments and disagreements over past wrongs are often deliberately linked to current political interests by leaders and thereby become a potential source of conflict. Nicholas Kristof described in 1998 how the "problem of memory" from World War II was still a source of mistrust between Japan and some Asian countries more than fifty years after the war.[24] He quoted the contested estimate of Chinese victims of World War II, ranging between 10 million and 35 million, and those of the so-called Rape of Nanking between 42,000 and 300,000.[25] A similar pattern of wide discrepancies was observed by the authors in Bosnia in 1992 at the outset of the civil war with respect to the estimated number of victims of atrocities committed by both by Ustashe and Chetnik forces during World War II in 1941–1945, fueling the nationalistic sentiment that contributed to the outbreak of violence at the time.[26]

Understandably, confronting past wrongs as a society—by victims, offenders, and third parties—is an extremely painful process, vividly witnessed in the exercise of the South African Truth and Reconciliation Commission, and is even potentially destabilizing. The former deputy chair of the South African Truth and Reconciliation Commission, Alex Boraine, described the four aspects of "truth of the past" that the Truth Commission addressed. First, there was factual or forensic truth, on which the Commission was mandated to prepare a comprehensive report on the basis of evidence it collected. Second, there was personal or narrative truth, recounted by both victims and perpetrators, then communicated via the media to the broader public. Third, there was social or "dialogical" truth, which was established through interaction, discussion, and debate between victims, offenders, and others in the postconflict society. Finally, there was healing and restorative truth, which can be achieved only by an official acknowledgment that the wrongs were committed. In analyzing the achievements and future challenges of reconciliation in South Africa, Boraine emphasizes that "the painful process of acquiring the truth is almost as important as the establishment of the truth. This process of dialogue points to a promotion of transparency, democracy and participation as a basis of affirming human dignity and integrity." He further stresses the "desperate need to create a common memory in South Africa," which in a sense is the measure of unity in the country.[27]

What the South African and other experiences demonstrate is that reconciliation is a process by which a postconflict society, including victims, offenders, and former parties to the conflict, comes to terms with the past conflict and agrees on the road to peaceful coexistence and eventual reconciliation. In this sense, it is a continuation of the peace process itself, which aims to make the peace sustainable and prevent the recurrence of violence. However, peaceful coexistence and reconciliation cannot be taken for granted. Truth or justice alone cannot automatically achieve reconciliation. Sufficient political will and deliberate efforts are required to initiate the process.

In this regard, postconflict justice and reconciliation may sometimes seem to be contradictory to the immediate objective of achieving peace, even if all parties recognize reconciliation as the ultimate goal or at least pay lip service to it. The political negotiations within which reconciliation processes need to be anchored are heavily influenced by elements such as the political-military balance of power, concerns of the personal fate of leaders, as well as mediators' overriding objective of arriving at a peace agreement. In the initial phase of peace or democratic transition, political trade-offs and compromises often need to be made. It is therefore crucial to analyze the sometimes competing demands for peace, truth, justice, and reconciliation and whether it is necessary to postpone the pursuit of one in order to achieve another. The situation in Sierra Leone is a case in point.

It is thus important that reconciliation be included as a long-term objective in the process of nation-building. Nonetheless, in the short term it is essential that care is taken not to damage the prospects for reconciliation by entrenching inappropriate or unrepresentative political structures on the basis of a poorly designed peace accord. Political conditions change over time as peacebuilding or democratization processes advance, as in Chile and Cambodia.

There are various instruments that can be utilized to promote reconciliation, such as different types of Truth Commissions, national or international justice mechanisms, human rights inquiry bodies, and other political measures. In initiating and designing reconciliation processes, there are four essential issues to be kept in mind. First, reconciliation processes must be initiated, driven, and owned by local actors, not only at the state level but also at the community level. The rules of engagement for the international community should therefore be based on a long-term and holistic approach that assists in the creation of an environment conducive to initiating these processes, one that takes into account the specific historical and cultural context in the country. Second, it should be clearly understood that reconciliation is a process that evolves over time and interacts with the dynamic and changing political postconflict situation. Third, no single measure will achieve reconciliation; although criminal prosecution is important in order to bring to justice those responsible for past wrongs, that alone will not reconcile the societies and communities devastated by war. Only a combination of measures, from the political acknowledgment of past wrongs to social healing, from the application of justice to the effective use of the media and education, will eventually help achieve reconciliation. Fourth, the timing and tempo of reconciliation should be balanced and harmonized with the consolidation of peace and democracy. This is particularly important in order not to destabilize the delicate process of consolidating peace and preventing the recurrence of violent conflict in the long run. Finally, a consensus should be achieved regarding impunity for certain kinds of war crimes, as defined by international law.

As numerous case studies demonstrate, reconciliation processes can take various paths. They can be initiated and imposed by foreign powers, as in the case of post–World War II Germany, or they can emerge as part of the process of democratic transition, as in the case of Latin America in the 1980s. Reconciliation processes can take the form of criminal prosecutions, as was the case in Greece in 1974 and Ethiopia after the fall of the Mengistu regime in 1991; or they could be based on a combination of international and national efforts, as in the case of Guatemala after 1998 and in the former Yugoslavia after the Dayton Peace Accords in 1995. One may even be able to design a South African model—that is, a comprehensive program for reconciliation—in which truth, justice, reparation and rehabilitation of victims, and reform of security forces are still being addressed. Although each postconflict society needs to choose its own avenue for reconciliation, one thing is clear: issues related to reconciliation—from an agreement on past history to future peace education policy, from the arrangements for political power-sharing between the former parties to the conflict to the future mechanisms and policies to ensure respect for human rights—are best addressed in the context of democratization processes.

In 1996, Mahmood Mamdani described the long and tragic history of Rwanda: "After 1994, the Tutsi want justice above all else, and the Hutu democracy above all else. The minority fears democracy. The minority fears that justice is a mask for finishing an unfinished genocide. The majority fears the demand for justice is a minority ploy to usurp power forever."[28] The challenge of democratization is well summarized in this statement. Substantive democracy is not about political dominance by a majority. A process toward democratic governance based on a liberal constitution and the rule of law is the only way to address all these seemingly conflicting demands for justice, reconciliation, political participation and representation, and the protection of minorities.

Conclusion

The case has been made as to why and how democracy and democratic institutions are important for conflict prevention. The United Nations, other international organizations, and the donor community need to adjust their strategies, approaches, and organizational structures to the requirements of the twenty-first century. These requirements include, on the one hand, an increased ability to respond rapidly to humanitarian and peacekeeping needs, and, on the other hand, a more process-oriented approach to peace-building and nation-building, development, and democracy support, which in turn will serve the cause of conflict prevention.

The time has come to achieve a broad consensus on a new, multifaceted, and integrated approach to the prevention of violent conflict. This new strategy should include both short- and long-term measures, and democracy assistance should be a core component of the longer-term approach. Such a strategy must be backed by commitment and engagement by the international community. A simplified operating procedure of elections held within a year or eighteen months after the mission deployment, followed by a rapid handover to the new authorities and a rapid departure of UN troops, can neither consolidate nor deepen peace and, in fact, presents the serious risk of causing a recurrence of violence. If the elections in Cambodia under the UNTAC administration in 1992 had to take place when they did for various reasons, they ought at least to have been backed by much more comprehensive support for creating a political environment conducive to democratization, including capacity-building for democratic institutions and facilitation of internal democratic political processes. More sustained and deeper engagement by the international community in Bosnia since 1995 also testifies to the importance of longer-term commitment. The same commitment and political will, needless to say, must be demonstrated by the international community in other parts of the world.

A long-term, process-oriented strategy aims to transform a society, slowly and over time, into a liberal democracy in which the rule of law prevails rather than a procedural democracy in which elections are merely held periodically. As Zakaria argues, our task at the outset of the new century is to "make democracy safe for the world" by promoting constitutional liberalism and the rule of law.[29]

This is obviously an enormous task that needs to be incorporated into development cooperation, peacekeeping, and peacebuilding. The United Nations cannot, and should not, be forced to do it alone. More substantive partnerships and a rational division of labor between the United Nations, regional organizations, and NGOs—both international and local—that build toward the shared objective of conflict prevention are necessary.

Democracy today has no enemies. The days of ideological wrangling over the definition of "democracy" that prevailed during the Cold War are over. In fact, most agree that there is no one model or definition of democracy. Rather, democracy is a political system of government that embodies, in a variety of institutions and mechanisms in a given cultural and historical setting, the ideal of political power based on the will of the people. Democratization is a process that leads to a more open, more participatory, and less authoritarian society.[30] It is also a process that leads to a peaceful, civilized, and humane society in which conflicts are managed in a constructive manner by opposing sides that handle their differences without recourse to violence. As has been suggested by Boutros Boutros-Ghali, the former UN Secretary-General, in *An Agenda for Democratization*, the time has come to initiate a serious policy debate on democracy and democratization at the United Nations.

Notes

1. Fareed Zakaria, "The Rise of Illiberal Democracy," *Foreign Affairs* 76 (1997): 22.
2. Edward Mansfield and Jack Snyder, "Democratization and War," *Foreign Affairs* 74 (1995).
3. See Carol Skalnik Leff's, "Democratization and Disintegration in Multinational States: The Breakup of the Communist Federations," *World Politics* 51 (January 1999): 205–235.
4. Nicholas Sambanis, "Partition as Solution to Ethnic War: An Empirical Critique of the Theoretical Literature," *World Politics* 52 (July 2000): 480.
5. Ibid., 481.
6. See Peter Harris and Ben Reilly, eds., *Democracy and Deep-Rooted Conflict: Options for Negotiators* (Stockholm: International Institute for Democracy and Electoral Assistance, 1998), 31–41, for details.
7. Operative paragraph 10 and 11 of UN Security Council Resolution 1244 of June 10, 1999, and operative paragraph 8 of UN Security Council Resolution 1272 of October 25, 1999, respectively.
8. The establishment of these political offices is normally "approved" by the Security Council in the form of a letter from the President of the Council addressed to the Secretary-General, which takes note of the information submitted by the Secretary-General.
9. Izumi Nakamitsu Lennartsson and Martin Wikfalk, *Democracy and Global Co-operation at the United Nations: Towards Peace, Development and Democratization,* a discussion paper before the UN Millennium Assembly (Stockholm: International IDEA, 2000), p. 7.
10. See Report of the International Crisis Group, "Elections in Kosovo: Moving Toward Democracy?" ICG Balkans Report No. 97 (Pristina/Washington/Brussels, July 2000).
11. Thomas Carothers, "Democracy Without Illusions," *Foreign Affairs* 76 (1997): 91.
12. Béatrice Pouligny articulates the problems of postconflict transformations in "Promoting Democratic Institutions in Post-Conflict Societies: Giving a Chance to Diversity," *International Peacekeeping* 7, 3 (autumn 2000), and "Peacekeepers

and Local Society Actors: The Need for Dynamic, Cross-Cultural Analysis," *Global Governance* 5, 4 (October-December 1999).

13. International IDEA, *Democracy and Global Co-operation at the United Nations*, 9. See also Béatrice Pouligny, "Promoting Democratic Institutions" and "Peacekeepers and Local Society Actors."

14. For details, see Peter Harris and Ben Reilly, eds., *Democracy and Deep-Rooted Conflict*, 191–204, and International IDEA, *The International IDEA Handbook of Electoral Systems Design* (Stockholm: International IDEA, n.d.).

15. See International IDEA, *Electoral Systems Design*, 27–35.

16. See Peter Harris and Ben Reilly, eds., *Democracy and Deep-Rooted Conflict*, 196–197.

17. The Sri Lankan system differs from the AV system in its counting of votes. In Sri Lanka, if no candidate receives a majority of first preference, all candidates except for the top two are eliminated, and the preferences for the top two determine the final winner.

18. AV was used in Papua New Guinea between 1964 and 1975, when it was an Australian territory. The country adopted FPTP since 1975, and according to the U.S. State Department Background Notes of November 2000 on the country, winners often gain less than 15 percent of the vote.

19. See Ben Reilly, "The Alternative Vote and Ethnic Accommodation: New Evidence from Papua New Guinea," *Electoral Studies* 16, 1 (1997): 1–11.

20. See Harris and Reilly, eds., *Democracy and Deep-Rooted Conflict*, esp. 198–199; and David Bloomfield, "Case Study: Northern Ireland," in ibid., 123–132.

21. Harris and Reilly, eds., *Democracy and Deep-Rooted Conflict*, 202.

22. For instance, persons who are illegally occupying apartments or homes belonging to refugees or displaced persons were banned from candidature. The issue of property is one of the most difficult political problems in Bosnia, preventing refugee returns to minority areas.

23. See Report of the International Crisis Group, "Bosnia's Municipal Elections 2000: Winners and Losers," ICG Balkans Report No. 91 (Sarajevo/Washington/Brussels, April 27, 2000).

24. See Nicholas Kristof, "The Problem of Memory," *Foreign Affairs* 77 (1998): 37–49.

25. Ibid., 42.

26. Neil Kritz, "Where We Are and How We Got Here: An Overview of Developments in the Search for Justice and Reconciliation," submitted to the Aspen Institute conference on November 10–12, 2000. He states that during the 1990s, Croat nationalists claimed that only 20,000 people died, mostly of disease at Jasenovac concentration camp in Croatia during World War II, whereas Serb nationalists insisted that up to 1 million were slaughtered.

27. Alex Boraine, "Truth and Reconciliation Commission in South Africa: The Third Way," paper presented to the International Seminar on Justice, Truth and Reconciliation: The Role of the Truth Commissions in Transitional Societies, Geneva, December 9–12, 1998.

28. Mahmood Mamdani, "From Conquest to Consent on the Basis of State Formation: Reflections on Rwanda," *New Left Review* 216 (1996): 3–36, quoted by the Organization of African Unity, International Panel of Eminent Personalities to Investigate the 1994 Genocide in Rwanda and the Surrounding Events, July 7, 2000, 202.

29. Zakaria, "The Rise of Illiberal Democracy," 22–43.

30. Boutros Boutros-Ghali, *An Agenda for Democratization,* UN Document A/51/761, 1996.

PART 4

Conclusion

16

Preventive Action at the United Nations: From Promise to Practice?

Chandra Lekha Sriram and Karin Wermester

The chapters in this volume seek to contribute to the scholarship and practice of conflict prevention, with a view toward strengthening the capacity of the United Nations system and its family of agencies. As such, they address several related aspects: the causes of and trends in violent conflict; the state of the art in preventive action and possible ways to strengthen institutional capacity and instruments; and the role that actors beyond the UN system play in conflict prevention. Taken together, they are instructive on what steps have been taken by different actors and at various levels to further the goal of conflict prevention, as well as on what lacunae in knowledge and practice remain.

Building on insights raised by authors in this volume, in the sections that follow we distill some key opportunities and challenges for the UN system and its agencies.

The Nature of Conflict Prevention

Broadly, "conflict prevention" refers to those initiatives that are undertaken to preempt the *eruption* of violence before armed conflict by international third parties to a dispute.[1] However, the relationship between means and ends is a complicated one, and conflict prevention is no exception. Very often, international actors engaged in countries or areas characterized by potential sources of conflict have mitigated or exacerbated the sources of conflict as an unintended by-product of their activities; other international initiatives that have explicitly sought to prevent the eruption or escalation of violence may in fact have been well-intentioned but targeted the sources of violence inappropriately. Furthermore, it may be difficult to identify what actions prevent conflict, even more so to prove that they were effective, given that success is often a nonevent. Frequently, "successful" prevention is likely to be circumscribed (containing conflict), small-scale (fostering of moderate local political forces), and/or of limited duration (e.g., Cambodia, Macedonia).

It is equally important to note what prevention—fuzzy and overstretched as the concept is becoming—is *not*; or, perhaps, should not be, especially as it pertains to the United Nations. Conflict prevention is not intervention but rather an attempt to forestall the need for forceful intervention with humanitarian aims and other forms of fire fighting action that tend to be difficult, expensive, run into reluctance by some member states to become too heavily involved, and simply come too little, too late. Preventive efforts do, nonetheless, seek to foster the *peaceful* management of disputes, under conditions of consent by relevant parties to the conflict. It is thus unrealistic to portray the activities of international preventive actors as impartial or neutral: as Barnett Rubin has noted, conflict prevention is an inherently and deeply political venture and necessarily penetrates via several entry points to affect different levels of activity, frequently within states.[2] However, interpretations of sovereignty are increasingly being relaxed by the processes of globalization. As a result, it has become increasingly accepted by many—but not all—states that their internal affairs can be, and at times are explicitly, the business of others. Although this is often fearfully perceived as carte blanche for domestic interference, it is equally true that no member state is likely to go on record at the United Nations as being categorically against the prevention of violent conflict in and of itself; what is contested, sometimes vehemently, is the nature and type of preventive action that is proposed or undertaken.[3]

Combining Incentives and Disincentives for Peace

Although it is a broadly desirable goal, conflict prevention is difficult in both theory and practice. The obstacles to its planning and implementation are real. At times, international actors will not be able to act preventively in convincing ways; and at times political realities will bar any kind of preventive action, not least by the Security Council. Even where conditions are relatively permissive, it is not self-evident how prevention *should* be managed. Although the overall goal of conflict prevention is to promote peaceful change, a narrower goal (or set of sector-specific objectives) toward which the international community can move concertedly, with the measured deployment of both carrots and sticks, is likely—but not guaranteed—to heighten the possibility of success.[4]

Timing and Sequencing

A general distinction has been made in much of the literature regarding "operational" versus "structural" prevention, terms coined by the large-scale study undertaken at the end of the 1990s by the Carnegie Commission on Preventing Deadly Conflict. Operational (sometimes referred to as "direct") conflict prevention is taken to reduce or eliminate the immediate manifestations of violence and is less focused on eliminating the conflict per se or addressing the underlying causes; in contrast, structural prevention seeks to address the underlying causes, very often through the use of development assistance.[5] As originally conceived, they are distinguished along the dimension of timing. Accordingly, direct prevention occurs at the urgent/late phase of potential or actual conflict, whereas structural prevention is deployed early and over the long term. This distinction is useful to the extent that it helps to disaggregate the actors, tools, and strategies of prevention according to the conflict cycle. However, when it comes to operationalizing preventive action, a focus on timing is not immediately instructive. When is the right moment for early prevention, and how do we know? How long should long-term deployments be? When are late preventive actions in fact too late to be of any remedy?

Perhaps a more useful approach for operationalizing prevention would be to distinguish the two types of preventive action according to the objectives they seek to accomplish or the kind of causes they seek to address (see Figure 16.1 and Table 16.1). Rather than view direct prevention as late prevention, then, it may be more fruitful to think of it as any preventive action that is designed to address the proximate sources of imminent or actual violence—regardless of when that violence threatens to or does occur. By the same token, structural prevention may be reconceptualized as any action that aims at redressing the permissive, root sources of conflict rather than as a set of policies that are restricted to the early stages of the conflict cycle. In this way, direct and structural prevention remain two distinct policy responses based on the kind of conflict cause they seek to address, yet each approach is potentially available to preventive actors at all points in the conflict cycle.[6]

One of the challenges for preventive efforts at the United Nations stems precisely from this disaggregation of roles between direct and structural prevention. Those actors engaged in so-called structural prevention have very little access to and knowledge of those direct preventive efforts that are being considered or undertaken. The converse is also true, although this has largely been due to disinterest on the part of the UN Secretariat and Security Council in particular. Although distinct strategies may be necessary at distinct phases, most practitioners agree that an integrated approach in which both types of prevention work in tandem or at least in informed

Figure 16.1 Causes of Conflict

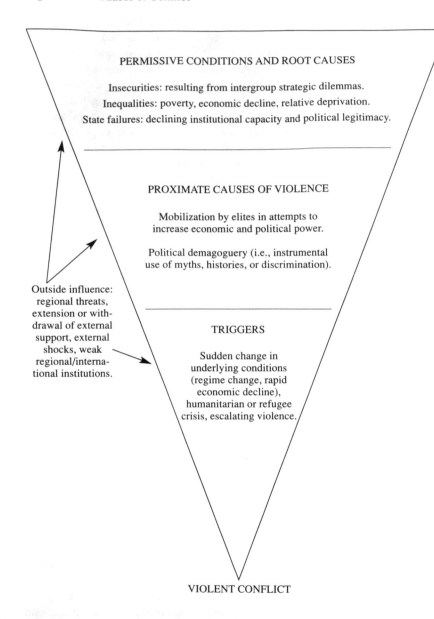

PERMISSIVE CONDITIONS AND ROOT CAUSES

Insecurities: resulting from intergroup strategic dilemmas.
Inequalities: poverty, economic decline, relative deprivation.
State failures: declining institutional capacity and political legitimacy.

PROXIMATE CAUSES OF VIOLENCE

Mobilization by elites in attempts to
increase economic and political power.

Political demagoguery (i.e., instrumental
use of myths, histories, or discrimination).

Outside influence:
regional threats,
extension or with-
drawal of external
support, external
shocks, weak
regional/interna-
tional institutions.

TRIGGERS

Sudden change in
underlying conditions
(regime change, rapid
economic decline),
humanitarian or refugee
crisis, escalating violence.

VIOLENT CONFLICT

Note: This chart was originally conceived by Anne-Marie Gardner.

Table 16.1 UN Capacity to Address the Causes of Conflict

Causes of Conflict	Instruments and Measures of Conflict Prevention	UN Institutional Capacity for Conflict Prevention	Organizational and Policy Recommendations Targeted at Specific Causal Factors
Permissive, Root Causes			
Insecurities resulting from intergroup strategic dilemmas	Preventive deployment and protective peacekeeping forces; international police; human rights monitors; confidence- and security-building measures (arms control, demobilization, mine clearance, etc.); security institutional reform (police and military); assistance with demobilization and reintegration of combatants; justice and reconciliation (war crimes tribunals, truth commissions)	Poor to fair due to political and resource constraints	• Strengthen preventive peacemaking via diplomatic dialogue and contact • Implement recommendations of the Brahimi Report to allow preventive peacekeeping deployments and better rapid reaction capability
State failures (declining institutional capacity and political legitimacy)	Democracy-building and governance (including electoral assistance, election monitoring, political party development, civil society capacity building, executive and civil service assistance, legislative support and assistance, judicial and legal reforms and assistance, local government capacity building, etc.); justice and reconciliation (war crimes tribunals, truth commissions)	Fair due to political and resource constraints	• Strengthen strategic planning and coordination within UN Secretariat, UN agencies and programs, and Bretton Woods institutions • Build on indigenous institutional capacity in conflict zones and promote governance and ownership through participation in rehabilitation and reconciliation • Ensure that elections are compatible with democratization and peacebuilding processes; timing of elections is particularly important and must be determined on a case-by-case basis with close attention to local political and civil society dynamics

(continues)

Table 16.1 continued

Causes of Conflict	Instruments and Measures of Conflict Prevention	UN Institutional Capacity for Conflict Prevention	Organizational and Policy Recommendations Targeted at Specific Causal Factors

Poverty, economic decline, horizontal inequalities, relative deprivation	Development assistance (including food security programs; targeted antipoverty programs; small enterprise, job creation, and microcredit projects; intergroup and community development projects; intergroup women's cooperation, etc.); land reform; conditional aid; structural adjustment programs that are sensitive to social justice and equity considerations	Poor due to organizational complexity and weak administrative, budgetary, and coordinating mechanisms among different UN agencies and programs and Bretton Woods institutions	• Involve Bretton Woods institutions, regional banks, and funds and, where appropriate, the private sector in prevention strategies
			• At the programmatic level, create labor intensive employment to rehabilitate infrastructure and private sector activity; restore key imports and social services that will facilitate private sector activity and provide resources for poverty alleviation
			• Institute donor guidelines for self-evaluation, including:
			  • Codes of conduct for ethical giving
			  • Donor observatory system
			  • Rules regarding the exercise of influence

Proximate Causes of Violence			
Elite mobilization in attempts to increase economic/political power	Targeted sanctions, conditional aid, special inquiries, and commissions of inquiry (naming and shaming)	Fair due to weak implementation mechanisms	• Maintain and strengthen recent hands-on practice of undertaking fact-finding and diplomatic missions to areas of tension • Use "naming and shaming" tactics to embarrass those engaged in illicit activities
Political demagoguery (i.e., instrumental use of myths, histories, or discrimination)	Targeted sanctions, conditional aid, special inquiries, and commissions of inquiry (naming and shaming)	Fair due to weak implementation mechanisms	• Maintain and strengthen recent hands-on practice of undertaking fact-finding and diplomatic missions to isolate and shame demagogic leaders • Utilize media and transnational advocacy networks to mobilize public opinion and strengthen moderate political forces

Causes of Conflict	Instruments and Measures of Conflict Prevention	UN Institutional Capacity for Conflict Prevention	Organizational and Policy Recommendations Targeted at Specific Causal Factors
Triggers			
Sudden change in underlying conditions (regime change, rapid economic decline)	Official and/or nonofficial diplomacy directed at defusing political tensions (including mediation, negotiations, good offices, conciliation, etc., and use of Article 99 in UN Charter); political and/or economic sanctions; fact-finding and monitoring	Fair	• Make better use of Secretary-General's capacity to offer "good offices" and other kinds of mediation services, recognizing that low profile diplomatic initiatives may be preferable to focusing the international spotlight on belligerents and making a bad situation worse • Work closely with regional and subregional organizations and bodies to help restore democracy
Humanitarian or refugee crisis	Humanitarian assistance (food; medicine; conditional relief aid; refugee assistance; reintegration, rehabilitation, and reconstruction; humanitarian law)	Fair to good depending upon resource availability	• Work harder to ensure that humanitarian interventions and assistance do not exacerbate conflict dynamics/processes over the medium-long term
Escalating intercommunal violence and terrorism	Official and/or nonofficial diplomacy directed at defusing political tensions (including mediation, negotiations, good offices, conciliation, etc., and use of Article 99 in UN Charter); fact-finding and monitoring	Fair	• Make better use of Secretary-General's capacity to offer "good offices" and other kinds of mediation services, recognizing that low profile diplomatic initiatives may be preferable to focusing the international spotlight on belligerents and making a bad situation worse • Rapid UN peacekeeping deployments to reduce tensions and avert violence (Brahimi Report)

Source: This figure was conceived and developed by Fen Osler Hampson.

and strategic sequence is likely to be the most effective course of action in any given conflict-affected area.

Moreover, very little attention has been paid to the gestation period between potential and imminent violence—often of long duration and which can also exist in some form after the eruption of conflict—as an entry point for integrated preventive action.[7] Some indicators of the precipitation of violence during this period include: an increase in state repression; a rising number of contentious political actors; low-level population movements; increased import and/or stockpiling of weapons; and the slow mobilization of the population. The gestation period is precisely when it is vital that the traditionally separate realms of peace and security, and economic and social development, work in tandem, or at least in strategic coordination.

Conversely, a lot—perhaps too much—of the literature and practice on conflict prevention has focused on preventing the recurrence of conflict, subsuming conflict prevention into the broader categorization of postconflict peacebuilding. This is an area in which the United Nations has had significant experience during the 1990s. There, specific preventive measures that could be, and are beginning to be, used to address the root causes of conflict are precisely those that were developed and deployed with increasing confidence in the 1990s for postconflict peacebuilding activities. Integrated preventive action at the preconflict stages has a lot to learn from the lessons, and pitfalls, learned from postconflict peacebuilding: the importance of civilian police; the need for demobilization, demilitarization, and reintegration of combatants and, more and more, civilians immediately after the signing of a peace agreement; the organizational and coordination problems that contribute to the pernicious gap between the downscaling of emergency relief and the beginning of longer-term development projects; and the difficulty of creating transparent and accountable political institutions and processes at all levels—from political elites to civil society. However, the usefulness of such insights for the UN system might be limited to the implementation of conflict prevention measures rather than informing the types of measures that could be deployed.

Addressing the Causes of Conflict: Comparative Advantages at the UN

The strategies, tools, and actors best suited to addressing the root causes of conflict would seem to naturally include aspects of the work of the United Nations Development Programme (UNDP), the international financial institutions (IFIs), and government donors. Capacity-building work at this stage might also involve a host of other UN actors, including the

Department for Economic and Social Affairs, the Office for the Coordination of Humanitarian Affairs, the UN High Commissioner for Refugees, and the UN High Commissioner for Human Rights. It is also liable to engage the work of a wide variety of nongovernmental organizations (NGOs) and international NGOs (INGOs). Conversely, the Secretary-General, the Security Council, and the General Assembly might be better placed to stem the imminent sources of violence. Their efforts might also be complemented by preventive peace operations or postconflict peacebuilding.

Proximate Violence

In addressing the proximate causes of conflict, the Security Council clearly has a prominent role to play. Potential tools within its purview include encouraging or, conversely, shaming, via presidential statements or resolutions, the authorization of sanctions regimes and the establishment of accompanying monitoring mechanisms,[8] preventive deployment missions,[9] and, in the final instance, the authorization of the use of force. Key prominent actors at this stage may also include the Secretary-General, formal or informal "contact groups" or "groups of friends" among member states (most often including one or several of the Council's permanent members), Special Representatives of the Secretary-General (SRSGs), and—potentially—the General Assembly.

The Secretary-General and/or SRSGs are sometimes well placed to affect the preferences of those local actors who are instrumental in precipitating conflict and whose cooperation is required to terminate it. The Secretary-General, especially the current incumbent, Kofi Annan, is widely perceived as having a high degree of moral authority. Moreover, SRSGs—often eminent international personalities—are uniquely placed to undertake the kind of quiet personal diplomacy that is most likely to be able to change the behavior of leaders fomenting or perpetuating conflict if the political/military situation makes resolution desirable or possible. Through the use of such "good offices," the United Nations has been quite effective despite, or perhaps because of, those efforts being largely underpublicized. Often, this lack of publicity is deliberate, especially when overt attention by the Secretary-General to countries of concern may be counterproductive, making a self-fulfilling prophecy of early warning alerts.

The General Assembly, as the body comprising the entire UN membership, could in the abstract have a role to play in conflict prevention and especially early warning, perhaps most especially during the gestation period. States where preventive action may be required likely sit in the Assembly and not the Council; General Assembly engagement might provide a useful venue for the voices of such states to be heard and for them to

hear from their peers. The General Assembly will most often be the appropriate body to mandate civilian missions (for example, human rights monitoring missions with preventive aim, as was the case in Haiti in the early
and mid-1990s). Specific roles for the General Assembly might well be harnessed by and channeled through more active involvement by the president
of the General Assembly in order to foster debate within the Assembly and
among the Assembly, the Secretary-General, and the Council. Such efforts
could allay concerns regarding the selective attention of not only the
Council but also the Secretary-General to areas of urgent concern.
Moreover, it would add an element of transparency to the United Nations'
preventive activity at the stage of imminent violence during which its
efforts are frequently shrouded in secrecy. However, even though the
General Assembly may enjoy broad legitimacy, its size and working methods mean that it may not be appropriate to take a more operational
approach to prevention.

Potential Conflict

The practice of targeting development assistance in ways that seek to
address the root causes of conflict and, at the very least, "do no harm" is
increasingly being operationalized and is showing promise.[10] Lenders and
donors, as well as those actors charged with humanitarian, development,
human rights, and refugee tasks, thus have an important role to play. They
are ideally placed to help create an integrated, long-term strategy for preventive action by assisting in the management of resources scarce and
abundant, processes of political transition and democratization, and socioeconomic issues such as horizontal inequality.

The kinds of preventive measures that might be usefully undertaken by
the United Nations to address the proximate causes of violence range from
the specific to the broad and include comprehensive, targeted development
assistance that focuses on: poverty alleviation; mitigating horizontal
inequality; preventive demobilization and demilitarization; promoting good
governance; supporting educational facilities and their development; capacity-building and technical support; strengthening civil society; and assisting
regional and international economic integration.[11] These measures could be
usefully accompanied by specific conflict management measures such as
data collection and risk assessment; the promotion of intergroup dialogue
and cooperation; official development assistance conditionality; support for
cross-sector networks; and the promotion of peace media and free speech
and press.

Almost all UN bodies have the tools with which to take on these tasks,
especially at the stages when conflict is not yet fully apparent. The main, or
lead, actors are UNDP and the World Bank, and likely the International
Monetary Fund, at different times.[12] UNDP has been engaged, since the

early to mid-1990s, in myriad activities aimed at preventing the *recurrence* of violent conflict; it became more explicitly engaged in preventing the *eruption* of violence at the end of the decade, especially through the work of the Emergency Response Division, which was changed to the Bureau for Crisis Prevention and Recovery as of December 2001.[13] Notable among UNDP efforts are its Early Warning Reports (for example on Bulgaria) and the mapping of high-risk areas (such as specific regions in Indonesia) that show a likelihood of violence.[14] The World Bank has also sought to engage more explicitly to prevent conflict and has developed an operational policy on development assistance and conflict, in addition to a rigorous conflict analysis methodology, to guide its lending practices in conflict-afflicted or -prone countries.[15] However, many of these developments can be described as nascent and, as yet, tentative. UNDP is obviously more constrained in its resource base and influence than the IFIs. The key to their collective impact is whether the UN system can, as a whole, undertake to prevent or mitigate violence coherently, in coordination with actors outside the UN system, over a long period of engagement, and across different stages in the conflict life cycle.

Scope of Prevention at the UN

It is clear from the schematic overview presented above that the United Nations has, potentially, vast scope to address the different sources of conflict and thereby prevent violence. However, even though the United Nations has a long-standing mandate for conflict prevention through Article 1 of the UN Charter, there remains considerable dispute as to the appropriate scope for preventive action. Some suggest that the United Nations, given its limited capacity, resources, and political will, should circumscribe its activities to direct measures. It may well be the case, however, that a central role of UN preventive action should be to address the root causes of potential conflict through development assistance and other measures. The realization of these broader objectives is, however, hampered by the myriad issues on which experts might and do disagree, including the efficacy of structural prevention generally and whether we can in particular identify, engage, and resolve the root causes of conflict and increase the funds available for structural prevention. The fact that other international actors such as the Development Assistance Committee (DAC) of the Organization for Economic Cooperation and Development (OECD), the G-8, and other regional actors have become increasingly engaged in conflict prevention is likely to influence the manner in which the United Nations processes the question of scope internally. Although the rhetoric of mainstreaming prevention has become common, it remains to be seen exactly what this might entail and whether the practice will ever become meaningfully embedded.

Implementing Prevention:
Action Within the United Nations and Beyond

Implementing prevention is a complex affair, engaging numerous actors in the UN system and beyond. Furthermore, UN efforts may be hamstrung by limits in political will and resources, making it important to also identify the central roles to be played by other actors, separately or in tandem with the United Nations.

Coordination Within the UN System

The mixture of communication failures and fierce competition for turf that characterizes the United Nations as much as, if not more than, most large bureaucracies means that the various departments and agencies have not always worked well together. At a minimum, preventive action at the United Nations engages those departments and agencies that are members of the Framework Team for Coordination, which has the explicit mandate of acting as a mechanism for early warning and preventive action.[16] Other notable mechanisms for the coordination of conflict prevention–related activities and others at headquarters level include the Executive Committees and the UN Development Assistance Framework (UNDAF). At the field level, coordination mechanisms include the Resident/ Humanitarian Coordinator System and UN Country Team Thematic Groups. Also of notable import in terms of coordination are the tools that exist for strategic assessment and planning, including the Common Country Assessment, which feeds into the work of UNDAF, the Consolidated Appeals Process, and strategic and integrated frameworks.[17] The Early Warning and Preventive Measures course, a one-week training course offered by the UN Staff College, is also an important mechanism that indirectly contributes to greater coordination by bringing together staff from headquarters and the field for simulation exercises of prevention cases. There is, however, room for significant improvement of all these mechanisms, but how such improvements ought to be made is subject to controversy. On the one hand, these mechanisms may well overlap to the point of canceling each other out. On the other hand, one major strategic framework for coordination of conflict prevention may prove unwieldy. Tragically, coordination within the United Nations is a perennial and oft-discussed problem, one that is likely to go unresolved short of a radical change in the structure of the organization itself.

Coordination with the Extended UN Family and Beyond

Equally important, the extended UN family and the actors beyond the UN system have a vital role to play in tandem or close collaboration with the main bodies of the United Nations. Vital roles include those played by, inter alia, regional organizations, the IFIs, government donors, and INGOs engaged in technical assistance. Some efforts to coordinate the IFIs, government donors, and the United Nations have begun with the creation of the Conflict Prevention and Post-Conflict Reconstruction Network, which engages all of these actors and within which some joint programming has been initiated.[18] However, more could be done with regard to UN coordination with regional and subregional organizations. Steps have been taken by the UN Secretariat to bridge these divides, notably through regular high-level meetings between the United Nations and regional organizations. However, the legislative bodies of the United Nations, notably the General Assembly, remain woefully behind the curve.[19] There may be situations in which regional organizations have greater experience, capacity, or legitimacy to act, and the United Nations could pay more attention to identifying opportunities to devolve more responsibility to them. Similarly, the World Bank and government donors are significant repositories of resources and knowledge; their practices could better inform and be informed by UN departments and agencies, especially UNDP. Finally, the United Nations still needs to move into more meaningful partnerships with NGOs and the business sector, implementing the repeated calls by the Secretary-General for such partnerships.

The Role of Experts

Experts from the academic world, NGOs, and other sources, particularly those based in the field, can play important roles in preventive action. Such experts can aid in the refinement and practice of prevention, through tools ranging from improved analysis to technical support. However, the UN system has been notoriously bad at engaging proactively with them. In fairness, one of the reasons that the United Nations fares so poorly in this respect is that ideas developed by scholars and practitioners do not always reach those responsible for specific issues at the United Nations or reach them in forms that are easy to apply to operational, much less political, challenges. However, there are several projects that seek to bridge this gap. One such initiative aims to bring together a network of experts from around the world: the Conflict Prevention and Peace Forum (CPPF). Based in New York, the CPPF is a small institution that aims to make available to the United Nations the best international expertise on impending crises of urgent concern as well as more generic prevention issues. Another initiative that seeks to fill the strategic information gap between actors at different levels at the United Nations is the Conflict Prevention Initiative, a web-based joint initiative between the United Nations and Harvard University. The project seeks to provide, in particular but not only, the Department of Political Affairs with efficient online access to existing research and practice from around the world and to provide an electronic forum that can facilitate the exchange of ideas on preventing and managing conflict.[20] Key to their success is whether the UN Secretariat and agencies, as well as Security Council members, actually wish to draw on expert knowledge and opinion.

Early Warning to Early Action

For some time, it was thought that effective preventive action would require greater information-gathering and early warning. Yet the creation of increasingly sophisticated early warning mechanisms have not necessarily been matched by action. Although it may be the case that intelligence and early warning signals are sporadic and generally difficult to translate into policy, the real problem seems to be a failure of comprehensive analysis combined with a lack of political will to act in risky situations. An oft-cited example of this failure is the early warning that emanated from Rwanda, in particular from Lt. Gen. Roméo Dallaire, force commander of the UN Observer Mission Uganda-Rwanda prior to the genocide of 1994.[21]

As many have advocated, a useful first step is to create a tighter link between early warning and early action.[22] The creation of an Executive Committee on Peace and Security Information and Strategic Analysis Secretariat, as proposed in the "Report of the Panel on UN Peace Operations" (the Brahimi Report), would have enhanced UN capacity for analysis of information, but fell prey to political opposition, particularly among developing countries.[23] It remains to be seen whether these functions will be re-created in another format within the United Nations or be undertaken outside the system, in particular by policy-oriented researchers. Perhaps more important, it remains to be seen whether the obstacles to analysis simply mask a more fundamental problem: a lack of combined will on the part of the member states to support the United Nations' potential to act preventively and systematically.

Directions for Future Research

The chapters in this volume seek to contribute to the theory and practice of conflict prevention. However, there remain several areas, especially at the practical, operational level that demand further attention in order to refine the tools and strategies of preventive action. The International Peace Academy's (IPA) prevention project, "From Promise to Practice: Strengthening UN Capacities for the Prevention of Violent Conflict," examines these issues in greater detail through research, policy events, and networking activities.[24]

There are areas that require more systematic attention; the IPA project will focus on some of these, including:

• *Phases of prevention: what tools, instruments, and strategies work and when?* The distinction between structural and operational, or direct, prevention may fail to capture sufficient nuance in the conflict cycle. For instance, a major gap in our understanding of the causes of conflict is the transition from the gestation period to a crisis. More generally, it is necessary to identify the relationship between tools, actors, and strategies and phases of potential conflict.

• *The need for and practice of structural prevention.* Chapters in this volume contribute to a better understanding of the role of development actors in preventing and mitigating violent conflict. However, there remain serious concerns that structural prevention may not work and in fact involve an unnecessary diversion of resources from other development goals. Further examination of practice will contribute to a greater understanding of the prospects for and limits of such structural prevention.

• *Coordination and collaboration.* We have discussed here some of the caveats and problems relating to coordination at the United Nations. Further work must ascertain how more dynamic, strategic partnerships can be developed for conflict prevention both within the extended UN family and among regional organizations, member states, donors, and NGOs and INGOs.

• *Regional dimensions of conflict prevention.* Even though it is increasingly clear that many internal conflicts feature significant regional dimensions, there is much to be refined with regard to the role of the United Nations, regional and subregional organizations and arrangements, and key member states in effective conflict prevention. Regional leaders, in conjunction with those of other countries, the UN Secretary-General, and heads of regional organizations, along with the IFIs, may have key roles to play. Further work might address the comparative advantages of such actors in different conflict situations, ways in which they might better coordinate their approaches, and lessons that may have implications for the United Nations' work.

Conclusion: Limits and Opportunities

The United Nations is uniquely placed to shift the normative framework of international action from reaction to prevention. However, it also has the potential to play a valuable role in the strategic coordination and implementation of an approach to conflict prevention that helps move forward horizontal (i.e., intersectoral plus interorganizational) and vertical (i.e., field to headquarters) integration. Nonetheless, there remain a number of daunting challenges for effective UN action to prevent conflict, including (1) mobilizing support and financial resources for complex, concerted, and often extended preventive action; (2) improving information flow and coordination within the organization; (3) developing a working relationship and division of labor with various regional and subregional organizations, many of which are likely to have an important role to play in collaboration with, or in lieu of, the United Nations; and (4) managing concerns about UN legitimacy, particularly those of developing states that object to the present composition of the Security Council. On this last point, there may be good reason for the United Nations not to act in instances where it lacks perceived legitimacy, political will, or necessary resources. In such instances, the United Nations might do better to defer to regional organizations and arrangements; NGOs, government donors, and the IFIs in the extended UN family may also, in certain circumstances, be better placed to take the lead. Conversely, legitimacy derives from success. Given the United Nations' broadly defined mandate, international presence, institutional strengths, and unparalleled moral authority and legitimacy, the possibilities for preventive action by the United Nations are great.

Notes

The authors are grateful for the insights and editorial acuity of Karen Ballentine, Fen Osler Hampson, David M. Malone, and George L. Sherry.

1. This is not to discount local actors—the preventive efforts of which are likely the key to effective conflict prevention—but simply to articulate the framework of the concept as it will be discussed in this chapter.

2. See Barnett R. Rubin and Susanna P. Campbell, "Introduction: Experience in Prevention," in *Cases and Strategies for Preventive Action,* ed. Barnett R. Rubin (New York: Century Foundation Press, 1998), 18–20.

3. Among the most vehement critics of the nature and type of conflict prevention initiatives undertaken by the UN system are India, Egypt, Russia, China, and Pakistan. However, even they agree at a general level that the prevention of conflict is a primary responsibility of the United Nations by virtue of Article 1 of the UN Charter—a minimal but important baseline of agreement. See, for instance, the statements by Council members during the open discussions on conflict prevention that were held under the Slovenian presidency in November 1999 (Security Council, 4072nd Meeting, S/PV.4072, November 29, 1999), and the Jamaican presidency in July 2000 (Security Council, 4174th Meeting, S/PV.4174, July 20, 2000).

4. These points were raised by participants at a workshop convened by the International Peace Academy (IPA) that gathered mainly members of the Security Council to discuss conflict prevention on February 9–10, 2001, at West Point, New York. See Chandra Lekha Sriram, "From Promise to Practice: Strengthening UN Capacities for the Prevention of Violent Conflict" (New York: IPA Workshop

Report, February 9–10, 2001). The notion of sector-specific objectives is raised by John Cockell in this volume (see Chapter 8).

5. The distinction is articulated as between structural and *operational* prevention in the Carnegie Commission on Preventing Deadly Conflict, *Preventing Deadly Conflict: Final Report* (New York: Carnegie Corporation of New York, December 1997), xvii-xlvi, but structural and *direct* prevention by Peter Wallensteen in this volume (see Chapter 9).

6. IPA's current project on conflict prevention, "From Promise to Practice: Strengthening UN Capacities for the Prevention of Violent Conflict," is seeking to examine not only timing but also the appropriate tools and actors that the UN system might bring to bear at different phases of conflict and of prevention. For more information on this project, see http://www.ipacademy.org.

7. This term was coined, to our knowledge, by Bruce D. Jones, Special Assistant to the Special Envoy to the Middle East.

8. For a sophisticated discussion of various sanctions regimes recently mandated by the UN Security Council, see David Cortright and George Lopez, *The Sanctions Decade: Assessing UN Sanctions in the 1990s,* a project of the International Peace Academy (Boulder: Lynne Rienner Publishers, 2000). The authors found a number of these sanctions regimes to have been effective, at least initially, but argue that sanctions are most useful when seen as an instrument to induce bargaining and compromise. Cortright and Lopez argue that without diplomatic give and take sanctions are unlikely to achieve their stated objectives.

9. See Abiodun Williams, *Preventing War: The United Nations and Macedonia* (Lanham, MD: Rowman and Littlefield, 2000).

10. Mary B. Anderson, *Do No Harm: How Aid Can Support Peace—or War* (Boulder: Lynne Rienner Publishers, 1999).

11. See Michael Lund's "toolkit" in Appendix 7.1 in this volume, especially the development, democratization and effective governance, security and human rights, and humanitarian assistance boxes.

12. See United Nations Staff College Project, *Rolling EWPM Project Reference Document*, on the website of the UN Department of Political Affairs, at http://www.un.org/Depts/dpa/docs/peacemak.htm, which elaborates on the roles that various UN bodies have to play at various stages of potential conflict and preventive action.

13. UNDP's activities in this area include: information, policy, and advocacy; area development and action at the community level; resettlement and reintegration of uprooted populations; disarmament, demobilization, and reintegration of former combatants; small arms; mine action; good governance, judicial systems, electoral assistance, and observance of human rights; strengthening the macroeconomic environment; rebuilding physical infrastructure; protection of the environment and natural disaster prevention, mitigation, and preparedness; and promotion of women. See Michèle Griffin, "Development, Peace and Security" (New York, UNDP, October 1999).

14. See Griffin, "Development, Peace, and Security," and United Nations Development Programme, "Working for Solutions to Crises: The Development Response," at http://www.undp.org/erd/archives/bridges2.htm; UNDP, "Governance and Conflict Prevention: Proceedings of Expert Group Meeting 7–8 March 2000" (New York: UNDP, Emergency Response Division, 2000); UNDP, "Promoting Conflict Prevention and Conflict Resolution Through Effective Governance: A Conceptual Survey and Literature Review," at http://www.magnet.undp.org/Docs/crisis/mapexercise.htm; UNDP Executive Board and the United Nations Population

Fund, "Role of UNDP in Crisis and Post-conflict Situations," UN Document DP/2001/4, November 27, 2000.

15. See Patricia Cleves, Nat Colletta, and Nicholas Sambanis, Chapter 14 in this volume.

16. At the time of writing, these are: the Department of Political Affairs, the Department of Peacekeeping Affairs, the UN Development Program, the Office for the Coordination of Humanitarian Affairs, the UN High Commission for Refugees, the UN High Commissioner for Human Rights, the United Nations Children's Fund, the World Food Program, the Food and Agriculture Organization, the World Health Organization, the World Bank, the Department of Economic and Social Affairs, and the Department of Disarmament Affairs. See UN Department of Political Affairs, "Note of Explanation on the Framework for Coordination Mechanism" (2000), on file with current authors.

17. See Colleen Duggan, "UN Strategic and Operational Coordination: Mechanisms for Preventing and Managing Violent Conflict" (Ottawa: International Development Research Center [IDRC], 2001).

18. See http://wbln0018.worldbank.org/ESSD/pc1.nsf/Home?OpenView.

19. Lessons Learned Unit, "Cooperation Between the United Nations and Regional Organizations/Arrangements in a Peacekeeping Environment: Suggested Principles and Mechanisms" (New York: United Nations, March 1999).

20. See http://www.preventconflict.org—part of the site is password-protected for UN access only, but the site contains a host of other research ready to download by the regular user.

21. For an accounting by the United Nations itself, see "Report of the Independent Inquiry into the Actions of the United Nations during the 1994 Genocide in Rwanda" (December 15, 1999), available online at http://www.un.org/News/ossg/rwanda_report.htm.

22. See, for example, Michael S. Lund, "Not Only When to Act, but How: From Early Warning to Rolling Prevention," in *Preventing Violent Conflicts: Past Record and Future Challenge,* ed. Peter Wallensteen (Stockholm: Department of Peace and Conflict Research, Uppsala University, Elanders Gotab, 1998), 155–166.

23. See United Nations, "Report of the Panel on United Nations Peace Operations," UN Document A/55/305-S/2000/809, August 21, 2000, and "Report of the Secretary-General on the Implementation of the Report of the Panel on United Nations Peace Operations," UN Document A/55/502, October 20, 2000.

24. For more information on this project, please see the IPA website at http://www.ipacademy.org.

Selected Bibliography

Alagappa, Muthiah, and Takashi Inoguchi (eds.). *International Security Management and the United Nations.* Tokyo: United Nations University Press, 1999.

Ali, Taisier M., and Robert O. Matthews (eds.). *Civil Wars in Africa: Roots and Resolution.* Montreal and Kingston: McGill-Queen's University Press, 1999.

Anderson, Mary B. *Do No Harm: How Aid Can Support Peace—or War.* Boulder: Lynne Rienner Publishers, 1999.

Annan, Kofi. "Two Concepts of Sovereignty." *The Economist,* September 18, 1999.

Auvinen, J., and E. W. Nafziger. "The Sources of Humanitarian Emergencies." *Journal of Conflict Resolution* 43 (1999): 267–290.

Ayers, R. William. "A World Flying Apart? Violent Nationalist Conflict and the End of the Cold War." *Journal of Peace Research* 37 (January 2000): 105–117.

Azar, Edward E. *The Management of Protracted Social Conflict.* Aldershot, UK: Dartmouth, 1990.

Bauwens, Werner, and Luc Reychler (eds.). *The Art of Conflict Prevention.* London: Brassey's, 1994.

Bercovitch, Jacob (ed.). *Resolving International Conflicts.* Boulder: Lynne Rienner Publishers, 1996.

Bercovitch, Jacob, and Jeffrey Langley. "The Nature of the Dispute and the Effectiveness of International Mediation." *Journal of Conflict Resolution* 37, 4 (1993): 670–691.

Berdal, Mats, and David Keen. "Violence and Economic Agendas in Civil Wars." *Millennium: Journal of International Studies* 26, 3 (1997).

Berdal, Mats, and David M. Malone (eds.). *Greed and Grievance: Economic Agendas in Civil Wars.* A Project of the International Peace Academy. Boulder: Lynne Rienner Publishers, 2000.

Boutros-Ghali, Boutros. *Unvanquished: A U.S.-UN Saga.* New York: Random House, 1999.

Brehio, Alys. "Good Offices of the Secretary-General as Preventive Measures." *New York University Journal of International Law and Politics* 30, 3–4 (1998): 589–643.

Brown, Michael E. (ed.). *Ethnic Conflict and International Security*. Princeton: Princeton University Press, 1993.

———. *The International Dimensions of Internal Conflict*. Cambridge: MIT Press, 1997.

Brown, Michael E., and Richard N. Rosecrance. *The Costs of Conflict: Prevention and Cure in the Global Arena*. Carnegie Commission on Preventing Deadly Conflict, Lanham, MD: Rowman and Littlefield, 1999.

Burton, John W. *Resolution and Prevention*. New York: St. Martin's, 1990.

Cahill, Kevin M. (ed.). *Preventive Diplomacy. Stopping Wars Before They Start*. New York: Basic, 1996.

Canadian International Development Agency (CIDA). *A Compendium of Operational Frameworks for Peacebuilding and Donor Coordination: Supplement on Conflict Prevention*. Hull, Quebec: CIDA, 2000.

Carment, David, and Patrick James (eds.). *Wars in the Midst of Peace: The International Politics of Ethnic Conflict*. Pittsburgh: University of Pittsburgh Press, 1997.

———. *Peace in the Midst of Wars: Preventing and Managing International Ethnic Conflicts*. Columbia: University of South Carolina Press, 1998.

Carment, David, and Albrecht Schnabel (eds.). *Conflict Prevention: Path to Peace or Grand Illusion?* Tokyo: United Nations University Press, 2001.

Carnegie Commission on Preventing Deadly Conflict. *Preventing Deadly Conflict: Final Report*. New York: Carnegie Corporation of New York, December 1997.

Chayes, Abram, and Antonia Handler Chayes (eds.). *Preventing Conflict in the Post-Communist World*. Washington, D.C.: Brookings Institution, 1996.

Chesterman, Simon (ed.). *Civilians in War*. A Project of the International Peace Academy. Boulder: Lynne Rienner, 2001.

———. *Just War or Just Peace? Humanitarian Intervention and International Law*. Oxford: Oxford University Press, 2001.

Cohen, J. *Conflict Prevention in the OSCE: An Assessment of Capacities*. The Hague: Clingendael Institute (Netherlands Institute of International Relations), 1999.

Colletta, Nat J., and Michelle L. Cullen. *Violent Conflict and the Transformation of Social Capital: Lessons from Cambodia, Rwanda, Guatemala, and Somalia. Conflict Prevention Series*. Washington, D.C.: World Bank Publication, July 9, 2000.

Collier, Paul. "Demobilization and Insecurity: A Study in the Economics of the Transition from War to Peace." *Journal of International Development* 6 (1994): 343–352.

Collier, Paul, and Anke Hoeffler. "On the Economic Causes of Civil War." *Oxford Economic Papers* 50 (1998): 563–573.

———. "Greed and Grievance in Civil War." World Bank Working Paper No. 2355 (May 2000).

Cortright, David. *The Price of Peace: Incentives and International Conflict Prevention*. Lanham, MD: Rowman and Littlefield, 1997.

Cortright, David, and George Lopez. *The Sanctions Decade: Assessing UN Sanctions in the 1990s*. A Project of the International Peace Academy. Boulder: Lynne Rienner Publishers, 2000.

Cousens, Elizabeth M., and Chetan Kumar with Karin Wermester (eds.). *Peacebuilding as Politics: Cultivating Peace in Fragile Societies*. A Project of the International Peace Academy. Boulder: Lynne Rienner Publishers, 2000.

Cranna, Michael, ed. *The True Cost of Conflict*. New York: New Press, 1994.

Crocker, Chester A., Fen Osler Hampson, and Pamela Aall (eds.). *Managing Global Chaos: Sources of and Responses to International Conflict.* Washington, D.C.: United States Institute of Peace Press, 1996.

———. *Herding Cats: Multiparty Mediation in a Complex World.* Washington, D.C.: United States Institute of Peace Press, 1999.

———. *Turbulent Peace: The Challenges of Managing International Conflict.* Washington, D.C.: United States Institute of Peace Press, 2001.

David, Stephen R. "Internal War: Causes and Cures." *World Politics* 49, 4 (1997): 552–576.

Davies, John L., and Ted Robert Gurr (eds.). *Preventive Measures: Building Risk Assessment and Crisis Early Warning Systems.* Lanham, MD: Rowman and Littlefield, 1998.

Douma, P., G. Frerks, and L. van de Goor. "Major Findings of the Research Project 'Causes of Conflict in the Third World.'" The Hague: Clingendael Institute (Netherlands Institute for International Relations), 1999.

Doyle, Michael W., and Nicholas Sambanis. "International Peacebuilding: A Theoretical and Quantitative Analysis." *American Political Science Review* 94, 4 (December 2000).

Elbadawi, Ibrahim A., and Nicholas Sambanis. "External Intervention and the Duration of Civil Wars." World Bank Working Paper No. 2433. Washington, D.C.: World Bank, September 2000.

Esty, Daniel C., et al. *Papers: State Failure Task Force Report.* McLean, VA: Science Applications International, 1995.

———. *State Failure Task Force Report: Phase II Findings.* McLean, VA: Science Applications International, 1998.

Forman, Shepard, and Stewart Patrick (eds.). *Good Intentions: Pledges of Aid for Postconflict Recovery.* Center on International Cooperation, Studies in Multilateralism. Boulder: Lynne Rienner Publishers, 2000.

Foundation on Inter-Ethnic Relations. *The Role of the High Commissioner on National Minorities in OSCE Conflict Prevention.* The Hague: Foundation on InterEthnic Relations, 1997.

G-8 Communiqué. "G8 Myazaki Initiatives for Conflict Prevention." Kyushu-Okinawa: Summit Meeting, July 13, 2000.

George, Alexander L. "Strategies for Preventive Diplomacy and Conflict Resolution: Scholarship for Policy-making." *Cooperation and Conflict* 34, 1 (1999): 9–19.

George, Alexander L., and Jane E. Holl. *The Warning-Response Problem and Missed Opportunities in Preventive Diplomacy: Report to the Carnegie Commission on Preventing Deadly Conflict.* New York: Carnegie Corporation of New York, 1997.

Ginifer, Jeremy, Espen Barth Eide, and Carsten Ronnfeldt (eds.). *Preventive Action in Theory and Practice: The Skopje Papers.* Oslo: Norwegian Institute of International Affairs, 1999.

Gurr, Ted Robert. *Minorities at Risk: A Global View of Ethnopolitical Conflicts.* Washington, D.C.: United States Institute of Peace Press, 1993.

———. "Testing and Using a Model of Communal Conflict for Early Warning." *Journal of Ethno-Development* 4, 1 (1994): 20–24.

———. *Peoples Versus States: Minorities at Risk in the New Century.* Washington, D.C.: United States Institute of Peace Press, 2000.

———. "Ethnic Warfare on the Wane." *Foreign Affairs* 79, 3 (May-June 2000): 52–64.

Gurr, Ted Robert, and Barbara Harff. *Ethnic Conflict in World Politics*. Boulder: Westview, 1994.

––––––. *Early Warning of Communal Conflicts and Genocide*. Tokyo: United Nations University, 1996.

Gurr, Ted Robert, Monty G. Marshall, and Deepa Khosla. *Peace and Conflict 2001: A Global Survey of Armed Conflicts, Self-Determination Movements, and Democracy*. College Park, MD: Center for International Development and Conflict Management, 2000.

Hampson, Fen Osler. *Nurturing Peace: Why Peace Settlements Succeed or Fail*. Washington, D.C.: United States Institute of Peace Press, 1996.

Harff, Barbara. "A Theoretical Model of Genocides and Politicides." *Journal of Ethno-Development* 4, 1 (1994): 25–30.

––––––. "Rescuing Endangered Peoples: Missed Opportunities." *Social Research* 62 (spring 1995): 23–40.

Harris, Peter, and Ben Reilly (eds.). *Democracy and Deep-Rooted Conflict: Options for Negotiators*. Stockholm: International IDEA, 1998.

Hooper, Rick, and Mark Taylor. "Command from the Saddle: Managing United Nations Peace-building Missions, Recommendations Report of the Forum on the Special Representative of the Secretary-General: Shaping the UN's Role in Peace Implementation." Fafo Report 266. Oslo: Fafo Institute for Applied Social Science, 1999.

Jentleson, Bruce W. (ed.). *Opportunities Missed, Opportunities Seized: Preventive Diplomacy in the Post–Cold War World*. Lanham, MD: Rowman and Littlefield, 2000.

––––––. "Coercive Prevention: Normative, Political, and Policy Dilemma." *Peaceworks* 35. Washington, D.C.: United States Institute of Peace, October 2000.

Jongman, A. J. "Downward Trend in Armed Conflicts Reversed." *PIOOM Newsletter* 9, 1 (2000): 28–34.

Kaufman, Chaim. "Possible and Impossible Solutions to Ethnic Wars." *International Security* 20, 4 (1996): 136.

Kaul, Inge, Isabelle Grunberg, and Marc A. Stern (eds.). *Global Public Goods: International Cooperation in the 21st Century*. Oxford: Oxford University Press, 1999.

Knight, W. Andy. "Towards a Subsidiarity Model for Peacemaking and Preventive Diplomacy: Making Chapter VIII of the UN Charter Operational." *Third World Quarterly* 17, 1 (1996): 31–52.

Kriesberg, Louis, and Stuart J. Thorson (eds.). *Timing the De-escalation of International Conflict*. Syracuse: Syracuse University Press, 1991.

Lake, David A., and Donald Rothchild (eds.). *The International Spread of Ethnic Conflict: Fear, Diffusion, and Escalation*. Princeton: Princeton University Press, 1998.

Lederach, John Paul. *Building Peace: Sustainable Reconciliation in Divided Societies*. Washington, D.C.: United States Institute of Peace Press, 1997.

Leonhardt, Manuela. "Conflict Impact Assessment of EU Development Co-operation with ACP Countries: A Review of Literature and Practice." London: International Alert and Saferworld, 2000.

Licklider, Roy. "The Consequences of Negotiated Settlements in Civil Wars, 1945–1993." *American Political Science Review* 89, 3 (1995): 685–687.

––––––, (ed.). *Stopping the Killing: How Civil Wars End*. New York: New York University Press, 1993.

Lund, Michael S. *Preventing Violent Conflicts. A Strategy for Preventive Diplomacy*. Washington, D.C.: United States Institute of Peace Press, 1996.

Lund, Michael S., and Andreas Mehler. *Peace-Building and Conflict Prevention in Developing Countries: A Practical Guide*. Brussels and Ebenhausen: Stiftung Wissenschaft und Politik, Conflict Prevention Network, 1999.

Lund, Michael S., and Guenola Rasmoelina (eds.). *The Impact of Conflict Prevention Policy: Cases, Measures and Assessments*. Stiftung Wissenschaft und Politik—Conflict Prevention Network Yearbook, 1999/2000. Baden-Baden, Germany: Nomos Verlagsgesellshaft, 2000.

Luttwak, Edward N. "Give War a Chance." *Foreign Affairs* 78, 4 (1999): 36–44.

Malone, David M. *Decision-Making in the UN Security Council: The Case of Haiti, 1990–1997*. Oxford: Clarendon, 1998.

Marshall, Monty G. *Third World War: System, Process, and Conflict Dynamics*. Boulder: Rowman and Littlefield, 1999.

———. "Current Status of the World's Major Episodes of Political Violence: Hot Wars and Hot Spots." *Report to the State Failure Task Force*. College Park, MD: Center for Systemic Peace, 2000.

Martin, Paul. "Regional Efforts at Preventive Measures: Four Case Studies on the Development of Conflict-Prevention Capabilities." *New York University Journal of International Law and Politics* 30, 3–4 (1998): 881–937.

Maynes, Charles William. "Containing Ethnic Conflict." *Foreign Policy* 90, 2 (spring 1993): 3–21.

Miall, Hugh, Oliver Ramsbotham, and Tom Woodhouse. *Contemporary Conflict Resolution*. Cambridge: Polity, 1999.

Miller, Laura L. "Do Soldiers Hate Peacekeeping? The Case of Preventive Diplomacy Operations in Macedonia." *Armed Forces and Society* 23, 3 (1997): 415–450.

Nafziger, E. Wayne, Frances Stewart, and Raimo Väyrynen (eds.). *War, Hunger, and Displacement: The Origins of Humanitarian Emergencies (Wider Studies in Development Economics)*, vols. 1 and 2. Oxford: Oxford University Press, 2000.

Narayan, Deepa, with Raj Patel, Kai Schafft, Anne Rademacher, and Sarah Koch-Schulte. *Voices of the Poor: Can Anyone Hear Us?* New York: Oxford University Press for the World Bank, 2000.

Nelson, Joan. "Poverty, Inequality, and Conflict in Developing Countries." New York: Project on World Security, Rockefeller Brothers Fund, 1998.

Organization for Economic Cooperation and Development (OECD)/Development Assistance Committee (DAC). *Conflict, Peace, and Development Co-operation on the Threshold of the 21st Century*. Paris: DAC/OECD Policy Statement, May 1997.

Ostrowski, Stephen. "Preventive Deployment of Troops as Preventive Measures: Macedonia and Beyond." *New York University Journal of International Law and Politics* 30, 3–4 (1998): 793–880.

Otunnu, Olara A., and Michael W. Doyle (eds.). *Peacemaking and Peacekeeping for the New Century*. Lanham, MD: Rowman and Littlefield, 1998.

Paris, Roland. "Peacebuilding and the Limits of Liberal Internationalism." *International Security* 22, 2 (fall 1997): 54–89.

Payne, Rodger A. "The Limits and Promise of Environmental Conflict Prevention: The Case of the GEF." *Journal of Peace Research* 35, 3 (1998): 363–380.

Peck, Connie. "Preventive Diplomacy: A More Effective Approach to International Disputes." *Ecumenical Review* 1, 74 (1995): 328–334.

————. *The United Nations as a Dispute Settlement System.* The Hague: Kluwer for UNITAR, 1996.

————. *Sustainable Peace: The Role of the UN and Regional Organizations in Preventing Conflict.* Carnegie Commission on Preventing Deadly Conflict, Lanham, MD: Rowman and Littlefield, 1998.

Pouligny, Béatrice. "Promoting Democratic Institutions in Post-Conflict Societies: Giving a Chance to Diversity." *International Peacekeeping* 7, 3 (autumn 2000).

Prendergast, John. *Crisis Response: Humanitarian Band-Aids in Sudan and Somalia.* London: Pluto, 1997.

Pugh, Michael (ed.). *Regeneration of War-Torn Societies.* London: Macmillan, 2000.

Rakita, Sara. "Early Warning as a Tool of Conflict Prevention." *New York University Journal of International Law and Politics* 30, 3–4 (1998): 539–589.

Satterthwaite, Margaret. "Human Rights Monitoring, Elections Monitoring, and Electoral Assistance as Preventive Measures." *NYU Journal of International Law and Politics* 30, 3–4 (1998).

Randel, Judith, and Tony German (eds.). *The Reality of Aid: An Independent Review of International Aid, 1996.* The Reality of Aid Management Group, Eurostep, and ICVA. London: Earthscan Publications, 1996.

Reinicke, Wolfgang H., and Francis Deng. *Critical Choices: The United Nations, Networks and the Future of Global Governance.* Ottawa: International Development Research Center, 2000.

Reychler, Luc. *Democratic Peace-building and Conflict Prevention: The Devil Is in the Transition.* Leuven: Leuven University Press, 1999.

Reychler, Luc, and Thania Paffenholz (eds.). *Peace-Building: A Field Guide.* Boulder: Lynne Rienner Publishers, 2001.

Rubin, Barnett R. (ed.). *Cases and Strategies for Preventive Action.* New York: Century Foundations, 1998.

Rupesinghe, Kumar, and Michiko Kuroda (eds.). *Early Warning and Conflict Resolution.* London: Macmillan, 1992.

Rupesinghe, Kumar. "Towards a Policy Framework for Preventive Diplomacy." *Security Dialogue* 26, 3 (1995): 113–114.

Sambanis, Nicholas. "Partition as a Solution to Ethnic War: An Empirical Critique of the Theoretical Literature." *World Politics* 52 (July 2000).

————. "Do Ethnic and Non-Ethnic Wars Have the Same Causes?" *Journal of Conflict Resolution* 43, 3 (June 2001): 259.

Schmid, Alex. P. "Thesaurus and Glossary of Early Warning and Conflict Prevention Terms." Leiden: Erasmus University, 2000.

Singer, J. David, and Melvin Small. *Correlates of War Project: International and Civil War Data, 1816–1992.* Ann Arbor, MI: Inter-University Consortium for Political and Social Research (ICPSR), 1994.

Singh, Daljit. "The Politics of Peace: Preventive Diplomacy in ASEAN." *Harvard International Review* 16, 2 (1994): 32–35.

Stavenhagen, R. (ed.). *Ethnic Conflict and the Nation State.* New York: St. Martin's, 1996.

Stedman, Stephen John. "International Actors and Internal Conflicts." Project on World Security. New York: Rockefeller Brothers Fund, 1999.

————. "Alchemy for a New World Order: Overselling 'Preventive Diplomacy.'" *Foreign Affairs* 73, 3 (1995).

Stedman, Stephen John, Donald Rothchild, and Elizabeth M. Cousens (eds.). *Ending Civil War: The Implementation of Peace Agreements.* A project the

International Peace Academy. Boulder: Lynne Rienner Publishers, forthcoming 2002.

Sucharipa-Behrmann, Lilly R., and Thomas M. Franck. "Preventive Measures." *New York University Journal of International Law and Politics* 30, 3–4 (1998).

Swedish Ministry of Foreign Affairs. *Preventing Violent Conflicts: A Swedish Action Plan.* Stockholm: The Printing Works of the Government Offices, 1999.

Tay, Simon S.C., with Obood Talib. "The ASEAN Regional Forum: Preparing for Preventive Diplomacy." *Contemporary Southeast Asia* 19, 3 (1997): 252–268.

Thakur, Ramesh (ed.). *Past Imperfect, Future Uncertain: The United Nations at Fifty.* London: Macmillan, 1998.

Townsend-Gault. "Preventive Diplomacy and Pro-activity in the South China Sea." *Contemporary Southeast Asia* 20, 2 (1998): 171–190.

David Turton (ed.). *War and Ethnicity: Global Connections and Local Violence.* Rochester, NY: University of Rochester Press, 1997.

United Nations Staff College Project. *Rolling EWPM Project Reference Document.* Available online at the website of the UN Department of Political Affairs, www.un.org/Depts/dpa/docs/peacemak.htm.

United Nations. "An Agenda for Peace: Preventive Diplomacy, Peacemaking, and Peace-keeping—Report of the Secretary-General." UN Doc. A/47/277-S/24111, June 17, 1992.

———. "Supplement to *An Agenda for Peace:* Position Paper of the Secretary-General." UN Doc. A/50/60-S/1995/1, January 3, 1995.

———. "The Role of the Security Council in the Prevention of Armed Conflicts." S/PV.4072. 4072nd Meeting of the Security Council, November 29, 1999.

———. "Statement by the President of the Security Council on the Prevention of Violent Conflict." S/PRST/1999/34, November 30, 1999.

———. "The Role of the Security Council in the Prevention of Armed Conflicts." S/PV.4174. 4174th Meeting of the Security Council, July 20, 2000.

———. "Statement by the President of the Security Council on the Prevention of Violent Conflict." S/PRST/2000/25, July 20, 2000.

———. *Report of the Panel on United Nations Peace Operations.* A/55/305-S/2000/809, August 21, 2000.

———. *Report of the Secretary-General on the Implementation of the Report of the Panel on United Nations Peace Operations.* A/55/502, A/55/507, October 20, 2000.

Urquhart, Brian. *Ralph Bunche: An American Life.* New York: W. W. Norton, 1993.

Uvin, Peter. "The Influence of Aid in Situations of Violent Conflict." Paris: Organization for Economic Cooperation and Development/Development Assistance Committee, Informal Task Force on Conflict, Peace, and Development Cooperation, September 1999.

Van de Goor, Luc, and Suzanne Verstegen. "Conflict Prognosis: A Conflict and Policy Assessment Framework, 2." The Hague: Clingendael Institute (Netherlands Institute for International Relations), 2000.

Van Walraven, Klaas, and Jurjen van der Vlugt. *Conflict Prevention and Early Warning in the Political Practice of International Organizations.* The Hague: Clingendael Institute (Netherlands Institute of International Relations), 1996.

Vance, Cyrus R., and David A. Hamburg. "Pathfinders for Peace: A Report to the UN Secretary-General on the Role of Special Representatives and Personal Envoys." Washington, D.C.: Carnegie Commission on Preventing Deadly Conflict, 1997.

Väyrynen, Raimo (ed.). *New Directions in Conflict Theory: Conflict Resolution and Conflict Transformation.* London: Sage, 1991.

Wallensteen, Peter (ed.). *Preventing Violent Conflicts: Past Record and Future Challenges.* Uppsala, Sweden: Uppsala University, Department of Peace and Conflict Research, 1998.

Wallensteen, Peter, and Margareta Sollenberg. "The End of International War? Armed Conflict, 1989–1995." *Journal of Peace Research* 33, 3 (1996): 353–370.

———. "Armed Conflict, 1989–1998." *Journal of Peace Research* 36 (1999): 593–606.

———. "Armed Conflict, 1989–1999." *Journal of Peace Research* 37 (2000): 635–649.

Wallensteen, Peter, with contributions from Birger Heldt, Mary B. Anderson, Stephen John Stedman, and Leonard Wantchekon. "Conflict Prevention Through Development Cooperation." Organization for Economic Cooperation and Development/Development Assistance Committee, Informal Task Force on Conflict, Peace, and Development Cooperation, Paris and the Department of Peace and Conflict Research, Uppsala University, Sweden, November 30, 2000.

Walter, Barbara F., and Jack Snyder (eds.). *Civil Wars, Insecurity, and Intervention.* New York: Columbia University Press, 1999.

Williams, Adiodun. *Preventing War: The United Nations and Macedonia.* Lanham, MD: Rowman and Littlefield, 2000.

Woodward, Susan. *Balkan Tragedy: Chaos and Dissolution After the Cold-War.* Washington, D.C.: Brookings Institution, 1995.

Zakaria, Fareed. "The Rise of Illiberal Democracy." *Foreign Affairs* 76, 6 (November/December 1997): 22.

Zartman, I. William. *Ripe for Resolution: Conflict and Intervention in Africa.* New York: Oxford University Press, 1989.

———. *Preventive Negotiation.* Lanham, MD: Rowman and Littlefield, 2000.

Zartman, I. William (ed.). *Elusive Peace: Negotiating an End to Civil Wars.* Washington, D.C.: Brookings Institution, 1996.

The Contributors

Patricia Cleves is a Colombian anthropologist. She has worked with the Colombian government on the 1987–1990 peace process and for the United Nations peace mission in El Salvador and Guatemala. Until recently, she was a member of the Post-Conflict Unit of the World Bank. Currently, she is a consultant in Bogotà, Colombia, working on conflict resolution and peace building.

John G. Cockell is currently an associate in the Conflict Analysis and Development Unit, London School of Economics. He served most recently as a political affairs officer with the United Nations Interim Administration Mission in Kosovo, where he managed political development programs. In 1998–1999, he was a member of the design team for the Early Warning and Preventive Measures project of the UN Department of Political Affairs/UN Staff College. He has also served as a policy adviser on conflict prevention to both the Canadian and UK delegations to the UN General Assembly.

Nat Colletta is the former head of the Post-Conflict Unit at the World Bank. Before joining the Bank in 1977, he lectured and wrote extensively on sociology, anthropology, education, and development. He has returned to teaching and consulting and is working on a new book entitled *Privatizing Peace: Responding to the Changing Nature of Armed Conflict*.

Tobi P. Dress is an attorney and specialist in conflict prevention and public policy. She works with international organizations including the UNDP (New York, Romania, and Moldova), UNDESA, UNESCO (Paris), IOM (Geneva), and ILO (Geneva), as well as the ICRC (Geneva and Moscow).

Recently, she has designed a conflict prevention program for Romania and Southeastern Europe and has taught peace and conflict studies and arms control law at New York University, Loyola Law School, and the University of Southern California. Currently she is a visiting lecturer at Ewha University (Seoul) and the Fondation Nationale des Sciences Politiques in Paris.

Anne-Marie Gardner is a Ph.D. candidate in the Department of Politics at Princeton University. She is the recipient of a National Science Foundation Graduate Research Fellowship and the Doreen C. Burbank Named PEO Scholar Award. Her primary research interests include international law and international relations theory.

Ted Robert Gurr is distinguished university professor at the University of Maryland–College Park and founding director of the Minorities at Risk Project, which tracks the political status and activities of more than 300 communal groups worldwide. He has written or edited twenty books and monographs, the most recent of which is *Peoples Versus States: Minorities at Risk in the New Century*. In 1993–1994, Gurr was president of the International Studies Association, and in 1996–1997 he held the Swedish government's Olof Palme Visiting Professorship at Uppsala University.

Fen Osler Hampson is professor of international affairs at the Norman Paterson School of International Affairs at Carleton University in Ottawa, Canada. In 1993–1994, he was a peace fellow at the United States Institute of Peace. He is author or coauthor of six books and editor or coeditor of twenty others. His most recent publication is *Madness in the Multitude: Human Security and World Disorder.*

Mukesh Kapila is head of the Conflict and Humanitarian Affairs Department in the UK Department for International Development (DFID). He has responsibility for the UK government's relations with international organizations dealing with conflict prevention, peacebuilding, and humanitarian assistance. He is also a stand-by member of the United Nations Disaster Assessment and Coordination Team. Previously, he worked for the Overseas Development Administration (which became DFID in May 1997) in Malawi and then as senior health and population adviser in London.

Izumi Nakamitsu Lennartsson is currently *chef de cabinet* at the International Institute for Democracy and Electoral Assistance. In 1998, she was part of the negotiation process leading to the adoption of the Statute of the International Criminal Court. She has also held a number of positions in UNHCR in New York, Geneva, Bosnia, Croatia, and Turkey, as well as in the office of the Special Representative of the Secretary-General to the former Yugoslavia and on the Secretary-General's UN Reform Team.

Edward C. Luck is director of the Center on International Organization in Columbia University's School of International and Public Affairs. His most recent publication is *Mixed Messages: American Politics and International Organization, 1919–1999.*

Michael S. Lund is senior associate at Management Systems International, Inc., professorial lecturer in Conflict Management at the Johns Hopkins University School of Advanced International Studies, and senior associate at the Center for Strategic and International Studies, all in Washington, D.C. He has researched, written, consulted, and trained extensively on the subject of conflict prevention regarding several regions. Recent publications include *Preventing Violent Conflicts: A Strategy for Preventive Diplomacy.*

David M. Malone is president of the International Peace Academy while on leave from the Canadian Foreign Service. He has served as director general of the Policy, International Organizations, and Global Issues Bureaus of the Canadian Foreign Ministry and as ambassador and deputy permanent representative of Canada to the United Nations. He has written extensively about the UN Security Council.

Monty G. Marshall is a faculty research scientist at the Center for International Development and Conflict Management at the University of Maryland, where he directs the Integrated Network for Societal Conflict Research program. He also established and directs the Center for Systemic Peace and is a senior consultant with the U.S. government's State Failure Task Force. He is author of *Third World War: System, Process, and Conflict Dynamics.*

Maureen O'Neil is president of Canada's International Development Research Centre. She currently serves on the board of directors of the International Institute for Democracy and Electoral Assistance. Her previous positions included chair of the board of the International Centre for Human Rights and Democratic Development, president of the North-South Institute, and deputy minister of citizenship for the government of Ontario. She has also represented Canada on the UN Commission on the Status of Women and on OECD committees and has been a member of the UN Committee for Development Planning and the UN Research Institute for Social Development.

Gay Rosenblum-Kumar is a public administration officer in the Governance and Public Administration Branch of the UN Department of Economic and Social Affairs. Currently, she manages governance projects aimed at strengthening the capacities of local institutions in developing countries to provide conflict transformation skills to development practitioners, government officials, and their civil society partners. Prior to joining the United Nations, she worked with several international NGOs on antiapartheid and development issues in sub-Saharan Africa.

Nicholas Sambanis is assistant professor in the Department of Political Science, Yale University. He held the position of economist at the World Bank's Development Economics Research Group until July 2001. His current research interests are in the political economy of civil violence and ethnic conflict. He has published in several journals, including the *American Political Science Review*, *World Politics*, and *Journal of Conflict Resolution*.

Bengt Säve-Söderbergh became the first secretary-general of the International Institute for Democracy and Electoral Assistance in March 1995. From 1967 to 1970, he worked in the Swedish International Development Authority and then joined the Swedish Ministry for Foreign Affairs. He headed the International Centre of the Swedish Labour Movement between 1978 and 1985, and in 1985 he was appointed undersecretary of state for international development cooperation at the Swedish Ministry for Foreign Affairs. In this capacity, he initiated and led the Nordic Project on reform of the UN system.

Frances Stewart is director of the International Development Centre, Queen Elizabeth House, and fellow of Somerville College at the University of Oxford. She is a development economist whose work focuses on poverty, adjustment, and conflict. Her publications include *Technology and Underdevelopment*, *Adjustment with a Human Face* (with Andrea Cornia and Richard Jolly), and *War and Underdevelopment: The Economic and Social Consequences of Conflict* (with Valpy Fitzgerald and others). She played a major role in the initiation and development of the Human Development Reports of the UNDP.

Chandra Lekha Sriram is an associate at the International Peace Academy, New York, where she directs the project on strengthening UN capacities for the prevention of violent conflict. She also holds a law degree from the University of California–Berkeley, Boalt Hall School of Law.

Necla Tschirgi recently joined the International Peace Academy as vice president. Previously, she headed the Peacebuilding and Reconstruction Program Initiative at the International Development Research Centre (IDRC) in Canada. Before joining IDRC in 1992, she was adjunct professor of political science at the American University in Cairo and coordinator of the Middle East Research Competition at the Cairo office of the Ford Foundation from 1991 to 1996. Her research interests lie at the intersection of security and development studies.

Peter Wallensteen has been the Dag Hammarskjöld Professor of Peace and Conflict Research at Uppsala University, Sweden, since 1985. He was the head of the Department of Peace and Conflict Research from 1972 to 1999. He directs the Uppsala Conflict Data Project, which gives annual reports on armed conflicts in the world. His recent publications include *Preventing Violent Conflicts: Past Record and Future Challenges.*

Karin Wermester is senior program officer at the International Peace Academy. She works primarily on the multiyear research and policy development project entitled From Promise to Practice: Strengthening UN Capacities for the Prevention of Violent Conflict. She is also a contributing editor of *Peacebuilding as Politics: Cultivating Peace in Fragile Societies.*

Index

hensiveness dilemma, 256–257;
through constitutional governance,
170; country-level multi-instrument
engagements, 171–174; current landscape of, 231–232; definition,
160–161, 180n6, 214; development
actors' role in, 297; doctrinal revi-
sions, 240–247; early action,
221–224; effectiveness of, 162–163,
166–168, 176; funding lack for, 255,
258, 260; future of, 232–235; G-8
initiatives, 254–255, 311; as global
public good, 289–292, 295n25;
holistic system of, 234; ICTs as aid
in, 290–291; identification of possible actions, 176; implementation of,
176–177; in-country planning and
implementation, 177–178; institutionalization of, 162–163, 171,
175–178; instrument toolbox for,
170, 179, 182n20; through international standard-setting, 170; knowledge base of, 277–282; lack of will
for, 165–166; lesson-learning framework for, 169–171; levels of,
168–169; liberal values as problem
in, 163–164; nature of, 381–382;
neutral venues for, 237–239; new
mechanisms for, 282–289; non-UN
actors in, 8–9; norms in, 310; paradox of, 279; phases of, 395; policy
directions for, 263–268; for poverty
reduction, 105; prediction of escalation, 221–224, 338; prioritizing
goals in, 172; regional dimensions,
395; technical cooperation approach
to, 240, 242; time-sensitive interventions, 170, 172; types of, 7–8; UN
coordination of, 392–395; UN role
in, 382–383, 385–396. See also
Preventive action
Conflict Prevention and Peace Forum
(CPPF), 295n21, 393
Conflict Prevention and Post-Conflict
Reconstruction Network (CPR), 177,
232, 275, 293n4, 330, 393
Conflict Prevention Initiative, 393
Conflict resolution, 140, 237–239, 241,
244–245, 278
Conflict(s): at-risk indicators, 9–10,
332–341, 353n15; causes of, 10,
30–31, 114–116, 132, 358–359, 384;
claim for self-rule as factor in, 359;
cost-benefit calculations in,
114–115; cultural factors in, 359;
decline in, 41–44; economic factors
in, 305–307, 359; global costs of,
319n40; global systemic factors in,
290; horizontal inequalities in, 106,
111–114; impact assessment of, 341;
indicators of, 334–335; intensity of,
337–338, 352n4, 352n9, 354n23;
liberal values as cause of, 163–165;
life cycles of, 181n7; measures of
escalation of, 221–224, 338; motivation for, 106–107; policy formulation for ending of, 125–132; political
disputes as cause of, 55, 261; political economy of, 305–307; predatory,
48–49; private incentives to,
129–130, 134n18; private-sector role
in, 128; public awareness of, 47–48;
regional frequency of, 344–345; separatist, 44–47, 60n5, 83; shift in
nature of, 229; stages of, 334; state-
formation, 219–220; targeting causal
complexity in, 186–191, 209n19;
trends in, 28–29, 31, 36; trigger
events for, 116; types of, 215; UN
capacity to address causes of,
239–247, 385–387. See also Ethnic
conflicts; Intrastate conflict;
Violence
Congo (Brazzaville): bad-neighborhood
effect, 83; 1997–1999 civil war, 42;
preventive diplomacy success in,
143; regional conflict effect on, 226;
regional organizations' role in, 160;
World Bank operations in, 324, 328
Congo, Democratic Republic of: civil
war, 3, 43; as failed state, 58, 321;
FEWER research on conflict in, 285;
foreign financing of conflicts in,
116; horizontal inequality in, 113;
illegal resource exploitation, 258;
IMF operations in, 324; Katanga
secession, 48; peacekeeping vs.
enforcement, 53; predation in, 56;
preventive diplomacy failure in, 143;
regional conflict effect on, 226;
World Bank operations in, 324, 328
Consociationalism, 367, 369

About the Book

Though the prevention of conflict is the first promise in the Charter of the United Nations, it is a promise constantly betrayed by international organizations, governments, and local actors alike. At the same time, and in a more positive vein, recent studies provide much-needed information about why and how today's conflicts start and what sustains them. This groundbreaking book presents some of the best scholarly and policy-relevant work on the practical challenges of conflict prevention within the UN system.

The authors consider the causes and dynamics of war, the tools that are being developed to predict the eruption of conflict, and what is being done—and what could be done better—in the effort to move from reaction to prevention.

Fen Osler Hampson is professor of international affairs at the Norman Paterson School of International Affairs, Carleton University (Canada). Most recent among his many publications are *Madness in the Multitude: Human Security and World Disorder* and *Nurturing Peace: Why Peace Settlements Succeed or Fail*. **David M. Malone** is president of the International Peace Academy. His recent publications include *Greed and Grievance: Economic Agendas in Civil Wars* and *Decision-making in the UN Security council: The Case of Haiti*.